Davis
best regards
16-3-99

Ecology, Politics and Violent Conflict

edited by
Mohamed Suliman

A Development and Peace Foundation book
in cooperation with
the Institute for African Alternatives (IFAA)

DEVELOPMENT AND PEACE FOUNDATION

INSTITUTE FOR AFRICAN ALTERNATIVES

ZED BOOKS
London & New York

To my wife Fatima, my daughter Azza,
my friends Günther Baechler and Mohamed Fathi Ibrahim,
and to Professor Adrian Newland and his medical team,
who saved my life

Ecology, Politics and Violent Conflict was first published by
Zed Books Ltd, 7 Cynthia Street, London N1 9JF, UK,
and Room 400, 175 Fifth Avenue, New York, NY 10010, USA in 1999

in association with
The Institute for African Alternatives,
Lyndhurst Hall, Warden Road, London NW5 4RE, UK
and the Development and Peace Foundation,
Gotenstrasse 152, D53175, Bonn, Germany

Distributed in the USA exclusively by St Martin's Press, Inc.,
175 Fifth Avenue, New York, NY 10010, USA

Typeset in Monotype Garamond
by Lucy Morton & Robin Gable, Grosmont
Cover designed by Andrew Corbett
Printed and bound in the United Kingdom
by Biddles Ltd, Guildford and King's Lynn

A catalogue record for this book is available from the British Library

Library of Congress Cataloging-in-Publication Data
Ecology, politics and violent conflict / edited by Mohamed Suliman
p. cm.
Includes bibliographical references (p.) and index.
ISBN 1–85649–601–5 (hb.). — ISBN 1–85649–602–3 (pbk.)
1. Environmental management—Developing countries. 2. Conflict management—Developing countries. 3. Violence—Developing countries. 4. Environmentalism—Developing countries. I. Suliman, Mohamed.
GE320.D44E25 1998 98–29914
363.7'009172'4—dc21 CIP

ISBN 1 85649 601 5 (Hb)
ISBN 1 85649 602 3 (Pb)

Contents

Preface

'In the rich fertile Nile valley of old Egypt, life followed an established and recurrent order, *an unfolding in time of what had been preordained from the beginning.*' The gods were powerful without being immoderately violent, and disputes between themselves or with mere mortals were usually resolved peacefully. 'However, in the rugged, wind-swept land of Mesopotamia, the divine assembly and its chosen champion, Marduk, had to wage a desperate and frantic fight against the powerful forces of chaos as contained in Tiamat, *the mother who brought forth gods and monsters in such profusion that her unbounded fruitfulness endangered the very existence of the universe.*'[1] Marduk killed her and mutilated her body.

Even in the cradle of civilization, the neighbouring Egyptian and Mesopotamian societies did not develop an identical *Weltanschauung*, nor share congruent existential problems. They certainly did not see eye to eye on how best to deal with them. In Egypt, peaceful assimilation of rivals, competitors and foes was the common practice to resolve conflicts. In Mesopotamia, it was bloodshed and annihilation. In Egypt, chaos was perceived as a friendly and cooperative Ogdoad, which gives birth to the creator, Sun. In Mesopotamia, chaos was the enemy of life and order. Tiamat, the Great Mother, was attacked atrociously and smashed into a thousand pieces. Two lands, two greatly contrasting ways of dealing with conflicts!

What chance do we have, then, in our turbulent and intricate time, to find that famous red thread that connects and goes through all aspects of such a complex social behaviour as violent conflict? Indeed, the complexity and variety of causes, perceptions and manifestations of group violence baffle rational thought. Complex social processes and phenomena, themselves dependent on a multitude of objective and subjective factors, impart uncertainty to the course of violent conflict as well as to our attempts to understand and judge it as the actual behaviour of actual people.

On first approximation, violence seems to be an irrational, chaotic behaviour *par excellence*. Yet we now know that chaos shows an inherent order that allows us to discern some repetitive patterns and that chance and necessity are indeed woven together. Even in the realm of the social, the inherent inner necessity articulates itself in the form of chance. It is not surprising, therefore, to find that in the very complex area of social violence, the objective has not been totally overrun by the subjective and that familiar patterns and similar traits may become discernible. Combining the cherished methods of social research with the development of general scientific theories of knowledge such as the theory of chaos, we have a good chance of discerning some of its rather murky substance as the concerted irrational but understandable behaviour of groups of people under stress.

This book is an attempt to understand group violence. It gives considerable attention to the social impact of negative changes in the natural environment. This is a growing factor in the complex web of causes that precipitate violent conflict. And since ecological degradation and scarcity can drastically affect how people live and work, it is important to tackle related economic issues and political decisions in order to assess their contribution to social violence.

This book brainstorms a complex area of social behaviour. I am glad that so many distinguished scientists have contributed to it. I am also grateful to the Development and Peace Foundation in Bonn for supporting its idea, and the editing and production processes. My thanks also to Gordon Lee, Marianne Biel and Rachel Houghton for excellent help with copy-editing. Zed Books were as competent and professional as ever.

Mohamed Suliman,
London

Note

1. These quotations are taken from Henry Frankfurt, H.A. Frankfurt, John A. Wilson and Thorkild Jacobsen, *Before Philosophy*, Pelican Books, Harmondsworth, 1954.

Part I

Theoretical and Historical Considerations

1

Blood, Babies and the Social Roots of Conflict

Nicholas Hildyard

'Blood' and 'babies' have long provided many people from all walks of life, in all parts of the world, with seemingly 'common-sense' explanations for far-off conflicts in which they themselves are not involved – and even for ones in which they are. I say 'common-sense' because explanations that ascribe the root causes of conflict to population pressure ('babies') or ethnic imperatives ('blood') play to assumptions that are so deeply embedded in contemporary global culture that they appear to be incontestable: they are simply, well, 'obvious'.

With satellite images showing widespread deforestation in West Africa, and census returns confirming rapid population growth in many African countries, an explanation of civil war in, say, Sierra Leone, as being the result of 'too many people' chopping down too many trees, leading to scarcity and hence conflict, somehow 'rings true'.[1] After all, Sierra Leone is in West Africa (and must therefore be deforested); it is in Africa (and must therefore be suffering from overpopulation); and it is 'well known' that in conditions of overcrowding and scarcity, people fight each other. Similarly, when confronted with the horrors of 'ethnic cleansing' in Yugoslavia or Rwanda, many people take it for granted that the explanation must lie in fixed, implacable, ingrained and ancient antagonisms: how else can one explain the sheer horror of neighbours who had previously lived together in seeming harmony hacking each other to pieces? Hatred between Muslim and Serb, Hutu and Tutsi must be in the 'blood' – let the two sides at each other's throats and genocide is inevitable. No other explanation would seem to be sufficient. Indeed, as one commentator astutely remarks, the horror is even 'somewhat mitigated' by the knowledge that Serbs and Croats, Muslims and Hindus, Northern Irish Catholics and Protestant Unionists, Africans (in general) and a host of 'others' have also always been prone to 'this kind of behaviour' (Keane 1996: 226).

Not surprisingly, when commentators (whether in the local pub or on television news) invoke 'blood' and 'babies' as explanations of conflict, they strike a chord which resonates with many people who do not know the intimate histories of those involved in these conflicts. The world becomes simple enough to understand again: rationality is restored to a seemingly irrational world. Yet, scratch below the surface of the violence that is increasingly 'explained' by labels such as 'population wars' or 'inter-tribal conflict' and the shallowness – and deceptiveness – of the 'blood and babies' line is soon revealed (Appadurai 1996).

More often than not, however, 'tribal hatred' (though a real and genuine emotion for some) emerges as the product not of 'nature' but of 'a complex web of politics, economics, history, psychology and a struggle for identity' (Keane 1996: 226); what commentators assume to be population-induced scarcity turns out to be socially induced scarcity, a very different phenomenon; and the 'objective truths' claimed for 'blood' and 'baby' explanations are revealed as the self-interested and highly partisan agendas of small groups within society. As Fergal Keane, a BBC Africa correspondent, writes of the genocide in Rwanda:

> Like many of my colleagues, I drove into [Rwanda] believing the short stocky ones had simply decided to turn on the tall thin ones because that was the way it has always been. Yet now, two years later … I think the answer is very different. What happened in Rwanda was the result of cynical manipulation by powerful political and military leaders. Faced with the choice of sharing some of their wealth and power with the [insurgent] Rwandan Patriotic Front, they chose to vilify that organisation's main support group, the Tutsis. The Tutsis were characterised as vermin. *Inyenzi in kinyarwanda* – cockroaches who should be stamped on without mercy … In much the same way as the Nazis exploited latent anti-Semitism in Germany, so did the forces of Hutu extremism identify and whip into murderous frenzy the historical sense of grievance against the Tutsis … This was not about tribalism first and foremost but about preserving the concentration of wealth and power in the hands of the elite. (Keane 1996: 226–30)

This is not to deny that ethnicity – be it in Rwanda or anywhere else in the world – can prove to be a murderous force. It is to insist, however, that the shared values, histories, customs and identities that generate 'ethnicity' are socially constructed, not biologically determined; and that, at root, ethnic conflicts result not from blood hatred but from socially generated divisions which, more often than not, reflect deep-seated conflicts over power and resources both *between* groups and (more pertinent still) *within* groups. Ethnicity is always grounded in an element of social imagination. Moreover, the 'imagined communities' which result, though defining particular groups as distinct and unique at any one given moment and in any one given context, are not unchanging: on the contrary, they are constantly being *re*-imagined as relationships within and between groups are reworked through everyday social interaction. Who is 'us' and who is 'them' is thus forever being subtly redefined as histories are told and retold; traditions invented and denied; statuses ascribed and challenged; allegiances forged and broken; and identities claimed and rejected (Hobsbawm and Ranger 1983).

Rwanda: Ethnicity and Repression

In the case of modern Rwanda, what it is to be 'Hutu' or 'Tutsi' not only reflects the experience of colonialism but also the practice of development in the post-colonial period: it also varies widely across classes and from one part of the country to another (Uvin 1996; de Waal 1994). Little is known for certain how ethnicity was conceived of prior to the advent of colonial rule, first under the Germans and later under the Belgians. The longest-established ethnic group in the region is the Twa, a hunter–gatherer group which, today, is both small in number and discriminated against by the majority of Hutus and Tutsis alike (Lewis and Knight 1995). The Hutu themselves are believed to have migrated into the region several centuries ago, certainly before the arrival of the cattle-rearing Tutsi during the fifteenth and sixteenth centuries. By the nineteenth century, according to some cultural historians, 'hundreds of years of cohabitation and intermarriage had produced an "integrated" social system wherein the categories of Hutu and Tutsi were largely occupationally defined: whoever acquired a sizeable herd of cattle was called Tutsi and was considered highly' (Uvin 1996: 4). Whilst this is disputed by some, it appears likely that, by the time it was colonized, Rwanda was a kingdom with a Tutsi king and the Hutu (or farmers, depending on one's perspective) were dominated by the Tutsis (or cattle-owners).

Whatever the nature of ethnicity in pre-colonial times, it is clear that the colonial powers made ethnic distinctions a fact of everyday life in Rwanda. Under colonial rule, ethnic identity cards were introduced, fixing identities – regardless of social context – on the basis of spurious racial science, such as skull size and nose measurements. New sources of power and privilege also emerged under colonial rule and these accrued almost exclusively to the white rulers and those designated Tutsi. Jobs in the administration and the army, for example, were reserved almost exclusively for 'Tutsi'. The Germans, and later the Belgians, justified such exclusion on the grounds that the Tutsis were somehow less African, more European and, by extension, superior to their Hutu fellow countrymen and women. As Keane reports:

> They cited the tallness of the Tutsis, their aquiline facial features, the fact that they preferred to raise cattle than till the land as evidence of a superior civilization. All manner of humiliating folly was employed in the name of proving this theory of innate Tutsi superiority. Skulls and noses were measured. Legends were invented to explain the presence of these superior beings in the centre of Africa. All of this was done less because the Belgians had any real desire to embrace the Tutsis as their equals, but rather because they needed the Tutsis as their allies to maintain a fundamentally unjust political dispensation. (Keane 1996: 228)

In other words, 'race and identity were used as a means to create and preserve an inherently unjust power structure' – a power structure with a clear hierarchy from whites to Tutsi to Hutu to Twa (Uvin 1996: 6).

The bottled-up sense of injustice felt by those at the bottom of the hierarchy exploded in 1958 after Rwanda became independent, not least because the departing Belgians abandoned their support for the Tutsi elite – who were increasingly seen as dangerous anti-colonial leftists – in favour of the Hutus (Prunier 1995: 49). The result was a series of brutal massacres as the new Hutu ruling elite – backed by Belgium – whipped up popular resentment against the Tutsi in order to consolidate its hold on power. It was a tactic that was to underpin the policies of successive post-colonial governments. Racism (the institutionalized discrimination against one group by another based on culturally and biologically ascribed differences) became embedded in government policy, just at it had been in the colonial period – only now, the targets were the Tutsi, the Twa and the Hutu opponents of the regime. The system of ethnic identity cards, introduced by the Belgians, was maintained: Tutsis were restricted from entering the army or the civil service through a discriminatory quota system; military personnel were forbidden from marrying Tutsis, an interdiction that also applied to those seeking political appointments. Daily, through legislation and other administrative 'proofs', people were 'reminded' that Tutsis were not only 'different' but potential 'enemies within' (Uvin 1996: 10). A pool of scapegoats was thus created that could be targeted in times of unrest – and targeted they were. In 1972–73, for example, when popular discontent with the regime's failure to address increasing levels of poverty threatened the government, mass anti-Tutsi campaigns were orchestrated by the leadership: thousands of Tutsi children were thrown out of school, whilst thousands of Tutsi adults lost their jobs (Uvin 1996: 10).

Despite such state-sponsored racism, Rwanda became a favoured client of international aid agencies,[2] praised for its 'political stability', 'sound economic policies' and (incredibly) for 'the cultural and social cohesion of its peoples'[3] (World Bank 1986, cited in Uvin 1996: 14). Millions of dollars of aid flowed into the country throughout the 1970s and 1980s. Yet, on the ground, conditions for the mass of people (Hutu, Tutsi and Twa alike) deteriorated – not least as a result of the development projects that the government and aid agencies instituted. By the early 1990s, according to Uvin (1996: 25), almost 50 per cent of the population were living in abject poverty, with a further 40 per cent only marginally above the poverty level. Meanwhile, the top one per cent of the population – the small clique of Hutus who were the favoured supporters of Juvenal Habyarimana, the country's president – lived in luxury.

By 1990, the pressure for political change had become intense. Internal dissent was on the increase as moderate Hutus began to organize against the authoritarianism and widespread corruption of the Habyarimana regime. The government also faced a growing military threat from the Rwandan Patriotic Front (RPF), a guerrilla army consisting largely of Tutsi exiles, which was now strong enough to invade the country from its bases in Uganda. And, with the Cold War over, the aid agencies on which the regime increasingly relied were beginning to put pressure on the regime to democratize and embrace power-sharing with the RPF and the growing domestic opposition.

Threatened from within and without, Habyarimana and his northern Hutu clique seized on the one element guaranteed to mobilize public support behind the government: hatred of Tutsis. As Keane reports:

> Newspapers and radio stations began to exhort the people to rally behind Hutuism. Drive the Tutsis out and show them no mercy, the virulent Radio Mille Collines demanded. A Hutu militia was established, the Interahamwe: those who stand together. The people were being conditioned for a final solution that would rid Rwanda of all political opposition to the government – all of the Tutsis and the moderate Hutus who opposed the regime. The Tutsis were convenient scapegoats and the more moderate Hutus could easily be condemned as traitors to their tribe. When Habyarimana himself seemed to weaken under international pressure and began to consider power sharing, his jet was blown out of the sky. Much as the burning of the Reichstag provided Hitler with a pretext for taking power, the murder of Habyarimana, very probably by his associates, gave the signal for the onset of Rwanda's final solution. On the evening of 6 April 1994, the killing began. (Keane 1996: 230)

The result, as the world now knows, was a bloodbath – a bloodbath rooted not in biology or some innate 'cultural' impulse of one ethnic group to butcher its neighbours, but in power and privilege. The initial violence in Kigali was not spontaneous: the killings on the night that Habyarimana was assassinated were carried out largely by the President's Guards, local militia and the army (Uvin 1996: 32). The vast majority of provincial governors, communal burgomasters and ordinary citizens did not join in the carnage for weeks – weeks in which they were bombarded daily with messages of hatred against 'Tutsis'. Ethnicity became the tool through which a small, but endangered, elite spread fear throughout Rwandan society, legitimizing violence and the suppression of opponents in the process and, ultimately, desensitizing people to violence (Uvin 1996: 31).

Culture as Biology: Naturalizing Conflict

Similar analyses hold for Yugoslavia (Chossudovsky 1997; Alund 1996), Cyprus (Hitchens 1997) and other sites of conflict where primordial tribal hostilities are assumed to be the root cause of the violence. Indeed, there are few 'ethnic' – or indeed 'religious' – conflicts where close analysis does not reveal supposedly ingrained 'tribal' hostilities to be grounded not so much in deep and ancient rivalries (though these may be played upon) but in very contemporary conflicts over power, justice, values, resources and rights. This is not surprising, for ethnicity – the 'conscious and imaginative construction and mobilization of differences' (Appadurai 1996: 14) – is always mediated and shaped by society, and its mobilization as a political and cultural force ineluctably reflects relationships of power.

The mobilization of ethnicity by social movements, elites and nation-states can take numerous forms, both negative and positive. It can be directed 'towards self-expression, autonomy and efforts at cultural survival, or [it] can be principally negative in form, characterized largely by hate, racism and the desire to dominate or eliminate other groups' (Appadurai 1996: 147). In some cases, it may involve attempts by minority groups to resist cultural identities imposed upon them by the majority: in effect, ethnicity becomes the vehicle for contesting imposed values about difference (Appadurai 1996: 14). Examples include the revival of suppressed cultural traditions by groups such as the Basques or Native American Indians (resisting the imposition of, respectively, mainsteam Spanish and US cultural values) or the invention of new traditions by black street gangs in an attempt to differentiate themselves from mainstream white US society.

In other cases, ethnicity may involve the mobilization of the majority around imagined (or re-imagined) national identities in an attempt to legitimize the suppression and colonization of minority cultures. In Indonesia, for example, the government-sponsored transmigration of peasant families from Java to the outer islands of the archipelago during the 1980s was part of a wider programme aimed at 'integrating all ethnic groups into one nation, the Indonesian nation' (Martono 1985). Indigenous inhabitants in the outer islands are officially viewed as *suku suku terasing* ('backward and alien'): in order to assimilate them into the 'Indonesian Nation', the authorities have broken up whole communities, dispersing individual families to separate transmigration camps. The aim, as stated by the Minister of Transmigration in 1985, is that 'different ethnic groups will in the long run disappear because of integration … there will be one kind of man' (Martono 1985). Ethnicity has been similarly mobilized in Thailand to blame cultivators shifting upland for environmental degradation and to justify the imposition of mainstream 'Thai' culture (Hirsch 1997: 25). Within Britain the ascription of pejorative ethnicities to the Scots and the Irish was put to the same brutal ends by the authorities to justify the clearances of the Highlands of Scotland in the nineteenth century, when hundreds of thousands of 'unproductive' crofters were forcibly removed from their lands (Prebble 1969) – and the starvation of millions of Irish peasants during the potato famine of the 1840s (Kinealy 1994, 1997; Woodham-Smith 1963). The same scapegoating mobilization of ethnicity is evident today within elite discourses – North and South – that ascribe stereotyped tendencies ('unproductiveness', 'backwardness', 'fecklessness' and 'laziness') to 'the poor', whose marginalization is explained through their 'culture of poverty'.

Such imposed cultural stereotypes have never gone unchallenged, as oppressed ethnic groups have demanded their right to self-determination and, critically, the right to define themselves, rather than be defined by others – demands which have long formed a central plank of anti-racist and human rights movements worldwide. Such calls have been based not only on the recognition of the diversity and equality of cultures, but also on the need to address the political and social basis of racism and xenophobia. Stripped of that commitment, however, the 'right to be different' – a political position whose value, in the words of Étienne Balibar (Balibar and Wallerstein 1991), 'has been confirmed by the contribution it made to the struggle against the hegemony of certain standardizing imperialisms and against the elimination of minority or dominated civilizations' – may take on very different overtones.

Within Europe, for example, the New Right (many of whose members are linked to neo-fascist groupings) has attempted – with considerable success in countries such as France – to appropriate the language of 'difference' in the cause of ethnic apartheid. The result is a twisting of the defence of ethnic differences into a new and subtle form of racism. In the hands of the New Right, culture – viewed as a fixed 'object', 'a thing, or substance, whether physical or metaphysical' (Appadurai 1996) – becomes a mechanism which, like genes, 'functions to lock individuals and groups *a priori* into a genealogy … that is immutable and intangible in origin' (Balibar, in Balibar and Wallerstein 1991: 22). 'Culture', in effect, becomes 'Nature' – the all-encompassing determinant to which, in the liberal, anti-racist canon, it has traditionally been opposed.

For the New Right, group 'difference' goes hand in hand, not with equity, but with separation (Axtmann 1996: 105). The result is 'a politics of exclusion, ranging from demands for "foreigners"/"aliens" to be sent "home" to genocide in the form of "ethnic cleansing"' (Axtmann 1996: 105). Unlike the racism of an earlier age, this new 'differentialist' racism insists on respect for ethnic and cultural diversity and the differences this implies. Indeed, a leading intellectual architect of the New Right in France, Alain de Benoist (Taguieffe 1993a), argues that 'racism is nothing but the denial of difference', be it in the form of xenophobia or in the form of liberal, "humanitarian" integrationist programmes. Yet, as Roland Axtmann of the University of Aberdeen points out,

> The flipside of this position is the claim that these differences have to be preserved at all cost: they must be cultivated, developed and defended against any attempt to abolish them. As a result, this particular version of the right to difference is organized around a 'mixophobic' core: it is 'haunted by the threat of the destruction of identities through interbreeding – physical and cultural cross-breeding'. (Axtmann 1996: 105)

In effect, it amounts to a politics of cultural separation which is informed by an obsession with avoiding contact (Taguieff 1993b). Even where that phobia is absent, the logical outcome is ethnic separation or the acceptance of cultural domination of one group by another.

In the case of Northern Ireland, for example, it has been argued that Catholics and Protestants constitute separate and implacably opposed 'tribal groups', whose differences are culturally insurmountable; the only lasting solution to the civil war that has periodically racked the country for several decades thus lies in splitting the two communities apart, forcibly if necessary. To quote from one commentator, writing three years after the most recent era of 'Troubles' first flared up in 1968:

> The Catholics and the Protestants in Northern Ireland … constitute two distinct ethnic groups, of different origin, with different manners and traditions and different motivations and capacities. They could occupy the same geographic area and form a single society if they were capable of living in cultural symbiosis with each other, which they have done up to now. The Catholics, however, are no longer willing to fill the lower echelons of the economic hierarchy, as the cultural pattern, which previously enabled them to do so has largely broken down. The only remaining solution is to separate them territorially. Ataturk

> separated Greeks and Turks very successfully, although there was a terrible outcry at the time and it undoubtedly caused considerable inconvenience to the people who were forced to migrate. But should we not be willing to accept measures of inconvenience in order to establish a stable society? (Goldsmith 1971)[4]

Entirely missing from such an account is any sense that the 'differences' in Northern Ireland are not reducible to those between 'Catholics' and 'Protestants' – even if it were possible (which it is not) to pigeonhole the peoples of the North of Ireland into such broad, homogenized camps. Not all Catholics, for example, are 'Republicans' (and thus supporters of a united Ireland), nor are all Protestants 'Unionists' (supporters of continued membership of the United Kingdom). Likewise, class differences may mean that middle-class Catholics have more in common with middle-class Protestants than with their working-class co-religionists – and vice versa. Moreover, even those class differences obscure wide divergences between and amongst individuals as to how they approach the conflict – and their willingness, or unwillingness, to renegotiate existing political structures.

Indeed, for a liberal like myself, one problem with approaches that argue for the enforced separation of Protestants and Catholics in the North of Ireland (or Hutus, Tutsis and Twa in Rwanda: Turkish and Greek Cypriots in Cyprus; or Hindus and Muslims in India) lies not only in its authoritarianism and disregard for human rights and history: it lies also in the way in which 'Culture-as-Natural Law' obscures the political forces that manipulate ethnicity to ferment violence or discrimination. A politics of negative, discriminatory ethnicity comes to be viewed as a 'natural' corollary of ethnic diversity – and ethnic scapegoating as an 'inevitable' (and excusable) response to economic and political insecurity. At a time when globalization and the imposition of top-down development programmes are disrupting livelihoods worldwide, people who find a home in racist/ethnic movements are 'provided' with an 'explanation' for the violence they inflict on 'the other' (Balibar, in Balibar and Wallerstein 1991: 23). Ethnic conflict becomes 'naturalized'.

In the process, other non-racist responses to inter-community violence are frequently rendered invisible. Yet such responses are widespread and – even in the midst of conflict – practised by numerous movements seeking 'more diverse forms of transnational allegiance and affiliation', based on equity, pluralism and a respect for the rights of peoples to self-determination (Kothari 1996, 1997; Appadurai 1996; Shiva 1996). The Peace Movement in Northern Ireland, for example, gets written out of the picture entirely by accounts which insist on the innate and irreconcilable differences between Protestants and Catholics.

Indeed, the very existence of such groupings, whether in the North of Ireland or elsewhere, provides powerful evidence to counter the view that racism, xenophobia and violent, discriminatory expressions of ethnicity are somehow 'natural', 'predetermined' and therefore excusable (if regrettable) responses to the tensions and insecurities that underlie most conflicts. Racism and xenophobia are indeed common responses to such insecurities but they represent only one set of responses among many – none of which is more 'natural' than the others. Far from providing an explanation for ethnic conflict, they are responses that themselves cry out for explanation. Indeed, the very fact that racist movements have to work so hard to manipulate ethnicity towards their own xenophobic ends belies the 'naturalist' arguments that ethnic warriors promote. In India, for example, the Hindu Right has assiduously cultivated the notion that Hindu and Muslim are irrevocably opposed, constructing hatred through a deliberate political programme that has involved infiltrating opposed movements in an attempt to appropriate their causes for xenophobic ends (McGuire et al. 1996). An 'explanation' of Hindu–Muslim conflicts that fails to address such manipulation, relying instead on the myth of predetermined hatreds, is no explanation at all.

None of this, I repeat, is to deny the existence of ethnicity as a social reality. It is, however, to deny that ethnicity is rooted in biology or in some 'authentic' set of unchanging cultural traditions. It is also to argue that much of what passes for ethnic violence results from the deliberate manipulation of ethnic differences for self-interested political motives or the contestation of ethnic differences by those who, for one reason or another, are seeking to resist the imposition of oppressive cultural stereotypes.

Naturalizing Scarcity

The discourse on 'overpopulation' – in effect, too many 'babies' being a cause of conflict – shares many of the same flaws as the discourse on 'blood', culture and ethnicity. Not least, by confusing two different forms of scarcity, it glosses over or obscures the very real political conflicts that result in groups of people being deemed surplus 'population'.

Scarcity – in the sense of a dearth of food or other necessities – is not a new phenomenon. Throughout history, communities have had to contend with times when harvests have failed or when wars and other disturbances have created insufficiencies. However, the experience of scarcity – who gets to eat and who doesn't – has always depended on the ability of households and individuals to command access to food (Sen 1981) and, hence, on the distribution of economic and political power within society.

Within most common regimes, for instance, where management of land is a communal affair, scarcity and its resulting hardship are a shared phenomenon. One reason lies in the limits that joint ownership and responsibilities place upon the ability of any one group or individual to exercise institutional power over others (*The Ecologist* 1992). Gender and class inequalities certainly exist, both between and within households, and should not be played down. Nonetheless, in general, a rough equity prevails in which everyone has some degree of bargaining power – the survival of all depends upon no one putting any one else in the community at risk. No one is thus likely to starve whilst others are comfortable.

Where common regimes give way to state or market-based regimes, the experience of scarcity is different. With the commodification or state expropriation of land, for example, control over subsistence is assigned to actors outside of the community, almost always to the detriment of those whose bargaining power is weak. In an undiluted market economy, for example, access to food is no longer dependent on being part of – and contributing to – a social network: instead, food goes to those who have money to buy it. Only those who, in the economists' jargon, have the income to translate their biological needs into 'effective demand' get to eat. In the global supermarket of today's world, people earning perhaps $25 a year – if they are lucky – must compete for the same food with people who earn $25 a hour, or even $25 a minute.

It is this market logic – and the power structures that drive it – that lies behind the paradox of people starving despite abundant local harvests; that explains why planeloads of vegetables were exported daily from the famine-stricken Sahelian region during the 1970s to feed already well-fed Europeans; that ensures that cats belonging to rich Europeans are often better fed than children of low-paid or unemployed European workers; that condemns an estimated 800 million people, including 2 million children in the UK alone, to malnutrition and hunger; and that ensures that, for the many, scarcity – previously a *temporary* phenomenon shared by all – is now a perennial feature of life (Xenon 1989).

Indeed, the deliberate manufacture of scarcity now provides one of the principal means through which powerful state and private interests 'monopolize resources, control markets and suppress the demographic majority'. Such brazen use of scarcity as an instrument of 'population control' – in its original sense of 'controlling people' – is not unique to free market economies or to any one historical era. It is, however, only possible in societies where elite interests – whether state apparatchiks, feudal landlords, colonial sahibs, military wannabes or corporate executives – have the ability to deny the majority control over the resources and markets on which their livelihoods depend.

Recognizing the existence of socially generated scarcity – insufficient necessities for some people and not others – is not to deny absolute scarcity – insufficient resources, no matter how equitably they are distributed. We live on a finite planet and there are, incontrovertibly, limits to the ability of the earth to accommodate human numbers, pollution, resource depletion and other demands on its 'ecological services'. It is, however, to insist that differentiating between socially generated scarcity and absolute scarcity is a *sine qua non* for any sensible discussion of the causes of ecological degradation, deprivation, food scarcity and other problems often attributed to 'overpopulation' – and hence the social upheaval, including violence, that they can help trigger. As Andrew Ross remarks:

> For more than two decades now, public consciousness has sustained complex assumptions about both kinds of scarcity. In that same period of time, however, neo-liberalism's austerity regime has ushered in what can only be described as a pro-scarcity climate, distinguished, economically, by deep concessions and cutbacks, and, politically, by the rollback of 'excessive' rights. As a result, the new concerns about natural scarcity have been paralleled, every step of the way, by a brutal imposition of social scarcity. More often than not, then, the two kinds of scarcity have been confused, either deliberately, in order to reinforce austerity measures against the poor, or else inadvertently, through lack of information and education about how natural resources are produced and distributed. (Ross 1996: 6)

Ross points out that it is important to distinguish the ways in which one type of scarcity is related to the other and the ways it is not, so as to forge appropriate responses. Resource shortages and ecological degradation, he argues, are primarily a result of the uneven social measures that 'manufacture scarcity all over the world for the economic and political gain of powerful interests'. The systematic inequalities that block peoples' access to income, health, education and democratic rights, for example, are primarily responsible for the geographical and sociological 'profile' of ecological degradation. Even in those instances where ecological scarcity appears unconnected to social scarcity, its character is nonetheless 'defined by economic forces, which are … fundamentally linked to the social and cultural tendencies that fuel pro-scarcity politics'. In sum, 'there is no easy separation of the two kinds of scarcity' (Ross 1996: 6).

Food scarcity provides just one of many examples that make Ross's point. Undoubtedly 'natural' events such as floods and droughts play a part in creating hunger and malnutrition: so too does the ecological degradation that results when people are crowded onto marginal lands. But, in an age of human-induced climate change and of projects that divert whole river systems, neither droughts nor floods can be viewed as entirely 'natural' events. Similarly, the forces that crowd people onto marginal lands cannot be separated from policies and practices that daily generate scarcity for poorer people by denying them control over land, inputs, markets and decision-making. Historically, control over land, for example, has always been vital to the livelihoods of the world's poorest people. Lack of access to land not only denies people the ability to grow or to gather their own food: it is also excludes them from a source of power. Who controls the land – and how they do so – affects how land is used and to whom the benefits of its use accrue. (Tansey and Worsley 1995: 87).

Highly concentrated land ownership is now a feature of agriculture in both North and South. In the USA, nearly half the country's farmland is held by just 124,000 corporations or individuals – just 4 per cent of the total number of farm owners (Krebs 1992: 60). In Guatemala, 65 per cent of the best agricultural land is owned by just two per cent of the population (Colchester 1993: 113) – a figure that is not atypical for other countries in Central America. In Brazil, a mere 340 of the largest landowners, many of whom are foreign-owned transnational companies, own more land than all the country's peasants put together. The 18 largest landowners own an area equivalent to that of the Netherlands, Portugal and Switzerland combined. In the Philippines, 5 per cent of all families control 80 per cent of the agricultural land, despite seven land reform laws since 1933 (Leonen 1993: 275).

The corollary of such concentration of land ownership in the hands of the few is land scarcity for the many. In the Philippines, about 72 per cent of rural households (three-fifths of the Philippine population) are landless or near-landless. Tenant farmers must contend with rents which account for between 25 and 90 per cent of their production costs. Usury at rates of 100 per cent in three months or 50 per cent in one month is common. Half of all those who make a living from agriculture are farm workers, often earning as little as $1 a day (Leonen 1993: 274).

In Central America as a whole, small and medium-sized farms producing for local consumption and local sale represent about 94 per cent of existing farms but use only 9 per cent of the farmland. Meanwhile, 85 per cent of the best farmland is used to grow crops for export (Barry 1987: xiv). In Costa Rica, 55 per cent of all rural households are landless or near-landless, whereas the cattle owned by two thousand politically powerful ranching families occupy more than half of the nation's arable, most fertile land (Durning 1989). As in other countries throughout the region, smallholders have been pushed from their land into areas where soils are poor and prone to erosion. In Guatemala, huge swathes of land owned by the biggest landlords – an estimated 1.2 million hectares – lie idle, either because the price of export crops is too low to justify planting or because the land is being held simply for speculation. Meanwhile, some 310,000 landless labourers over 20 years of age are without permanent employment (Colchester 1993: 114). A complicating factor is that ownership or continued access to land is not secure for many people. Some 22 per cent of farms in the country are held by squatters with limited rights.

Landlessness and poverty go hand in hand. Eight out of ten farmers in Central America do not own enough land to sustain their families, forcing them to look for seasonal jobs. In Guatemala, government figures from the mid-1980s estimated that 86 per cent of families were living below the official poverty line, with 55 per cent classified as 'extremely poor'. Rates of malnutrition reflect these figures: a national survey in 1980 found that only 27 per cent of all children between 6 months and 5 years showed normal physical development, with 45 per cent showing moderate to severe retardation in their growth (Colchester 1993: 114).

Land concentration in the Third World is not accidental. It has always been resisted, not least by popular movements demanding land redistribution. Imbalances of power, however, have enabled landowners to ensure that, by and large, land reform programmes have either been put on hold, subverted or short-lived. In other instances, they have been framed, not as a means of addressing insecurity of tenure, but as a means of replacing peasant systems of farming with industrialized agriculture.

By defining rural poverty in terms of insufficient productivity (solution: high-yielding crop varieties and agrochemicals) rather than a lack of access to sufficient land (solution: agrarian reform), some governments, in alliance with richer farmers and international development agencies, used 'land reform' to appropriate land for the Green Revolution instead of freeing it up for peasant agriculture. The ultimate aim of such 'reforms' was to transform Third World farming into 'a dynamic productive sector' (Alexandratos 1988) by extending export crop production and by drawing peasants still further into the cash economy where they were at a disadvantage.

The promotion of off-farm inputs – chemical fertilizers, pesticides and improved seeds – has forced farmers to buy what was previously free, in addition to locking them into a cycle of diminishing returns on fertilizers and increasing pesticide use. As a result, thousands of small farmers – including those who had gained land under previous land reform programmes – have fallen into debt, their land holdings bought up by richer neighbours. In South Korea, where the army was mobilized to rip up traditional varieties of rice and to compel farmers to plant Green Revolution varieties, the number of rural households in debt rose 'from 76 per cent in 1971 to 90 per cent in 1983 and to an astounding 98 per cent in 1985' (Bello and Rosenfeld 1990: 86). As a result, farmers have left the land in droves: 34,000 migrated to the cities in 1986, 41,000 in 1987 and 50,000 in 1988. Many of the farmers who remain have now abandoned the new varieties and are returning to planting traditional seeds.

Thus, for marginal groups of people, the promotion of Green Revolution technologies – the hallmark of 'efficient' farming – has generated yet more scarcity of land and of food as the land becomes further concentrated in fewer and fewer hands. In India, the resulting social conflicts have been cited as one of the major causes of violence against the Sikhs – rich farmers in the Punjab having benefited most, economically, from the Green Revolution – conflicts which have frequently been ascribed to ethnic differences (Shiva 1989).

Widespread ecological degradation has also followed the systematic undermining of ecologically sound systems of agriculture and the adoption of Green Revolution techniques. Such degradation is now in itself a major cause of socially generated scarcity. In the Sudan, for example, the combination of mechanized farming, monoculture and the search for quick profits has caused an estimated 17 million hectares of rainfed arable land – almost half the country's potential arable land – to lose its topsoil. As Mohamed Suliman reports:

> Traditional agriculture in the Sudan follows crop rotation systems and fallow periods to conserve and regenerate the fragile land. The absentee owners of mechanized farms, however, are interested in quick economic returns: knowing that they can move on to new areas, migrant workers employed on these farms tend to neglect the fallow period prescribed by the government and grow the same crop on the same piece of land for several years. (Suliman 1993: 106)

Productivity is high in the first two to four years, after which yields start to decline: the severely exhausted and eroded land is abandoned around the seventh year when yields fall below profitable levels. The area east of the Nile has been most affected. Loss of tree and plant cover there has exposed the clay soils to wind erosion and compaction, enhancing surface run-off, particularly in the three months when rain falls, often in heavy storms. As the land becomes degraded, so the mechanized farms have sought to expand onto lands farmed or grazed by local subsistence farmers, creating land scarcity for those who previously had sufficient land. In many cases, the result has been open conflict – conflict which again has usually been ascribed, wrongly, to ethnicity and overpopulation.

As land and water become increasingly degraded, and control over such resources increasingly concentrated, so the livelihoods of peasant farmers, the landless and the near-landless become increasingly precarious. No longer able to rely on growing their food, the vast majority have to buy it instead. How much and what they get to eat depends on their ability to earn money or on the state's willingness to support them. For the World Bank and other development agencies, this necessity has frequently been interpreted as evidence of the need to integrate Third World agriculture still further into the global economy so as to increase the income of farmers and to generate rural and urban employment.

Yet, as economist Amartya Sen points out, the creation of famine and hunger results not from the exclusion of the marginalized from markets (they have always marketed goods) but from the normal working of markets. In his classic text, *Poverty and Famines*, Sen stresses that the famines which decimated peasants in India in 1943 and in Ethiopia, the Sahel and Bangladesh in 1974 were not the result of market failures, but of those market and non-market mechanisms (including the ownership of resources) which undermine the ability of poorer sections of the community to command goods on the market (Sen 1981; Mackintosh 1990). The terms on which people come to the market – and in particular their ability to exercise control over resources and trade – are thus critical to whether they experience scarcity as starvation and famine (Mackintosh 1990)

The development policies pursued by Third World countries, under the tutelage of the IMF and the World Bank, have dramatically undercut the bargaining power of poorer people within the market. The growing pool of landless labourers, many of whom are women, means that the rural poor must compete for jobs in a 'buyer's market', giving employers the upper hand in determining wages and working conditions. Real wages for labourers have been rapidly declining in many Third World countries. As writer and researcher Jon Bennet remarks of the estimated 1.75 million seasonal labourers who compete for work in the cotton-growing areas of Sudan:

> Stripped of their traditional means of support, farmworkers [have] become simply components of production ... increasingly vulnerable to the shifting fortunes of an economy outside their control. As a seemingly limitless resource with minimal bargaining power, they [can] now be hired or fired at will. (Bennet 1987: 59)

Those working as labourers in export-crop plantations have been particularly vulnerable to exploitative wages and working conditions. Because exporters rely on markets abroad rather than at home for the sale of their crops, low wages are not 'necessarily so bad for business' since 'profits do not significantly depend on the ability to sell domestic products to wage earners or peasants' (O'Brien and Gruenbaum 1991: 178).

Even where peasant producers do have access to land, they may be hardly better off than landless labourers in an economy over which they have little control. Increasingly, large corporate producers are moving away from direct ownership of land towards indirect control through contracts with peasant smallholders. Under the terms of the contract, a company agrees to buy given quantities of crops of particular specifications at a fixed price in return for supplying inputs and advice. The peasants retain ownership of their land, but have to abide by the conditions set by the company regarding cultivation, marketing and pricing, if they are to sell the crop (Halfani and Baker 1984: 48). The risks of production, heightened by unstable global markets, are thus transferred to the peasant, who becomes, in effect, a tied-labourer for the company (Raikes 1988: 57).

Moreover, because the onus of finding and organizing the labour force is placed on the contracted grower – generally the male head of household – contract farming often leads to increased domestic violence as family and marital responsibilities are forcibly 'renegotiated' (Watts 1994: 130). The resulting intra-household tensions can particularly disadvantage women, whose access to food within households, even within relatively equitable commons regimes, has historically been skewed by gender biases. Food owned by the household, for example, is not always shared equally: gender subordination results in women often being the last to eat and explains why, in a number of recent incidents of famine, food shortages have resulted in women being neglected, abandoned and 'sold into prostitution in the interests of male survival' (Downs et al. 1991).

Eight hundred million people worldwide now experience socially induced food scarcity – and the violence that this often entails. Rather than address the inequitable power relations that lie behind such scarcity, however, 'solutions' that minimize disruption to the status quo are put forward by the generators of such scarcity.

One tactic has been to reduce the problem to abstract mathematical equations in which projected agricultural output is set against projected human numbers to justify the continuance of current forms of food production. Factors that do not compute – a wide range of different and interacting power relationships, systems of land tenure, food grown and traded outside the formal markets, and so on – are simply left out of the equation.

Backed by 'the amoral authority of numbers' (Ross 1996: 20), such quantitative assessments of global food budgets are powerful tools in colonizing the future for specific interest groups. Legitimate concerns about future rates of population growth, for example, are regularly harnessed to insist that current policies aimed at industrializing agriculture must be pursued more aggressively. Estimated projections for population increases are thus set alongside figures of declining output (usually guesstimates based on officially marketed agricultural produce) to argue the case for an overall increase in pesticide and fertilizer use and the employment of genetically engineered crops – or to dismiss traditional 'low external input technologies' as inadequate to meet the challenge of feeding an extra 2.5 billion people in the next thirty years (World Bank 1996: 1). The myriad ways in which production could be increased using labour-intensive, organic methods of agriculture are steadfastly ignored, as is the increasing tendency for many peasants to sell their crops on the black market or to consume the food themselves – produce which is not accounted for in official output estimates.

In the absence of radical change to current economic and social structures, however, increased output – whatever way it is achieved – will not translate into increased numbers of people fed. In a world in which scarcity is continually generated as an unavoidable – some would argue, deliberate – feature of the food system, the experience of hunger will only increase. In addition, by inexorably undermining the capacity of land to produce food, the ecological damage caused by intensive farming is creating the conditions for absolute scarcity – where even equitable economic and social arrangements may prove insufficient to prevent widespread human impoverishment. Artificial fertilizers and chemical sprays, for example, have disastrously undermined the natural fertility of soils. As farmers have ceased to apply manure and other organic material to the land, so the soil's structure in many areas has begun to break down, increasing its vulnerability to erosion – an estimated 24 billion tonnes of soil being eroded from the world's agricultural lands every year. This is enough soil to fill a train of freight cars stretching from the earth to the moon – and back again – five times.

Yet, genuine concerns about the impacts of environmental degradation, coupled with equally genuine concerns over population growth, are being reworked by some policymakers to legitimize yet further land enclosure. The UN Food and Agriculture Organization (FAO), for example, has proposed that, in the interests of 'environmental protection' and 'sustainability', all national governments should 'zone' agricultural lands, rangelands and forests. Under this policy, 'high potential areas' (that is, the most fertile areas) would be set aside for intensive export crop monocultures or livestock rearing and the 'carrying and population supporting capacity of major agricultural areas' assessed. Where such areas are deemed to be 'overpopulated', steps should be taken to change 'the man/land ratio' by 'facilitating the accommodation of migrating populations in better endowed areas' (FAO 1992: 16) Peasants who have been forced on to marginal lands as a result of 'high potential areas' being taken over for intensive export-orientated agriculture would thus be liable to resettlement at the whim of any government which deemed them a threat to 'the environment'. The FAO does not even consider the possibility that ecological stress could be better relieved by reclaiming 'high potential areas' for peasant agriculture.

Conclusion

Discussions of population and food supply which leave out relationships will always mask the true nature of food scarcity – who gets to eat and who doesn't – and lead to 'solutions' that are simplistic, technocratic, frequently oppressive and gender-blind – all of which, ultimately, reinforce the very structures that create ecological damage and hunger. Indeed, so long as one person has the power to deny food to another, even two people may be judged 'too many'. Recognizing that fact – and putting equity at the centre of the debate – is a *sine qua non* for any sensible discussion of the causes of food insecurity and food scarcity.

It is also a *sine qua non* of any sensible discussion on conflict. The violence that is increasingly 'explained' by labels such as 'population wars' or 'inter-tribal conflict' is generally not the product of 'ingrained' hatreds or 'too many babies' but of 'a complex web of politics, economics, history, psychology and a struggle for identity'. Indeed, more nuanced accounts of such conflicts almost invariably reveal the 'objective truths' claimed for 'blood' and 'baby' explanations of ethnic violence as the self-interested and highly partisan agendas of small groups within society whose preoccupation with ethnicity is rooted not in a celebration of cultural diversity but in a desire to dominate others.

Notes

The author would like to thank Sarah Sexton and Larry Lohmann for their invaluable comments on earlier drafts of this chapter. I would also like to thank the programme in Agrarian Studies at Yale University for financial support.

1. For a critique of this view as it applies to Sierra Leone, see Richards 1996.
2. As Uvin (1996: 15) records: 'Until the genocide, and in accordance with its positive and popular image [among donors], Rwanda was one of the most aided countries in the world. According to the OECD, official development aid accounted for 11.4 per cent of its GNP in 1989–90; above the already very high average for Africa and the least developed countries.'
3. Uvin (1996: 14) notes how international aid agencies consistently ignored the institutionalized racism in Rwanda. Following Ferguson (1990), he notes how the country's development problems were predominantly analysed in terms of the

technical 'solutions' which the aid agencies (notably the World Bank) were set up to provide. The result was a depoliticized image of Rwanda that reflected the institutional priorities of the aid agencies and which downplayed (or deliberately obscured) pervasive human rights violations and state-organized racism within the country – to the benefit of the Hutu ruling elite and at tragic cost to the Tutsis.

4. More recently, Edward Goldsmith has similarly argued for the separation of Hutus and Tutsis in Rwanda. Just about every country in Africa, he maintains, is a 'time-bomb waiting to explode, precisely because each one has been created without any regard whatsoever for the ethnic differences among the people within its borders – and it is a question of time before the various ethnic groups that make up these artificial countries seek to obtain their independence'. There is undoubted truth in this. Most African states were created by the colonial powers without consideration for ethnic self-identification, with the result that many groups found themselves divided between different countries by arbitrarily imposed boundaries: many have since struggled to assert their right to self-determination. The Biafran civil war is just one example. However, the narrative of the African 'time-bomb' fails to explain many of the conflicts in contemporary Africa, the majority of which reflect a much more complex politics than that suggested by Goldsmith. In many cases, pre-colonial ethnic identities have evolved into new (and different) identities which may or may not even identify with the supposedly 'authentic', 'natural' ethnic units of the pre-colonial era. Moreover, the demands of rebel groups in many of the conflicts are not necessarily centred on asserting the rights of one ethnic group to the exclusion of others, nor on the redrawing of existing boundaries to create new 'mini-states': on the contrary, many movements seek a fairer deal for all ethnic groups within existing state boundaries. The accent is thus on challenging the current political structures that foster ethnic exclusion today, rather than making such exclusion the basis for a new political geography for the future. For further discussion, see Richards 1996.

Bibliography

Alexandratos, N. (ed.), 1988, *World Agriculture: Toward 2000, An FAO Study*, Belhaven Press, by arrangement with FAO, London.

Alund, A., 1996, 'The Stranger: Ethnicity, Identity and Belonging', in S. Gustavsson and L. Lewin, *The Future of the Nation-State: Essays on Cultural Pluralism and Political Integration*, Routledge, London.

Anderson, B., 1991, *Imagined Communities*, Verso, London.

Appadurai, A., 1996, *Modernity at Large: Cultural Dimensions of Globalization*, University of Minnesota Press, Minneapolis.

Axtmann, R., 1996, *Liberal Democracy into the 21st Century: Globalization, Integration and the Nation State*, Manchester University Press, Manchester.

Balibar, É. and I. Wallerstein, 1991, *Race, Nation, Class: Ambiguous Identities*, Verso, London.

Bandyopadhyay, J., 1988, 'The Ecology of Drought and Water Scarcity', *The Ecologist*, vol. 18, nos 2/3.

Barry, T., 1987, *Roots of Rebellion: Land and Hunger in Central America*, South End Press, Boston MA.

Bello, W. and S. Rosenfeld, 1990, *Dragons in Distress: Asia's Miracle Economies in Crisis*, Institute of Food and Development Policy, Food First, San Francisco.

Bennet, J., with S. George, 1987, *The Hunger Machine*, Polity Press, Cambridge.

Chossudovsky, M., 1997, *The Globalisation of Poverty: Impacts of IMF and World Bank Reforms*, Zed Books/Third World Network, London.

Colchester, M., 1993, 'Guatemala: The Clamour for Land and the Fate of the Forests', in M. Colchester and L. Lohmann (eds), *The Struggle for Land and the Fate of the Forests*, World Rainforest Movement/The Ecologist, Zed Books, London.

Downs, R.E., D.O. Kerner and S.P. Reyna, 1991, *The Political Economy of African Famine*, Gordon & Breach, Reading.

Durning, A.B., 1989, *Poverty and the Environment: Reversing the Downward Spiral*, Worldwatch Paper 92, Washington DC.

The Ecologist, 1992, 'Whose Common Future? Reclaiming the Commons', vol. 22, no. 3.

FAO (Food and Agriculture Organization of the United Nations), 1993, *Agriculture: Towards 2010*, FAO, Rome.

FAO/Ministry of Agriculture, Nature Management and Fisheries of The Netherlands, 1992a, *Sustainable Agriculture and Rural Development*, Draft Proposals, 's-Hertenbosch, The Netherlands.

FAO/Ministry of Agriculture, Nature Management and Fisheries of The Netherlands, 1992b, *The Den Bosch Declaration and Agenda for Action on Sustainable Agriculture and Rural Development*, 's-Hertenbosch, The Netherlands.

Ferguson, J., 1990, *The Anti-politics Machine: 'Development', Depoliticization and Bureaucratic Power in Lesotho*, Cambridge University Press, Cambridge.

Goldsmith, E., 1971, 'Basic Principles of Cultural Ecology', *The Ecologist*, vol. 2, no. 5.

Halfani, M.S. and J. Baker, 1984, 'Agribusiness and Agrarian Change', in J. Barker (ed.), *The Politics of Agriculture in Tropical Africa*, Sage Series on African Modernization and Development, Volume 9, Sage Publications, London.

Hirsch, P., 1997, 'Seeking Culprits: Ethnicity and Resource Conflict', *Watershed*, vol. 3, no. 1, July–October 1997.

Hitchens, C., 1997, *Hostage to History: Cyprus from the Ottomans to Kissinger*, Verso, London.

Hobsbawm, E. and T. Ranger, 1983, *The Invention of Tradition*, Columbia University Press, New York.

Keane, F., 1996, 'No Man is an Island', in *Letter to Daniel*, Penguin, Harmondsworth.

Kinealy, C., 1994, *This Great Calamity: The Irish Famine 1845–52*, Gill & Macmillan, Dublin.

Kinealy, C., 1997, *A Death-Dealing Famine: The Great Hunger in Ireland*, Pluto Press, London.

Kothari, S., 1996, 'Rising from the Margins: The Awakening of Civil Society in the Third World', *Development*, no. 3.

Kothari, S., 1997, 'Whose Independence? The Social Impact of Economic Reform in India', *Journal of International Affairs*, vol. 51, no. 1, Summer.

Krebs, A.V., 1992, *The Corporate Reapers: The Book of Agribusiness*, Essential Books, Washington DC.

Leonen, M., 1993, 'The Philippines: Dwindling Frontiers and Agrarian Reform', in M. Colchester and L. Lohmann (eds), *The Struggle for Land and the Fate of the Forests*, World Rainforest Movement/The Ecologist, Zed Books, London.

Lewis, J. and J. Knight, 1995, *The Twa of Rwanda: Assessment of the Situation of the Twa and Promotion of Twa Rights in Post-War Rwanda*, World Rainforest Movement and International Work Group for Indigenous Affairs, Oxford.

Mackintosh, M., 1990, 'Abstract Markets and Real Needs', in H. Berstein, B. Crow, M. Mackintosh and C. Martin, *The Food Question: Profits versus People?*, Earthscan, London.

Martono, 1985, Proceedings of the Meeting between the Department of Transmigration and the Inter-Governmental Group on Indonesia, Jakarta, 20 March 1985; quoted in M. Colchester, 'Unity and Diversity: Indonesia's Policy towards Tribal People', *The Ecologist*, vol. 16, nos 2/3, 1986, p. 59.

McGuire, J., P. Reeves and H. Brasted (eds), 1996, *Politics of Violence: From Ayodhya to Behrampada*, Sage, New Delhi.

O'Brien, J. and E. Gruenbaum, 1991, 'A Social History of Food, Famine and Gender in Twentieth-Century Sudan', in R.E. Downs, D.O. Kerner and S.P. Reyna, *The Political Economy of African Famine*, Gordon & Breach, Reading.

Prebble, J., 1969, *The Highland Clearances*, Penguin, Harmondsworth.

Prunier, G, 1995, *The Rwanda Crisis: History of a Genocide*, Columbia University Press, New York.

Putzel, J. and J. Cunningham, 1989, *Gaining Ground: Agrarian Reform in the Philippines*, War on Want, London.

Raikes, P., 1988, *Modernizing Hunger*, Catholic Institute for International Relations, in collaboration with James Currey, London.

Richards, P., 1996, *Fighting for the Rain Forest: War, Youth and Resources in Sierra Leone*, James Currey/Heinemann/International African Institute, Oxford.

Ross, A., 1996, 'The Lonely Hour of Scarcity', *Capitalism, Nature, Socialism*, vol. 7, no. 3, September.

Sen, A., 1981, *Poverty and Famines: An Essay on Entitlement and Deprivation*, Clarendon Press, Oxford.

Shiva, V., 1989, *The Violence of the Green Revolution: Ecological Degradation and Political Conflict in Punjab*, Codal, Dehra Dun.

Shiva, V., 1996, 'The Alternative to Corporate Protectionism', *Bija – The Seed*, nos 15/16.

Suliman, M., 1993, 'Civil War in the Sudan: From Ethnic to Ecological Conflict', *The Ecologist*, vol. 23, no. 3, May/June.

Taguieff, P.-A., 1993a, 'The Case of Alain de Benoist', *Telos*, nos 98–99, Winter.

Taguieff, P.-A., 1993b, 'The New Right on European Identity', *Telos*, nos 98–99, Winter.

Tansey, G. and T. Worsley, 1995, *The Food System: A Guide*, Earthscan, London.

Uvin, P., 1996, *Development, Aid and Conflict: Reflections from the Case of Rwanda*, Research for Action 24, United Nations University/WIDER, Helsinki.

de Waal, A., 1994, 'Genocide in Rwanda', *Anthropology Today*, vol. 10, no. 3, June.

Wachter, D. and N. North, 1996, *Land Tenure and Sustainable Management of Agricultural Soils*, Centre for Development and Environment, Institute of Geography, University of Berne, Switzerland.

Watts, M.J., 1994, 'Living Under Contract: The Social Impacts of Contract Farming in West Africa', *The Ecologist*, vol. 24, no. 4, July/August.

Woodham-Smith, C., 1963, *The Great Hunger: Ireland 1845–9*, Hamish Hamilton, London.

World Bank, 1996, 'Agricultural Action Plan – From Vision to Action in the Rural Sector', Office Memorandum from Caio Koch-Weser to James Wolfensohn, 23 February, Washington DC.

World Bank, 1986, *Rwandese Republic: A Third Education Project*, Staff Appraisal Report, South, Central and Indian Ocean Department, Washington DC.

Xenon, N., 1989, *Scarcity and Modernity*, Routledge, London.

2

The Rationality and Irrationality of Violence in Sub-Saharan Africa

Mohamed Suliman

Group violence is a phenomenon that appears baffling to rational thought. Complex social processes and phenomena, themselves dependent on a multitude of objective and subjective factors, impart uncertainty to the course of violent conflict as well as to our attempts to understand and judge it as the actual behaviour of actual people.

On first approximation, violence seems to be irrational, chaotic behaviour *par excellence*. It defies the practical principle that in the case of dispute over conflicting interests, cooperation is, in the long term, the most rewarding course of action. Yet history is replete with incidents of violence. We now know that irrationality and chaos do show an inherent order that allows us to discern certain repetitive patterns and to observe that chance and necessity are indeed woven together. Even in the realm of the social, the inherent inner necessity articulates itself in the form of chance. It is not surprising, therefore, to find that in the very complex area of social violence, the objective has not been totally overrun by the subjective and that familiar patterns and common traits may become discernible.

Thus, we may not be able to understand the rationality of social violence at the level of the individual participants, but we have a better chance of discerning some of its opaque reality as the concerted behaviour of a large number of people, so-called group violence. The rationality and irrationality of violence are thus two facets of the same reality.

Violent Conflict in Sub-Saharan Africa

In sub-Saharan Africa today there are no raging interstate armed conflicts. Irredentist and secessionist conflicts have receded, the Cold War and apartheid conflicts fought by proxy are on their way out, and liberation wars are relegated to the past. But internal violent conflicts are growing in number and ferocity.

Traditional conflict analysis, relying almost entirely on ethnic, religious and cultural dichotomies, has been unable to explain the spread of internal conflicts and has also failed to provide useful advice in the most important area of conflict research, namely conflict resolution. This approach to violent conflict often confuses causes, perceptions, manifestations, triggers and catalysts. It tends to overemphasize one or two elements in the complex web of causes of violent conflict, usually ethnicity, culture or religion. It has, therefore, been unable to appreciate fully the importance of economic and ecological factors in precipitating violent conflicts.

Historical Background

When the colonial powers introduced the market economy in sub-Saharan Africa at the beginning of the century, they simultaneously restricted its development and expansion by indigenous Africans in order to maintain economic and political control of the continent. After independence, however, an African 'bourgeoisie' began to evolve from a primarily mercantile social class now ostensibly freed from colonial control. There were, nevertheless, several strong barriers to the development and progress of a middle class such as that in Europe which had brought about the Industrial Revolution. Business people in sub-Saharan Africa lacked the major prerequisites for industrialization – namely capital, technical and scientific know-how, and markets – and so their focus shifted from manufacturing production to the extraction of natural resources and primary commodity production. The collapse of attempts at industrialization – mainly import-substitution industrialization – led to the exploitation of natural resources in a manner so thoughtless and unscrupulous that it soon endangered the traditional peasant and pastoral societies in many parts of the continent.

Since the 1970s, countries in sub-Saharan Africa have suffered from unfavourable terms of trade, servicing and repayment of foreign debt, structural adjustment programmes (SAPs) and persistent capital flight. This pressure has in turn been transmitted by the governing elite to the people and their natural environment. Unfair terms of trade at the international level are reflected in unfair terms of trade at the national level and more aggressive exploitation of natural resources. Just as poor developing countries were exporting more and importing less, so African peasants and pastoralists were forced to produce more and buy less in the local market. This invariably led to an acceleration of the rate of exploitation of all available natural resources. For example, forests were decimated by the expansion of large-scale mechanized farming, by commercial logging, mining operations, fires, wars, and the increasing demand for fuel wood.

Wherever human-made and natural adversities combine, as is the case in the Sahel with its persistent drought, subsistence economies begin to collapse. The assimilation of the African elite into the international free-market economy in the restricted role of resource extractors has received an enormous boost from the IMF and the World Bank. Their loan conditionalities have accelerated considerably the restructuring of resource utilization away from local needs and the local market towards the demands of the international market. Despite the rapid increase in the area of land in use and increased export capacity, the overall effect of the new export-oriented policies was negative. The value of primary commodities in the international market steadily declined and poverty worsened in the urban slums and in rural Africa.

To prosper, the African elite needed to export more. To survive, the African poor were forced to learn how to extract their basic needs from a shrinking resource base. In the process, conflicts tended to multiply and intensify. This economic/ecological dimension in the prevailing spectrum of conflict is steadily gaining in importance, both as cause and catalyst.

Conflicts are historical processes, not static events. Therefore, when the wealth of a nation is dwindling because of intensive exploitation and degradation, it is only logical to assume that this situation will have far-reaching negative repercussions on the social fabric, leading to conflict. To continue treating conflicts in Africa as purely ethnic, tribal or religious, ignoring in the process the growing impact of restricting or denying access to resources and the growing ecological degradation and depletion of the renewable resource base, could, ultimately, lead to a distorted understanding of the real situation and, consequently, limit the possibility of genuine conflict resolution.

An analysis of the civil war in the Sudan confirms the viability of this approach and the need to extend it to other African conflicts. Ecological degradation in northern Sudan, caused by large-scale mechanized cultivation, has had a significant role in the return of the civil war between the North and South of the country and in the gross destabilization of traditional agriculture and pastoralism in the most populous regions of the Sudan (Suliman 1992). The Sudan offers a prime example of how an African elite driven to specialize in resource extraction has degraded its resource base to the extent that its expansion becomes a necessity, justifying aggression against its own people and its neighbours.

A factor additional to both the socio-economic decline and the degradation of the natural environment is the militarization of rural poverty. Life in Africa revolves around the land, and when the land is degraded or access to it limited or denied the quality of people's lives is directly affected. And whenever land inadequacy and degradation are coupled with other push and pull factors such as political pressure, armed conflict, ethnic tension, deteriorating services and infrastructure, as well as physical insecurity, people begin to move to the safety of urban areas or they take up arms against the perceived enemy.

A Century of Increasing Violence

In the past, rural Africans faced with deteriorating living conditions would not have had to move far to find a richer ecozone. This exit option is now drastically limited, especially within the Sahel and Horn regions, because of the general worsening of the environmental situation, compounded by higher population densities, large-scale mechanized farming restricting access to land, and the growing poverty of rural life. Weakened governmental control of law and order has left many people with no option other than to join the militia of burgeoning mini-states and their civilian or military warlords, to challenge the central government, to destabilize neighbouring ones, to attack weaker communities, or simply to thrive on banditry and smuggling.

Early African clan societies seldom resorted to large-scale violence to settle disputes with neighbouring clans. The movie images of the savage warrior are grossly misleading and should not tempt us into believing that the early history of humanity was a continuous battle of survival of the fittest. Unfortunately, historians were and still are more interested in war than in peace. Long before the classic game of 'Prisoner's Dilemma' emerged people had learnt from hard experience the important lesson that cooperation brings about the best results for all concerned. The basic instinct is not to kill but to preserve life. Apprehension and fear dominated over recklessness and violence.

Early human groups were strong collectives, where the common goods were shared and where group solidarity and reciprocity were paramount. Neither on the individual nor on the social level did group violence play any significant role in the life of these early human societies. Early humans had a capacity but no need for aggression. The 'savage' was indeed peaceful!

Social or group violence is almost everywhere a product of the social division of labour and the consequent appearance of family and group competition over material and cultural resources. Even then, people tended to choose cooperation most of the time, because cooperation brings long-term rewards, while confrontation carries the risk of retaliation. Unfortunately, not all people choose cooperation all the time. Human beings have the tendency to undervalue future rewards and penalties. In *Passion within Reason* Robert Frank cites psychological evidence that people usually do not equate present rewards with future rewards. Thus, while there is genuine gain from cooperation over long periods of time, the temptation of short-term gains can be too strong to resist. People then break the rules and cheat. Violence can erupt, not because it is rewarding in the long run, nor because the future penalties will be light, but because the immediate gains are too tempting to resist. Most coup plotters lose out instantly or in the longer term. Yet the attraction of immediate rewards still lures many a soldier into giving it a try.

The Present Situation

The international constellation of power in the 1960s bore many advantages for the newly independent African countries. Governments could play off the rival superpowers in their bid to attract development aid and military hardware, while accomplished tacticians such as Siad Barre of Somalia or Mobutu Sese Seko of former Zaïre succeeded in establishing complex patrimonial states, in which benefits were allocated from the top down in return for political support. By encouraging factionalism and sectarianism, this process undermined both the institutional base and the development effort, with serious ramifications for the internal stability of many countries. When resource flows declined, under the combined effects of the oil shock and falling primary commodity prices – the principal exports of most African countries – many patrimonial states were no longer able to meet the demands made upon them. As the state had since independence claimed the monopoly on modernity and dominated the economy, there were few private sector or civil society mechanisms to absorb the shock of state recession. Unable to deliver on the promise of development, many African states, further racked by structural adjustment policies in the 1980s, faced a severe crisis of legitimacy. Groups and sections excluded from the benefits of the receding patrimonial state were increasingly taking up arms to enforce their claims to a shrinking and contested resource base, often with international support. This was provided, as long as it fitted the designs of Cold War strategists, and across Africa insurgency leaders and government politicians alike became adept at dressing their causes in the language of the opposing ideologies of Right and Left, of East and West.

The collapse of the Eastern Bloc deprived some African politicians of a coveted advantage. Aid flows declined as the strategic pertinence of their countries diminished, and the triumphant and aid-fatigued West turned its economic ambitions towards the former foe. In Africa, however, civil wars, insurgencies and low-level conflict continued unabated. Political analysts in industrialized countries began to revise their assessments of African warfare in keeping with the tremendous changes that have taken place since the 'end of history'. From the early 1990s onwards, three major schools of thought have dominated the approach to African conflict in the West: cultural essentialism, neo-Malthusianism, and natural disaster theory.

Borrowing heavily from cultural anthropology, the proponents of cultural essentialism (Huntingdon 1993; Kaplan 1994) reduce African conflicts to ethnic differences, the absence of overarching political institutions in sub-Saharan Africa, and a primordial propensity to violence. In the envisaged global realignment into cultural blocs, Africa occupies a residual category with the state portrayed as the helpless victim of deep-seated centrifugal tendencies. This school of thought is supported by the findings of the neo-Malthusians (Chase, Hill and Kennedy 1996; Homer-Dixon 1994), who link the volatility of African politics to the progressive degradation of the natural resource base, in this case, the unsustainable extraction of natural renewable resources, which in turn can be traced back to population growth and the lack of economic diversification.

Followers of another school counsel Western powers to help reduce unsustainable exploitation of renewable resources, mainly soil, water and forests, and to slow the rate of population growth in these countries as the remedy for the pernicious violent conflicts in Africa.

The advice of the essentialist school, however, is to disengage from this inscrutable and self-made web of problems. With African warfare presented as the by-product of a lower culture, the development project is doomed, and scarce resources are better spent on more promising candidates. Moral qualms are laid to rest by reference to the internal generation of scarcity, which absolves colonial and post-colonial actors of any remaining shred of responsibility.

At first sight, a more sympathetic reading is offered by the natural disaster theoreticians, prominent in the development industry. Here, the humanitarian approach is writ large, and incorporated into the development paradigm. Irrepressibly optimistic, adherents of this school regard conflict as a transitory setback in the development process, on a par with natural catastrophes, and open to similar remedial measures: airlifts, distribution centres and provision of basic commodities.

This chapter will try to show that the reduction of such complex social phenomena, as violent conflict truly is, to simple causal explanations is not scientifically defensible and can also encourage misguided and even counterproductive response patterns. It argues that violent conflict is usually the outcome of interconnected, political, economic and ecological processes that take place in a given historical, cultural and spiritual matrix.

Even in the environmentally degraded, socially impoverished and highly populated regions of Africa, people prefer cooperation to violent confrontation most of the time. Only a combination of unfavourable factors will make them cross the threshold between war and peace. The most pernicious among these are the denial or limiting of people's access to renewable natural resources, and ecological degradation.

Denying Access to Natural and Social Resources

Work carried out on environment and conflict by a number of research groups has shown that ecological degradation can act as the cause or catalyst of violent conflicts. Greater emphasis, however, has been given in the research to the impact of ecological degradation than to the implications of denying or limiting access to renewable resources. This focus on the degradation of the renewable resource base imparts by default greater significance to the causes of environmental degradation, namely human and animal population growth, climatic variations and so on. Such conflict analysis tends to limit conflict resolution to tackling the causes of ecological degradation and in the process neglects or belittles the implications of limiting people's access to vital resources. With environmental degradation as the focal point, the proposed conflict-resolution mechanisms are thus more technical than economic or political.

This school emphasizes issues of environmental conservation and rehabilitation as conflict management mechanisms: for example, better water management, soil conservation, reforestation, family planning to curb population growth. The crucial issues of the economy, state power and politics are inadvertently pushed aside. The persistent inequity in resource allocation, which is inherently political and economic, and the role of the beneficiaries and perpetrators of the status quo are thus taken out of the spotlight.

In order to assess properly the impact of denying or limiting access to renewable resources in sub-Saharan African countries, with their economies largely confined to primary commodity production, such very important issues as structural adjustment programmes and export agriculture; the collapse of the terms of trade as a consequence of the deterioration of the prices of primary commodities; the economic, social and ecological implications of foreign debt and of capital flight; the reversal of investment trends and so on, must be taken into full consideration as integral to understanding the causes of violent conflicts and ultimately to conflict resolution.

In all the group conflicts we scrutinized in the Sahel and the Horn regions, access to natural and social resources expressed in terms of justice, fairness, equitable sharing and equal development was the primary concern of people in arms.

With resource access, conflict research enters the realm of politics, the economy and the state. Technical solutions to violent conflict situations are no longer adequate. Both conflict analysis and conflict resolution must critique the conventional wisdom in this area and strive to be interdisciplinary.

The Environmental Factor

Environmental scarcity of renewable resources, especially cropland, fresh water, marine resources and forests, is becoming more and more significant as cause and catalyst of armed conflict, especially in the developing world. Scarcity of renewable resources such as soil, water, fauna and flora does not inevitably lead to violent confrontation and could well bring about desirable cooperation among the affected parties. Yet in situations where this scarcity is aggravated by social and economic upheavals, as is the case in many poor Third World and most sub-Saharan African countries, the confrontational aspect of environmental scarcity appears to gain predominance.

In spite of its growing impact, researchers in the field of environment and conflict concede that environmental scarcity is but one in a complex web of causes that collectively precipitate violent conflicts. Environmental scarcity functions within the given multi-layered matrix of history, economy and politics and is most acute where human and livestock population pressures are reinforced by unequal resource access. Environmental scarcity is widespread in sub-Saharan Africa.

The African natural environment is fragile. The movie image of Africa as a continent overflowing with fertility is seriously misleading. In fact the African environment is the most fragile on earth, and its vulnerability has been pushed to the limit over the past hundred years. Although the land and the people often demonstrate remarkable resilience in adversity, all too often the pressures of unsustainable exploitation of renewable resources have been enormously destructive. A spiral of human and environmental disasters has been the result.

No other continent suffers the same degree of separation of agriculture and livestock. No other continent has such a high proportion of soils that are infertile and so easily degraded. No other continent has a climate of such unpredictability. These factors, made more potent still by their combination, have severely handicapped African agriculture (Harrison, 1987). In the web of causes that precipitate violent conflicts in sub-Saharan Africa, environmental scarcity (understood as degradation of and the denial or limiting of access to renewable natural resources) stands out as probably the most important factor. That is, violent conflicts arise mainly out of ecological and economic distortions.

The traditional assumption, that violent conflicts in Africa emanate from ethnic/tribal, religious, and/or cultural differences, is seriously limited. Except for 'old', so-called traditional conflicts, ethnic dichotomies appear to be rather a consequence of violent conflicts than a cause of them. However, ethnic, religious and cultural dichotomies are very potent in people's perceptions of violent conflicts – perceptions held by many fighters on both sides of the conflict divide – but are weak or non-existent as root causes of 'new' conflicts. However, the longer a conflict persists, the more these ethnic, religious and cultural factors come into play. In an old conflict, when even the initial causes have petered out or died away, that 'abstract', ideological ethnicity becomes an active material and social force.

Somalia is a land of great ethnic, religious and cultural homogeneity. However, when competition intensified over control of the state and the economy and for a greater share of renewable resources – mainly land and water – the contestants evoked sub-ethnic, clan differences and fought along these clan lines for economic gain and state control. Wars have rarely proclaimed their true motivation and the Somali conflict is no exception. However, if the violent conflict in Somalia continues unabated for a number of years, these weak clan barriers will harden into strong ethnic divides and will eventually become material causes of violence in their own right. That is why it is generally easier to resolve new violent conflicts than settle old ones.

The Case of the Horn of Africa

The Horn has been a conflict-prone area for centuries. However, sources of and actors in war have changed significantly over time. Today, the Horn countries are confronted with a variety of endemic and protracted conflicts as well as with numerous potential conflicts at all levels: inter-state, sub-national, ethnic, clan-based. The IGAD countries not only belong to the poorest countries in the world; in the *Human Development Index* they figure in the lowest ranks. Various types of environmental problem – such as drought, water scarcity, soil erosion, desertification, erratic precipitation pattern, and the overuse of scarce renewable resources – also affect them. Wars of the recent past, widespread poverty and environmental degradation form a triangle, each angle of which has a causal impact on each of the others.

What is more, war-torn societies and degraded resources can aggravate protracted conflicts, provoke new ones and finally lead to violent clashes and war. In this multi-causal setting, environmentally induced conflicts may be defined as conflicts that involve environmental degradation whether as a cause, as a consequence or as an intervening variable – most often appearing in combination with social, ethnic or political elements (Dokken and Graeger 1995).

Nevertheless, environmentally induced conflicts manifest themselves as political, social, economic, ethnic, religious or territorial conflicts, and as such differ from resource wars. Since conflicts over non-renewables such as oil, gas and minerals are historically well-known events, environmentally induced conflicts over renewables have not been known until recently, at least not as a phenomenon on a global scale. In fact, the sources of conflicts are not unequal distribution or scarcity as such. They arise from growing supply-side restrictions, resulting from either degradation, pollution or depletion of resources.

Environmental scarcity, which has always been the result of violence and war and an instrument put to their use, has recently become in itself a source of violence in all of the IGAD countries. The denial or limiting of access to renewable resources, water scarcity and soil erosion are the major threats to environmental security in the Horn countries. The farmer-pastoralist conflict in Jebel Marra massif in the western Sudan province of Darfur is a good example of environmentally induced conflict. In particular, since the drought of 1983–84 the nomads have been increasing their pressure on the Fur farmers, penetrating the semi-arid and humid mountain areas with their herds much deeper, longer, and in greater numbers than they ever did in the past (Suliman 1996). Another example is the clashes between the Baggara Arab pastoralists in south Kordofan and the Dinka of Bahr el Ghazal province in Sudan. A third example is the migration of farmers from the degraded highlands in Eritrea to the lowlands of Gash Setit, where the Kunama minority protests against the threatening growth of an alien population in this area (Barentu and neighbouring villages such as Shambiko). The pastures of the Haud in the eastern Ogaden are the object of contention between two Somali clans: the Ogaden from Ethiopia and the Ishaq from northern Somalia. To the north of Somalia, a long-standing conflict over land has made struggling parties of the Issa Somali and the Afar, both pastoralists.

Too Many People Doing the Same Thing

The armed conflicts that have afflicted the Horn region over the last three decades, have usually been interpreted as typical ethnic/tribal and/or religious/cultural conflicts. While these categorizations may have served as plausible descriptions of earlier conflicts, and may still have some bearing on how current conflicts are being conducted and perceived, the reality is that conflict causes tend to change and diversify. Changes in the economic, political, social and ecological background do gradually, if imperceptibly, influence the nature of conflicts, and so it is justifiable to assume that the far-reaching ecological changes that have beset the Horn must have had a profound effect on social conflicts in the region.

Prolonged, severe climatic desiccation coupled with intensive exploitation of soil, water, forests and other renewable resources, compounded by the huge increase in human and livestock populations, have so degraded the inherently fragile environment of the region that conflicts were bound to arise. Four factors have contributed substantially to this state of affairs.

Countries in the region have been suffering from too slow a rate of structural differentiation of their economies; that is, too many people are doing the same thing. This scant differentiation has drastically limited the opportunities to engage people profitably in activities other than traditional agriculture and pastoralism. The too-many-people-doing-the-same-thing economy intensifies the effects of environmentally damaging practices. The damage to the environment is being reinforced and aggravated year in, year out by repeated land-use practices. The lack of economic differentiation also limits the possibility of rescue coming from other quarters of the economy, in case of emergency or sectoral crisis. While land resources have remained fairly inelastic as the population continued to grow, the person-to-resource ratio has continuously increased. As a consequence, the carrying capacity of the regional ecosystem has almost reached the limit.

The most menacing consequence of the inelasticity of both the economic system and the resource base is the decline in food security. In the Horn, food scarcity and conflict seem to go together, as vultures follow hyenas. Environmental security in the Horn is thus directly, but not exclusively, a function of the intensity of resource exploitation, which in turn depends on the availability of resources, mainly the endowment of renewable resources, and on the number of people competing for these resources – that is, the person-to-resource ratio. The distribution of resources is dependent on the political and land tenure systems in each country. Huge increases in commercial agriculture, mainly for export purposes, are pushing more and more people and livestock into marginal lands and into fierce competition for meagre resources.

The structure of the production and distribution systems is largely determined by the technology used (the external factor) and the degree of social equity reached (the civil society factor), respectively. Development projects that rely on scarce resources, for example water and soil, increase competition for these resources and can be a cause or catalyst of social conflict. In general, development efforts that do not cater for the needs of the local communities, or that favour one local group over others, do not reduce the conflict potential but may, in fact, drastically increase it.

The overall situation is further complicated by the fact that resource endowment in the Horn is far from being uniform, with, for example, highlanders enjoying relative abundance in rainfall and good soils, while their immediate neighbours in the plains suffer persistent droughts. This dichotomy increases the potential for intergroup conflict: what we have termed the desert-versus-the-oasis syndrome. The general implication of all these factors is chronic disruption of both the social and the natural environments. Social disruption, because the material needs of the population, not to mention their cultural, social and spiritual needs, are not secure; environmental disruption, because the sustainable use of the ecosystems is constantly being hampered by increasing numbers of people doing the same thing in an inelastic resource base. In fact, ecological degradation in the Horn has been so severe that traditional means and agreements for the settlement of occasional ethno-political disputes have been rendered virtually unworkable.

It is therefore not surprising to find that many current disputes are taking place not along traditional political borders, but along the ecological borders that divide richer and poorer ecozones. This fact highlights the need for a broader approach to the analysis and interpretation of active and potential armed conflicts in the region, one which takes into consideration the impact of environmental scarcity and climate variation, thus enabling the parties concerned to deal effectively with a very complex situation.

To continue to treat conflicts in Africa as religious/cultural and/or ethnic/tribal and ignore the growing impact of degradation and depletion of the renewable resource base can only lead to a distorted understanding of the real situation and consequently drastically limit the possibility of genuine conflict resolution.

Ethnicity

For decades, the notion of ethnic (tribal) difference dominated most attempts to explain violent conflicts in sub-Saharan Africa. By pairing the rich spectrum of ethnic diversity found in the continent with the culture of competition induced by a harsh environment and restricted access to natural and social resources, intra-ethnic violence came to be regarded as the natural state of affairs (Fukui and Turton 1979). In this view, ethnic conflict was part of the historical baggage modernizing states had been saddled with, both product and indicator of the cultural conservatism and traditionalism found among the rural population.

However, the standard interpretation of African ethnicity as a leftover from primordial conditions attracted criticism from the 1960s onwards. Anthropologists came to challenge existing assumptions about ethnicity as a quasi-ontological base of human identity, with reference to such phenomena as cultural conversion, situational identity, the uneven distribution of cultural properties and the invention of tradition (Barth 1969; Hobsbawm and Ranger 1983; Holy 1987; Eriksen 1993). Ethnicity, far from presenting a historical leftover, has been recast as a modern phenomenon, with people re-tribalizing in the face of pressure, so that ethnicity was no longer seen as a cause, but rather as a consequence of war (Fukui and Markakis 1994; Gurr and Harff 1994). However, with the passage of time an inversion of ethnicity, from being an effect to being a cause, is indeed possible.

However, ethnic, religious and cultural dichotomies remain very potent in people's perception of violent conflict. While they are weak as root causes, they come into play the longer a conflict persists, fuelling the violence long after the initial causes have petered out. A combination of factors – climate variations, increases in human and animal population, capture of traditional resources by the state elite – has triggered the migration of peoples from different ecological production systems into the 'empty' corridors that once separated them.

Adaptations to variant ecological habitats produce corresponding contrasts in material culture, in aspects of social organization, in dress and language. These differences become critical as soon as quarrels arise over the allocation of resources in the newly occupied land. As a result, marginal lands are often the flashpoint of much larger structural conflicts between neighbouring groups. As each contender seeks to attract maximum support, ethnicity is the loudest rallying cry. As Markakis notes, of all the ideological weapons used in African warfare – nationalism, socialism, religion and ethnicity – it is ethnicity that has proved superior as a principle of political solidarity and mobilization, as well as a dominant political force (Fukui and Markakis 1994; also Baechler 1993; Molvaer 1991). The outcome is that discord over material resources, once clothed in the symbolism of ethnic survival and fuelled by the vicious circle of revenge, can simmer long after the initial resource dispute has been settled.

The Effect of Time

Many violent conflicts continue over a long period of time, hence there is a need to understand what time does to causes, perceptions and manifestations of a violent conflict. The passage of time blurs some processes, enforces others and obliterates some altogether. We can only guess what the consequences of today's acts will be, given the number of subjective factors in action and the very real possibility that a subjective factor may invert and become an objective one and vice versa.

We shall deal here only with the possibility inherent in enduring violent conflicts that some factors, like ethnicity, and cultural and religious affiliations, which were initially abstract ideological or philosophical categories effective mainly in the realm of perception, can be transformed by the passage of time into objective, 'material' social forces. Ethnicity, for example, often the product of violent conflict, can end up becoming an objective cause of enduring or future violence, proving that, with time, effects can become causes.

The possibility of this transformation has already been demonstrated by the armed conflict in northern Darfur, Sudan, between the Fur people of Jebel Marra and the Zaghawa and other Arab tribes. I have written elsewhere that,

> The enemies confronting each other in this bloody conflict have a long history of guarded cooperation. Their current conspicuously polarized and antagonistic ethnic stand is more a product of the war, than a cause of it. The low ethnic barriers that existed among them were friendly and easily surmountable by intermarriage or similar processes of assimilation in a fluid exchange of ethnic affiliation. (Suliman 1996)

Fifteen years after the conflict began, the ethnic divide between the Fur and the Zaghawa has become a concrete social reality contributing its share to conflict causation. The longer a conflict goes on, the more its ethnic divide hardens and the more that divide functions as a tangible cause of violence, augmenting its initial causes, which may in turn gradually decrease in importance and topicality.

Ecological and Ethnic Borders

Ecological borders are, in most cases, also ethnic and cultural borders. Different ecozones demand different social production systems. In Africa, this means different land-use systems. In semi-arid zones, the pastoral mode of production is viable and can survive. Over the years, pastoralists acquire distinctive cultural and ethnic traits, compared with their neighbouring sedentary peasants. Ecological borders become ethnic and cultural lines of demarcation, where people meet to cooperate or to fight.

In the past, the prevailing tendency was for people to cooperate, exchanging goods and services and sharing the use of renewable resources. These were borders of cooperation, not confrontation. However, competition over resources and natural services has intensified, because of environmental, social and economic pressures, and the equilibrium of war and peace has gradually, sometimes abruptly, shifted towards confrontation. In the process, people and livestock, tanks and tractors cross these ecological and ethnic/cultural frontiers. The Zaghawa pastoralists in the Sudan, suffering from persistent drought in the plains, enter the Jebel Marra massif planning to stay as long as it is necessary. The Baggara want similar privileges for themselves in the Nuba mountains. The Tuareg conflict in Niger and Mali, the Casamance conflict in Senegal, the turbulence in the Boran region in southern Ethiopia – all are examples of local violent conflicts. Conflicts over economic and renewable natural resources are thus sometimes incorrectly seen as ethnic/cultural, simply because the warring factions come from diverse ethnic/cultural backgrounds.

An additional complication is the spread of modern weapons, which has transformed African warfare from a mere demonstration of power to large-scale killing. The new weapons kill many people so quickly that the available time for mediation and intervention is drastically reduced, compounding the difficulties facing peacemakers in current internal conflicts.

The State

After centuries of exploitation and colonialism, the independent African state emerged as the torchbearer of development, setting out to modernize and transform societies in the shortest possible time. Land tenure systems were altered to facilitate private ownership, mechanized farming introduced, cash crop production intensified and rudimentary industries established. In contrast to the rhetoric, which advocated the pursuit of national development, economic strategies soon prioritized the capture of vital resources by the national elite. In the face of a dwindling private sector, control of the organs of government became vital for economic prosperity, as the state, however 'soft' or 'impoverished' by international standards, was the custodian of national wealth and recipient of foreign inflows. Competition between elite factions intensified as a declining economy combined with international pressure to curtail government spending. Harvest failure, drought, and a steady fall in terms of trade for primary producers intensified the struggle for control of the centre, sparking off intra-elite conflict over access to, and control over, the state. The groups involved in this critical competition also extended their sway over ever-larger parts of the country. In the guise of national development, and often with the intellectual encouragement and financial backing of multilateral donors, national governments would appropriate natural resources, for redistribution among members of the elite. Paying no heed to local demands, economic strategies were implemented which pushed smallholding peasants off the land, and intersected nomadic migration routes.

As the political circles in Khartoum, Addis Ababa and Mogadishu were equally impervious to rural discontent, protests turned into violent uprisings, which became conflicts against the state and the modernizing impetus, as was illustrated by the SPLA attacks on the construction site of the Jonglei Canal in the Sudan (Salih 1991; Baechler, Bellwald and Suliman 1996). Where sectional differences coincided with sectarian faultlines, the resulting conflict was ideologically informed: for example, in the Sudan northern Muslims are fighting southern Christians; in Ethiopia, Eritreans, Tigrayans and Oromos fought for greater degrees of regional autonomy against the central Amharic state. Once unleashed, conflict is exacerbated by the involvement of outside interests – the superpowers during the Cold War; Islamic brotherhoods channelling money from the Gulf states today.

While the promise of natural resources attracts the attention of central government – such as the penetration of the south by the northern elite in the Sudan – regions of little economic or political significance are abandoned and frequently revert to local rule. Such mini-states are, however, too small to maintain their economic and political independence (with the possible exception of Somaliland) for long, and tend to grow by mutual agreement or by devouring one another. This is a sure recipe for violent conflict – witness the fighting among Eritrean rebel groups, between Sudanese militias and the SPLA, and among Somali clans.

A Typology of Violent Conflicts

In our research on the state of war and peace in Africa, we identify four types of armed conflicts: (1) national conflicts mainly over state political power; (2) regional conflicts usually over local political power (warlordism); (3) local conflicts, typically over renewable natural resources; and (4) banditry.

National conflicts take place among the so-called national elite over control of the central state, which in many sub-Saharan African countries is almost equivalent to controlling the economic, social and political levers of power and all tools of coercion. Wars in Liberia, the Democratic Republic of Congo (formerly Zaïre) and Somalia are clear examples. This type of conflict has received great attention and interests Western governments most. The accepted wisdom is that mediation coupled with diplomatic or military intervention and the use of economic carrot-and-stick policies is likely to bring about good results. It is certainly possible to resolve, but not transform, such conflicts using the mediation/intervention approach. Occasionally, the conflict is resolved temporarily by a popular uprising, which, not infrequently, is subsequently hijacked by a section of the elite.

Most power transfers of the 1990s are examples of such conflict resolution. Usually an agreement is reached among the competing sections of the national elite to share the state's political power among themselves. An example is the Addis Ababa Accord (1972), between the Sudanese government and the southern rebels, which catered only for political power-sharing. Neither the people nor the natural environment is considered important in the agreement. In this type of conflict, the peace agreements reached are as easily concluded among the warring elite groups as they are broken. Generally, dissatisfaction soon creeps in and topples the fragile equilibrium and war is resumed (the return of civil war in the Sudan in 1983). Violent conflicts among the African national elite will continue as long as economic, political and military powers are controlled almost entirely by the central state.

Paradoxically, the second type, regional conflict, is an outcome of the weakening of central state power, especially in large countries like the Democratic Republic of Congo, Chad and the Sudan. Regions of little economic and political significance are abandoned by the state and business people and left to their own fate. In the main, local leadership tends to revert to traditional rule, with some success. The problem, however, is that these mini-states are too small to maintain their economic and political independence for a long period, and the tendency among them is to grow by mutual agreement or by one devouring the other – a sure recipe for violent conflict.

The third type of conflict takes place among people competing over renewable resources – mainly soil, water, fauna and flora – which have become scarcer through environmental degradation and/or through the limiting or denial of access to these resources. As mentioned earlier, it is this type that needs greater scrutiny, because incidents are growing in number and intensity, especially in the Sahel and Horn regions. Conflicts in Senegal, Mali, Niger, Sudan and Ethiopia are examples.

In the past, faced with deteriorating natural conditions, people moved to a nearby richer ecozone. There were enough empty corridors then. Now there are practically none. Climatic variations, large-scale mechanization for export agriculture encouraged by the IMF's SAPs and demanded by the World Bank's policies, as well as huge increases in human and livestock populations, have all conspired to limit or deny access to renewable resources. And so these marginal, no man's lands are gradually losing their distinction as borders of cooperation to become borders of confrontation (Suliman 1994a).

Traditional Conflict Management

In the area of immediate conflict management, we share the conviction with many researchers that indigenous means of conflict resolution are more important than alien ones. The point of departure should always be that, left to themselves, most people tend to choose cooperation most of the time, and if provided with the right assistance all people will choose cooperation all the time.

The direct and local solutions have, therefore, the better chance of success. Whenever possible, aliens to the conflict, even the elite on both sides of the conflict divide, should not be major players. The elite tends to favour its own interests. For example, given the chance they will usually negotiate how to share political power among themselves, rather than consider how their people can share the sustainable use of the disputed resources.

Generally, we are also for equitable (not necessarily symmetric), sustainable sharing of contested resources. To achieve success in this process it is important not to insist on the Western concept of ownership, usually postulated by the educated and by jurists, who insist on so-called historic rights and private ownership. The traditional African mode of production is based on collective ownership, understood as the right to use, rather than the right to have. Insistence on historic rights and similar notions can only aggravate the situation. For example, the insistence of the Fur elite that Jebel Marra massif is now and always has been their own is one big barrier facing peace efforts in that part of the Sudan.

The Borana of southern Ethiopia have been able to resolve a violent conflict with their neighbours through asymmetrical sharing of resources. The neighbours acknowledged the right of the Borana over the land, understood as the right to use rather than own the land, while the Borana accepted the right of their neighbours, as well as their animals, to survive. Reconciling the two rights has made peace possible.

Ecological degradation, large-scale primary commodity production for export, human and animal population growth, inelastic natural and economic resource bases, the most-people-doing-the-same-thing syndrome: all these and other factors have conspired to raise the intensity of competition over dwindling renewable resources. The so-called corridors of security are no longer empty. There is scarcely any empty space left. In the Sahel and the Horn regions, cooperation is giving way to confrontation.

It is also possible to resolve political conflicts through mediation, persuasion and intervention. However, the economic–ecological conflicts which are likely to dominate the African scene in the years to come demand that more attention be given, not to perceptions and manifestations of the conflict, but to its root causes. These internal violent conflicts are especially tragic because they are wars of the weak against the weak and because they are inherently avoidable: the economy of rural Africa relies almost exclusively on available renewable resources. Bad economic and ecological policies threaten the very survival of rural people. In response to ecological and economic stress, many people take up arms and fight against their perceived enemy, who is often none other than their neighbour.

Bibliography

Adams, M. and M. Bradbury, 1995, *Conflict and Development: Organisational Adaptations in Conflict Situations*, Oxfam Discussion Paper No. 4, Oxford.

Assefa, H., 1996, 'Ethnic Conflict in the Horn of Africa: Myth and Reality', in K. Rupesinghe and V. Atchikov (eds), *Ethnicity and Power in the Contemporary World*, UN University Press.

Baechler, G. 1993, *Conflict and Cooperation in the Light of Human–Ecological Transformation*, ENCOP Occasional Paper No. 9, Swiss Peace Foundation, Bern.

Baechler, G., S. Bellwald and M. Suliman, 1996, *Environmental Conflict: Management Approach and Implementation in the Horn of Africa*, ETH, Zürich.

Baechler, G., V. Böge, S. Klötli and S. Libiszewski, 1993, *Umweltzerstörung: Krieg oder Kooperation?*, Agenda Verlag, Münster.

Barth, F. (ed.), 1969,. *Ethnic Groups and Boundaries: The Social Organisation of Cultural Difference*, Universitetsforlaget, Bergen.

Bennet, O. (ed.), 1989, *Greenwar: Environment and Conflict*, Panos Institute, London.

Bratton, M., 1989, 'Beyond the State: Civil Society and Associational Life in Africa', *World Politics*, vol. 41, no. 3.

Chase, R.S., E.B. Hill and P. Kennedy, 1996, 'Pivotal States and US Strategy', *Foreign Affairs*, vol. 75, no. 1, pp. 33–51.

Cohen, A., 1969, *Customs and Politics in Urban Africa*, Routledge, London.

Diamond, L., 1995, 'Nigeria: The Uncivic Society and the Descent into Praetorianism', in L. Diamond, J. Linz and S. Lipset, *Politics in Developing Countries: Comparing Experiences with Democracies*, Lynne Rienner, Boulder CO.

Dokken, K. and N. Graeger, 1995, *The Concept of Environmental Security: Political Slogan or Analytical Tool?*, report prepared by the Royal Ministry of Foreign Affairs, Oslo.

Duffield, M., 1994a, 'Complex Emergencies and the Crisis of Developmentalism', *IDS Bulletin*, vol. 25, no. 4, pp. 37–45.

Duffield, M., 1994b, *War and Famine in Africa*, Oxfam Discussion Paper No. 5.

Eriksen, T., 1993, *Ethnicity and Nationalism: Anthropological Perspectives*, Pluto, London.

Frank, H. Robert, 1991, *Passions within Reason*, Norton, New York.

Fukui, K. and J. Markakis, 1994, *Ethnicity and Conflict in the Horn of Africa*, James Currey and Ohio University Press, London and Athens.

Fukui, K., and D. Turton (eds), 1979, *Warfare among East African Herders*, Osaka, Senre, Ethological Centre, No. 3, National Museum of Ethnology.

Gurr, T.R. and B. Harff, 1994, *Ethnic Conflict in World Politics*, Westview Press, Bounder CO.

Harrison, P., 1987, *The Greening of Africa*, Paladin Books, London.

el Hinnawi, H., 1985, *Environmental Refugees*, UNDP Publications.

Hobsbawm, E. and T. Ranger, 1983, *The Invention of Tradition*, Columbia University Press, New York.

Holy, L. (ed.), 1987, *Comparative Anthropology*, Blackwell, Oxford.

Homer-Dixon, Thomas, 1994, 'Environmental Scarcities and Violent Conflict', *International Security*, vol. 19, no. 1.

Huntingdon, S.P., 1993, 'The Clash of Civilizations', *Foreign Affairs*, 72.

Kaplan, R.D., 1994, 'The Coming Anarchy: How Scarcity, Crime, Overpopulation and Disease are Rapidly Destroying the Social Fabric of Our Planet', *Atlantic Monthly*, February, pp. 44–76.

Keen, D., 1994, *The Benefits of Famine: A Political Economy of Famine in South-western Sudan, 1983–1989*, Princeton University Press, Princeton NJ.

Markakis, J., 1991, *Environmental Stress and Security in the Horn of Africa*, Sigruna.

Mohamed Salih, M.A., 1991, 'Generation and Migration: Identity Crisis and Political Change among the Moro of the Nuba Mountains', *GeoJournal*, vol. 25, no. 1.

Molvaer, R.K., 1991, 'Environmentally Induced Conflicts?', *Bulletin of Peace Proposals*, vol. 22, no. 2.

Richard, P., 1996, *Fighting for Rainforest: War, Youth and Resources in Sierra Leone*, International African Institute, Oxford.

Suliman, M., 1992, *Civil War in the Sudan: The Impact of Ecological Degradation*, ENCOP Occasional Paper No. 4, Swiss Peace Foundation, Bern.

Suliman, M., 1994, *War in Darfur*, IFAA Publications, London.

Suliman, M., 1996, ''War in Darfur', in G. Baechler and Kurt R. Spillmann (eds), *Environmental Degradation as Cause of War*, Verlag Rüegger, Zürich.

Suliman, M., and Axel Klein, 1998, *Inversion der Ethnizität: Von Wahrnehmung zur Kinfliktursache*, Friedensbericht, Verlang Rüegger, Zürich.

Young, P., 1996, 'The MNR/RENAMO: External and Internal Dynamics', *African Affairs*, vol. 89, no. 357, pp. 491–509.

3

The Gender Impact of War, Environmental Disruption and Displacement

Fatima Babiker Mahmoud

Environment and Gender

There is a close relationship between gender and environment as scientific disciplines. Both are new areas of investigation and are still in the process of formulating their theoretical frameworks of analysis. Gender, for example, was not an inherent part of traditional political science. When interest in women's issues emerged, the focus was almost entirely on minor aspects of their role in politics, for example their voting behaviour.

The natural environment was likewise absent in political science. When interest in the environment began to grow, especially after the Stockholm Conference in 1972, political scientists became increasingly aware of the need to incorporate it in their discipline. However, in almost all attempts to achieve this goal, they were oblivious of the interrelationship of women and the environment. Human ecology was, predominantly, male ecology. Women were not an inherent part of the research goal, nor of its methodology. The newly discovered natural environment was thus women-free!

Both disciplines call for the abolition of all forms of oppression and wanton destruction. In the case of the science of the environment, the aim is the 'liberation' of nature from depletion and destruction; in the case of gender studies, the aim is liberation of almost half of humanity from all forms of inequality and oppression. This includes their right to a fair share in using, enjoying and conserving the natural environment itself. Because of this common interest in liberation, both are disciplines of the future. This is an important commonality, because both disciplines strive to reshape the present and bring about a better future. Both disciplines are thus resentful of the misuse and destruction of natural and social wealth. They rise and thrive with the sustainable progress of all humankind.

> To say that women and nature are intimately associated is not to say anything revolutionary. After all, it was precisely just such an assumption that allowed the domination of both women and nature. The new insight provided by rural women in the Third World is that women and nature are associated not in passivity but in creativity and in the maintenance of life. (Shiva 1989)

There are, however, a few theoretical problems in defining the relationship between gender and the environment. One such problem arises out of the definition, by some eco-feminists, of women not as intimately associated, but as identical or synonymous with nature. Irrespective of its ambiguous theoretical justification, one of its inappropriate practical implications is that women are considered the part of society most responsible for nature's preservation and management. Such a definition does not serve women well and inevitably adds to their other responsibilities as bearers of cultural good and the well-being of the family. The environment, however, is the responsibility of all humanity. There is a growing awareness of the necessity to 'return', albeit at a higher level, to our previously intimate relationship with nature.

Former development of human societies appears as a process characterized by the continuous alienation of human beings from nature and subsequently from each other. The primeval oneness with nature gave way to two confronting worlds, to the separation of the subjective from the objective.

> Nature was perceived as the totality of all things in the universe which were alive and have wills of their own. In a world made up of a multitude of wills, which could be friendly or unfriendly, thorough knowledge of all surrounding wills was a prerequisite for survival. This dramatic conception of nature as a continuous strife among living wills demanded from all human beings continuous alertness, continuous readiness to wage battle against the wills of evil and support the wills of good. Human beings were not mere spectators, but active participants in the cosmic drama. Even when the process of alienation turned nature into a collection of dead objects, there still lingered in our cultures and in our hearts a relationship with nature whereby she was an inherent part of ourselves, full of life and strife, akin to fighting lovers. (Suliman 1993, author's translation)

There is, however, no going back to the primeval oneness of human beings with nature. The original oneness and continuous struggle of wills that determined our relationship with nature has been superseded by a willed unity and a continuous striving for sustainable living.

It is therefore important to broaden our understanding of environmental issues and to adopt a socially holistic approach regarding their sustainability. This broadening necessitates that women, as a social category, should not be studied outside social relations; that is, they must be regarded as members of social classes as well as being a social category in their own right. A study of gender and environment should look at gender relations as a set of power relations operating at the level of the household, the economy, society, and its links with the outside world.

The second misconception is that which makes women the agents responsible for environmental destruction through activities related to their reproductive role and to their efforts to maintain a living for their families. To blame women for environmental damage is to shift responsibility from the real perpetrators, namely the power and business elite and their partners in resource mining – the big international companies.

A specific example will illustrate this point. Since the beginning of environmental studies in the Sudan in the early 1960s, it was assumed that the environment has little, if anything, to do with economic, social or even political relations. When, in the early 1980s, a linkage was assumed between environment and gender, heads of environment departments (all men) recruited women researchers to explore the link. They advised them to go to neighbouring villages to collect data about how women destroy woodland by cutting trees and generally fail to sustain environmental resources! This is one of many examples of how male environmental scientists overlook the role of women in environmental management and preservation.

Gender and Violent Conflict

Susan Brownmiller, in common with other eco-feminists, falls into the same trap of positing the biological as a determinant of female destiny. While she correctly proposes that in all societies war and warfare is man's work, she nevertheless goes on to suggest that the origin of this specialization is biological. In her paper 'The Spoils of War', she writes that,

> War evolves as a man's work for a variety of obvious biological reasons. The male of the human species is larger, stronger, possessed of superior upper body strength and greater natural musculature, the product of the Y chromosome and testosterone, a hormone with additional implications of restlessness, excitability, irritability, and possibly of aggression. Science has not yet determined whether physical aggression is attributable to testosterone, but I do not rule it out. (Brownmiller 1995)

By proposing that men have greater 'natural' musculature and by not ruling out the relationship between testosterone and aggression,

Brownmiller has overlooked the contributions of feminist thought, especially those of the 1960s, which distinguish in a convincing way between sex and gender – the former being biological, the latter referring to the social construction of gender. This was put in a nutshell by Simone de Beauvoir, when she wrote: 'I was born a human being, I became a woman.'

It is thus not surprising that Brownmiller and certain other Western feminists call upon women to boycott everything to do with war. Her contention is that war is the domain of the male sex. Since both men and women are victims in war, the important issue is not whether women are engaged in war activities or not. Even if it is men that wage wars – and this is by no means the case in many violent conflicts in Third World countries – women nevertheless suffer more than their fair share. Women suffer twice: as active participants in the war effort and as carers of children, they manage the natural environment and secure food for the family. This dual role is a reflection of the social division of labour in the realm of warfare.

While there is no doubt that most of the violence against women, especially killing, torture and rape, takes place during the war itself, the central focus of this chapter is the forms of violence perpetrated against women in the aftermath of war. It is especially concerned with the implications of internal displacement of women in my own country, the Sudan. Following prolonged periods of environmental degradation and war, new approaches are needed to their social understanding. Persistent droughts and brutal wars have become so complex, they are almost unfathomable even to those most affected by them.

The Deprivations of Women Displaced by Drought and War

In the post-1967 period, the Sahel's average annual rainfall has halved. It has also experienced two major periods of drought, in 1972–74 and 1982–84.

> The flux of environmental refugees and displaced people that followed the last drought was the largest ever witnessed in Africa. By early 1984 more than 150 million people in 24 African countries were affected and more than 10 million of them had to abandon their homelands in search of food and water. (Suliman 1994)

This environmental crisis, coupled with the renewal of the war in southern Sudan in 1983, has made large-scale displacement a serious social problem. The number of people displaced by war and drought – known as *naziheen* – exceeded by far the total of traditional cross-border refugees (Table 3.1).

Table 3.1 *Naziheen* by area

Area	No. of *naziheen*
Khartoum	1,617,500
Kordofan	300,000
Darfur	170,000
Central provinces	400,000
Northern province	165,000
Eastern provinces	175,000
Upper Nile province	180,000
Bahr Algazal province	170,000
Equatorial province	350,000
Total	3,527,500

The new term *naziheen* gave expression to a new pattern of migration caused by environmental crisis. Before the advent of this type of migration, migrants were referred to as *igleemiyeen* (rural people). This word gives no indication of the cause of migration, its nature or its length. The term *naziheen* has more specific connotations. First, it means migration of whole communities; second, it means the settlement of these communities in a different natural environment; third, it also signifies that their future in the new areas is unknown or unsettled. When the term *muhagireen* was used to refer to the prophet Mohammed and his followers, migrating from Mecca to Medina, it indicated a planned migration from one settlement to another. The term *naziheen* also differentiates between migrants and refugees in the sense that when a person is a *nazih*, he or she is moving within national boundaries, whereas the word *lagi*, meaning refugee, refers to a person who has left his or her country to seek refuge, *luguo*, in another. The term *naziheen* is so specific to the drought-displaced that, in general usage, the war-displaced, who are mainly from southern Sudan, are not referred to as *naziheen*. They are referred to simply as Southerners. This reflects the ethnic dimension with regard to migrants from the south and also implies that the migration of southerners to the north was a process that started prior to the drought, which reached its peak in 1984.

The Displaced *Naziheen*

Umbada (1991) gives an estimate of 2 million war-displaced and 1.8 million drought-displaced, while El-Fahal (1990) estimates the total number of displaced as 3,527,500, distributed as shown in Table 3.1. Of this total, more than 80 per cent are women and children. In addition to these *naziheen*, there are some 942,000 refugees living in the Sudan today (the figure might decrease following the independence of Eritrea). Most refugees receive assistance from the UNHCR; the *naziheen*, however, are not entitled to official help from the Sudanese government or UNHCR. Even the support in kind offered by relief organizations is subject to theft by government officials before any of it reaches the *naziheen*.

Khartoum, the Displaced-Receiving Province

Of the total number of displaced people, Khartoum province alone received over 1.6 million. This was to be expected since Khartoum is the capital and largest city in Sudan, and the second and third largest cities, Khartoum North and Omdurman, are also in Khartoum province. The movement to Khartoum is understandable, given that Khartoum has the largest specialized hospitals in Sudan, with 60 per cent of the country's specialist doctors, 70 per cent of the private clinics, 85 per cent of all business establishments, 80 per cent of the industry as well as the lion's share of educational institutions, in addition to the availability of other services such as water and electricity.

Yet, in Khartoum province the displaced people live in poor conditions, in slums or camps far away from the city centre, and lack facilities such as water, electricity, medical services, public transport and educational institutions. The displaced millions live in shacks constructed of old garments, cardboard boxes and whatever suitable waste materials they can lay their hands on. In Khartoum province, there are 49 camps of displaced people: 19 in Khartoum itself, 20 in Omdurman and 10 in Khartoum North. The inhabitants of these camps are grouped according to the areas they come from. Those who are displaced as a result of the war in the south live together according to their ethnic or tribal origin. The same goes for those who migrated from the west as a result of the drought.

The influx of the displaced to towns has caused a number of conflicts, some manifest, others latent. The urban population, especially in the capital towns of Khartoum, Omdurman and Khartoum North, are divided between sympathy and unjustified fear in the face of the sudden influx of hundreds of thousands of displaced people. A number of research projects were conducted to survey and analyse the problems of the displaced population in the Sudan. Understandably, most have dealt with the displaced in Greater Khartoum. None of the studies was gender alert although a few dealt with women and their conditions. These latter analyses, however, do not take a gender perspective. It is my contention that without studying women's conditions and all relevant gender aspects in the community under investigation, policy-makers will not make adequate recommendations. Indeed, their policies will suffer severe shortcomings and be of little help to about 80 per cent of the community under survey.

Displaced Sudanese Women and Post-war Problems

In the aftermath of environmental degradation and war, 4 million Sudanese women, men, children and elderly became war displaced, or drought *naziheen*. This has brought a host of problems to family life and to the division of power between the sexes. So far as women are concerned, they specifically enter into conflict, which – in some cases – results in violence inflicted on them by male members of the household, especially husbands. Traditional forms of the marriage institution begin to dissolve and the women experience social harassment and rape outside their homes, in the workplace, in prison or in custody.

The Disintegration of the Family

The war-displaced and environment *naziheen* face economic hardships in alien natural and social environments. In Sohair Khalil's (1987) study of the displaced in Greater Khartoum, she reported a considerable degree of family disintegration. Some family members moved to Khartoum from the south, while other members of the same family joined the refugee camps in Kenya or Uganda. Some family members reported that they had received no news from the rest of the family. Also reported is a remarkable increase in deserted and widowed women. Khalil recorded a high rate of divorce among the *naziheen* families. Table 3.2 summarizes her findings in this area.

The organization of production within the displaced groups in general, and in the household as a unit of production and consumption in particular, has changed dramatically. The former division of labour within subsistence and pastoral production societies has turned into open competition between all members of the group for available work opportunities. This is especially so in the informal sector, where no particular formal skills or training are necessary. The single-mother families, the widowed and the divorced make up 41 per cent of the families (see Table 3.2). This is a high proportion indeed. If we also consider women who are unmarried and unable to trace their families, or who had left their families behind, the picture becomes even bleaker. The 31 per cent rate of divorce is comparatively high, almost ten times the average divorce rate

Table 3.2 Status of displaced women

Marital status	%
Married	13.7
Deserted	14.7
Divorced	11.6
Single	37.9
Widowed	22.1

in the Sudan. This high ratio reflects the threat posed to marriage and family relations by the new social composition of the family.

Arriving in a predominantly Islamic territory (i.e. northern Sudan), displaced families, especially non-Muslims from the south and the Nuba Mountains, are confronted by a brutal fundamentalist state. Especially brutal is the so-called *kasha*, a rounding-up by police of displaced people, especially southerners and Nuba, who are detained randomly. Arrested children are sent to camps where they are trained for military service under harsh conditions in which maltreatment, abuse and rape are practised by the police and supervising personnel. African Rights (1995) traced seven of these camps, where arrested children, mainly boys, were sent for military training. African Rights was able to collect information on five of these camps. The total number of children held was reported to be 2,661. Families of these children are not informed of their whereabouts, and at times not even of their arrest (usually without charge). These children do not know where they will be taken. Women and men are also forcibly taken in the same fashion, mainly to agricultural areas to serve as cheap agricultural labourers. They are not paid wages and are forced to live and work in poor conditions and subject to harsh treatment.

During the 1994 harvest and as part of the so-called government repatriation scheme, the state radio announced that: 'A train carrying about 2,000 migrants is expected to leave Khartoum for Renk in Upper Nile State to take part in the harvest campaign there. For the same purpose, some 7,000 migrants will be transported to Kordofan in the coming few days' (African Rights 1995). Judging by this official announcement, families are broken up by the thousand every time cheap labour is needed. The disappearance of family members is a common expectation in the community of the displaced. In most cases, there is no pretence that those relocated for cheap labour will be returned home. Indeed, many disappear never to come back. For example, five women from the south disappeared from Jebel Aulia camp and were never traced.

Displaced Women, Harassment, Violence and Rape

Violence against displaced women takes a variety of forms: (i) abuse and violence during demolition of squatter areas by the state police; (ii) sexual harassment; (iii) abuse and rape in the street and place of work; (iv) harassment and rape in prison and in detention; (v) the imposition of Islamic dress on women in an attempt to force them to abandon traditional clothing.

Housing Demolition, Abuse and Harassment

Under the 1990 Act, the present Islamic fundamentalist government incorporated a plan recommended by the Squatter Resettlement Committee, which proposed two types of relocation sites: transit sites for the displaced and resettlement camps known as peace sites for squatters. This reflects the racist nature of the distinction between the displaced and the squatters. Squatters are generally those who squatted prior to the arrival of the displaced in the 1980s and the 1990s; they are mainly workers of Arab origin. The displaced are mainly southerners and westerners who moved to Khartoum province in response to environmental degradation and war. However, squatters are not exclusively northerners. A considerable number of them are southerners, who came to Khartoum as early as the first civil war in 1953–72. In 1992 there were an estimated 873,000 squatters in Khartoum province alone.

The policy of demolishing shelters built by squatters affects displaced women and children in a number of ways. First, 41 per cent of all heads of household are women, which means that they are the ones who encounter the police and resist demolition. In this process, abuse, harassment and rape take place. In one such demolition operation which took place in the Alkadier area in Omdurman in 1994, reports estimated the death toll at between seven and fourteen and the number arrested at about ninety. Second, after being made homeless again, the children and the elderly usually follow the mothers, who now face the responsibility of feeding and finding alternative shelter for them. Third, on the arrival of the police, the family members present are usually women and children. The anticipation of a raid at any time puts the women under severe psychological stress. Single women are also badly affected, as they face greater problems in finding a place to live when they become homeless.

Landlords are reluctant to rent to them because they prefer to deal with men rather than women, especially unmarried women.

Compulsory Islamic Dress

New laws initiated by the present government of the Sudan demand that women must wear Islamic dress. A committee of eight, all men, was established to design such dress. The committee opted for a long dress that is loose and opaque so that the woman's figure cannot be discerned. The dress must cover the whole body and enough of the head to cover the woman's hair. This law is enforced on all female public employees and students regardless of their age, cultural background or religious affiliation. As such, this law hits both settled and displaced women. All traditional dresses are considered incompatible with Islam. Those who wear them are subject to harassment and flogging. As for the displaced women, who are not accustomed to covering themselves totally, wearing Islamic dress is a hardship even if they are willing and can afford to buy it. For them it is an alien dress, quite different from their tradition. Furthermore, arguing with the members of the People's Police can itself lead to flogging or imprisonment. An educated southern woman, who lives in Khartoum, described her experience as follows:

> Finishing the university, I found myself forced to work in Khartoum, as the security situation in the South had deteriorated. Luckily, I was able to find a job in a very progressive institution. My problems started after the 1989 coup. The government recruited young men into the People's Police with instructions to stop any women they consider indecently dressed. One day, I was on my way to work, and had reached the market (Souk al-Arabi), when I was stopped by a young member of the People's Police, who accused me of being indecently dressed. I was dressed in long baggy trousers and a long-sleeved blouse, but he maintained that I had not covered my head. I argued that as a non-Moslem I was not obliged to do so, and that I had neither orders from my employers nor seen notices in the streets to tell me that it is now compulsory to do so. I asked them to let me go as I had classes to teach. But they refused. As a result, I missed my class, and was left feeling angry and nervous for the rest of the day. Similar incidents meant that my journey to and from work had become a daily ordeal. (African Rights 1995)

Harassment in the Street and Violence at Work

Displaced women are easily distinguished by their looks, style and standard of dress and their accent. Because they are alien, they are singled out by men for verbal and sexual abuse. Men expect displaced women, because they know them to be defencelesss, to be available to them and to accept these abuses. Harassment takes place in the street, at the marketplace and at transport centres and in vehicles, where the turbulence and cacophony make it easy for men to harass women sexually with impunity.

As a considerable number of women work as domestics in north Sudanese households, most sexual abuse and rape takes place in homes. Employers exploit displaced women by overworking them for little money. They are denied leave or days off, even when their children are sick. The testimony of a former domestic worker describes such a situation:

> I came to the North in order to take my sick father to Khartoum for treatment. As this treatment took ages, I decided to work as a housemaid for an Arab woman. When my employer wanted to take me abroad with her, I did not mind as everyone told me it was a good idea for me to go and send foreign currency back to my sick father. I went abroad with my employer, but then she turned nasty towards me. I was forced to manage the whole house and look after the children. When I was paid, I found she had deducted sums from my wages. I complained to her husband but he referred me back to her. I felt like a prisoner, trapped inside, with no knowledge of the city where I was living. When I demanded to leave them they wouldn't let me go, and held on to my passport. Later I found that this is not the first time they had done this, because when we moved houses I came across the passports of two former employees. (African Rights 1995)

These domestic workers are often taken advantage of by male members of the household, and even by relatives and neighbours. One repercussion of this particular kind of work on displaced married women is the dramatic change in power relations between wife and husband. Husbands feel jealous that their wives are mixing with strange town men. In many cases, this causes quarrels and even divorces or desertion. Moreover, these domestic workers are serving other women and children while their own children are left behind to roam the streets, since there is no member of the family or of the extended family to look after them. Displacement disintegrates or weakens formerly extended family structures and inter-family solidarity. Working mothers cannot take their children to work, especially not to domestic work. Left to their fate, many of these unattended children become thieves or beggars, susceptible to the *kasha* and to police raids.

Another type of work in which displaced women become engaged, and which is an extension of their former activities, is beer brewing and alcohol distillation, albeit now for commercial purposes. This is one of the crimes non-Arab displaced women are most frequently charged with. Besides brewing for economic gain, there are also social reasons. Local beer plays an important role in traditional ceremonies, such as harvest, cooperation in home building (*nafir*), in funeral ceremonies or child blessing by the clan elderly. Beer is considered an integral part of food in traditional Sudanese societies. Women involved in brewing now face police raids. The police usually confiscate their equipment and take them to court, after which they go to prison. They are taken advantage of by the police personnel there, sexually abused and in many cases raped. Some policemen raid displaced households to threaten the women with imprisonment unless they pay them money.

Sexual Abuse and Prostitution Charges

I refrain from using the term 'prostitution' and prefer the term 'sexual exploitation', because the former is loaded with negative moral judgement. In the case of displaced women, sexual exploitation is even more relevant. Many displaced women are either driven to prostitution by the desperate need for money, or are charged without evidence. According to the present Sudan penal code: 'Those shall be deemed to have committed the offence of prostitution whoever are found in a place of prostitution where it is likely they may exercise sex or earn therefrom.' A place of prostitution is described as: 'A place designated for the meeting of men and women who are not in a marital relationship or persons with whom no legal marriage can take place in circumstances in which the exercise of sexual act is likely to occur.'

As the term 'likely' in the above description is vague, it is open to subjective interpretation by the police or the judge, thereby placing the burden of proof of innocence on the accused. As a rule, any woman found in a place arbitrarily designated as a potential place of prostitution can automatically be assumed to be guilty of prostitution. Unlimited police powers and the nature of the courts, manned by prejudiced judges, have resulted in numerous unfair convictions. For example, Batoul Musa, aged 17 years and Nuba by birth, was convicted of prostitution. 'A policeman alleged that she was dressed in trousers, which he described as indecent and unacceptable as a woman's dress. But to her, the fact of the matter was that she refused the policeman's demand for sex' (African Rights 1995).

The legal definition of prostitution allows wide interpretation and enables the police to frame a case of prostitution. Language difficulties, ignorance of the law, and the widespread use of unrecorded verbal testimonies give the police the chance to frame suspects. Also, the ignorance of the police about the cultural differences between Arabs and non-Arabs with regard to the relationships between men and women exposes displaced women to unfounded convictions for prostitution. This vulnerability is further intensified by the fact that displaced women can hardly afford legal representation and the police usually win cases against them as a result. Once convicted, they are imprisoned in sub-standard conditions. Non-Arab migrant women are the main victims of this prostitution law.

Imprisoned Displaced Women

Approximately 80 per cent of women imprisoned are between 17 and 43 years of age, with half of them between 14 and 35. They are mainly convicted of the following offences: brewing beer, the majority offence of those imprisoned; prostitution; theft and bribery; resistance to home demolition. Others, the majority of whom are young females, are rounded up (*kasha*) as displaced people.

Prison conditions are very poor and the treatment is harsh and cruel. There is practically no medical care for the women prisoners, or for their children. In fact, children are not even provided with food; they have to share with their mothers. Rape in prison is an everyday occurrence. An account given by a woman doctor, who was jailed for her political beliefs, confirms this. She also noted the fact that victims usually hide incidents of rape for social reasons. She gave me the following account about sexual abuse and rape in Omdurman Prison:

> Life in Omdurman prison had opened my eyes to the abuses against women prisoners in the Sudan. I used to hear about rape but I did not take it seriously. In prison, I was told by inmates that several women had been raped in their cells by policemen while awaiting trial; others were either raped or coerced into sexual intercourse by wardens in exchange for a visit by relatives or for such small things as a piece of soap. One woman told me about her experience when she knew that I was a doctor. She asked me to examine her to find out if she was pregnant. She told me that she had been raped in the police cell awaiting trial. She mentioned that she was raped by several men but she could not tell how many, because the attacks happened at night when the lights had been turned off. (Author's unpublished material)

It is clear from this prison account that rape and violence against displaced women is by no means confined to times of conflict.

Displaced women encounter violence both during war and in peacetime. When women become displaced in a culturally and economically harsh and alien environment, they encounter violence, abuse and rape because they are culturally and ethnically different and defenceless, and because they are poor. Most of the crimes are committed against them by employers, prison and security personnel and males in the household where they work as domestics – that is, by men in positions of power. They were born human beings; they became Sudanese women in a fundamentalist state and have, therefore, to suffer twice.

Bibliography

African Rights, 1995, *Sudan's Invisible Citizens*, African Rights, London.

Brownmiller, S., 1995, *War against Women*, Swiss Peace Foundation, Bern.

El-Fahal, T.I., 1990, *Displaced Women and Children in the Sudan*, Conference Proceedings, Vienna, July.

Khalil, S. El-Sayed, 1987, *The Socio-economic and Political Implications of Environmental Refugees in the Vicinity of Omdourman*, Environmental Monograph series, No. 6, Institute of Environmental Studies, University of Khartoum.

Shiva, V., 1989, *Staying Alive: Women, Ecology and Development*, Zed Books, London.

Suliman, M., 1993, *Weltanschaung aus dem Labor: Uber die Herausbildung und popularisierung von wissenschaftliched Leitbildern am beispiel der Eine-Welt Symbolik*, Evangelische Akademie Loccum, Rehburg-Loccum.

Suliman, M., 1994, 'The Predicament of Displaced People inside the Sudan', in G. Baechler (ed.), *Umweltfluchtlinge: Das Konfliktpotential von morgen?*, Agenda Verlag, Münster.

Umbada, S., 1991, *The Naziheen: Drought and Civil War Victims in the Sudan*, Second Study, Group on Population and Resettlement in the Middle East, Yarmouk University, Jordan, March.

4

Social Justice and Environmental Sustainability in the Post-Development Era

Wolfgang Sachs

At the Dawn of the Post-Development Era

It appears that today, near the close of the century, a cycle is coming to an end which was started by Columbus as he set out on his journey across the Atlantic ocean more than five hundred years ago. With his departure from Cadiz in search of a direct route to Asia, thinking of God, spices and gold, he unknowingly set the course for the expansion of Europe to the ends of the world. First, ships discovered ever more remote coastlines, then expeditions penetrated into the innermost regions of countries. Voyage after voyage the Europeans progressed, until barely any uncharted area was left on the map.

Missions and trading posts established early global interconnections while the hunger for raw materials spurred later colonial empires. More recently CNN and Mondovision have finally created the global experience. Many departures were to follow; as a result, innumerable separate civilizations have been integrated within a single world as European civilization has circumnavigated the globe in the wake of Columbus.

Until recently, the burden of the unification of the world had been borne virtually exclusively by the peoples of the Southern hemisphere: starting with the plague that killed millions of Aztecs and Mayans in South America following the white man's arrival, through the deportation of generations of blacks as slaves to America, to the slums and *favelas* in today's mega-cities in the Third World. And those who were spared such calamities often had to struggle with political dependence, economic disadvantage and cultural degradation. Whatever achievements have been brought to the last corner of the globe by the gradual integration of the world, they shrink into insignificance in the light of the bitter consequences of the process. The countries of the North, for their part, were able to monopolize the gains from the unification of the world. Notwithstanding financial failure and humiliating retreat at times, it is sufficiently obvious that the rise of the West has in part been fuelled by the riches drained from the South through the network of global interconnections.

But, after five hundred years, this inequality cannot be relied upon any longer. The bitter consequences of global unification have now begun to affect the North as well and the tide is slowly turning. For the first time since Columbus's departure the painful effects of worldwide interdependence are returning to haunt the North. Consider, for example, the increasing economic strength of some countries in what used to be the Third World. Over the last twenty years the competitive edge of some of those countries has sharpened, putting considerable pressure on jobs and entire branches of the economy in the North as the pupils of yesterday prepare to outdistance their masters. A similar constellation has also emerged in another area: ever since Saddam Hussein's attack on Kuwait on 2 August 1990, if not before, the North has woken up to the fact that the many years spent arming the South threaten to backfire on the North. Since then governments have nervously watched the accumulation of mega-arms in several countries of the South – and of the East as well. Moreover, the population in the North feels alarmed at the steady flow of immigrants and refugees that arrive every day, legally and illegally, in the northern belt of prosperity. The fear of migration and population pressure rising from the South has firmly taken root in the subconscious of the rich countries. And, last but not least, environmental dangers are also building up in the South – dangers that threaten in the long run to engulf and to destabilize even the countries of the North. After all, the rainforests in the tropics act as the lungs of the global (and, by implication, the Northern) climate, the loss of biodiversity impinges upon the high hopes placed on a bio-technological future in the wealthy countries, and an unfettered motorization in China and India would finally transform the entire globe into a greenhouse.

Taking everything together, the boomerang seems to be a suitable metaphor for understanding the novel features of a rising epoch in North–South relations. The increasing integration of the world engenders consequences that threaten to rebound upon the North like a boomerang. Although the reasons for this turn reach far back into the history of colonialism, two principal chronic conflicts have built up in the last fifty years of accelerated world integration after the Second World War, the effects of which are increasingly spreading around the globe.

The Crisis of Justice

Epochs rise slowly, but the opening of the development era happened on a certain date and hour. On 20 January 1949, President Harry Truman, in his inauguration speech before Congress in which he drew the attention of his audience to the conditions of the poorer countries, for the first time defined them as 'underdeveloped areas'. All of a sudden this concept, which has been present ever since, was established, cramming the immeasurable diversity of the globe's South into one single category: the underdeveloped. That Truman coined a new word is not a matter of accident but the precise expression of a world-view: for him all the peoples of the world were moving along the same track, some faster, some slower, but all in the same direction. The Northern countries, and in particular the USA, were running ahead while the rest of the world, with its ridiculously low per-capita income, lagged behind. An image the economic societies of the North had increasingly acquired about themselves was thus projected upon the rest of the world: the degree of civilization in a country is determined by the level of its production. Starting from that premiss, Truman conceived of the world as an economic arena where nations attempted to increase their gross national product (GNP). No matter what ideals inspired the Kikuyus, Peruvians or Filipinos, Truman recognized them only as stragglers whose historic task was to partake in the development race and catch up with the lead runners. Consequently, it became the objective of development policy to bring all nations into the same global arena and to enable them to compete in the race.

After forty years of development, the state of affairs is dismal. The gap between frontrunners and stragglers has not been bridged; on the contrary, it has widened to the extent that it has become unimaginable that it could ever be closed. The aspiration to catch up has ended in a blunder of planetary proportions. The figures speak for themselves: during the 1980s the contribution of developing countries, where two-thirds of humanity live, to the world's GNP shrank to 15 per cent, while the share of the industrial countries, with 20 per cent of the world's population, has risen to 80 per cent. To be sure, upon closer inspection the picture is far from homogeneous, but neither the Southeast Asian showcases nor the oil-producing countries alter the conclusion that the development race has ended in disarray. The world may have developed, but it has done so in two opposing directions.

This is especially true if one considers the destiny of large majorities of people within most countries, as the polarization between nations repeats itself within each country. On the global as well as on the national level, there are polarizing dynamics at work which create an economically excited middle class on the one side and large swathes of the socially excluded on the other. The best one can say is that development has created a global middle class of those with cars, bank accounts and career aspirations. This is made up of the majority in the North and a small elite in the South, and its size equals roughly the 8 per cent of the world's population which owns an automobile. This 8 per cent is beyond all national boundaries, increasingly integrated into the worldwide circuit of goods, communications and travel. An invisible border separates the rich from the poor in all nations, in the North as well as in the South; entire categories of people in the North, such as the unemployed, the elderly and the economically weak, and entire regions in the South, such as rural areas, tribal zones and urban settlements, find themselves increasingly excluded from the circuits of the world economy. 'North' and 'South' are therefore less and less geographical categories than socio-economic ones, referring to the line which divides the strong world market sectors from the competitively weak, economically superfluous sectors in society. A new bipolarism pervades the globe and reaches into every nation; it is no longer the East–West division that leaves its imprint on every society, but the North–South division.

The Crisis of Nature

Another dramatic result of the development era is that Truman's premiss of social superiority has today been fully and finally shattered by the ecological predicament. For instance, much of the glorious rise in productivity is fuelled by a gigantic throughput of fossil energy, which requires mining the earth on the one side and covering her with waste on the other. By now, however, the global economy has outgrown the capacity of the earth to serve as both mine and dumping ground. After all, the world economy increases every two years by about US$60 billion, the figure it had reached in 1900 after centuries of growth.

Although only a small proportion of the world's regions have experienced economic expansion on a large scale, the world economy already weighs down nature to the extent that nature has had in part to give in. If all countries followed the industrial example, five or six planets would be needed to serve as 'sources' for the inputs and as 'sinks' for the waste of economic progress. Therefore a situation has emerged where the certainty which ruled for two centuries has been exposed as a serious illusion: that growth is a show with an open end. Economic expansion has already come up against its biophysical limits; recognizing the finite nature of the earth is a fatal blow to the idea of development envisaged by Truman.

Five hundred years of protected status for the North seem to be drawing to an end. Europe's journey to the ends of the earth, initiated in the fifteenth century and completed in the twentieth, has created a rich history, but at the same time has produced a configuration of conflicts which will inevitably shape the face of the twenty-first century. A world divided and a nature ill-treated are the heritage that casts its shadow forward. It is not that these conflicts as such are new, but their impact potentially spreads worldwide as the pace of globalization accelerates. For the unification of the world increasingly shows its seamy side; the globalization of goods is accompanied by the globalization of troubles. What is new, in fact, is that the North is increasingly less protected by spatial and temporal distances from the unpleasant long-term consequences of its actions.

For several centuries the North could avoid dealing with the reality of a divided world, since the suffering occurred far away. Long distances separated the places of exploitation from the places of accumulation. However, as distances shrink and as the distance between loser and winner shortens, the North is exposed to the threats of a divided world. Globalization not only joins the haughty North with the South but also the chaotic South with the North. Likewise, the bitter consequences of the ill-treatment of nature now make themselves felt daily. Many generations could afford to neglect the limits of nature as a resource and as a sink; the costs of the present have been transferred to the future. However, the more the rate of exploitation increases, the faster the limits of nature make themselves felt on a global scale. Since the distance in time, which for so long bolstered industrialism against its effects, is shrinking, the biophysical limits of nature have forcefully emerged in the present. For these reasons, time and space, delay and distance, have ceased to provide a protective shell for the world's rich; as globalization promises the simultaneity and ubiquity of goods, so the simultaneity and ubiquity of troubles is to be expected. The departure of Columbus is followed, after a long cycle, by the return of menace.

The Horns of the Dilemma

'Development', as a way of thinking, is on its way out. It is slowly becoming common sense that the two founding assumptions of the development promise have lost their validity. For the promise rested on the belief, first, that development could be universalized in space and, second, that it would be durable in time. In both regards, however, development has revealed itself as finite, and it is precisely this insight which constitutes the dilemma that has pervaded many international debates since the United Nations Conference on the Environment in Stockholm in 1972. The crisis of justice and the crisis of nature stand, with the received notion of development, in an inverse relation to each other. In other words, any attempt to ease the crisis of justice threatens to aggravate the crisis of nature; and vice versa. Whoever demands more agricultural land, energy, housing, services or, in general, more purchasing power for the poor, finds him/herself in contradiction with those who would like to protect the soil, animals, forests, human health or the atmosphere. And whoever calls for less energy or less transport and opposes clear-cutting or input-intensive agriculture for the sake of nature, finds him/herself in contradiction with those who insist on their equal right to the fruits of progress. It is easy, however, to see that the base upon which the dilemma rises is the conventional notion of development: for if there were development which used less nature and included more people, a way out of the dilemma would open up. It is small wonder, therefore, that in the last two decades committed minds from all corners of the world have been calling for an 'alternative model of development'.

The comet-like appearance of the concept 'sustainable development' is to be understood in the light of that background. It promises nothing less than to square the circle: to identify a type of development that promotes both ecological sustainability and international justice. Since the times of the Club of Rome study *Limits to Growth*, two camps of political discourse had emerged, one under the banner of 'environment' and the other under the banner of 'development'. The voices from the North mostly emphasized the rights of nature, while voices from the South tended to bring the claims for justice to the fore.[1] In 1987, the World Commission for Environment and Development (the Brundtland Commission) appeared to have succeeded in building a conceptual bridge between the two camps, offering the definition which has become canonical: sustainable development is development that 'meets the needs of the present without compromising the ability of future generations to meet their own needs.[2]

A quick glance, however, reveals that the formula is designed to maximize consensus rather than provide clarity. As with any compromise, that is no small achievement, because the definition works like an all-purpose cement which glues all parts together, friends and foes alike. The opponents of the 1970s and 1980s have found themselves pinned down to a common ground, and since then everything has revolved around the notion of 'sustainable development'. Nevertheless, the price paid for this consensus was considerable. Dozens of definitions have been and continue to be passed around among experts and politicians, because many and diverse interests and visions hide behind the common key idea. As so often happens, deep political and ethical controversies make definition of the concept a contested area.

The formula is based upon the notion of time. It invites the reader to raise his or her eyes, to look at the future, and to pay due consideration to the generations of tomorrow. The definition officially confirms that the continuity of development in time has become a world problem. The egoism of the present is under accusation – as an egoism which sells off nature for short-term gain. In a way, the phrase is reminiscent of the words by which Gifford Pinchot, the steward of Theodore Roosevelt's conservation programme, sought to bring utilitarianism up to date: 'conservation means the greatest good for the greatest number for the longest time'. But upon closer inspection, it will be noted that the definition of the Brundtland Commission makes no reference to 'the greatest number', but focuses instead on the 'needs of the present' and those of 'future generations'. While the crisis of nature has been constitutive for the concept of 'sustainable development', the crisis of justice finds only a faint echo in the notions of 'development' and 'needs'. In the definition, attention to the dimension of time is not counterbalanced by an equal attention to the dimension of space. It is therefore no exaggeration to say that the canonical definition has resolved the dilemma of nature versus justice in favour of nature. Yet two crucial questions remain open. What needs? And whose needs? To leave these questions unanswered in the face of a divided world is to sidestep the crisis of justice. Is sustainable development supposed to meet the needs for water, land and economic security, or the needs for air travel and bank deposits? Is it concerned with survival needs or with luxury needs? Are the needs in question those of the global consumer class or those of the enormous numbers of have-nots? The Brundtland report remains undecided throughout and therefore avoids facing up to the crisis of justice.[3]

Environmental action and environmental discourse, when carried on in the name of 'sustainable development', implicitly or explicitly position themselves with respect to the crisis of justice and the crisis of nature. Different actors produce different types of knowledge: they highlight certain issues and underplay others. How attention is focused, what implicit assumptions are cultivated, which hopes are entertained, and what agents are privileged, depends on the way the debate on sustainability is framed. What is common to all these discourses, I would submit, is the hunch that the era of infinite development hopes has passed, giving way to an era in which the finite nature of development becomes an accepted truth. What renders them deeply different, however, is the way they understand finiteness; either they emphasize the finiteness of development in the global space and disregard its finiteness in terms of time, or they emphasize the finiteness of development with regard to time and consider irrelevant its finiteness in terms of global space.

The contest perspective works with the silent assumption that development, unfortunately, will have to remain spatially restricted, but can be made durable for the richer parts of the world. It neglects the fact that the range of harmful effects produced by the North now covers the entire globe and limits the responsibility of the North to its own affairs. The astronaut's perspective takes a different view. It recognizes that development is precarious in time and seeks global adjustment to deal with the crisis of nature and the crisis of justice. As a response to the global reach of harmful effects, it favours the extension of the range of responsibility, until it covers the entire globe. The home perspective, in turn, accepts the finiteness of development in time and suggests delinking the question of justice from the pursuit of development. It draws a different conclusion from the fact that the range of effects produced by the North has vastly outgrown the radius of Northern responsibility, and advocates reducing the effects until they remain within the given radius of responsibility. It is quite possible that the relative strength of these perspectives will shape the future of North–South relations.

The contest perspective

Recently, the French author Jean Christophe Rufin, in a book entitled *The Empire and the New Barbarians*, proposed a telling metaphor to describe the changing mood in rich societies and sub-societies that face the globalization of threats. Reaching deep into European memory, he evoked the archetype of all frontiers, the *limes*, to describe the new perception of North–South relations. Much as the Romans erected the *limes* to separate themselves from the barbarians beyond their empire, present powers, Rufin suggests, are busy drawing a perceptual wall between the market-integrated parts of the world and the rest. Indeed, large parts of the Southern countries are now no longer considered laboratories of the future, but zones of potential turbulence. All kinds of dangers are expected: violent flare-ups, hurricanes, immigration threats, cheap products flooding the market, and the population bomb ticking away. As the finiteness of development in terms of space enters consciousness, perception changes: the countries of the South change from places where hope resides to places where threats arise.

Having been for a long time the economic masters of the world, the Northern elite feel the pressure rising, as the newly industrialized countries become players on the world market. For these reasons, the attention of economic actors is firmly focused on international competitiveness; to counter global threats with the particular weapon of 'competitive strength' is their primary concern. Given the obsession to get ahead in the competitive struggle between the USA, Europe and East Asia, achieving some ecological modernization along the way is all that seems conceivable.

In the light of the contest perspective, environmental concern emerges as a force propelling economic growth. Shifting consumer demand spurs innovation; trimming down resource use lowers production costs; and environmental technology opens up new markets. Ecology and economics appear to be compatible; and the pursuit of both promises to be, as the magic formula goes, a positive-sum game. Growth is regarded as part of the solution, no longer as part of the problem (e.g. Reilly 1990; Fritsch et al. 1993). Indeed, it was perhaps this conceptual innovation that has done most to propel environmentalism into mainstream thought. Ever since the early 1980s when the OECD (Organization for Economic Cooperation and Development) raised the prospects of an ecological modernization of industrial economies (Hajer 1995), advocating a new mix of resources, a changed structure of growth, and an emphasis on prevention, a language linking business and environmental concerns has been developing. It centres around the redefinition of the environmental predicament as a problem of efficient resource allocation. Natural resources are considered grossly undervalued and therefore wastefully allocated, while human resources along with technology are underutilized; redressing the balance would basically do the job. Thus, achieving 'eco-efficiency' (Schmidheiny 1992) is proposed as the key strategy for business – a strategy of considerable innovative power. The contest perspective goes further, however: by transferring the principle from the micro-economic to the macro-political level, society is viewed as if it were a corporation; and political regulations which do not aim at efficiency are regarded as pointless or even wrong-headed. Issues such as legislation controlling multinationals, the evaluation of technologies in the public interest, or a sustainable GATT (General Agreement on Tariffs and Trade, now the World Trade Organization) were pushed off the agenda. For instance, through the Business Council on Sustainable Development, whose membership list reads like the *Who's Who* of the chemical, steel and automobile industry, this perspective largely shaped the results of the UN Conference on Environment and Development at Rio de Janeiro in 1992. Public authority in the realm of business activities remained a taboo – an outcome which, however, fits nicely in the neo-liberal utopia of those years which purported to bypass collective human decisions (Hobsbawm 1994).

The contest perspective likes to put a price tag on nature. This has found its logical conclusion at the epistemological level, as nature is redefined as capital (El Serafy 1991). With this conceptual operation, it becomes possible to compare natural capital with economic capital, to assess the costs and benefits of substituting one with the other, and to combine the two in an optimal fashion. In the light of the all-pervasive cost–benefit logic, anything – not only nature but also human life – turns into a variable which can in principle be traded off against something else. As a consequence, supporters of this view may consider climate protection, for instance, sub-optimal in comparison to future adjustment to adverse climate effects, which appears to be more a lesson in the sustainability of money than of the environment. But even the contest perspective needs to look beyond the arena of competition. After all, the rich economies require more land and natural resources than are available for them within their own boundaries. Plugging into the 'syntropy islands' (Altvater 1992) of the South had for centuries fuelled accumulation in the North, a scheme which is increasingly threatened as biophysical limits to exploitation come to the fore. As natural resources become scarce, some new regime, based either on the price mechanism or on political agreements, is mandated in order to cool down exploitation and to keep it at an optimal level. Moreover, in the 1980s the concern for nature as a resource was complemented by the concern for nature as a sink. The absorptive capacity of the biosphere for chlorofluorocarbons (CFCs) and carbon dioxide seemed to be exhausted, suggesting that the scarcity of sinks is even more pressing than the scarcity of resources. Whereas, however, access to sources could classically be secured bilaterally through occupation or trade, securing the access to sinks required limiting the emissions of a large number of countries. Making all utilize less can only be achieved multilaterally. For that reason, a new domain of international politics has emerged, in which international conventions are negotiated with the purpose of containing the claims to the biosphere. As a consequence, multilateral negotiations no longer centre on the redistribution of growth, as in the negotiations about the new economic order in the 1970s, but on the redistribution of reductions. However, given that all governments feel obliged to maximize their space for economic development, any reduction is seen as a loss. As a consequence, the ensuing conflicts are usually heated, up to a point that the environmental objectives fall by the wayside, as has happened with most of the Rio agreements.

The search for competitive strength can live with the insight about the finiteness of development in space, but cannot go along with the notion of finiteness of development in time. In this view, therefore, the growth civilization, and its further diffusion through 'free trade', remains unquestioned in terms of time, while its limitation in geographical space is secretly accepted. Though the bitter environmental effects produced in the North reach the far corners of the globe, the radius of responsibility remains restricted. As generally in the contest perspective, it is the South which emerges as the major arena for environmental adjustment. The strategic goal prevails to minimize the burden for the North and to shift the cost of environmental adjustment as much as possible to the South. Obviously, the population question figures prominently on such an agenda. After all, no issue lends itself so easily than taking the South to task on this subject; no issue grants the status of innocence so clearly to the North as this one. The inclination to define environmental problems in the Third World in such a way that their solution can only come from the North is a benign variant of the tendency to project responsibility onto the South. For example, the bulky 'Agenda 21' – UNCED's plan of action of about 800 pages – has been largely drafted in this spirit. It divides the world ecologically into deficit countries and high-performance countries. Environmental problems in the South are framed as the result of insufficient capital, outdated technology, lack of expertise and slackening economic growth. And the definition of the problem already implies its solution: the North has to increase its investments in the South to provide technology transfer, to bring in competence in eco-engineering, and to act as a locomotive of growth for the South. It is easy to see how the conventions of development thinking shape this outlook; once again the South is pictured as the home of incompetence and the North as the stronghold of excellence.

The astronaut's perspective

Many environmentalists proclaim that they wish to save nothing less than the planet. For them, the blue earth, that suggestive globe suspended in the dark universe, delicately furnished with clouds, oceans and continents, has become the reality that ultimately matters. Since the 1970s the world has been increasingly perceived as a physical body maintained by a variety of bio-geochemical processes rather than as a collection of states and cultures. As did the world models which led to 'Limits to Growth', so too does the bio-physical conception of the earth as a system project a transnational space where the existence of nations, the aspirations of communities or other human realities fade into irrelevance when compared to the overwhelming presence of the natural earth. In this way, especially within an epistemic community of scientists around the globe (Haas 1990), a discourse has developed which constructs the planet as a scientific and political object. This community thinks in planetary terms; they frame 'sustainable development' through an astronaut's perspective.

Without the photographs of the earth it would scarcely have been possible to view the planet as an object of management (Sachs 1994). But there is a political, a scientific and a technological reason as well. Only during the course of the 1980s, with the ozone hole, acid rain and the greenhouse effect, did the border-crossing, global impact of pollution by industrial societies force itself into the foreground. Furthermore, scientists have made enormous headway in representing the biosphere as an all-embracing eco-system, linking biota with processes in the atmosphere, oceans and the earth's crust. And finally, as happens so frequently in the history of science, a new generation of instruments and equipment created the possibility of measuring global processes. During the past decade, satellites, sensors and computers provided the means for calibrating the biosphere and displaying it in models. In fact, research on the biosphere is rapidly becoming big science; spurred by a number of international programmes (Malone 1986), 'planetary sciences', including satellite observation, deep-sea expeditions and worldwide data processing, are being institutionalized in many countries. With this trend, sustainability is increasingly conceived of as a challenge for global management. Experts set out to identify on a planetary scale the balance between human extractions/emissions on the one hand, and the regenerative capacities of nature on the other, mapping and monitoring, measuring and calculating resource flows and bio-geochemical cycles around the globe. 'This is essential', says Agenda 21 (Chapter 5.1), 'if a more accurate estimate is to be provided of the carrying capacity of the planet Earth and of its resilience under the many stresses placed upon it by human activities'. Feeling the pulse of the earth seems to be the implicit objective of a new geoscience: the planet is put under sophisticated observation like a patient in an intensive care unit. The management of resource budgets has become a matter of world politics.

The image of the circular earth underscores the assumption, fundamental to this perspective, that since the effects of industrial civilization spread globally, the range of responsibility of the North should also embrace the entire globe. As a consequence, the entire globe is considered the proper arena for environmental adjustment, and not mainly the South, as in the contest perspective. Security against global threats is sought primarily in the rational planning of planetary conditions, not in the defence of the empires of wealth. The fragility of the biosphere under stress by human action is the story-line of this approach. It is recognized that economic development is threatened along the dimension of time. Since, however, the rational design of global conditions can never be achieved without the cooperation of many political actors, some new balance between North and South has to be found. To put it more delicately, at least some of the expectations of the less privileged parts of the global middle class have to be met if a new global order is to be achieved. In this perspective, the commitment to countering the crisis of nature does not allow neglecting the crisis of justice.

Since the inclusion of the South is imperative for such a strategy, calls for a 'global Marshall Plan' arise (Gore 1992). Such a plan seeks to concentrate all efforts on stabilizing the world population, developing environmentally sound technologies, modifying the economic rules of the game, concluding collective treaties, and launching an information campaign for the citizens of the globe. On the horizon is the noble vision of making ecology the centrepiece of a domestic world politics, which would carry out the rational organization of global affairs.

The local livelihoods perspective

'Sustainable development' in this perspective is neither about economic excellence nor about biosphere stability, but about local livelihoods. From this angle, the environment suffers in the first place from *overdevelopment* and not from an inefficient allocation of resources or the proliferation of the human species. At the centre of attention is the goal and structure of development, which in the South is seen as disempowering communities, in the North as diminishing well-being, and in both instances as environmentally disruptive. 'Sustainable development' is therefore suspected to be an oxymoron; in one way or the other, practical and theoretical efforts aim at alternatives to economic development. What is more, it is only in that perspective that the crisis of justice figures prominently in the debate. Internationally, 'conserver' societies in the North are expected to make room for Southern societies to flourish, while nationally sustainable lifestyles for the urban middle classes would leave for peasant and tribal communities more control over their resources. Consequently, the question of whose needs and what needs sustainable development is addressing looms large in this perspective; most inquiries in the last analysis turn around the question: how much is enough? (Durning 1992). Despite their differences, the indigenous and rural populations in the hinterlands of the global middle classes often share the common fate of being threatened by the claims of urban industrial developers on their resources. For when water sources dry up, fields get lost, animals vanish, forests dwindle and harvests decrease, the very basis of their livelihood is undermined, pushing them onto the market, for which they have no sufficient purchasing power. Misery is frequently the result of enclosed or destroyed commons. Wherever communities base their subsistence on the renewable resources of soil, water, plant and animal life, the growth economy threatens nature and justice at the same time; the environment and the people's life-support are equally degraded (Gadgil and Guha 1992). In that context, for many communities, sustainability means nothing less than resistance against development (Tandon 1993). To protect both the rights of nature and the rights of people, the enclosure of extractive development, a federal state with village democracy (Agarwal and Narain 1989) and an affirmation of people's 'moral economies' are called for. Searching for sustainable livelihoods in this sense means searching for decentralized, and not accumulation-centred, forms of society.

Smaller non-governmental organizations, social movements and dissident intellectuals comprise most of the social base of the local livelihoods perspective. What links the efforts of Southern groups with those in rich countries is that both expect the North to retreat from utilizing other people's nature and to reduce the amount of global environmental space it occupies. After all, most of the Northern countries leave an 'ecological footprint' (Wackernagel and Rees 1995) on the world which is considerably larger than their territories. They occupy foreign soils to provide themselves with all the materials they need; and they utilize the global commons – like the oceans and the atmosphere – far beyond their share. The Northern use of the globally available environmental space is blown out of proportion; the style of affluence in the North cannot be generalized around the globe – it is oligarchic in its very structure. From the home perspective, the North is called upon to reduce the environmental burden it places on other countries and to repay the ecological debt accumulated from the excessive use of the biosphere over decades and centuries. The principal arena for ecological adjustment is thus neither the Southern hemisphere nor the entire globe, but the North itself. It is the reduction of the global effects of the North to the reach of domestic responsibility which is at the centre of attention, not the extension of Northern responsibility to coincide with the radius of the effects, as from the astronaut's perspective. The local livelihoods perspective believes in making room for others by means of an orderly retreat; it proposes a new kind of rationality, which could be called 'the rationality of shortened chains of effect', for meeting the crises of justice and of nature. Good global neighbourhood, in this view, requires above all the reform of home out of a cosmopolitan spirit. But the reform of home is a major challenge, particularly in industrial countries. According to the current rule of thumb, only a cutback of between 70 and 90 per cent in the throughput of energy and materials over the next forty to fifty years would live up to the challenge (Schmidt-Bleek 1994). Therefore the perspective hesitates to overemphasize efficient resource management and attempts to focus the social imagination on the revision of goals rather than on the revision of means. For over the longer term, saving effects are invariably swallowed up by the quantity effects involved, if the overall dynamics of growth are not slowed down. Consider the example of the fuel-efficient car. Today's automobile engines are definitely more efficient than in the past; yet the relentless growth in the number of cars and miles driven has cancelled out that gain. In fact what really matters is the overall physical scale of the economy with respect to nature, not only the efficient allocation of resources (Daly and Cobb 1989). Efficiency without sufficiency is counterproductive; the latter has to define the boundaries of the former.

There are indications, however, that many industrial societies passed a threshold in the 1970s, after which growth in GNP no longer corresponded to a growth in quality of life (Cobb and Cobb 1994). This is good news for the local livelihoods perspective, because it encourages these voices to assume that even a shrinking volume of production would not necessarily lead to a decline in well-being; on the contrary, it could make livelihoods flourish through more common wealth. Such a civilization transition, however, implies new models of prosperity which are ultimately not based on permanent growth (Trainer 1995). At the dawn of the twenty-first century, it is argued, it may be conceivable that the aspirations of the nineteenth century, 'faster, farther and more', lose importance. Intermediate speeds that favour an unhurried society, shorter distances that strengthen regional economies, intelligent services that replace throwaway goods, and selective consumption that decreases the volume of commodities: these are signposts for the route towards a sustainable civilization (Bund and Misereor 1996). Still, whether the principle of capital accumulation can be made compatible with the principles of a conserver society remains the conundrum of this perspective (Altvater 1992). No doubt a politics of self-limitation in the end always implies a loss of power, even if it is sought in the name of a new prosperity.

Notes

1. For an overview of the international discussion see: John McCormick, *Reclaiming Paradise: The Global Environmental Movement*, Indiana University Press, Bloomington, 1989. Hans-Jürgen Harbordt, *Dauerhafte Entwicklung statt globaler Selbstzerstörung: Eine Einführung in das Konzept des 'Sustainable Development'*, Berlin, 1991; Peter Moll, *From Scarcity to Sustainability: Future Studies and the Environment: The Role of the Club of Rome*, Frankfurt, 1991.

2. World Commission on Environment and Development, 1987, *Our Common*

Future, Oxford University Press, Oxford, p. 8.

3. Paul Ekins ('Making Development Sustainable', in Wolfgang Sachs (ed.), *Global Ecology: A New Arena of Political Conflict*, Zed Books, London, 1993, p. 91) suggests a similar reading. The same analysis is explicitly formulated in The Ecologist, *Whose Common Future?*, Earthscan, London, 1992.

Bibliography

Agarwal, A. and S. Narain, 1989, *Towards Green Villages: A Strategy for Environmentally Sound and Participatory Rural Development*, Centre for Science and Environment, New Delhi.

Agenda 21, 1992, *Programme of Action for Sustainable Development*, United Nations Department of Public Information, New York.

Altvater, E., 1992, *Der Preis des Wohlstands*, Westfälisches Dampfboot, Münster.

Arndt, H.W., 1981, 'Economic Development: A Semantic History', *Economic Development and Cultural Change*, vol. 26, April, pp. 463–84.

Bund and Misereor (eds), 1996, *Zukunftsfähiges Deutschland*, Birkhäuser, Basle and Berlin.

Clark, W.C. and R. Munn (ed.), 1986, *Sustainable Development of the Biosphere*, Cambridge University Press, Cambridge.

Cobb, C. and J. Cobb (eds), 1994, *The Green National Product: A Proposed Index of Sustainable Economic Welfare*, University Press of America, New York.

Daly, H.E. and J. Cobb, 1989, *For the Common Good*, Beacon Press and Penguin, Boston MA and Delhi.

Durning, A., 1992, *How Much Is Enough?*, Earthscan, London.

The Ecologist, 1992, *Whose Common Future?*, Earthscan, London.

El Serafy, S., 1991, 'The Environment as Capital', in R. Costanza (ed.), *Ecological Economics: The Science and Management of Sustainability*, Columbia University Press, New York.

Fritsch, B., S. Schmidheiny and W. Seifritz, 1993, *Towards an Ecologically Sustainable Growth Society*, Springer, Berlin.

Gadgil, Madhav and R. Guha, 1992, *This Fissured Land: An Ecological History of India*, Oxford University Press, Delhi.

George, S., 1992, *The Debt Boomerang*, Pluto, London.

Gore, Al, 1992, *Earth in the Balance: Ecology and the Human Spirit*, Houghton Mifflin, Boston MA.

Haas, P., 1990, 'Obtaining International Environmental Protection through Epistemic Consensus', *Millennium*, vol. 19, pp. 347–63.

Hajer, M.A., 1995, *The Politics of Environmental Discourse*, Clarendon Press, Oxford.

Harbordt, H.J., 1991, *Dauerhafte Entwicklung statt globaler Selbstzerstörung*, Sigma, Berlin.

Hays, S., 1979, *Conservation and the Gospel of Efficiency – The Progressive Conservation Movement 1890–1920*, Atheneum, New York.

Hobsbawm, E., 1994, *The Age of Extremes: A History of the World, 1914–1991*, Pantheon, New York.

Kehr, K., 1993, 'Nachhaltig denken. Zum sprachgeschichtlichen Hintergrund und zur Bedeutungsentwicklung des forstlichen Begriffs der Nachhaltigkeit', *Schweizerische Zeitschrift für Forstwesen*, vol. 144.

Kothari, R., 1993, *Growing Amnesia: An Essay on Poverty and Human Consciousness*, Penguin, New Delhi.

Lovelock, J., 1979, *Gaia – A New Look at Planet Earth*, Oxford University Press, Oxford.

Malone, T.F., 1986, 'Mission to Planet Earth: Integrating Studies of Global Change', *Environment*, vol. 28, no. 8, pp. 6–11, 39–41.

McCormick, J., 1986, 'The Origins of the World Conservation Strategy', *Environmental Review*, 10, pp. 177–87.

McCormick, J., 1989, *Reclaiming Paradise: The Global Environmental Movement*, Indiana University Press, Bloomington.

Moll, P., 1991, *From Scarcity to Sustainability. Future Studies and the Environment: The Role of the Club of Rome*, Peter Lang, Frankfurt.

Rambler, M., L. Margulis and R. Fester (eds), 1989, *Global Ecology: Towards a Science of the Biosphere*, Academic Press, San Diego CA.

Reilly, W.K., 1990, 'The Environmental Benefits of Sustainable Growth', *Policy Review*, Fall, pp. 16–21.

Sachs, W. (ed.), 1992, *The Development Dictionary. A Guide to Knowledge as Power*, Zed Books, London.

Sachs, W. (ed.), 1993, *Global Ecology: A New Arena of Political Conflict*, Zed Books, London.

Sachs, W., 1994, 'The Blue Planet: An Ambiguous Modern Icon', *The Ecologist*, vol. 24, no. 5, September–October, pp. 170–75.

Schmidheiny, S., 1992, *Changing Course: A Global Business Perspective on Development and the Environment*, MIT Press, Cambridge MA.

Schmidt-Bleek, F., 1994, *Wieviel Umwelt braucht der Mensch?*, Birkhäuser, Berlin and Basle.

Scientific American, 1990, *Managing Planet Earth: Readings from Scientific American*, Freeman, New York.

Tandon, Y., 1993, 'Village Contradictions in Africa', in W. Sachs (ed.), *Global Ecology: A New Arena of Political Conflict*, Zed Books, London.

Trainer, Ted, 1995, *The Conserver Society*, Zed Books, London.

Wackernagel, M. and W. Rees, 1995, *Our Ecological Footprint: Reducing Human Impact on the Earth*, New Society Publishers, Gabriola Island (Canada).

World Commission on Environment and Development, 1987, *Our Common Future*, Oxford University Press, New York.

5

Environmental Degradation and Violent Conflict: Hypotheses, Research Agendas and Theory-building

Günther Baechler

A basic assumption of this chapter[1] is that under certain conditions environmental degradation may cause violent conflict or war. Indeed, recent years have seen an ever-growing discussion about 'eco-conflicts' or green wars caused by the global environmental crisis. While environmentalists among peace and conflict researchers argue that eco-conflicts will be the wars of the foreseeable future, traditionalists refuse to accept that the phenomenon really exists. Others argue that throughout human history there have been conflicts over natural resources; thus environmental conflicts or wars are hardly new. 'Green wars' do not exist in isolation: wars seldom have a single cause; most have a complex and multilayered background. What is striking, however, is the regular appearance of transformation in the genesis of violent conflicts. We will examine the role the natural environment plays in precipitating violent conflicts, and how it is perceived by the parties concerned.

The discussion about environmental security and environmentally induced conflicts has intensified in the last few years (Dokken and Graeger 1995; Lonergan 1996; Gleditsch 1997), despite the fact that virtually everywhere government interest in environmental foreign-policy issues has diminished. The time lag involved is perhaps not surprising: the issue emerged only at a very late stage of the debate on global environmental change. It must also be remembered that the debate has been conducted among members of quite different scientific communities – environmentalists, security experts, development sociologists, conflict researchers – since 1989 and the end of the Cold War. There is, on the one hand, a growing body of literature that either concentrates on more theoretical issues or deals with methodological questions and criticism of existing studies (Gleditsch 1997; Matthew 1997). On the other hand, very little emphasis is put on empirical work, case studies, or field research. The somewhat ideologically coloured debate on environmental security has led to repeated attempts to redefine security. At the same time, attempts to reject the concept as either too narrow or too encompassing are no less persistent. An unusual situation has developed: while scholars throughout the world try to define what a new security threat is, military and defence ministries are pressuring government leaders to define their security priorities.

It is important to note the twin biases in the debate on environmental conflicts among scholars and experts. The first I call 'the discovery of a new issue' bias: whenever a new issue emerges, there is a tendency to ignore history. This leads either to rather alarming statements about future events such as 'water wars' and similar disasters, or to an ahistorical approach which neglects the root causes of present developments. Regarding the issue of environmental transformation and violent conflict or war, these shortcomings are critical in so far as environmental history should not, and indeed cannot, be separated from socio-economic and political history. The second bias is 'environmental determinism', which tends to overestimate the significance of geographical structures, demographic data and resource dependence at the expense of cultural, socio-economic and political capacities or shortcomings, respectively, in order to deal with environmental degradation as well as discrimination. Even if correlations between resource degradation and physical violence can be made, there are no linear cause/effect relationships between the environment and the collective decision to resort to violence.

This chapter does not set out to provide an exhaustive survey of the growing literature dealing with environmental security in one form or another (Baechler et al. 1996). It concentrates instead on: (1) an early contribution that conceptualized well the interrelationship between environmental transformation, underdevelopment and socio-political conflict – the UN Founex Report of 1971; (2) recent studies which focus on resource scarcity and environmental degradation as a major security issue or as a trigger of various types of serious conflicts.

Founex Report on Environmental Change and Underdevelopment

The United Nations Conference on the Human Environment, which took place in Stockholm in 1972, created for the first time a broader awareness of international and global environmental problems (Kilian 1987). This conference – or, rather, prior discussions – was the starting point of debates on so-called environmental foreign policy, international environmental cooperation, and poverty as the biggest polluter. These discussions that preceded the UN conference were held by a group of experts, chaired by Maurice Strong, to address the issue of environmental change and underdevelopment from a global perspective. The group produced the Founex Report on Environment and Development, which was prepared by Mahbub ul Haq (Founex Report 1971). This formed a cornerstone for decisions taken by the UN, international agencies, and member states in Stockholm in 1972 and beyond. In the Report the point is made for the first time that the environmental problems of the developing countries are predominantly problems that reflect both rural and urban poverty and the lack of development in their societies. 'In both towns and in the countryside, not merely the "quality of life", but life itself is endangered by poor water, housing, sanitation and nutrition, by sickness and disease and by natural disasters' (Founex Report 1971). While most environmental problems of the industrialized countries were held to be related to development, it was maintained that environmental disruptions in the South could be overcome by the process of development itself. However, since many developing countries were experiencing the same problems as the industrialized countries, development itself would have to be broadened by new aims and qualitative measures to cater for the 'environmental side-effects that have been known to accompany, in varying degrees, the process of development' (Founex Report 1971). The participants acknowledged the role of socio-ecological variables, recognizing that deviant social behaviour, and hence social conflict, can emerge from a loss of community and social organization. 'Many developing societies', the report states, 'display a high degree of social organization and a considerable sense of community, even in urban settings, as a result of the transplantation of traditional social structures in the process of rural–urban interactions' (Founex Report 1971). The Founex Report goes on to discuss specific problem areas, addressing the world economic order, and providing detailed policy recommendations. However, what is of particular note are two statements made by participants.

First, the members were well aware that poverty-related environmental change could induce heavy degradation of socio-ecological structures, which in turn could lead to social conflicts in developing countries. If consideration is given to the growing trend over the last two decades or so of internal violent conflicts and wars in the South – mainly in the least developed countries (LDCs) – it would seem that this view can be confirmed today. Second, and as a consequence, the participants called for a broader and redefined concept, not of security but of development.

They assumed a causal linkage between environmental and socio-political deterioration and therefore put an emphasis on a broader concept of development. If this assumption holds, environmental conflicts may be understood as a failure of both socio-economic development and sustainable resource use over the last decades or at least over the time span between the UN conferences of Stockholm in 1972 and of Rio de Janeiro in 1992.

The Linkage between Environmental Change, Security and Conflict

It was only in the late 1980s and early 1990s that the debate on war-related environmental destruction shifted away from classical military security topics. Previously, environmental destruction was treated as a side-effect of military training (Krusewitz 1985); as a means of warfare (Westing 1976, 1984); as a by-product of wars (Weizsäcker 1971; Westing 1980, 1985); or as the catastrophic outcome of a future war carried out with weapons of mass destruction (Westing 1977; Ehrlich et al. 1985). The debate moved on to 'environmental factors in strategic policy and action' (Westing 1986; Brown 1990), which focused on 'redefining security' by bringing into the picture new threats such as global environmental change (Ullman 1983; Mathews 1989, 1991b; Gleick 1991). This resulted in introducing environmental degradation as a major cause of violent conflict and war (Lipschutz 1989; Renner 1989; Baechler 1990a, 1990b; Brock 1991; Homer-Dixon 1991a, 1991b).[2]

In the meantime there have been a myriad arguments and activities associated with 'environment and security' (Simmons 1995), and there are sharp disputes over how to define the linkages between environment and security (Brock 1991; Deudney 1991; Gleick 1991; Bruynincks 1993).[3] As a recent report states, 'one of the difficulties in assessing the nature of the linkage is caused by the ambiguity surrounding the term 'security' (Lonergan 1996). For Westing, for instance, comprehensive security consists of two intertwined components: political security, with its military, economic and humanitarian sub-components; and environmental security, which includes protection and use of nature (Westing 1989). The United Nations Development Programme (UNDP), on the other hand, simply lists seven components of 'human security', such as economic security, food security, health and the environment. Some sceptics completely reject the association of environment and security for several reasons. Daniel Deudney (1990) claims that it is analytically misleading to think of environmental degradation as a national security threat. First, the traditional focus of national security – namely interstate violence – has little in common with either environmental problems or their solution. Second, the effort to harness the 'emotive power of nationalism' to help mobilize environmental awareness and action is counterproductive, because it would undermine global political sensibility. Third, environmental degradation is not very likely to cause interstate wars.

Linkages between Environment and Security

The problem, it seems, is not redefining security but rather how to define security adequately. This difficulty is shared with other normative terms or general social categories such as development or peace. There is no way out of the normative trap of being either too broad and therefore vague or too narrow and hence necessarily exclusive. If one defines security in the most general way, it means the absence of any threats in the foreseeable future (Kaufmann 1973). To break this general statement down to a specific type of threat in a given period of time, we must identify the linkages in question.

In principle, four sets of linkages between environment and security have to be distinguished (see Figure 5.1). In the first row (environmental transformation) are events with empirical evidence; the impact of the various linkages can be measured, at least in principle. In the second row (environmental security) there are normative statements on ideal situations or concepts that should be achieved; it means wishful thinking, strategic planning, or practice-oriented theory. The notion of security, narrowly or broadly defined, will remain in dispute, because it is only one normative approach to managing threats and dangers concerning both societies and individuals. Some critics prefer to replace it with other terms, which indicate alternative or even more appropriate problem-solving concepts, such as peace or sustainable development. Therefore a false hope underlies attempts to redefine security: namely, the use of environmental concerns as a means of order to overcome the controversies both within and among different communities concerned with national security issues. Even redefined security may be designed to deal with non-conventional threats in a very conventional manner and with traditional means. It does not necessarily induce major shifts from curative (end-of-pipe) thinking to preventive actions and to therapies of the root causes of problems. The same is of course true for causal linkage as well. If environmental disruption does lead to violence, it is not sufficient to concentrate on how to mitigate or stop violence. In an integrated approach one must rather provide concepts connected to global linkage. The absence of a threat to human security or, more precisely, to human habitat is a necessary prerequisite for sustainable conflict resolution and resource use.

Figure 5.1 Taxonomy of environmental transformation linkages

	Global linkage	Functional linkage	Intentional linkage	Causal linkage
Environmental transformation	as a threat to human security	as a consequence of war	as a means of warfare	as a cause of violent conflict and war
Environmental security/peace with nature/ sustainable development	absence of threat to human security	no environ-mental damage through war	environment is not/should not be used as a means of warfare	environmental transformation does/should not cause violent conflicts/wars

This study concentrates on the upper segment of causal linkage (see Figure 5.1): namely, environmental transformation as a cause of current violent conflict and war. Only in the conclusions drawn can environmental conflicts be examined more in the light of the security dilemma between states or within states. A third option suggested here could be the integration of security and development issues into one concept.

Discussion of the Causal Linkage

Why is causal linkage so important? First, if it were possible to identify environmental transformation as a major cause of present conflicts in many of the poor countries, this might help to redirect both political awareness and financial contributions to address a hitherto little understood root cause of domestic violence. If this happened, conflict management would be more successful than it is today. This is evident in the case of Rwanda/Burundi, where the third parties involved totally failed to address the root causes of the protracted conflict. Second, 'eco-conflict' is predicted to become a major threat to humankind at the threshold of the next century. Therefore it is crucial for policy-makers to deal with 'global linkage' in order to get precise analytical tools and to highlight causal relationships, as well as to improve both predictability and preventive measures. Both factors point to the need for major research efforts in the domain of transformation, poverty and violent conflicts.

A first major step in the exploration of causal linkage is the 'Studies in Environmental Security', which resulted from a joint venture of the United Nations Environment Programme (UNEP) and the Oslo Peace Research Institute (PRIO). Part of the programme concentrated on the Horn of Africa, where causal linkage was analysed in great detail:

> A degraded environment has, in the context of the Greater Horn of Africa, frequently led to war and competition over scant resources. Taking up the challenge of promoting the resolution of the complex problems of the region would require identifying the linkages that undoubtedly exist between environmental stress, the clash of economic interests and the tensions inherent in political conflicts that escalate to armed confrontations. (Imru 1990)[4]

Another participant in the Horn project states:

> Indeed, the environment itself is among the causalities of war. Nevertheless, it is generally recognized that competition over scarce resources is frequently a contributing cause of conflict, because it generates insecurity. War itself is very wasteful of resources and destroys the environment that produces them, thereby increasing scarcity and insecurity and aggravating conflict. (Markakis 1990)

Markakis finds it legitimate 'to examine the role scarcity and competition for basic resources play in the generation of conflict', even though 'this role may, or may not, be clearly perceived by the embattled parties' (Markakis 1990). Consequently, while highlighting the environmental dimension of the 'tragedy in the Horn', he suggests including socio-economic and political factors that have environmental impact.

The Horn study group concluded that the task was not easily resolvable, despite the availability of a great deal of information on environmental change. As a member of the group pointed out: 'It may be difficult or impossible to prove, in a scientific way, that wars or conflicts or hostilities between nations are caused by environmental degradation' (Molvaer 1989). Indeed, even though the literature widely accepts that such a connection or linkage often exists, not as a sole factor but as a contributing one that may trigger unrest, few attempts to 'prove' this linkage have been made. The study group provided empirically rich area studies and identified fields of environmental cooperation. Nevertheless, it failed to identify the causes of environmental conflicts.

This is not to say that the UNEP/PRIO programme would not have worked out on the basis of a widely defined environmental security concept, stating for instance that 'while military activities can have a severe and debilitating effect on the environment, environmental factors can, in turn, have a profound effect on security and prospects for peace' (Ulrich 1989).

However, the concept has its benefits as well as its shortcomings on empirical terrain. One definite advantage is that it sheds light on an emerging issue, considering simultaneously data on wars as well as on victims (refugees), on political events, and on the devastating effects of warfare on the environment. On the other hand, the socio-economic, institutional, and actor-oriented variables which affect the causal relationship linking environment and conflict tend to be underestimated. The Horn project, like a number of others listed by Gleditsch in his critical overview of the scholarly literature, suffered from a lack of clear definition of the concept of environmental conflict. Furthermore, there is no clear distinction between internal and international conflict and therefore no consistency in the level of analysis (Gleditsch 1997). This criticism applies to most scholarship in this domain. It is still not clear, for instance, if the degree or severity of environmental degradation in a certain area has a direct relation to the intensity of conflict behaviour by the actors involved. Some studies presume a linear relationship; others do not. Socio-economic effects of environmental change are commonly cited as being responsible for violent outbreaks of conflict, though it is not indicated which effects. Hume's question – same cause (leads to) same effect? – remains to be answered.

The notion of environmental conflict has often been criticized as being unable to prove the interrelationship between environmental degradation and violent conflict. The main problem that arises repeatedly seems to be the impulse to 'prove' causality (Molvaer 1989).[5] This, however, is not a shortcoming of social science in general, nor of the environmental conflict programme in particular. It is by no means proven which factors other than environment – such as economy, ethnicity, or contention for state power – cause violent conflict. Even in the 'hard' discipline of medicine it would be very difficult to obtain proof that a small number of precisely described factors trigger cancer or heart attacks. If successful methods were developed in distinct domains, then nothing would be easier than adopting them. However, the problem is that there is little ongoing empirical research that has led to testable hypotheses (Lane and Ersson 1994). Theories claiming to provide testable hypotheses, such as rational choice theory, have not so far carried out many empirical tests (Green and Shapiro 1994).

The term 'proof' raises methodological expectations that cannot be fulfilled, and therefore leads to rationalizations and defensive research strategies; grapes that cannot be grasped are sour. That is why, after careful exploration of environmental disruptions, conclusions drawn are quite often weak and somewhat unimpressive. In many publications causes of conflicts are described rather vaguely; they are considered to be complex and multifaceted – the environment being a contributor to this complexity. Who would oppose this? More differentiated statements contend that environmental change either contributes to instability, heightens political tensions, aggravates existing conflict, or is a catalyst for hostilities (Ulrich 1989). Such observations on trigger mechanisms are much more helpful; however, they are rarely empirically grounded or systematically related to specific events. So far, little emphasis has been placed on tracing causal pathways accurately. The myriad arguments quite often get stuck in the marshy ideological battlefield where people fight for definitions. Thus linkage between environment and conflict must be clearly distinguished from linkage between environment and violent conflict or war in particular. A clear-cut distinction exists between the two different kinds of linkages, the analysis of which requires specific tools.

A further problem is that many studies hedge their conclusions by failing to distinguish clearly between past and future developments. A common statement, and indeed a truism, is that population growth and migration may lead to conflict. Instead one must argue that both population growth and migration always lead to some sort of conflict. Yet the interesting questions, in terms of predictability, could be how, where and why the two factors lead to serious social and political problems which tend to become violent. In which cases does this problem syndrome also exist but not lead or contribute to violence, and why?

The environment is often seen as a background variable that only indirectly influences or intensifies an already existing and often more comprehensive conflict situation (Dokken and Graeger 1995). Although it is widely acknowledged that research has addressed existing linkages between environmental degradation and conflict, 'establishing one causal element in a conflict situation, e.g. the environment, does not preclude other elements from being equally important' (Dokken and Graeger 1995). Here again analysts seem to question whether environment really matters by suggesting that it contributes to a given event or state of affairs rather than serves as a necessary precondition. An overview concludes that 'the threshold for when environmental degradation becomes intolerable and erupts into violent conflict is difficult to assess in general terms and must be decided on a case by case basis' (Dokken and Graeger 1995). Against this background, a widely shared view holds that the environmental conflict approach cultivates rich case studies which help to justify the environmental dimension of security empirically and therefore make it more applicable to the political community and the general public.

In conclusion, I suggest there must be a position between the two poles of scientific proof and case-by-case studies. If proof of linkage does indeed overstate the claim made by (social) science and myriad case studies, why give up the search for common denominators, for well-selected indicators going beyond single-case description, and for allowing certain generalizations which could be integrated within more general approaches in conflict research? By considering the state of the art as well as methodological constraints, several distinct options arise in which the results of general evidence can be gained without ignoring empirical evidence. How to deal with this is the focus of the next two sections.

Methodological Dilemmas in the Study of Causal Linkage

Several analysts provide differing taxonomies and typologies of linkage between environment and security in general and causal linkage in particular. The following section will examine the relationship between some of the most important systematic orders in order to learn more about the specifics of the approaches under consideration. Sometimes the taxonomies give the impression of being mutually exclusive. In fact, this is not the case at all, as a comparison of them demonstrates.

Peter Gleick (1990) concentrates more on general linkages, distinguishing four ways of using or manipulating the environment in terms of security issues. His taxonomy (see Figure 5.2) is more or less at the same level of generalization as the four linkages mentioned earlier (see Figure 5.1). Since this study is focusing on causal linkage, I will refer only to the four different taxonomies listed under 'root of conflict' (see Figure 5.2). These are located at the same level of analysis. This does not mean that they mutually exclude each other. Indeed, the opposite is the case: they are highly complementary, because all deal with the same syndrome but from a different angle. They highlight a series of aspects of a transformation which supposedly induces environmental conflicts.

Steven Lonergan (1996) addresses five trigger mechanisms, encompassing almost all factors that cause disruptions in society–nature relationships, which he represents as a curve ranging from unintended to intended or planned activities. Michael Renner (1989) prefers a politico-geographical approach that allows him to analyse the effect environmental change could have on political entities at different levels of the international system. The two approaches could easily be integrated. For instance, we can ask if cumulative changes (Lonergan) affect regional commons as a whole or only an eco-region on a sub-national level (Renner). The geography of environmental transformation determines the level of conflict in the international system. Thomas Homer-Dixon (1991b) identifies categories of renewables, the degradation of which is supposed to induce violent conflict. Finally ENCOP (Libiszewski 1992; Baechler et al. 1996) focuses on the historical dimension of changes in society–nature relationships, addressing the transformation of renewables as a cause of environmental conflicts and wars.

As can be demonstrated through case studies (carried out mainly by the third and fourth groups in the taxonomy in Figure 5.2), it is impossible

Figure 5.2 Environment, security threat and conflict setting

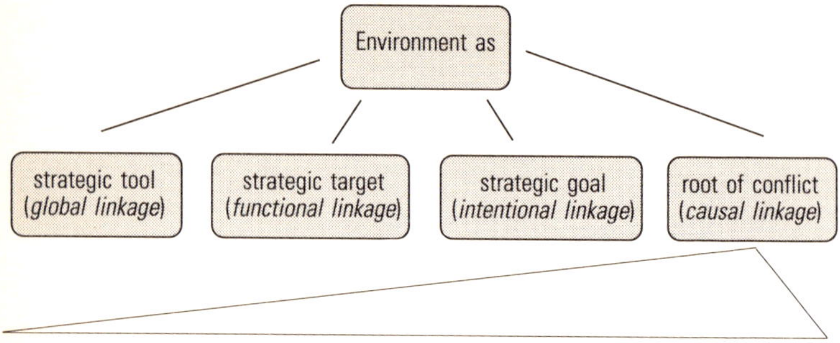

Trigger mechanisms[1]	Geographical boundaries[2]	Renewable resources[3]	Anthropogenic transformation[4]
1. Natural disasters 2. Cumulative changes 3. Accidental disruptions 4. Development projects 5. Conflict and warfare	1. Global environ-mental effects 2. Regional effects 3. Bilateral effects 4. Nationwide effects 5. Sub-national effects	1. Climate change 2. Ozone layer depletion 3. Degradation of land 4. Degradation of forests 5. Water depletion 6. Depletion of fisheries	1. Overuse of renewables 2. Overstrain of sink capacity 3. Impoverishment of space of living

[1] Lonergan 1996 [2] Renner 1989 [3] Homer-Dickson 1991b [4] ENCOP 1992

to focus on one classification exclusively because each deals with specific aspects of the problem as a whole. For instance, overuse of a renewable resource (ENCOP) can consist of the degradation of land (Homer-Dixon). The degradation of land may affect a sub-national or a transboundary area (Renner), the transformation of which may be caused by cumulative anthropogenic changes or by natural disasters or by both – that is, drought (Lonergan). The result of this comparison is not at all surprising: every renewable resource (Homer-Dixon) is geographically bound (Renner), forms part of the historical transformation of societal-nature relationships (ENCOP), and belongs to a broader societal environment (Lonergan).

The three elements of the ENCOP taxonomy can be formulated in an encompassing way, integrating the crucial aspects of the other classification schemes. The first dimension of the synthesis consists of transformation in both physical form and chemical substance. To these processes belong: (a) the deterioration of the sources – that is, of renewable resources based on industrial exploitation of non-renewable resources; this may occur through drilling for fossil energy and open-cast or underground mining, or through large-scale industry and extensive or intensive agricultural use of land. Increasing demand put upon resources by rapidly growing populations accelerates transformation of nature's sources; (b) overuse of nature's sink capacity, namely through the introduction of anthropogenic pollutants – that is, pollution of waters, deposits of hazardous wastes, deterioration of soils by chemicals, emission of greenhouse gases and so on.

The second dimension consists of transformation in an eco-geographical setting. This refers to the destabilization of well-adjusted living orders through a syndrome of transformation processes. For instance, soil erosion and drought deprive farmers and stock breeders of their means of production and encourage urban settlements. These are processes that lead inevitably to impoverishment of society–nature relationships. Impoverishment expresses itself, too, in the resettlement of populations forced to abandon their original living space as a result of industrial development projects, accidental disruption, or natural disasters.

The inherent tendency of local transformation to have consequences in a wider eco-geographical area may easily cause environmental deterioration throughout the world. Simultaneously, globalized transformation may induce serious regional or local damage. Greenhouse gas emissions are blamed for global climate change, inducing regional as well as local transformation, such as erratic precipitation patterns. Human action affects resources, whether it be home-made environmental deterioration or due to the impact of externalization caused by third parties. There is that which affects eco-regions within a single country (for example soil erosion, deforestation and mining activities); that which affects eco-regions touching two or more neighbouring states (for example, transboundary waterways, mining activities); that which does not directly affect eco-regions within one state or shared by two states, but regional commons in a wider geographical area (for example acid rain, air pollution and dumping of hazardous waste); and that which affects global commons, which in turn has an impact on both eco-regions within states and extra-territorial eco-regions (for example, depletion of the stratospheric ozone layer, global warming and rising sea levels).

Whereas the taxonomies deal with the independent variable, there are typologies concerned with the dependent variable, namely environmental conflict and war. The typologies on conflicts are far less complementary than the taxonomies on the independent variable (see Figure 5.3). Peter Wallensteen's (1992) concept aims at identifying the different stages during

Figure 5.3 Typologies of environmentally caused conflicts

Wallensteen (1992)

1. Reduced resources available results in more contention in society at large
2. Shift in power between already existing parties
3. Formation of new parties as a reaction
4. Environment becomes more important for established parties
5. Environment becomes central in political affairs
6. Involvement of environmentally based groups

Homer-Dixon (1991b, 1994)

1. Simple scarcity conflicts
2. Group identity conflicts
3. Relative deprivation conflicts
4. Environmental scarcity conflicts (1994)
   (Population growth + resource distribution)

Baechler et al. (1996)

1. Centre–periphery conflicts
2. Ethno-political conflicts
3. Interregional migration conflicts
4. Transboundary migration conflicts
5. Demographically induced conflicts
6. International water conflicts
7. Long-distance conflicts (cumulative effects)

---

which ecological concerns emerge as a topic of political competition in democratic societies rather than a typology of distinct conflicts. However, it indicates that the environment matters in terms of inducing changes in both political institutions and the priority-setting of political actors.

Thomas Homer-Dixon (1991b, 1994) distinguishes environmental conflicts in Third World countries with the help of hypotheses provided by three general theories well established in social science and psychology – namely, economy dealing with scarcity of commodities, group-identity theory, and relative-deprivation theory. Although it seems a plausible approach to explain three types of conflicts with three theories, the approach is in fact too linear. The three theories do not necessarily explain three distinct types of conflict but rather three different stages in the genesis of one and the same conflict. An example may help to illustrate this. Environmentally induced migration does not exclusively and necessarily cause typical group-identity conflicts (Homer-Dixon 1994). A group-identity conflict may initially have been caused by a simple scarcity conflict

– for example, about access to fertile land. In a second phase, violent reactions may have urged people to flee to another area where they got into trouble with people belonging to another ethnic group. Migration could also have resulted in clashes between refugees and border police or the armed forces of a neighbouring state. Thus, by tracing a specific conflict, we recognize that one and the same conflict passes through different stages, probably with different actors involved. At the same time, the pathways may be quite complex.

ENCOP (Baechler et al. 1996) provides a typology, which is inductively drawn from a set of some forty area studies. It indicates the amalgamation of actor-oriented analyses and structurally defined arenas of conflict in terms of socio-political, ethno-political and regional geography of environmental conflicts and wars. ENCOP did not start with complex theories and models but aimed at applying what is called 'a gradualist approach to model-building' (Gleditsch 1997). Only in a second step did examination of each of the seven types lead to explanations that referred to hypotheses drawn from several theories such as *dependencia*, political geography, anthropology, or development sociology. In order to understand and explain complex cases, the configuration of several approaches was stressed rather than the linear connection between an individual type and a single theory.

Different Angles from which a Conflict Story Can Be Told

Some critics use these shortcomings or 'methodological flaws' in order to neglect the environmental conflict approach as such, maintaining that there are no interesting mechanisms that are purely and discretely environmental, because environmental factors interact with a variety of other factors to spawn violent conflict (Levy 1995). According to Levy, one has to focus on the 'contention' for state power as a fundamental factor of present violent conflicts. It is evident that power contention increased sharply after 1987, and it is evident that power contention was and is the source of much more severe conflicts than ethno-nationalism or indigenous rights (Gurr 1994). However, only eighteen out of fifty ethno-political conflicts fall into the category 'contention for power' (Gurr 1994), which means that there are other important issues to study as well. After Gurr, a strong case can be made linking ecological stress, inequalities and conflict affecting indigenous peoples. It would therefore be 'unwise to discount the present or future significance of economic factors … because conflicts tend to be more numerous and intense in regions and countries where systemic poverty is greatest' (Gurr 1994).

The suggestion (Levy 1995) that analysts should concentrate on 'how nations get into war' and not on structural root causes is somewhat biased. Stories of proximate events are tremendously important in understanding the dynamics of a conflict, but there is a tendency to confuse the outward appearance of a conflict with its root causes. Focusing, for instance, on political or military leadership without an understanding of the deep motivation of the actors contributes to disasters, as was experienced by hundreds of thousands of refugees in the triangle between eastern Zaïre, Burundi and Rwanda in 1996. Rwanda, Somalia, Liberia and Afghanistan remind us to ask why there are actually no nations going to war but nevertheless many ongoing violent conflicts and wars. Certainly the struggle for power is a crucial problem, above all in the young states of the international system where the starting point was in the mid-1950s for social, economic and ecological transformation as well as modern leadership (that is, only forty years ago) (Lane and Ersson 1994). Since these transformation processes began only a few decades ago, it is all the more important to understand and explain them in the light of historically shaped socio-economic and cultural-ecological factors, these being closely intertwined. Hence, explaining the encompassing patterns of current conflicts is not inconsistent with the strategy to trace particular factors as part of the causation process of violence.

Thus far, relatively little research has been done on violent conflict and war as a chronic development problem, although there are exceptions (Arnold 1991; Matthies, 1988, 1994, 1995a, 1995b; Senghaas 1989). The association between conflict and poverty has often been excluded in development sociology and economics. Only recently Dan Smith provided a study which focused on this very relationship, recognizing the problem that exists in identifying single causes of current violent conflicts and wars in the South without being accused of 'mono-causality' (Smith 1994). Although it treats foreign debt and domestic poverty as causes of conflict, the approach is nonetheless helpful in many ways to the study presented here. First of all, Smith insists on both the uniqueness of each conflict and its shared features. Concentrating systematically on the causal relationship between violent conflict and foreign debt structure shows that there is 'in some cases at least, a connection between debt and violent conflict based on the mechanism of response to economic reform and austerity measures' (Smith 1994). The problem here is not monocausal explanation, but rather the failure to realize that pure statistical analysis is only the very first step in explaining causes – causes that may even change over time. Only dense case studies which focus on certain causes in a multidimensional approach can fill this gap.

Second, Smith stresses the fact that the multiplicity of conflict causes underlines the need for 'more focused, comparative studies of conflicts, tracing their genesis within the full context – social and political, economic and environmental, domestic and international' (Smith 1994). Even though one may agree fully with this statement, difficulties remain in translating it into practical research. Full-context studies can only build on an extremely complex model of linear and non-linear causalities, adding to the picture a great number of variables. If, for instance, the programme is to trace the 'strong association of poverty and conflict' (Smith 1994), we can do so by correlating violent internal conflicts and the country ranking of the Human Development Index of UNDP. However, a country's rank is determined by only five indicators, excluding many other variables that could indicate the status of a country in a broader framework.

The full context turns out to be a fiction. It consists of images, shared meanings and conventional wisdom, and depends on data provided by agencies, which try hard to get more valid and, above all, comparable data from each country. This is especially difficult in the hot spots, which are the very cases conflict research is normally most interested in.

'Someone's Cow Ate Someone Else's Crop'

Another point is that even parties in conflict may not fully understand the causes of their own struggle or war. This happens because of 'a difference between the causes for which they fight and what it is that causes them to fight' (Smith 1994). This difference is well understood by Beth Roy (1994) in her rich empirical field study carried out in Bangladesh. I will briefly summarize her case, which fits well into the argument. According to Roy the causation of the conflict under consideration was that 'in a remote village somewhere in South Asia, someone's cow ate someone else's crop' (Roy 1994). Was this the cause that explains why the villagers were ready to fight an almost all-out war on a community level? It is not. The villagers were ready to fight because they got a green light from both political and traditional leaders to do so. The leaders did not mediate, because they perceived that the times 'have changed' (Roy 1994). Indeed, local leaders had information about similar fights going on elsewhere in the country. This meant that 'waves of history' swept over into a normally quiet place. What happened far away was that Bangladesh, where the village is located, after separation first from India and then Pakistan, has become an independent state. The Muslims, among them the owner of the cow, started to complain: 'The Muslim did not have any existence, the Hindus have all. The elderly Muslims had all suffered a lot of loss during the pre-partition days. But they could not make any protest during British time' (Roy 1994). The implication is clear: the cohesion of oppression, or of the collectively shared feeling of being oppressed, had created bitterness among Muslims, so they didn't care to compromise any more. They developed a strong feeling of 'now the state is ours, it is our turn. Now we'll teach them a lesson'; or, as Beth Roy concludes, 'to translate power on a state level into power on a local level was the task of the day' (Roy 1994). Hence, step by step, an atmosphere was created that made violence acceptable, possible, and even necessary:

> People knew, however vaguely and inaccurately, that outside their village forces were at work which corresponded to their own experience. Pakistan was formed. Pakistan represented the culmination of other Muslims' grievances. They knew those wrongs had to do with a state unfavorable to their people. Precisely in what way it was unfavorable was only vaguely understood. It had something to do with job discrimination and exclusion from schools. All that part of the story took place in a class universe far distant from the villagers. But it harmonized with their own experience. They too felt excluded and oppressed. Their landlord and moneylenders, the economic powers in their world, were Hindu, and the erstwhile state was somehow felt to be a Hindu state, even though it was known to have been British. In any case, now the state was Muslim. Those Muslims so far away in town, so far away across India, speaking another tongue and wearing a different garb, those Muslims had risen and won a new state. Such monumental events struck chords of harmony with the desires of the villagers in Panipur.... Between the winds of history and the storm in Panipur came some process of synthesis and decision.

Roy provides a good example of how to study both the gap between causation and causes, or reasons and the genesis of a conflict in a certain arena, which is heavily influenced by events and perceptions stemming from within or outside this arena. An arena made up of individual and collective actors who aim to mobilize their cultural, social and economic capital in the hope of playing an active role in policy design and aiming to receive a significant part of the cake (either material or power). The causal pathway between cow-eats-crop and almost all-out war on a local scale consists of different pieces. There is the economically motivated fight among neighbouring farmers about scarce resources. There is also an element of a social class struggle between top-dog caste Hindu and underdog Muslims. There is a local political component, because the leaders, in whom people trusted, tolerated the resort to violence. There is an ethno-political dimension induced by the historically developed cohesion of oppression within the Muslim community. Finally, there is an important shift in regional power in South Asia which led to the creation of a new state by the underdogs. The proximate trigger which caused them to fight, namely cow-eats-crop, is not difficult to explain.

However, the other pieces indicate that strong distant triggers are at work, causes which peoples found it worthwhile fighting for. The distant trigger is found somewhere in history, not only in political history (this would be too reductionist an approach) but also in social and environmental history. The rural population has played a crucial role throughout Indian history. The cow-eats-crop conflict is just one of thousands of similar conflicts. This explains why it is not only interesting as an individual case but is also interesting as an indicator of heavy socio-economic pressure felt by struggling neighbours when the cow started eating the crops. Rural poverty, unproductive agriculture and land degradation through overuse or mismanagement, and not 'simple scarcity', have induced social and political conflict in India over centuries; the syndrome of factors is, therefore, supposed to act as a crucial distant trigger. One can further assume that the farmers in the story were not directly struggling for a change of power in South Asia; instead, their ultimate interest concerned land and crops. And it is further known that in India especially there were major obstacles to rebellion, explained by Barrington Moore within the structure of the predominant type of village society (Moore 1966). However, this is why the intervening variable foundation of a new state in Roy's story cannot be overestimated. The state was far away and could not intervene in favour of the Muslim community. That is why the cow owner could summon the courage to protest against the Hindu neighbour capturing his crop-eating cow and why he had the collective support of both the Muslim community and its leaders.

Against the background of Muslim farmers versus Hindu neighbours, the foundation of Pakistan must be viewed as a necessary condition too. Some crucial observations concerning the environment and violent conflict can be made in this regard:

- even though full-context analysis may be a fiction, it is obvious that single root causes to a conflict must be seen in the multidimensional arena where the play occurs;
- the cause of a conflict is not necessarily identical to the causes the parties involved believe they must fight for;
- the perception of causes can change during the genesis of a conflict; ethical deterioration driven by external events can create new fault lines during the escalation period, which at a certain stage may be perceived by the actors as the 'real' causes they fight for;
- the conditions contributing to a conflict are not interesting in terms of scientific analysis; what counts is whether, in a certain arena, necessary or sufficient conditions (or both) exist;
- the analysis of causal pathways, and therefore determination of root causes, depends heavily on the subjective decision of the analyst (the 'storyteller'), on where the pathway starts in history.

The Effects of Persistent Drought

The last point can be illustrated by a well-documented conflict which quite often serves as an example in the debate on environmental conflict: the Mauritania/Senegal border conflict that broke out in 1989. The effects of persistent drought in the Sahel, occurring mainly in the mid-1980s, led to the governmental decision to build a dam and a barrage in the Senegal river valley. The decision, once taken, created unintended consequences (in the terms of Lonergan's taxonomy): land prices in the region increased significantly. Thus the Mauritanian Arab elite did not hesitate to change the land tenure system immediately after becoming aware of the possible future benefits of denying black African farmers, herders and fishermen use of their resources, as they had done for ages before.

Now let us analyse the genesis of the conflict. As perceived by analysts, the genesis of the conflict was usually seen to begin with the phrase: 'the effects of persistent drought…' The question arises whether this beginning suffices. Is it correct to start the story with persistent drought? If so, does it lead to the conclusion that in this case we are confronted with a typical environmental conflict? Was it not the change in the land law by the white elite that was responsible for the brink-of-war situation? On the other hand, it could also have been ethnic division induced by the expected significant increase in land prices that triggered the escalation of the conflict. This explanation is viable too. Or was it the clear decision to build a dam? Or could it have been the somewhat unintended consequences of the elite's decision? Depending on the answers to these questions the conflict might be classified as either a group-identity conflict, as contention for power in the state, as a modernization conflict, or as a simple scarcity or environmental scarcity conflict (Smith 1994). If we maintain this to be a typical environmental conflict caused by drought and probably triggered by the decision to build dams, then we are confronted with a problem of definition. Since environmental conflicts are caused by anthropogenic transformation of the environment, at least in the approach chosen in this study, the question arises whether the Sahel drought of the 1970s and 1980s resulted from anthropogenic climate change or 'natural' influences upon the climate. If the latter is the case, does it still constitute an environmental conflict? The question is of some significance, because the Senegal valley served as a case of reference in the analyses of most participants to the discussion on environmental security and violent conflict (Dokken and Graeger 1995; Smith 1994; Homer-Dixon 1994; Dessler 1994; Baechler and Spillmann 1996). Since there is still much uncertainty about the regional impact of climate change, the answer to the question is rather pragmatic. Causation – both man-made and natural – may be perceived as a natural catastrophe by human beings affected by a persistent drought, in which case the perception of actors in the arena may be more important in terms of conflict dynamics than the best scholarly explanation. On the other hand, as soon as a means of problem-solving is found, it makes a difference. In the case of anthropogenic transformation, it may be easier to find ways out of the trap of unsustainable resource-use than to deal adequately with the challenge of 'natural' climate change.

This leads finally to the question of how best to escape the problems of causal analysis addressed in the example of Mauritania versus Senegal. Three answers present themselves. First, one must carefully trace causal pathways. This must be done by highlighting the syndrome of factors involved within a given arena and in a historical perspective. Concerning the Senegal example, this means one must look behind the decision to build a dam and analyse the political and societal processes that led to the decision. Was it really persistent drought? Or was it the expectation of benefits in terms of land price? Perhaps there would have been better strategies than building a dam in order to compete with drought in the Sahel, strategies that might not have fuelled an existing syndrome. Second, one must identify the different but interacting roles played by a syndrome of factors in a given arena. The third answer concerns the rejection of any attempt at a quasi-functional analysis of causes, in the sense that the Sahel drought would have the function of modernizing rural societies, which would have to be seen, *per se*, as a violent transformation process.

Any study of causal linkage must focus on an institutional and actor-oriented approach by dealing with positions and perceptions, interests and decision-making processes.

Causation in Complex Politico-ecological Systems

The Environmental Change and Acute Conflict Project (ECACP) took a major step forward in the tracing of pathways and the interacting roles of causes. It aimed at combining empirical research by carrying out a set of case studies with a systematic approach focusing predominantly on causal linkages (Homer-Dixon 1991b, 1994). The ECACP study group was definitely not interested in the whole range of factors that currently cause changes in the value of the dependent variable 'conflict'; instead, it wanted to know whether and how a hypothesized independent variable, in particular 'environmental scarcity', causes conflict (Homer-Dixon 1995). The research team identified four social effects of ecological degradation which may lead to violent conflict, namely decreasing agricultural productivity; economic decline; migration; and disruption of political institutions and social relationships. Against the background of eight case studies carried out, they drew the following conclusion: 'Scarcities of renewable resources are already contributing to violent conflicts in many parts of the developing world' (Homer-Dixon et al. 1993). Environmental degradation is supposed to trigger internal violent conflicts and wars; only under exceptional circumstances does it lead to wars at an interstate level. This is because resource conflicts are mainly related to degradation of renewables such as land, water, forests and fisheries in a local or regional context, whereas the hypothesis that ozone layer depletion or climate change induce violent international conflicts was falsified.

Acknowledging that environmental scarcity always operates together with other political, socio-economic and cultural causes, the analysts are confronted with the problem that all these causes may be contributory or necessary conditions, but not necessarily sufficient ones. Therefore multi-causality as such is not the most challenging problem, but rather the relationship between the variables, ranging from being fully endogenous to being fully exogenous. David Dessler (1994) confirms that 'the central epistemological issue does not concern the presence of environmental change in these causal processes. No one denies that environmental change is somehow involved. The issue is rather the *importance* of environmental change in producing violent conflict' (Dessler 1994).

There are three different standpoints concerning the role of environmental scarcity. First, environmental scarcity can be an important force behind changes in the politics and economics governing resource use (see Figure 5.4a; Figures 5.4a, b, c, taken and modified from Homer-Dixon 1995).

Figure 5.4 Degrees of causal independence

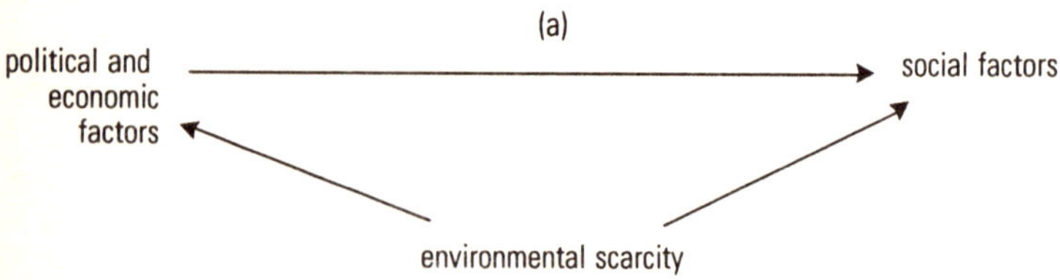

Second, ecosystem vulnerability is often an important variable contributing to environmental scarcity, and this vulnerability is, at least partly, an external physical factor that is not a function of human social institutions or behaviour (see Figure 5.4b).

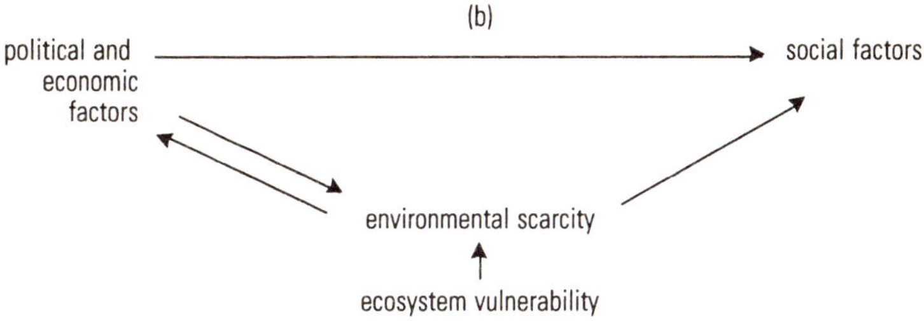

Third, in many parts of the world environmental degradation has crossed a threshold of irreversibility. Even if enlightened social change removes the original political, economic and cultural causes of degradation, it will be a continuing burden on society: 'Once irreversible, in other words, environmental degradation becomes an exogenous variable' (Homer-Dixon 1995; see Figure 5.4c).

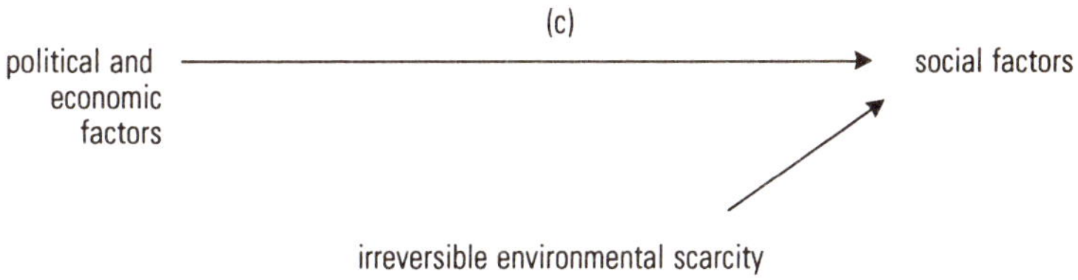

The degree of exogeneity/endogeneity of the independent variables is only to be determined by tracing back the causal linkage through rich case studies, and/or by model testing. But to come back to the Mauritania/Senegal case: what is the degree of exogeneity of the Sahel drought: is it (a), (b) or (c)? One might come to the following conclusion: (a) is to be excluded because each analysis starts with 'persistent Sahel drought' stressing predominantly the fact of ecosystem vulnerability. There seems to be ample evidence that the drought is an independent variable rather than a contributing factor to the syndrome; it is supposed to play a major role in the arena. However, if it is (b), it could also be (c), namely irreversible environmental scarcity perceived as a fully exogenous variable, the role of which dominates the arena. It is difficult to decide whether it is (b) or (c) because there are no scientific tools available so far to predict irreversibility.[6]

Hence the choice depends heavily on perceptions of the actors in the arena. If, let us say, a community of farmers perceives drought and its effects on fertile land as irreversible and they act accordingly by abandoning the fields, one may choose (c) as the degree of independence we have to deal with. As demonstrated by a huge comparative study in the Shewa-Wello province, one of the most drought-prone parts of the highlands of Ethiopia, the farmers firmly believe they suffer 'under God's environment'. Indeed, the deep-rooted belief in God as 'the fountain of authority and power' insulates those in power from any accountability to the people. 'In famine or war, the peasants almost never charge any government or institution with responsibility. Nothing, including their abject poverty and suffering, happens without God's will' (Wolde-Mariam 1991). And since people are prepared to accept responsibility for their conditions, the situation does not end in social action, 'because the basis of responsibility is personal rather than social' (Wolde Mariam 1991). This is a good example of how drought perceived exclusively in terms of a sequence of crop failures over time can become a fully exogenous variable a rural population tries to compete with.

Causal Relationship Between Independent and Dependent Variables

The previous section outlined a scheme which can help clarify the connection between the independent and the dependent variable. The distinct conditions involved (see Figure 5.4a–c), according to system models (Easton 1965), are contributing, necessary and sufficient conditions. A contributing or c-condition (see Figure 5.4a) is a condition that contributes to the occurrence of some event or state of affairs. In comparative politics, economic factors, for instance, are supposed to be without exception conditions 'which means that other factors need to be recognized, allowing for complexity' (Lane and Ersson 1994). A necessary or n-condition (see Figure 5.4b) for an event or state of affairs posits that, if the event takes place or the state of affairs holds, the condition will certainly be present. To put it the other way round, if the condition is not there, the event will not occur that way. A condition is both necessary and sufficient, an s-condition, when in its absence an event or state of affairs would simply not occur (see Figure 5.4c). If we could identify conditions that are both necessary and sufficient, we would have come a long way toward explaining causes of violent conflicts. Most often we have to be content with identifying c-conditions only (Lane and Ersson 1994).

In order to illustrate the difference between c-, n-, and s-conditions I refer to the dependent variable (I) of this study, namely violent conflict and war, and to independent variables listed under (II):

(I) Dependent variable:

  (a) Violent conflict and war.

(II) Independent variables:

  (a) Physical conditions: environmental degradation.
  (b) Economic conditions: affluence, structure and growth.
  (c) Social conditions: homogeneity versus heterogeneity.
  (d) Cultural conditions: family structure.
  (e) Political conditions: institutions, rules and actors.

Focusing on the question what kind of condition environmental degradation (independent variable (IIa)) in a specific conflict consists of, we find the following alternatives:

- If variable (IIa) is a c-condition, then it necessarily has an impact on either variable (IIb), or on (IIc), or on (IId) etc., or on all other variables (IIb-e). All those factors being together with (IIa) c-conditions cause (I).
- If variable (IIa) is an n-condition, then it has an impact on either variable (IIb), or on (IIc), or on (IId) etc., or on all other variables (Iib-e). At the same time it independently has a direct impact on variable (I) as well.
- If variable (IIa) is an n- as well as an s-condition, then it has a direct impact on variable (I), whereas the impact on variables (IIb-e) is only minor and is thus to be ignored.

If there are any interactions between I and II, and the correlations are rather weak, then we are confronted with either c- or n-conditions. Although it is obviously difficult to identify the set of causally relevant factors in a definitive way, we emphasize that we have to focus on cases of environmental conflicts where degradation is an n-condition. Interestingly enough, newer approaches in comparative politics found that physical variables do matter concerning state stability and performance. There is, for instance, statistical confirmation for a combined socio-ecological model dealing with climatic impact and family structures. The correlations between dry climate, traditional family structures, and a weak state 'are so pronounced that these factors have to be looked into. Even though there is no obvious causal mechanism at work here, these findings require more interpretation' (Lane and Ersson 1994). But it is not only the question to what extent environment matters that is crucial (in terms of regression coefficients) but also how it matters. It is still an open question to what extent the degree or severity of environmental scarcity directly influences the dependent variable. I assume this can only be determined in the light of rich case studies combined with generalizations and model building.

A further problem concerning domestic conflicts is to determine relevant indicators and to quantify them. Mesfin Wolde Mariam's survey (1991) in the Ethiopian highlands was confronted with this very problem when he asked: 'How do we measure total environmental quality? And how do we relate the cultivation of crops and the animal and human population to this environmental quality and measure the strain on it? This is something that requires the cooperation of individuals from various disciplines as well as field experience.' Not only states but also parapolitical systems such as local and regional governments, kinship groups and NGOs all play a role of one kind or another in a given arena.

A final point to be addressed concerns criticism of the procedure for selecting the dependent variable. Critics maintain that one should not just select cases in which environmental scarcity and conflict both occur, but also engage in controlled testing of hypothetical cases without conflicts. Homer-Dixon rejected this kind of criticism by justifying the case selection with the complexity of the environmental conflict programme. Since many other issues in conflict research are complex too, there must be found a more convincing counter-argument. More importantly, there is no such thing as a zero-hypothesis in the sense that 'environmental degradation does not lead to conflicts'. The reason is that scarcity, as a notion drawn from economic theory *per se*, implies some sort of conflict. If resources are perceived to be scarce by more than one actor, there is conflict. Therefore, in order to fulfil the postulate of introducing control cases, one has to be more precise on what is meant by conflict. The adequate procedure after all is to choose cases where environmental scarcity is either linked to non-violent conflict (zero-hypothesis) or to violent conflict. This distinction is designed to help explain the why and the how of the difference it makes (see Figure 5.5).

To summarize: in the first step of a cumulative research programme involving many projects, it is methodologically legitimate to focus the first empirical programmes on the causal linkage (B), environmental scarcity and violent conflict. This is important for two reasons: first, most violent conflicts that can now be analysed occur in the South. The causation of violent conflict there is in general ill-understood. This is true for environmental scarcity and violent conflict in particular. Linkage (A), which is a very common one in industrialized countries and to some extent also in developing countries, is far better documented. Concentration on violent conflict is important in order to provide both a better understanding of the dynamics and adequate tools to prevent or mitigate violence. Only sound empirical ground enables analysts to compare linkage

Figure 5.5 Independent and dependent variables

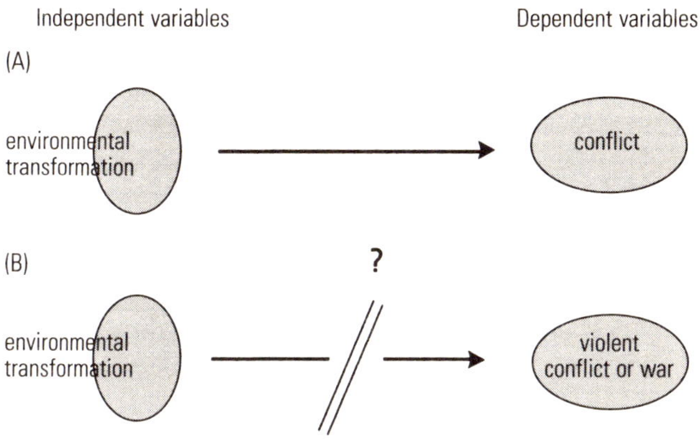

(A) as control cases with linkage (B) constituting the area studies. Thereafter we will hopefully be able to answer why some countries succeed in peaceful conflict and resource management and others do not.

Sorting Out Causes by Attributing Specific Roles to Them

Since the causal contribution of environmental transformation to any given conflict can only be analysed as part of a syndrome of factors in a given arena, the analytical task is to develop a method to determine the contribution of a particular factor, for example environmental transformation, to a specified type of outcome, such as violent conflict.

Different ways exist to determine the importance of a factor. For instance, the concept of probability trajectory as discussed by David Dessler (1994); this is a causal pathway along which some probability of the outbreak of violent conflict exists. In other words, a causal factor is to be considered important in proportion to its quantitative contribution to the probability of violent conflict breaking out. The problem with this method is that 'we have no way of accurately measuring the probability of conflict at a particular point in time, nor of making fine-grained judgments as to changes in the probability of conflict from one moment to the next' (Dessler 1994). Neither trajectories of causal pathways nor accurate constructions of counter-factual pathways would provide a viable basis for sorting causes in empirical analysis (Dessler 1994). Moreover,

Figure 5.6 Action as the result of two filters
(adapted from Baechler et al. 1996)

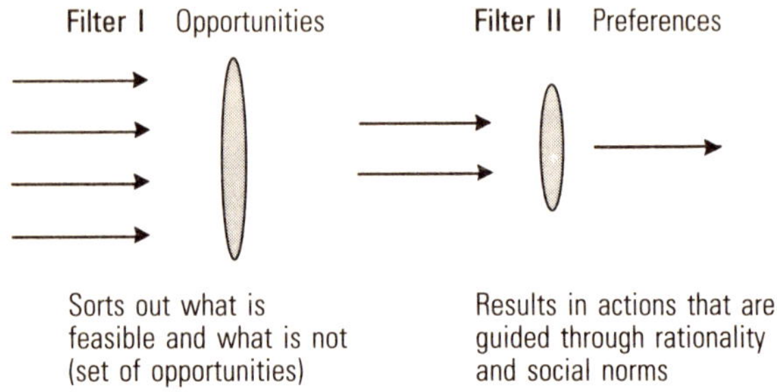

multiple causation would appear to be a major problem at every point along the curve.

There is another trap to fall into, well known in social science as the *post hoc ergo propter hoc* trap. Why should we believe that an event (a) and an event (b) relate to each other as cause and effect? For instance, how can we know that it was the Sahel drought of the mid-1970s that triggered violent conflicts between farmers and nomads in the Jebel Marra mountains a few years later? It is only theory that enables us to link two events substantially and not only occasionally. We must have certain knowledge and understanding of the situation and the link must be analytically plausible.

Dessler (1994) proposes an intentional-actor model of human behaviour in order to achieve robust and testable results in environmental conflict studies. Thereafter, human action is the product of two successive filtering operations (see Figure 5.6). The first filter separates what is feasible from what is not; it determines the content of the feasibility or opportunity set of an actor. As such, feasibility indicates a hard separation between what is physically, psychologically, economically and socially possible for a person or a collective actor from what is not. The second filtering operation results in an action drawn from the opportunity set. In other words, two mechanisms co-react in this process: the first one is rooted in individual and collective rationality, the second in social norms. Through these double-filtering mechanisms, an individual or collective actor selects a certain course of behaviour. Against this background, a choice is seen as rational when it is perceived as the best means of reaching a given goal and when it is chosen because this goal exists (Dessler 1994). The distinction between rationally and normatively guided action seems to be crucial regarding rural actors in developing countries. Belonging to traditional communities, they are believed to share strong beliefs in traditional rights. Since there is some evidence that primary organizations, or ascriptive structures, such as kinship, are more important than secondary organizations of such unions (Lane and Ersson 1994), one has to bear in mind that social norms are shared beliefs about proper and improper behaviour in defined circumstances. 'An action is norm-guided when it is meant to conform to such beliefs, rather than to serve an instrumental goal. Social norms encompass standards of behaviour directly relevant to the dynamics of intergroup conflict, such as norms of revenge for instance' (Dessler 1994; see also Elster 1987, 1989). We may call this approach 'soft rational choice', because it hypothesizes neither totally objective rationality nor complete rationality (Zürn 1993). Simultaneously and even more importantly, it is focused on collective actors and not exclusively on individuals. Regarding a particular case study, we would ask about how individual behaviour results in collective action and how collectively shared views become a social phenomenon that can precipitate some individual reactions.

Both independent and dependent variables influence the options of action and the set of preferences in various ways. Actors may understand the social and economic constraints of resource depletion as a major challenge and concentrate the available human capital on development of new technologies to compete with the challenge. On the other hand, they may have a completely different order of preferences and therefore decide to fight against those actors they perceive as responsible for resource degradation, discriminated resource access, or general mismanagement of natural resources. The different options depend heavily on the feasibility set or on the perceived capacities to compete with a problem.

If we break the general theory down to our research programme, we get two problem areas: first, in view of the opportunities and constraints, there is the question of how environmental transformation leads to violent conflict and war; and second, concerning preferences, why environmental transformation causes violent conflicts and wars. Both questions lead to complete causal–intentional explanations of action including their effects, be they intended or not (Zürn 1993).

Questions and Step-by-Step Programme

It is legitimate to isolate one cause of a multiple-cause event if one bears firmly in mind that it is only part of a syndrome analysis in a given arena. It is not whether the environment matters that is interesting, but how it matters and what specific contributions it imparts on a given violent conflict or war. Causal analysis of political and social events or states of affairs is confronted with a range of difficulties related to multi-causality, to identification of appropriate indicators, as well as to availability of data. Acknowledging the probability nature of social science knowledge, we should try to find traces of connections between variables, which make sense in a causal interpretation. Since there is no widely accepted single paradigm for conduct of research in this field, we suggest a cumulative step-by-step approach, which combines the advantages each single methodology provides. It is acknowledged in the literature, especially in comparative politics, that various methods from multivariate modelling to single case studies should be tested for whatever usefulness they may offer (Lijphart 1971).

The first step starts by hypothesizing simple correlations, tracing a first clue, which may already bear some circumstantial evidence. This can only suggest where to look for causes. Correlation simply means that there is some kind of interaction between the dependent and the independent variable. There is a strong possibility that the interaction is spurious, meaning that some other variable accounts for the interaction. Nevertheless, we must interpret the empirical associations so that they make sense from a theoretical point of view even though co-variation is not a safe tool to justify causal hypotheses (Lane and Ersson 1994).

Therefore this step can be complemented by the conventional approach dealing with configurative descriptions. One should by no means underestimate the heuristic value of the case studies approach, especially in a relatively new field of research where major constraints always develop because of a lack of sufficient data to build models and test them. Case studies support behavioural analysis of actors by looking into the action that really occurs behind political ideologies. Political phenomena are substantially affected by other kinds of social phenomena such as economic development, physical environment, social stratification and cultural system. However, socio-economic and ecological conditions do not affect political behaviour in a direct way. There is a crucial property of politics to consider: the behaviour of political leaders, their capacity for adaptation and innovation, and their significance for explaining properties of political systems such as stability and conflict regulation. Besides structure we therefore have to account for institutions and actors too (Lane and Ersson 1994).

It is necessary to trace causal relationships in order to provide insights into a specific conflict history and to generalize the findings of a single analysis. Causal analysis is therefore necessary but not sufficient. In order to avoid the *post hoc ergo propter hoc* trap, the tracing of pathways of conflicts has to be combined with an actor-oriented approach that conceptualizes

Figure 5.7 Two sets of research questions

	Opportunities	Preferences
Environmental transformation	How does environmental transformation influence the opportunity sets of the actors?	Why does environmental transformation influence the preferences of the actors?
Violent conflict and war	How do violent conflict and war influence the opportunity sets of the actors?	Why do violent conflict and war influence the preferences of the actors?

the positions, interests (aims) and perceptions of both individual and collective actors; that is, actions undertaken by actors in the light of certain aims, interests and perceptions, as well as outcomes resulting in interplay between those actions. This should lead to a generation of inductively produced typologies drawn from area studies, as well as to general causal patterns which may provide ample evidence of the supposed causal linkage. The two filter models of 'soft' rational behaviour of both individuals and collective actors leads us to formulate two pairs of research questions; these are as shown in Figure 5.7.

The Different Roles Causes Can Play

Having formulated the four research-guiding questions, a systematic approach to trigger mechanisms is still missing. Considering the role environmental change plays in causal linkage there are, as we have seen above, assumptions that the deteriorating environment either contributes to instability, heightens political tensions, aggravates existing conflict, or is a catalyst for hostilities (Ulrich 1989). Only recently have the fuzzy 'folk' concepts of causal verbs such as aggravate, amplify and trigger been problematized (Homer-Dixon 1995). In order to overcome cloudy concepts, David Dessler (1994) provides a helpful system of four different roles that causes play in a given arena. I adapt this concept by linking it to a case study on Rwanda in East-Central Africa. This area study is designed to demonstrate how helpful identification of roles is empirically, and whether it leads to explanations of a more systematic character.

Concerning the first role, the trigger of a conflict, Dessler's distinction between a distant trigger and a later or proximate trigger is somewhat problematic. An earlier or distant trigger is considered to be low on the probability curve. It should create situations in which later or proximate triggers lead to events much closer to the outbreak of violence and therefore supposedly higher on the probability curve. If a trigger is seen as 'any event causing actions that increase the probability of conflict', Dessler is unintentionally confronted with the same difficulties that led him to reject the concept of the probability trajectory. As he pointed out correctly, we cannot describe any event that increases the probability of violence without having precise tools to measure it.

There is a further problem related to the first one: if a trigger is the intended result of a choice made by actors who prefer violence instead of other means to reach a goal, why then is the distant trigger considered to be very low on the probability curve? In the distant/proximate trigger concept, distant triggers are always considered weak, fading away in the clouds of the past, whereas proximate triggers are supposed to be strong in all cases because they just occurred. First, this is not necessarily so, and second, this concept bears the risk of an endless regression. Any later trigger mechanism can be explained by a previous trigger mechanism and this one by another one that occurred earlier, and so forth; it is a never-ending story of triggers becoming ever weaker over a growing passage of time. To avoid this I suggest distinguishing between reasons and triggers as time-neutral concepts. Dessler's slightly modified concept consists now of five causal roles, which are defined as follows:

1. A reason is a combination of actions that are perceived by an actor as 'historical problems' (traumata, history of oppression, injustice, former wars, etc.) which influence his preferences in a way he thinks justifies the resort to violence historically. The reason, however distant or immediate it may be, could be a strong factor in mechanisms leading to the outbreak of violence. Reasons rely on the background role which shapes normative behaviour more than rational behaviour. A reason works on both the content and dynamics of a conflict.
2. A trigger of an action is an event which causes that very action to become the most favoured alternative in someone's feasibility set. In terms of violent conflict, a trigger causes an actor who previously preferred nonviolent solutions to a problem to favour violent action instead. A trigger must always be seen near the outbreak of the violent conflict or war under consideration. It is part of the cause, whereas reasons are, by contrast, the causes actors fight for. Triggers are the outcome of decisions that lead to violence, even though the latter is not necessarily intended. Violence could also be the unintended result of a strategic threat by an actor or of a perceived threat by another one. A trigger works foremost on the dynamics of a conflict.

3. A target is an actor's objective, aim or goal. The target is what the conflict is about (Dessler 1994), at least in the eyes of the parties to the conflict. If the target(s) can be defined, the purpose of the conflict can be explained and it becomes clear why an actor prefers to resort to violence. A target works on the content of a conflict more than on its dynamics.
4. 'A channel is a line of political, social, economic or national cleavage.... To cite a channel is to explain the social, political, economic, and/or cultural structures that cause individuals to fall into the groups they do' (Dessler 1994). Channels are designed to form the group identity. They figure primarily in sub-intentional explanations (why actors have certain beliefs and desires) and supra-intentional explanation (why individual actions have certain collective or cumulative effects), whereas triggers and targets figure in explanation of intentional action. For instance, a reason can be, and often is, a strong motive to stress fault lines that can be traced back to both recent or ancient history and that are ideal to build channels along which groups can more easily be divided. A channel can be strong enough to influence causal linkages so that new reasons arise during the genesis of a conflict. A channel is working on both the dynamics and content of a conflict.
5. 'A catalyst is any factor that controls the rate or intensity and the duration of a conflict, once initiated' (Dessler 1994). A catalyst might serve to lengthen a conflict if it stabilizes opportunities and preferences for violence in a given conflict. It might cause a conflict to become extremely violent. Ethical deterioration in a conflict can itself be a catalyst that induces more violence. Together with channelling, a catalyst can transform reasons too. For instance, ethnic groups that may have had an economic reason to fight each other may, as ethical deterioration goes on, perceive differing ethnicity as the cause, rather than the resources for which they fight. A catalyst works on both the dynamics of a conflict and its content.

The five trigger mechanisms give us the tools to formulate simple correlation hypotheses. This is achieved by associating current conflicts with data on significant patterns of socio-economic development and on disruption of the environment. This is useful in re-evaluating case studies provided by research projects such as ENCOP and ECACP. It is also appropriate to in-depth study of the conflict syndrome in specific cases such as Rwanda, and in building a model of environmental conflicts and wars based on empirical results, as well as in checking the model with the help of further case studies.

It is time for the environmental conflict research programme to proceed with elaborate case studies, to develop its theoretical premisses as well as to link its results with other conflict research dealing with crucial issues such as poverty, ethnicity and state.

Notes

1. This chapter is a slightly modified version of Chapter 2 in Baechler 1997.
2. For an extraordinary early contribution on 'redefining security', see Brown 1977; and on environmentally caused conflicts, see Earthscan 1984.
3. An excellent overview is provided by the PRIO Report on 'The Concept of Environmental Security', Dokken and Graeger 1995. The ENCOP team refers to the debate in more detail in Baechler et al. 1993, pp. 10lff.
4. Most of the papers on the Horn are unpublished. I quote here from manuscripts gathered in six volumes and owned by the individual formerly responsible for the programme with UNEP, Ato Naigzi Gebremedhin, Asmara/Nairobi.
5. Many of those sceptical of the ECACP and ENCOP programmes argued that both projects failed to explain how environmental change 'really' matters in terms of conflict. This is why Dessler's caveat concerning explanatory relativity, citing as an example the explanation of a lunar eclipse, is worth noting here. He argues that scientists cannot explain the eclipse *tout court.* They explain its timing, its duration, its visibility from certain parts of the earth, etc. They only select certain aspects. These are the aspects which really matter. However, the quality of these aspects or indicators is important for a common understanding of the *explanandum* (Dessler 1994).
6. There is a tendency in international discussion to state that environmental degradation is in principle reversible in terms of physical or chemical recovery. However, from the perspective of chaos theory, for instance, which stresses linearity of time, every single impact induced by human action is irreversible; change is always and everywhere cumulative, one reason why the term transformation was introduced.

Bibliography

Arnold, Guy, 1991, *Wars in the Third World since 1945*, Cassell, London.

Baechler, Günther, 1990a, 'Kollaps und Konflikt: Zur Konfliktdimension globaler ökologischer Zerstörung', *Antimilitarismus Information*, no. 12, pp. 5–14.

Baechler, Günther, 1990b, 'Ökologische Sicherheit und Konflikt', *Arbeitspapiere der Schweizerischen Friedensstiftung* No. 5, Bern.

Baechler, Günther, 1999, *Violence through Environmental Discrimination*, Kluwer, Dordrecht, Boston MA and London.

Baechler, Günther, et al., 1993, *Umweltzerstörung: Kriek oder Kooperation? Ökologische Konflicte im internationalen System und Möglichkeiten der friedlichen Bearbeitung*, Agenda Verlag, Münster.

Baechler, Günther, Volker Böge, Stefan Klötzli, Stephan Libiszewski and Kurt R. Spillmann, 1996, *Kriegsursache Umweltzerstörung: Ökologische Konflikte in der Dritten Welt und Wege ihrer friedlichen Bearbeitung*, Vol. 1, Verlag Rüegger, Zürich.

Baechler, Günther and Kurt R. Spillmann (eds), 1996, 'Kriegsursache Umweltzerstörung' (Environmental Degradation as a Cause of War), *Regional- und Länder-*

studien von Projektmitarbeitern (Regional and Country Studies of Research Fellows), Vol. II, *Länderstudien von externen Experten* (Country Studies of External Experts), Vol. III, Rüegger, Zürich.

Brock, Lothar, 1991, 'Peace through Parks: The Environment on the Peace Research Agenda', *Journal of Peace Research*, vol. 28, no. 4, pp. 407–23.

Brown, Janet W. (ed.), 1990, *In the US Interest: Resources, Growth, and Security in the Developing World*, Westview Press, Boulder CO, San Francisco and London.

Brown, Lester R., 1977, *Redefining National Security*, Worldwatch Paper No. 14, Worldwatch Institute, Washington DC.

Brown, Michael E. (ed.), 1996, *The International Dimensions of Internal Conflict*, MIT Press, Cambridge MA.

Bruynincks, Hans, 1993, 'Environmental Security: A Conceptual Assessment', paper presented at the Second Conference of the European Peace Research Association, Budapest, 12–14 November 1993.

Dessler, David, 1994, 'How to Sort Causes in the Study of Environmental Change and Violent Conflict', in Nina Graeger and Dan Smith (eds), *Environment, Poverty, Conflict*, PRIO Report No. 2. Oslo, pp. 91–112.

Deudney, Daniel, 1990, 'The Case Against Linking Environmental Degradation and National Security', *Millennium: Journal of International Studies*, vol. 19, no. 3, pp. 461–76.

Deudney, Daniel, 1991, 'Environment and Security: Muddled Thinking', *The Bulletin of the Atomic Scientists*, vol. 47, no. 3, pp. 22–8.

Dokken, Karin and Nina Graeger, 1995, *The Concept of Environmental Security – Political Slogan or Analytical Tool?*, report prepared for the Royal Ministry of Foreign Affairs, PRIO, Oslo.

Earthscan (ed.), 1984, *Environment and Conflict: Links between Ecological Decay, Environmental Bankruptcy and Political and Military Instability*, Earthscan Briefing Document No. 40, Earthscan, London.

Easton, David, 1965, *A Systems Analysis of Political Life*, Wiley, New York.

Ehrlich, Paul et al., 1985, *The Cold and the Dark: The World After Nuclear War*, New York.

Elster, Jon, 1987, *Subversion der Rationalität*, Campus, New York.

Elster, Jon, 1989, *Nuts and Bolts for the Social Sciences*, Cambridge University Press, Cambridge.

Founex Report on Development and Environment, 1971, United Nations Conference on the Human Environment, Founex, Switzerland.

Gleditsch, Nil P., 1997, 'Armed Conflict and The Environment: A Critique of the Literature', paper presented to the NATO/CCMS Pilot Study meeting in Ankara, 11–12 November 1996; revised version for the meeting in Washington DC, 21–22 January 1997, PRIO, Oslo.

Gleick, Peter H., 1990, *Environment, Resources, and Security: Arenas for Conflict, Areas for Cooperation*, Pacific Institute for Studies in Development, Environment and Security, Berkley CA.

Gleick, Peter H., 1991, 'Environment and Security: The Clear Connections', *The Bulletin of the Atomic Scientists*, vol. 47, no. 3, pp. 17–21.

Green, Donald P. and Ian Shapiro, 1994, *Pathologies of Rational Choice Theory: A Critique of Applications in Political Science*, Yale University Press, New Haven and London.

Gurr, Ted R., 1994, *Ethnic Conflict in World Politics*, Westview Press, Boulder CO, San Francisco and Oxford.

Homer-Dixon, Thomas F., 1991a, 'Environmental Change and Economic Decline', *International Studies Notes*, vol. 16, no. 1, pp. 18–23.

Homer-Dixon, Thomas F., 1991b, 'On the Threshold: Environmental Change as Causes of Acute Conflict', *International Security*, vol. 16, no. 1, pp. 76–116.

Homer-Dixon, Thomas F., 1994, 'Across the Threshold: Empirical Evidence on Environmental Scarcities as Causes of Violent Conflict', *International Security*, vol. 19, no. 1, pp. 5–40.

Homer-Dixon, Thomas F., 1995, *Strategies for Studying Causation in Complex Ecological Political Systems: The Project on Environmental Population and Security*, Toronto University College, Toronto.

Homer-Dixon, Thomas F., Jeffrey H. Boutwell and George W. Rathjens, 1993, 'Environmental Change and Violent Conflict', *Scientific American*, February, pp. 38–45.

Imru, Mikael, 1990, 'Environmental Security for the Horn of Africa', in UNEP (ed.), *Horn of Africa* (vol. I) (unpublished).

Kaufmann, Franz-Xaver, 1973, *Sicherheit als soziologisches und sozialpolitisches Problem*, Ferdinand Enke Verlag, Stuttgart.

Kilian, Michael, 1987, *Umweltschutz durch Internationale Organisationen: Die Antwort des Völkerrechts auf die Krise der Umwelt?*, Duncker & Humblot, Berlin.

Krusewitz, Knut, 1985, *Umweltkrieg: Militär, Oekologie und Gesellschaft*, Athenaeum, Königstein/Ts.

Lane, Jan-Erik and Svante Ersson, 1994, *Comparative Politics: An Introduction and New Approach*, Polity Press, Cambridge.

Levy, Marc A., 1995, 'Time for a Third Wave of Environment and Security Scholarship?', *Environmental Change and Security Project Report*, no. 1, Spring, pp. 44–6.

Libiszewski, Stephan, 1992, *What is an Environmental Conflict?*, ENCOP Occasional Paper No. 1, Swiss Federal Institute of Technology/Swiss Peace Foundation, Zurich/Berne.

Lijphart, A., 1971, 'Comparative Politics and the Comparative Method', *American Political Science Review*, 65, pp. 682–93.

Lipschutz, Ronnie D., 1989, 'Global Resources and Environment: Arenas for Conflict, Opportunities for Cooperation', paper prepared for the East–West Workshop on Common Security, Institute for Peace Research and Security Policy at the University of Hamburg, Hamburg, 4–5 December.

Lonergan, S., 1996, *Environment and Security: An Overview of Issues and Research Priorities for Canada*, Canadian Global Change Program, Technical Report No. 96-1, Royal Society of Canada.

Markakis, John, 1990, *National and Class Conflict in the Horn of Africa*, Cambridge University Press, Cambridge.

Mathews, Jessica T., 1989, 'Redefining Security', *Foreign Affairs*, vol. 68, no. 2, pp. 162–77.

Mathews, Jessica T., 1991a, 'The Environment and International Security', in Michael T. Klare and Daniel C. Thomas (eds), *World Security*, New York.

Mathews, Jessica T., 1991b, 'Environment and Security: The Clear Connections', *The Bulletin of the Atomic Scientists*, vol. 47, no. 3, pp. 17–21.

Matthew, Richard A., 1997, 'Rethinking Environmental Security', paper prepared for 1997 ISA Annual Meeting, Toronto.

Matthies, Volker, 1988, *Kriegsschauplatz Dritte Welt*, C.H. Beck, Munich.

Matthies, Volker, 1994, *Immer wieder Krieg? Eindämmen – beenden – verhüten?*, Schutz und Hilfe für die Menschen, Opladen.

Matthies, Volker, 1995a, 'Nicht mehr Krieg und noch nicht Frieden: Schlichtung und Wiederaufbau als Aufgaben der Entwicklungspolitik', *Der Überblick*, vol. 31, no. 1, pp. 94–6.

Matthies, Volker (ed.), 1995b, *Vom Krieg zum Frieden: Kriegsbeendigung und Friedenskonsolidierung*, Bremen.

Molvaer, Reidulf K., 1989, 'Environmental Cooperation in the Horn of Africa', in UNEP (ed.), *Horn of Africa*, Vol. I, Nairobi (unpublished).

Moore, Barrington, Jr, 1966, *Social Origins of Dictatorship and Democracy: Lord and Peasant in the Making of the Modern World*, Beacon Press, Boston MA.

Renner, Michael, 1989, *National Security: The Economic and Environmental Dimensions*, Worldwatch Paper No. 89, Worldwatch Institute, Washington DC.

Research Panel on Environment and Security of the Canadian Global Change Program, 1996, *Environment and Security: An Overview of Issues and Research Priorities for Canada*, Canadian Global Change Program Technical Report No. 96–1, Royal Society of Canada.

Roy, Beth, 1994, *Some Trouble with Cows: Making Sense of Social Conflict*, University of California Press, Berkeley.

Senghaas, Dieter (ed.), 1989, *Regionalkonflikte in der Dritten Welt: Autonomie und Fremdbestimmung*, Nomos Verlagsgesellschaft, Baden-Baden.

Simmons, P.J. (ed.), 1995, *Environment and Security Debates: An Introduction*, Report of the Environmental Change and Security Project No. 1, Spring, Woodrow Wilson Center, Washington DC.

Smith, Dan, 1994, 'Dynamics of Contemporary Conflict: Consequences for Development Strategies', in Nina Graeger and Dan Smith (eds), *Environment, Poverty, Conflict*, PRIO Report No. 2, Oslo, pp. 47–90.

Ullmann, Richard H., 1993, 'Redefining Security', *International Security*, 8, pp. 129–53.

Ulrich, Rita, 1989, 'Environment and Security in the Horn of Africa: A Report Prepared for the United Nations Environment Programme Peace, Security and the Environment Programme Regional Cooperation in the Horn of Africa', in UNEP (ed.), *Horn of Africa*, Vol. I, Nairobi (unpublished).

UNDP, 1994, *Human Development Report 1994*, Oxford University Press, New York.

Wallensteen, Peter, 1992, 'Environmental Destruction and Serious Social Conflict: Developing a Research Design', in Sverre Lodgaard and Anders Hjort af Ornäs (eds), *The Environment and International Security*, PRIO Report No. 3, Oslo, pp. 47–54.

Weizsäcker, Carl Friedrich von (ed.), 1971, *Kriegsfolgen und Kriegsverhütung*, Hanser, Munich.

Westing, Arthur H., 1976, *Ecological Consequences of the Second Indochina War*, Almqvist & Wiksell, Stockholm.

Westing, Arthur H., 1977, *Weapons of Mass Destruction and the Environment*, Taylor & Francis, London.

Westing, Arthur H., 1980, *Warfare in a Fragile World: Military Impact on the Human Environment*, Taylor & Francis, London.

Westing, Arthur H., 1986, 'Environmental Factors in Strategic Policy and Action: An Overview', in Arthur H. Westing (ed.), *Global Resources and International Conflict: Environmental Factors in Strategic Policy and Action*, Oxford University Press, Oxford and New York.

Westing, Arthur, 1989, 'The Environmental Component of Comprehensive Security', *Bulletin of Peace Proposals*, vol. 20, no. 2, pp. 129–34.

Westing, Arthur H. (ed.), 1984, *Environmental Warfare: A Technical, Legal and Policy Appraisal*, Taylor & Francis, London and Philadelphia.

Westing, Arthur H. (ed.), 1985, *Explosive Remnants of War: Mitigating the Environmental Effects*, Taylor & Francis, London.

Wolde-Mariam, Mesfin, 1991, *Suffering Under God's Environment: A Vertical Study of the Predicament of Peasants in North-Central Ethiopia*, Walsworth Press, Marceline MS.

Zürn, Michael, 1993, 'Interessen und Institutionen in der internationalen Politik: Grundlegung und Anwendungen des situationsstrukturellen Ansatzes', dissertation, Opladen.

Part II

Environmental Sector Case Studies

6

International Conflicts over Freshwater Resources

Stephan Libiszewski

Water is not only the central natural resource upon which all biological life is predicated; it is also of paramount significance for the 'societal metabolism' (Falkenmark and Lindth 1993). Indeed, only a fraction of global fresh water consumption goes to meet immediate human needs within private households. Worldwide daily water consumption amounts to several thousand litres per head, of which 92 per cent is accounted for by economic activities. Securing an adequate water supply is therefore an essential precondition of socio-economic development, as well as a central aspect of the social contract between people and the state.

The most extensive application of water resources is found in agriculture. Artificial irrigation is required wherever the water required for crop cultivation cannot be sufficiently provided by natural precipitation. The quantities of water required by irrigation schemes in arid or semi-arid areas can easily reach 10,000 cubic metres per hectare – that is, 1,000 litres per square metre of land. Given expression in the simple equation of water input to agricultural output, this translates into 120 litres of irrigation water needed for the production of a single kilogram of Jordanian tomatoes. Citrus fruits cultivated under similar conditions contain 418 litres of water, bananas 1,383 and cereals 2,352 litres per kilogram (Schiffler 1993). Modern irrigation methods can only achieve limited savings. In Israel, one of the pioneers in developing cost-effective irrigation techniques, the average irrigation rate remains at an annual 6,000 cubic metres per hectare (Kliot 1994).

Table 6.1 Worldwide water consumption by sector of usage (%)

	Agriculture	Industry and commerce	Private households
World	69	23	8
Africa	88	5	7
Asia	86	8	6
CIS (former Soviet Union)	65	27	7
South America	59	23	18
North and Central America	49	42	9
Oceania	34	2	64
Europe	33	54	13

Source: World Resources Institute 1994.

In the industrial sector variations are even greater, depending upon demand and the process in question. However, as a rule of thumb, the typical demand for a tonne of cement, for example, is 4,500 litres of water; for a tonne of leather it is 50,000 litres; for a tonne of steel around 280,000 litres (Clarke 1991). In contrast to agricultural use patterns, industrial water use is by and large non-consumptive. That is to say, though large quantities of water are extracted, they are normally returned to the natural cycle after having been used for cooling or cleaning purposes. The problems arising from industrial water use therefore mainly lie in pollution level and temperature changes. This affects ecological systems and can impair subsequent water use. Similar problems are caused by and the damming of water streams for the purposes of electricity-generation and flow regulation.

Private and personal water consumption in households is therefore low when compared to industrial and agricultural usage. However, even here dramatic discrepancies can be found, from the mere 20 litres per head per day used by Bedouins, to the 200–300 daily litres used in Western Europe, and the 500 litres average consumption in North America. The WHO has fixed the daily minimum requirement for healthy living conditions of settled populations at 100 litres per person per day.

The world's renewable water resources are coming under increasing pressure from population growth, economic development and wastage. Theoretically, global resources would cover the private and economic requirements of 20 billion people at current consumption rates (Maurits la Rivière 1990). What these figures conceal, however, are the glaring inequalities of water resources across regions and countries. Canada and Iceland, for example, enjoy respectively 106,000 and 654,000 cubic metres of fresh water per head, while an entire range of countries has less than the 1,000 cubic metres of natural fresh water that is the designated cut-off point of water shortage (Falkenmark and Lindth 1993). At the beginning of the 1990s, twenty-six countries fell into this category. Several of them had even less then 500 cubic metres per head, and had to be considered as chronically poor in water resources. Currently most of these countries are to be found in the Middle East and North Africa; but were present demographic trends set to continue, large countries like China, India and Nigeria would also come precariously close. By the year 2025 the number of people living in a situation of chronic water shortage would have increased from 300 million to 3 billion.

Besides natural reasons, water shortages can frequently be adduced to socio-economic causes. This is when the technological and organizational infrastructure for the collection, storage and distribution of water is inadequate or distribution patterns are uneven among economic sectors or social classes. In spite of efforts undertaken during the 1980s under the auspices of the United Nations' water programme, the number of people without access to clean drinking water remains at 1.3 billion, while 1.7 billion suffer from insufficient sanitary installations. The majority of the people included in these figures live in countries with sufficient water resources.

Water as an Element of Conflict

The central importance of water for physical survival as well as for socio-economic development necessarily implies that crises in the natural water cycle entail serious political consequences. Water cannot be substituted, and making up local shortfalls with imports is of only limited use. For once, the costs of transport are in most cases exorbitant in comparison to the intrinsic economic value of the water. This applies to canalization as well as to desalination. As an ecological dilemma, then, water shortage can be compared only to the degradation of farmland, which equally undermines the nutritional base of societies and countries.

Moreover, the fluid and trans-spatial qualities of water streams almost seem to predetermine it to play a crucial role as both trigger and object of inter-state conflict. Running water bodies present a clear demonstration of the contradiction between the natural borders of eco-regions and the political borders of nation-states. Water links ecological regions that lie in different political domains.

Table 6.2 States with a high dependency on exogenous water resources

	Dependency rate (%)	Main river basin concerned	Other riparian states
Asia			
Turkmenistan	98	Aral Sea basin (Amu Darja and Syr Darja)	Kyrgyzstan, Afghanistan
Uzbekistan	91		
Tajikistan	50		
Kazakhstan	49		
Cambodia	82	Mekong basin	China, Laos, Myanmar
Vietnam	>50		
Thailand	39		
Azerbaijan	72	Kura/Araks	Armenia, Georgia, Iran, Turkey
Bangladesh	42	Ganges–Brahmaputra	Nepal, Bhutan, India
Pakistan	36	Indus	India
Africa			
Egypt	97	Nile	Ethiopia, Rwanda, Burundi, Tanzania, Uganda, Kenya, Zaïre
Sudan	77		
Mauritania	95	Senegal river	Guinea, Mali
Senegal	34		
Botswana	94	Limpopo	South Africa, Zimbabwe
Mozambique	>50		
Gambia	86	Gambia river	Guinea, Senegal
Congo	77	Congo basin	Zaïre, Central African Republic, Cameroon
Niger	68	Niger	Guinea, Ivory Coast, Nigeria
Mali	>50		
Chad	>50	Lake Chad basin	Sudan, Central African Republic, Nigeria, Cameroon, Niger
Mozambique	>50	Zambesi basin	Angola, Zambia, Zimbabwe, Malawi, Botswana, Tanzania, Namibia
Namibia	>50	Oranje	South Africa, Botswana, Lesotho
Somalia	>50	Djuba/Webi Shebeli	Ethiopia, Kenya

Table 6.2 (*continued*)

	Dependency rate (%)	Main river basin concerned	Other riparian states
Middle East			
Syria	79	Euphrates–Tigris	Turkey, Iran
Iraq	66		
Israel (*'67 border*)	>50	Jordan/Yarmuk	Syria, Lebanon, Palestine
Jordan	36		
Europe			
Hungary	95	Danube	Germany, Switzerland, Italy
Bulgaria	91		
Romania	82		
Slovakia	>50		
Yugoslavia	>50		
Moldavia	93		
Austria	38		
Moldavia	93	Dnestr	Ukraine
Netherlands	89	Rhine	Switzerland, Austria, France,
Germany	44		Luxembourg, Belgium
Luxembourg	80	Mosel	France, Germany
Albania	53	Drin/Vjosë	Yugoslavia, Greece
Lettland	52	Düna	Russia
Portugal	48	Tejo/Guadania/Duero	Spain
Lithuania	45	Memel	Russia
Ukraine	39	Dnjepr	Russia, Belarus
The Americas			
Paraguay	70	Paraguay/Paraná	Brazil, Argentina, Bolivia
Uruguay	52	Uruguay/Rio Negro	Brazil, Argentina
Venezuela	35	Orinoco	Colombia

Source: World Resources Institute 1994. The calculations are by the author.

Currently, the world counts around 240 major international water basins. However, in view of the continuous creation of new states, this number is likely to rise even further. An estimated 40 per cent of the global population lives within these international river basins. One indication for this high degree of hydrological interrelation can be found in the dependency of many countries on exogenous water resources; that is, a dependency on water that springs from sources outside their national territory. Countries like Egypt, Turkmenistan and Hungary, for instance, are almost entirely dependent upon exogenous water supplies. But even a dependency rate of 30 per cent has to be characterized as high, especially in regions where external water dependency coincides with water shortage. Such countries are likely to be extremely sensitive about any quantitative or qualitative alteration to their water supply. High dependency rates therefore contain conflict potential. On the other hand, the ecological interdependence of such states points to the direction of co-operation and joint water management.

Water conflicts arise from the externalities which one riparian shifts onto the other. This inevitably leads to conflict and competition over access to water, as well as over rights to use rivers for energy generation and as a 'sink' for waste. The directionality of river water flow, however, creates a further asymmetry: upper riparians always transmit the consequences of their economic activity to those living down river, thus being in a privileged position.

Over the past hundred years, the human capacity to manipulate water cycles has increased exponentially. As a consequence, there are today over 8,000 dams of over 30 metres in height around the world (World Resources Institute 1992) and hardly one larger river basin has been spared this kind of intervention in its natural flow. Due to this kind of technological progress, it is now possible to redirect entire rivers with pumps and canals and turn deserts into gardens. On the other hand, water levels in the original basins are falling, sometimes to the point of running dry. This can lead to the transformation of entire eco-regions, while the emission of pollutants by mechanized farming, urban conglomerations and industry often has equally detrimental effects.

Up to now the codification of international law regarding water use has pertained mainly to bilateral treaties governing the uses of individual river basins. Where the parties concerned are unable to agree on quotas and usage-modality, a lawless condition prevails. Upper riparians can insist upon their territorial sovereignty when redirecting or damming the watercourses crossing their territory. Lower riparians, by contrast, appeal to 'territorial integrity', and the undisturbed effluence of the natural water flow. This lack of legal unanimity carries enormous conflict potential.

Attempts in 1996 to introduce the 'Helsinki Rules' and the so-called principle of 'equitable utilization' as a regulatory regime under the auspices of the UN were torpedoed by a group of upstream countries, including Ethiopia, Turkey, China, India, France, and others. Several of the states concerned also tried to delay negotiations until the completion of upstream engineering projects within their territory.

For analytical purposes, we shall now develop a topology of water conflicts, with reference to the variant water uses outlined above: (1) conflicts over the absolute distribution of water resources; (2) conflicts over the relative distribution of water resources; and (3) conflicts over pollution or degradation of water resources. These are to be understood as ideal types, while actual conflicts usually contain combined elements.

Conflicts over the absolute distribution of water resources

Conflicts emerge in the changing pattern of water demand and utilization within an international river basin. The most obvious instance is the removal of water resources from their natural circulation for irrigation projects or to supply urban needs. Water that has been *consumed* is definitively taken out of the natural cycle and is therefore no longer available to competitors downstream. Conflicts over absolute water distributions are therefore a zero-sum game.

This type of conflict mainly occurs in regions where water scarcity is conditioned by climate and high demand levels. The latter can be measured by the ratio between water availability and per-capita water utilization. High utilization intensity can be the result of scarcity and/or of particularly high demand, for example on the part of agriculture. Seasonal variations place further constraints upon the optimal use of resources. Thus in some regions the utilization of a third of existing resources can be an indicator of scarcity, with serious repercussions for the ecosystems adjacent to the course of the river.

A chronic water crisis exists in situations when the utilization ratio comes close to or is even above 100 per cent. In these cases the entire renewable fresh water supply is taken out of the natural system, leaving no margin for the extension of water consumption. Ratios over 100 per cent can only be borne by tapping into non-conventional sources of water supply, such as 'fossil' water resources (non-renewable underground aquifers), or through the use of desalination, methods found in Libya and the Gulf states. Others achieve this through the over-exploitation of renewable ground-water supplies, as in Israel, Jordan and Palestine. High levels of exploitation are also being reached in North Africa, the Mediterranean, and Central Asia.

Table 6.3 Freshwater availability and utilization ratio
(countries with a utilization ratio exceeding 33%)

Country	Water supplies per capita (m^3)	Utilization ratio (%)	Annual population growth 1990–95 (%)
Libya	140	374	3.5
United Arab Emirates	180	299	2.3
Saudi Arabia	140	164	3.4
Kuwait	–	>100	5.8
Yemen	200	136	3.5
Palestine (West Bank/Gaza)	100	*c.* 120	3.2
Jordan	220	110	3.4
Israel	370	110	4.7
Egypt	1,000	97	2.2
Malta	80	92	0.7
Uzbekistan	4,700	76	2.1
Belgium	1,250	72	0.1
Cyprus	1,300	60	1.0
Azerbaijan	3,750	56	0.8
Tunisia	490	53	2.1
Afghanistan	2,150	52	6.7
Armenia	2,200	46	2.3
Iraq	4,700	43	3.2
South Korea	1,470	42	0.8
Spain	2,800	41	0.2
Madagascar	2,820	41	3.3
Ukraine	1,650	40	0.2
Iran	1,760	39	2.7
Morocco	1,060	36	2.4
Pakistan	3,500	33	2.7
Turkmenistan	16,800	33	2.5

Source: World Resources Institute 1994; Gleick 1993.

In many of these countries, especially in the developing world, high rates of water utilization coincide with high population growth. Their water supplies per capita will therefore further diminish within the coming years. Apart from the desert countries of the Arabian peninsula and some island states, most of these countries are riparians of international river systems and therefore rely on their supply from shared resources. The basins concerned are thus highly exposed to the likelihood of absolute water conflicts.

In the absence of substitutes or alternatives to water, the conflicts over absolute distribution are the most difficult to resolve. Concerned states will regard water as a question of national interest, or even survival. This may in their view justify the use of military means to prevent the withholding of water, or changes in the quantity of supply by other riparians. Additionally, where governments include the diplomatic fallout of water projects in the equation, water distribution conflicts can become bound up with with other political conflicts (Spillmann 1994; Mandel 1992).

Conflicts over relative water distribution

The manipulation of water courses for the purposes of energy generation, navigation or flood protection normally do not definitively withdraw water resources from the natural cycle, but it effects alterations in the seasonal pattern of water discharge. In this sense, the problem relates to the relative distribution of run-off over the year. For downstream countries such interventions spell the possibility of significant socio-economic and ecological changes. When the downstream country does not possess storage possibilities, rescheduling the run-off period from the dry to the wet period can cause severe water scarcity. On the other hand, during the wet seasons the danger of flooding may increase.

A further consequence of the damming of rivers is the increase in water loss and salinity through evaporation. Nutrients contained in the water are lost to sedimentation. The redirection of the run-off can also affect the geomorphology of estuaries, leading to the advance of sea water and the salination of ground water. The reduction of sediment flow can increase the risk of marine flooding, while the construction of barrages hampers navigation and blocks the migration of fish.

As dam construction projects are frequently prestige projects, symbolic for national development aspirations, the commissioning government will insist upon its sovereign rights to dispose of natural endowments. Neighbouring downstream states, in turn, are bound to react sharply to alterations in the hydrological cycle.

However, generalizations about conflicts over relative distribution of water resources are more difficult than for the first type (absolute distribution). While interventions in the hydrological cycle can inflict damages tantamount to the absolute withdrawal of water, it does not necessarily have to be so. Levelling the volume of run-off over the annual cycle, for example, can assist lower riparians in flood control, in bridging drought periods, and in regulating its own power generation. Losses in the water supply of the downstream country can, for example, be compensated by electricity supply from the upstream neighbour. Depending upon climatic, ecological and economic requirements, dam projects along transboundary rivers can therefore encourage neighbouring countries towards cooperation and sharing development benefits. Such corrective measures should be

Table 6.4 Riparians of international river basins with a great dependency on hydropower

Dependency on hydropower (%)		Primary basin concerned
Africa		
Uganda	96	Nile
Rwanda	93	
Burundi	74	
Kenya	69	
Tanzania	59	
Ethiopia	58	
Sudan	45	
Egypt	23	
Mauritania	58	Senegal river
Mali	52	
Guinea	27	
Nigeria	47	Niger, Lake Chad basin
Zaïre	98	Congo basin
Congo	81	
Central African Republic	51	
Zambia	92	Zambesi, Limpopo
Mozambique	88	
Malawi	79	
Angola	67	
Zimbabwe	31	
The Americas		
Canada	57	St Lawrence, Great Lakes
Costa Rica	81	Rio San Juan
Paraguay	100	Paraguay, Paraná
Brazil	86	
Uruguay	71	Uruguay, Rio Negro
Brazil	86	
Colombia	77	Orinoco
Venezuela	42	
Asia		
Kyrgyzstan	>50	Aral Sea basin
Tajikistan	>50	
Laos	89	Mekong, Saluen
Cambodia	29	
Vietnam	24	
China	31	
Myanmar	24	
Thailand	23	
Bhutan	97	Ganges–Brahmaputra, Indus
Nepal	85	
Pakistan	32	
India	25	
Bangladesh	9	
Europe		
Austria	65	Danube
Yugoslavia	>30	
Romania	24	
Switzerland	78	Rhine, Rhône, Po
Luxembourg	91	Mosel
Albania	89	Drin, Vjosë
Portugal	46	Tejo, Guadania, Duero
Spain	37	
Middle East		
Turkey	41	Euphrates–Tigris
Syria	24	

Source: UN Energy Statistics Yearbook 1990 (1992); calculations by the author.

incorporated at the planning stage of the project, when compromises are reached more readily than upon completion.

In the absence of consultation and negotiation between neighbouring states, however, large-scale dam projects will inevitably reinforce existing political problems and are likely to escalate regional conflict. Downstream countries will assume that their neighbours have included the damage inflicted upon them in their cost–benefit analysis. Where neighbours coexist in a state of hostility the intervention in the hydrological cycle can amount to as grave an assault upon the national interest as the absolute withdrawal of water for consumption. Dam construction on a transboundary river can then be used as a political weapon (Frey 1993). In the Middle East or in South Asia, where numerous inter-state conflicts remain unresolved, any dam project will appear in a political light regardless of the original motivation.

Conflicts over river pollution

Industry, mining, urbanization and the use of fertilizer and pesticide in modern agriculture are the principle causes of water pollution. However, the nature and extent of river pollution vary between different regions. Although it was the industrialized countries of the OECD that were initially most affected, they possess the financial means and the technological and institutional capacity to contain water pollution. In particular, the North American and Western European countries have succeeded in cutting industrial emissions at source, and improved treatment facilities for urban sewage (Lean et al. 1990).

A very different situation obtains in Eastern Europe, the former Soviet Union and the rapidly growing mega-cities of the developing world. Sewage treatment facilities are underdeveloped in these regions and, where available, often lack proper maintenance. Mining and industry in developing countries put additional pressure upon water resources, as the rapid uncoordinated development process is not met by the setting up of corresponding infrastructure for environmental protection. It is no mean task to assert the protection of water resources against the demand for economic growth. As a result of this, among the 148 rivers with pollution levels above the benchmarks given in the GEMS/Water programmes of the UNEP are most international river systems of the developing world, including the Ganges, the Indus, the Euphrates–Tigris, the Nile, the Niger, the Senegal and the Paraná.

The fundamental difference between distribution and pollution conflicts is that the latter revolve not around the quantitative availability of water resources but its quality. Though pollution can render water unusable, with practically identical effects to withdrawal itself, the form of conflict is not that of a 'zero-sum game', but rather a 'tragedy of the commons' (Hardin 1968). Accordingly, the rearrangement of costs and benefits of a common good will provide sectoral advantages in the short term, but in the long run all parties (including those responsible for the pollution) are negatively affected. So, in spite of variously patterned needs, all participants share an interest in the protection of the water basin. At least in principle, the 'commons' offer incentives for cooperative resolutions between neighbouring states.

Another distinguishing factor of pollution conflicts is the question of intention. Pollution is rarely the outcome of single large-scale projects undertaken by government agencies, though an individual industry or mining enterprise in a developing country can have environmentally severe consequences for an entire region. Usually pollution is the cumulative outcome of innumerable acts on the part of private-sector operators. The responsibility of the government is of a more passive nature, in neglecting to interrupt the polluting process. The general thesis therefore attributes a lower degree of inter-state conflict potential to such cumulative acts of pollution. The conflict potential is much more diffuse and uneven, and is often escalated by secondary phenomena such as migration. Open inter-state conflicts are far more likely to escalate from clearly identifiable state-run projects such as large dams or river redirection (Spillmann 1994).

Further characteristics of water pollution lie in the gradual process of occurrence, the wider range of consequences, and the subsequent options for technical resolution (Mandel 1992). Even degraded water retains a number of economic uses (e.g. cooling, power generation, and even agriculture). Conflicts over transboundary water pollution thus take the form of a conflict over the distribution of economic costs and benefits, rather than over the physical use and availability of the resource itself. A much wider range of technological solutions is theoretically available, especially where the know-how and the financial resources are in place. Industrial and urban pollution, for example, can be contained through closed cycles and treatment plants, while agricultural pollution can be limited through improved irrigation methods and adequate drainage. But for developing countries, which meet neither condition, water pollution can take on an existential dimension.

A Model for International Water Conflicts

It is becoming apparent that conflicts over the utilization of international water basins have to be set within a wider socio-economic and political context. Notions such as 'water scarcity' and 'supply crises' do not have absolute value but are dependent upon the level of development and the lifestyle of the society in question, and its ability to respond to shortages. Not even in arid zones do water conflicts automatically lead to armed hostilities, as some writers seem to assume (Starr 1991; Bulloch and Darwish 1993). When evaluating the conflict potential of an international water basin the following factors, in addition to the hydrological situation, need to be considered.

The economic and institutional ability of the state

This will depend on a range of economic, social and institutional factors, including the GDP, economic diversification, and the level and efficiency of the administration. This enables industrialized nations to cope with water problems more ably than developing countries, which are largely dependent on agriculture. Developing-country agriculture takes a terrible toll in manipulations with the hydrologic regime, where the state is powerless to respond. Wealthy countries, by contrast, experience water problems as an economic cost factor, rather than as an existential dilemma. Under these conditions there is far more room for manoeuvre in inter-societal compensation and compromise.

Population growth in the basin concerned

The pressure put on water resources by high rates of population growth is twofold. On the one hand demand rises, and with it the instances of pollution. On the other, it complicates the ability of the state to cope with crises. Rising demand for housing, education, social services and income opportunities confront many governments in developing countries with challenges that they find hard to meet. This further diminishes their ability to act.

Political relationships and tradition of conflict in the basin

Where a water basin straddles several antagonistic countries the control of this essential element is likely to be used as a means of applying political pressure. In situations of unresolved, historic conflict, water becomes sucked into the spiral of conflict. This is particularly the case in the Middle East and on the Indian subcontinent. Conversely, the escalation of conflict can be contained where a tradition of cooperation exists in other policy fields (e.g. in Western Europe).

Institutional infrastructure between the conflicting parties

Conflict and cooperation are not mutually exclusive, but mostly occur simultaneously. Where there is precedence of successful compromise formulation this reduces the dangers of escalating water conflict. Empirical analysis has shown that international accords over the use of transboundary rivers have been concluded more expeditiously within politically and economically integrated regions than in non-integrated ones (Durth 1995). The most favourable scenario for resolution is a situation where new conflicts can be negotiated within an existing institutional and legal framework.

Distribution of power between riparian states

Conflicts are largely determined by the power relations between the parties involved. However, the influence of the distribution of power varies depending on the political context. In situations where a high degree of institutional integration coincides with a tradition of cooperation, conflicts are more likely to be contained within a legally defined code of conduct (Müller 1993). Even the hegemony of one player can allow a mutually satisfactory solution when the principle of good neighbourliness is adhered to. This has been the case, for example, in the resolution of water conflicts between the USA and Mexico over the Colorado river.

On the one hand, in situations of antagonism the distribution of power often determines the choice of methods to resolve the issue. The crucial issue here is which of the adjacent states is militarily and politically dominant. Where the dominant state lies upstream, it holds all the cards (e.g. Turkey in the Euphrates–Tigris basin; Israel versus the Palestinians in the Jordan basin). This very dominance may also preclude the use of military means, as the militarily weaker state has no hope of improving its position. This may instead produce a situation of low-intensity conflict at a sub-state level, eventually triggered by secondary processes such as migration, and subsequent ethnic discrimination (e.g. the ethno-political conflicts in the Ganges–Brahmaputra basin).

On the other hand, where the more powerful state is located downstream it can compensate for geographical disadvantages by military means and may even become a trigger for military conflict (e.g. Egypt's policy towards the upstream countries of the Nile). Equally escalatory is the potential of undecided power relations. An example of the latter is the situation between Israel and the Arab states in the run-up to the Six Day War, where control over regional water resources played a major role.

International water conflicts are staked out between the nature of socio-economic problems, the degree of dependency on exogenous water resources, the distribution of power between adjacent states, and the relationship of an antagonistic versus cooperative tradition in inter-state relations. The composition of socio-economic problems is in turn a function of ecological challenges, such as population growth, and the capacity of the state itself.

Figure 6.1 A model of international water conflicts

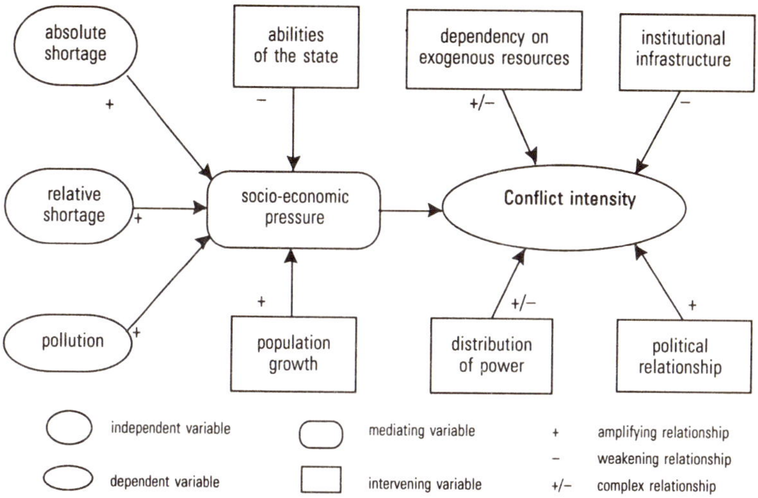

In view of these considerations the following rough assessment regarding the probability of water conflict can be put forward: the most conflict-prone are absolute and relative distribution conflicts in regions of political crisis and water disputes in regions of absolute poverty. In the first case, water distribution appears as a 'zero-sum game' and inevitably interacts with other causes of conflict. Upstream states will exploit their geographic position, while shortages due to climate and demographic factors will eventually intensify the situation. In this arena the outbreak of armed conflict is most probable, though it is difficult to extricate water as a single root cause from the wider political context. Water utilization is at the same time at the source of conflicting interests, and the instrument of antagonism within a frame of wider rivalries.

In regions of absolute poverty, on the other hand, the potential for conflict stems from the powerlessness of the state to cope with problems of scarcity and/or pollution. Though this may not lead to open inter-state conflict, it results in chronic economic marginalization, dislocation and violence at the sub-state level.

Case Studies

Threatening gestures in the Nile basin

Egypt is probably the most extreme example of a country's total dependence upon a single water body. The Nile traverses the entire length of the country. Although the valley represents only 4 per cent of the state's territory, 95 per cent of the population dwells along its banks. Apart from a few non-renewable water resources in the desert, the Nile constitutes the sole water resource of the country. These extraordinary circumstances have shaped the civilization of the Nile valley for millennia. Egyptian agriculture today, which takes up about 90 per cent of the available water, could not dispense with the Nile. But electricity generation, which covers 27 per cent of national demand with the energy generated by the Aswan dam, is likewise dependent upon a regular flow of water. Egypt already uses 97 per cent of its available renewable resources. On the other hand, almost 100 per cent of the Nile's discharge originates outside the country, thus resulting in Egypt's total dependency on exogenous water resources.

Nine other states share the Nile basin with Egypt, namely Sudan, Ethiopia, Zaïre, Burundi, Rwanda, Tanzania, Kenya, Uganda and Eritrea. Egypt is the lowest riparian and the entire water collection occurs outside its territory. This high degree of dependency explains the attention paid by the Egyptian government to developments in upstream countries, especially in Ethiopia, where 85 per cent of the waterflow originates. Events in neighbouring Sudan are watched with equal interest and mounting concern. As the country with the largest population and considerable military and political clout, Egypt plays the role of a regional power. As such, it is the only state that has undertaken major water construction projects in recent decades. The other countries have not been in a position to do so.

The distribution of water resources has been regulated by a number of bilateral treaties going back to 1902, when Emperor Menelik II of Ethiopia was enjoined by the Sudan, then under Anglo-Egyptian administration, not to undertake any dam construction along the Nile and its tributaries. The current Ethiopian government has abjured the binding powers of this treaty on the grounds that it was drawn up during the colonial era (Beschorner 1992). Another treaty between the Sudan and Egypt drawn up in 1929 obliges the Sudan, represented at the time by Great Britain, not to undertake any construction which would interfere with the run-off to Egypt.

Egypt was forced to reconsider this latter treaty in 1959, when the newly independent Sudanese government disputed its validity, and initiated construction work on the Roseires Dam along the Blue Nile. The Egyptian president, Nasser, was dissuaded from taking extreme measures by international pressure. At the same time, Egypt herself wished to continue with plans for the Aswan Dam, which foresaw the inclusion of Sudanese territory in the reservoir. A total of 165 km^2 of Sudanese territory were to be flooded, forcing the dislocation of 70,000 people. The Sudanese government agreed with the plan in return for financial compensation. In the same treaty the water distribution between the two countries was renegotiated, with Egypt now being allocated 55 billion cubic metres, and the Sudan 18.5 billion. A 'Permanent Joint Technical Committee' was set up in Khartoum, and possibilities for raising the water supply into the Nile investigated. These concentrated upon the Jonglei canal, which was meant to divert the waters of the Sudd swamps in southern Sudan to raise an additional 9 billion cubic metres of water per annum. Though the project was begun, the renewed outbreak of civil war in Sudan has since interrupted construction.

Although the treaty is resented in political Sudanese circles, the war-torn government has not been in a position to challenge its clauses. In any case, the country has not even been able to utilize fully the allocated quota. While water is unlikely to become a bone of contention in the near future, it has become implicated in the political conflict of the two states. These include the support extended by the Sudanese government to Egyptian Islamic fundamentalists, and border disputes in Halaib. The water issue is a regular feature in the political posturing of both sides.

The greatest single drawback in the regulative management of the Nile, however, is the mere bilateral nature of the Egypt–Sudan treaty. Other upstream countries, for example Ethiopia, have not been included in the water distribution agreements. This has not been an issue so far, as Ethiopia never moved to implement an American-backed feasibility study undertaken in the 1950s for the construction of thirty-three dams. Crippled by a series of wars against external and internal opponents, the Ethiopian government has never been able to realize these aspirations, but has always reserved the right to return to these plans one day.

Although the Ethiopian plans never came close to implementation, the Egyptian reaction to the announcement of such plans has always been extremely sharp. When Soviet hydrologists began investigating the possibilities for extended irrigation projects in the 1970s, the Egyptian president, Sadat, threatened the bombing of building sites. During the nine-year drought of 1979–88, when the water level of the Aswan Dam dropped dramatically, Egypt accused the upstream countries of 'non-cooperation'. The foreign minister at the time, later to become UN general secretary, Boutros Ghali, coined the phrase that 'the next war in our region will be over the waters of the Nile, not politics' (*International Herald Tribune*, 2 February 1985).

Although such threats are partly of a rhetorical nature, serving to divert political attention from internal difficulties, a very real possibility of conflict remains. Egypt's interest in maintaining existing water distribution patterns are diametrically opposed to those of Ethiopia and Sudan, who face a great population growth too, and aspire to increase their irrigated surface.

Should the political situation in these countries stabilize, and if the finances were mobilized, the development of national water resources would return to the political agenda. As Egypt's opposition can be taken for granted, only an international ruling could pre-empt the outbreak of acute conflict.

A further unknown factor in the water situation of the Nile basin has been the development of rainfall patterns as an outcome of global climate change. For the past thirty years the average water volume lay below the 84 billion cubic metres which were the 1959 benchmark, itself the average volume for the 1900–1959 period. Though no conclusion can be drawn about the actual effects of climate change, it is safe to predict that any long-term reduction in the volume of water will intensify distribution conflicts.

Efforts by the OAU and the UN to set up a forum for technical consultation between all beneficiaries of the Nile waters had long been dogged by Ethiopia's stubborn refusal to participate. This situation changed with the overthrow of the Mengistu regime in December 1991, when the new Ethiopian government concluded an agreement with the Egyptian government to participate in water-related initiatives in the Nile basin. A series of conferences, called 'Nile 2002', was launched in 1993 with the participation of all Nile countries. Although this encouraged the exchange of scientific data, no political solutions have as yet been formulated. The Ethiopian rejection of a proposal for an international water convention under the auspices of the United Nations was indicative of the gulf still separating the different governments. Attempts to intensify cooperation are hampered by the low degree of economic integration between the countries of the Nile basin, where intra-regional trade remains negligible.

Water surplus versus water scarcity: the conflict pattern in the Ganges–Brahmaputra basin

The river system of the Ganges–Brahmaputra, the fourth largest river system in the world, drains the south-eastern part of the Himalayan range, and traverses Nepal, Bhutan, China, India and Bangladesh. The morphology of Bangladesh, which is located in the Delta, is largely determined by the two rivers and their countless tributaries. An estimated 9.7 per cent of Bangladesh's territory is covered by rivers, which have been changing their course throughout history. Though annual rainfall reaches a maximum of 6 m in the north-east, and a steady 1.1 m in the west, 85 per cent of this occurs during the monsoon period in the summer. Heavy seasonal floods are, therefore, succeeded by the dry winter months, when the smaller streams dry up entirely and the water level of the main rivers falls drastically (Hafiz and Islam 1993). The impact of these seasonal tribulations could theoretically be contained by the construction of reservoirs, in which the excess water during the summer would be reserved for domestic and agricultural uses in the winter. But scarce economic resources compound the topographic obstacles set by an extremely flat country to the construction of large dams. The exploitation of groundwater reserves has also been held back by financial constraints.

Bangladesh is the most densely populated country in the world, with over 120 million people on a territory of 144,000 square kilometres. At the same time, the country counts among the poorest in the world. The race between population growth and increased food production is one of the most important challenges facing the government.

All the rivers traversing Bangladesh originate abroad and move through India, which encloses the country almost completely. The relationship between the two neighbours is highly asymmetrical. India, although suffering from a small per capita income compared to the world average, has reached the status of an economic power due to its size, and has achieved a high level of technological competence. Therefore it plays the role of a regional power, treating Bangladesh, which it supported during the 1971 war of independence against Pakistan, as a client. The large Bengali population in the north-eastern part of India, and tensions between fundamentalist Hindus and Muslims within the Indian state, as well as wrangling over border demarcation, further complicate the relationship (Hafiz and Islam 1993).

The water-use conflict concerns a number of dams which India has constructed along the upper course of the Ganges over the last decades. The largest of these is the Farakka Dam. A mere 18 kilometres from the Bangladeshi border, this dam diverts part of the Ganges water into the neighbouring Bhagirathi–Hooghly river. The diversion serves mainly to maintain the water level of the port of Calcutta in winter and to supply a number of irrigation projects.

As a result of this dam Bangladesh has lost 90 per cent of the previous water flow during the dry season. The resulting water scarcity has cut short the agricultural cycle and reduced the harvest. Since the completion of the dam the south-western part of Bangladesh suffers from severe drought in the winter. UN experts have explained the famine of 1982 as a direct outcome of the reduced water flow in the Ganges (Swain 1993). In the estuary, falling water levels have led to the intrusion of sea water, resulting in turn in the salinization of ground water and coastal soils and impairment of the water supply of southern towns. Using water with high saline levels for irrigation causes the further degradation of soils (Hafiz and Islam 1993). A further result of reduced water volume is the sedimentation of the river-beds in the delta. This is compounded by deforestation in the Himalayas and the subsequent erosion. Bangladeshi experts maintain that these two causes have led to river-beds becoming increasingly narrow and shallow, and more likely to burst banks during the rainy season (Hafiz and Islam 1993).

Since the completion of the Farakka Dam in 1975 the use of river water has been subject to numerous short-term treaties between the two neighbours. In 1977 the dry season allocation was fixed at 60:40 in favour of Bangladesh. It was drawn up on the assumption that measures to increase the overall water volume of the river would be implemented. A definitive treaty was to be signed once these had been finalized, but owing to financial constraints and political differences they were never realized. The provisional agreement was therefore repeatedly extended, but in 1988 negotiations broke down when the two sides again failed to agree on measures for increasing the total water volume. While Bangladesh was seeking to include Nepal in the negotiations, by proposing the construction of dams along the upper river, India insisted upon a bilateral solution and suggested raising water levels in the Ganges with water drawn by canal from the Brahmaputra. Bangladesh rejected this, as the canal would divide the country in two, take up valuable land, and require the resettlement of a large number of people (Hafiz and Islam 1993; Swain 1993).

In December 1996 a breakthrough was achieved with the negotiation of a new accord over water use. This was made possible by a shift in India's position. Having established its status as the regional heavyweight, India moved away from an insistence on bilateral reciprocity as a principle of diplomatic relations. A more complex rhythm of water use could therefore be agreed upon, with water being shared out in ten-day cycles during the dry period, to the detriment of India's interior waterways. Attempts are under way to compensate for the resulting shortages by deepening the channel of Calcutta harbour.

In sum, despite the existential dimension of the problem, the conflict has not led to inter-state violence. An open war between the countries has never been a realistic scenario, due to the discrepancy in power between them. At a sub-state level, however, the consequences of water scarcity have increased conflict and violent confrontation. Increasing numbers of Bangladeshi people who have lost their subsistence basis in the aftermath of the droughts and flood catastrophes, have migrated into the uplands of the Indian states of West Bengal and Assam. The regional government of the Bangladesh province of Khulna, the region most affected by the redirection of water flows, is actively supporting such emigration.

In Assam locals have reacted with hostility to these new migrants. In turn, migrants from Bangladesh have organized themselves to resist forced deportations. As a result violent clashes have occurred between immigrants, nationalist Hindus and the police. As the Bangladeshi immigrants are ethnically related to the population of West Bengal, the increasing tension has fuelled demands for autonomy. This represents a threat to the unity of the Indian state and could in future become a serious source of internal tension. According to Swain (1993) the date of these migrations in the mid-1970s indicates clearly the causal relationship between the ecological transformation of the Ganges basin and ethnically motivated conflicts and demands for autonomy in Assam and other parts of western India (Hafiz and Islam 1993).

The political ecology of the conflicts in the Senegal basin

The valley of the lower Senegal is a fertile wetland in the middle of a semi-arid region. The Senegal river forms the border between Mauritania in the north and Senegal in the south. At the same time, the Senegal valley is the transition zone between two distinct eco-regions and their respective peoples: the Sahel in the north, mostly populated by Arab nomads, and the tropical Savannah in the south, mostly populated by settled farmers of black-African descent. Conflicts between the two countries and between the different ethnic groups within both states are narrowly related to water issues, but in different ways from the two previous cases, where it was the construction of two dams that triggered the disputes, which had their roots in the impact of ecological changes upon the political relations between two ethnic groups within both states.

In Mauritania, the land along the Senegal river has traditionally provided the arid Sahel state with a narrow strip of great fertility. The economy in the valley used to revolve around the exchange relationship between farmers of black-African descent settling on both banks of the river valley and the nomadic pastoralists living in the north. Both groups had adapted to the ecological circumstances. They had developed a system of interdependence to the benefit of both. The pastoralists employed their mobility for the conservation of the delicate grazing ranges. The farmers took advantage of river flooding for a second harvest. After the second harvest had been gathered, the nomads took the animals into the valley to feed on the stalks and in turn fertilize the ground. Animal produce and trading goods were exchanged for farming produce. These traditional relationships were reinforced by family and cultural ties and survived the political independence of the two states. Mauritanian pastoralists enjoyed grazing rights on both sides of the river (Horowitz 1991).

Since the end of the 1960s, however, this symbiosis has been undermined by successive Sahel droughts. The cluster of causes for this process of desertification are deforestation and overgrazing of pastures, a consequence of population growth as well as of misguided development policy which encourages disproportionate increase of herds; in the restriction of nomadic mobility as the by-product of political borders; and in global climate change. Displaced from their traditional habitat by the erosion of the resource base, the pastoralists increasingly pushed into the Senegal valley. The herds would arrive earlier in the year and stay longer; some even settled and entered into competition with the black-African farming population. The Mauritanian state, dominated by a segment of the Arab majority, the northern Bidan, encouraged expansion of the nomads.

Thus the advance of the desert was the trigger for the redefinition of the economic and political relations between the ethnic groups in the country. Deprived of their traditional pastures and trade, the Arabic elite began to focus upon the fertile land of the Senegal valley. Mauritania joined Senegal and Mali in the 'Senegal Valley Development Organization' to develop the economic potential of the river for irrigation, power generation and navigation. Two dams were completed in 1988, at Manantali on the upper river in Mali, to regulate the run-off, and at Diama in the estuary, to prevent saline intrusion.

The possibilities provided by irrigation caused the value of real estate in the valley to shoot up exponentially. While the Mauritania elite had hitherto treated agriculture with disdain, it was now recognized as a source of potential wealth. Under pressure from the international financial institutions which had financed the projects, a policy of privatization was introduced in the agricultural sector in 1983. Outside investors rushed into the valley, while many traditional cultivators, with no documentary proof of ownership, lost out. Finally, the government of Mauritania declared illegal the cultivation of valley land by 'foreigners'. This affected not only Senegalese citizens living on the Mauritanian side of the border but also many black-African Mauritanians, whose citizenship was suspended and whose property was expropriated.

The murder of two farmers in 1989 triggered a programme directed against the black-African population in the country. The Senegalese response came immediately: the border was closed to Mauritanian pastoralists, and the persecution began of the Mauritanian minority in the country, which was mainly active in trade and commerce. The death toll in Mauritania reached over 200, while 50–60 people were killed in Senegal. About 60,000 Senegalese and 120,000 Mauritanians subsequently returned to their own countries. Citizens belonging to a different ethnic group were simply stripped of their citizenship (Horowitz 1991).

This form of 'ethnic cleansing' has raised the temperature between the two neighbouring states. The armies of both countries face each other in the valley. Cross-border raids for cattle and for other property lost in the expropriation are launched from the Senegalese side of the border, and border patrols engage in occasional clashes. Old rivalries have been resurrected, with Senegal raising claims to both sides of the river.

Bibliography

Baechler, Günther and Kurt R. Spillmann (eds), 1996, *Environmental Degradation as a Cause of War*, vols 1–3, Verlag Rüegger, Zürich.

Beschorner, Natasha, 1992, *Water and Instability in the Middle East*, Adelphi Paper No. 273, London.

Bulloch, John, and Adel Darwish, 1993, *Water Wars: Coming Conflicts in the Middle East*, Victor Gollancz, London.

Clarke, Robin, 1991, *Water: The International Crisis*, Earthscan, London.

Durth, Rainer, 1995, 'Internationale Oberlauf-Unterlauf-Probleme und regionale Integration: Zur politischen Ökonomie von Umweltproblemen an grenzüberschreitenden Flüssen', dissertation, Bundeswehr University, Hamburg.

Falkenmark, Malin and Gunnar Lindth, 1993, 'Water and Economic Development', in Peter H. Gleick (ed.), *Water in Crisis: A Guide to the World's Fresh Water Resources*, Oxford University Press, New York.

Frey, Frederick W., 1993, 'The Political Context of Conflict and Cooperation Over International River Basins', *Water International*, vol. 18, no. 1, pp. 54–68.

Gleick, Peter H. (ed.), 1993, *Water in Crisis: A Guide to the World's Fresh Water Resources*, Oxford University Press, New York.

Hafiz, M. Abdul and Nahid Islam, 1993, 'Environmental Degradation and Intra/Interstate Conflicts in Bangladesh', ENCOP Occasional Paper No. 6, ETH Zürich and SFS Bern, Zürich and Bern.

Hardin, Garrett, 1968, 'The Tragedy of the Commons', *Science*, vol. 162, no. 3859, pp. 1243–8.

Horowitz, Michael M., 1991, 'Victims Upstream and Down', *Journal of Refugee Studies*, vol. 4, no. 2, pp. 164–80.

Kliot, Nurit, 1994, *Water Resources and Conflict in the Middle East*, Routledge, London and New York.

Lean, Geoffrey, Don Hinrichsen and Adam Markham, 1990, *WWF Atlas of the Environment*, Prentice Hall, New York, London and Toronto.

Libiszewski, Stephan, 1995, 'Water Disputes in the Jordan Basin Region and their Role in the Resolution of the Arab–Israeli Conflict', ENCOP Occasional Paper No. 13, Swiss Peace Foundation, Swiss Federal Institute of Technology, Zürich and Bern.

Mandel, Robert, 1992, 'Sources of International River Basin Disputes', *Conflict Quarterly*, vol. 12, no. 4, pp. 25–56.

Maurits la Rivière, J.W., 1990, 'Bedrohung des Wasserhaushalts', *Spektrum der Wissenschaft*, Sonderheft 9, pp. 34–41.

Müller, Harald, 1993, *Die Chance der Kooperation: Regime in den internationalen Beziehungen*, Wissenschaftliche Buchgesellschaft, Darmstadt.

Schiffler, Manuel, 1993, 'Nachhaltige Wassernutzung in Jordanien: Determinanten, Handlungsfelder und Beiträge der Entwicklungszusammenarbeit', *Berichte und Gutachten des DIE*, no. 7, Deutsches Institut für Entwicklungspolitik, Berlin.

Spillmann, Kurt R., 1994, 'Eine andere Konfliktdimension im Nahen und Mittleren Osten: Wasser!', in Kurt R. Spillmann (ed.), *Zeitgeschichtliche Hintergründe aktueller Konflikte III*, Zürcher Beiträge zur Sicherheitspolitik und Konfliktforschung, no. 31, Forschungsstelle für Sicherheitspolitik und Konfliktanalyse an der ETH Zürich, Zürich, pp. 153–73.

Starr, Joyce R, 1991, 'Water Wars', *Foreign Policy*, no. 82, pp. 17–36.

Swain, Ashok, 1993, 'Conflicts over Water: The Ganges Water Dispute', *Security Dialogue*, vol. 24, no. 4, pp. 429–39.

UN Energy Statistics Yearbook 1990, *1992*, United Nations, New York.

World Resources Institute, UNEP, UNDP, 1992, *World Resources 1992–93*, Oxford University Press, New York and Oxford.

World Resources Institute, UNEP, UNDP, 1994, *World Resources 1994–95*, Oxford University Press, New York and Oxford.

7

Fisheries: Confrontation and Violence in the Management of Marine Resources

Simon Fairlie

> Third Fisherman: Master, I marvel how the fishes live in the sea.
>
> First Fisherman: Why as men do a-land – the great ones eat up the little ones.
>
> William Shakespeare, *Pericles*

Many wars have been fought between people competing for the right to exploit the resources of the land. Few, if any, have been fought by people competing for the right to harvest the ocean. There have been skirmishes between fishing communities, and the occasional feud; there have been diplomatic incidents that have acquired pretentious titles, such as the 'Cod Wars' between Britain and Iceland. There has been one recorded 'battle' involving some fifty fishing boats. But there has never been a conflict over the resources of the sea to match the conquest of America by white settlers or the collectivization of Russian farmland.

Reasons for peaceful marine coexistence are not difficult to identify. First, until recently, fishing technologies were often not sufficiently advanced to exhaust fish stocks; and where stocks have been exhausted there has often been an untapped supply to turn to further afield. Thus the potential for conflict as the waters around the British Isles became overfished at the beginning of this century was averted by the creation of ocean-going fleets extending their reach to Iceland, Greenland and the coast of Canada. Second, the seas are not inhabited in the same way that land masses are, and so aggressive fisheries have been less likely to cause conflict with indigenous inhabitants (in the manner that aggressive gold-mining has, for example).

Yet paradoxically, fishing can be viewed as an inherently conflictual activity, at least when it is pursued within a capitalist context. Fishermen compete for a limited resource. A peasant growing maize will not suffer a poor crop because a neighbour's harvest is plentiful – on the contrary their good fortune is likely to be mutual. But a fisherman who locates an abundance of cod is likely to be wary of informing colleagues, since their gain might be his loss. In capitalist fisheries communication between fishermen, both on land and over the radio, can involve sophisticated levels of badinage, ambiguity and deception – a serious game where each skipper attempts to extract the maximum amount of information about where the fish are, whilst giving as little as possible away (Pálsson 1991).

Indeed, it could be surmised that fishers, as a profession, are adept at conflict resolution, because of their familiarity with conflict. Disputes between different classes of fishermen over fishing grounds or the placing of gear are frequent, but they are rarely bloody. When, for example, Alaskan crab fishermen dumped wrecked cars on the sea bed to tear the nets of trawlers that might otherwise sever the lines of their crab pots, the rivalry was serious, but impish in spirit, rather than bitter. Similarly when the fisherfolk of Pongwe village in Zanzibar overexploited the octopus on the stretch of reef which they customarily use and had to request permission from the neighbouring village of Uroa to share resources, they then 'had to bear the brunt of great teasing by the Uroa fisherfolk because they had not managed their own resource wisely' (Bryceson 1994). Fishing conflicts, from the first protest against the Wondychroun trawl net in London in the fourteenth century to the recent confrontation between Namibian authorities and Spanish trawlers, have not been noticeably bloody and have sometimes been tinged with farce. The fisherman's main rival is the sea itself, and in the face of the dangers presented by the elements, fishermen do not forget that ultimately they are 'all in the same boat'.

However, the conditions under which fisherfolk live and work are changing rapidly, and this may be having an effect upon the ways in which conflict is managed. As fisheries become increasingly overexploited and the opportunities for fishing further afield decline, the potential for conflict increases; and as fisheries become increasingly differentiated between a highly capitalized industrial sector and a hard-pressed artisanal sector, the opportunities for communication and conflict resolution diminish. Fishing conflicts have received considerable coverage in the developed world's press recently. Resource disputes between Spain and Canada, between Spain and France, between Spain and England, and between the USA and Mexico, have impressed upon the public that the fishing industry is facing an ecological crisis.

These disputes have been almost entirely bloodless. Less well reported in the North have been the conflicts between inshore fishermen and offshore trawling fleets in the Third World. Over the last thirty years these disputes have cost the lives of several hundred fishermen – the equivalent of the human loss resulting from two or three or three plane crashes, and a casualty rate far lower than the number of fishermen dying at sea from accidents or shipwreck.

A human toll of these proportions in the Third World does not attract international press attention. But in an intrinsically good-natured industry it in fact masks a great deal of human suffering and an ecological crisis of severe proportions. Fishing provides a livelihood for over one hundred million people throughout the world. There is a great deal of evidence that the methods of production that are coming to dominate are not only diminishing the resource base of the industry and causing food insecurity for large numbers of people; they are also undermining well-supported traditions for conflict resolution and replacing them with state-managed institutions and mechanisms whose track-record on land, if we judge it by the number of people killed in conflicts over resources, has been lamentable.

Traditional Systems

There is a surprisingly large body of literature covering traditional methods of managing natural resources; and a high proportion of this literature relates to marine ecosystems. In one of the key studies, *The Question of the Commons* (McCay and Acheson 1987), no fewer than ten out of seventeen case studies concentrate upon fisheries – a proportion which suggests, not that marine ecosystems have traditionally been more comprehensively managed in the past than land-based ecosystems, but these management systems have survived better (McCay and Acheson 1987). From such studies it is clear that two salient factors have ensured, until recently, a relatively sound management of fishery resources.

The first of these has been a customary restriction upon tenure. Far from being a free-for-all or open-access situation, as Garret Hardin and other protagonists of the 'tragedy of the commons' theory have insisted (Hardin 1968), access and control of fisheries has frequently been limited. In some communities, such as the Marovo of the Solomon Islands (Ruddle et al. 1992) or the Cree Indians in Canada (Berkes 1987), access is controlled by a 'fishing boss' or a tribal elder, whose decisions are largely subject to the approval of other members of the group. Lobstermen in Maine have evolved an informal system of harbour gangs which operate self-proclaimed and self-policed communal territories (Acheson 1987). In more complex social situations fishing may be the accepted domain of a certain caste or ethnic group. In Southern India, where Hindu, Muslim, and Christian religions are intermingled, fishing has until recently been regarded as a lower-caste activity; and in the Batticaloa district of Sri Lanka, prior to the civil war, fishing was a caste-based vocation practised largely by the Karayar in the Tamil community and the Karawa in the Sinhalese. The breaking out of the conflict ensured that Sinhalese migrant fishermen no longer visit Batticaloa. This ended a mutually beneficial relationship (Rajasingam 1994).

In West Africa, marine fishing is pursued by only about a dozen of the many ethnic groups in the region: the Ga, the Fante, the Uwe, the Kru and the Nominkha are among those who have established a reputation for certain methods of fishing. The Fante are a mobile people originating from Ghana who have established themselves in Liberia and other countries along the West African coast as operators of highly efficient canoes employing about twelve men and operating drift, seine or set nets. The Kru, in Liberia, operate from small one- or two-manned canoes and use mainly handlines. One observer in Liberia, also writing in the midst of a civil war, comments:

> Most Fante would scoff at the mere suggestion of hiring a Kru crew member on their canoes, but on the other hand, a Kru would never accept to lower himself to be ruled by a bosun and adhere to a company contract. Yet there appears to be little animosity between the two groups, each does its own fishing and not only is there no conflict between the two, they even complement each other. (Haakonsen 1992)

However, by no means all traditional fisheries are customarily reserved for one group of people. Equally prevalent are formal or informal management systems that control the methods of fishing or the times of year and places at which fishing activities can take place. These methods of regulating marine commons have been well documented, not, alas, by fishery biologists, but mainly by anthropologists, and are widespread both in industrial and in Third World countries.

According to R.E. Johannes almost every basic conservation measure devised in the West was in use in the tropical Pacific centuries ago.[1] Among the measures he lists are closure of areas, closed seasons, bans on taking small fish, provisions allowing a portion of the catch to escape, and restrictions on the amount of gear. The same wide range of measures is found in other parts of the world. Ade Olomola of the Nigerian Institute of Social Relations lists nine different mechanisms used by Nigerian communities to control their fisheries, including restrictions concerning gear, area, timing, and size of fish and the prohibition of the use of chemicals and magic. Olomola (1993) highlights one Nigerian community, the Kaiama living near Lake Ou in southern Nigeria, who open the lake for fishing for a two-day period only once every seven years. The date is announced beforehand on the regional radio station and the fishery is open to anyone; it is free to members of the community while outsiders pay a fee. The event, which is a source of high income both for the fishers and for the community, is a festive affair which attracts hundreds of participants (Olomola 1993).

Some conservation measures adopted by local fisheries can be quite sophisticated. Berkes (1987) cites the net restrictions respected by Cree fishermen: for distant fishing grounds which are only fished once every few years a large mesh net is specified so as to catch only fully grown specimens; but for closer waters which are fished more regularly a variety of smaller mesh sizes are used in order to thin the population across all the age classes. These two strategies are the most productive way of ensuring the survival of breeding stock in respect of the fishing rhythm employed.

The objective of maintaining natural equilibrium is closely allied to that of maintaining social harmony, and many of the measures employed by fishing communities are more directly oriented towards this end. Very similar customs have been recorded in different parts of the world. Amongst the Cree and in communities in Donegal, Ireland, fishermen competing on a given day for a particularly propitious stretch of water form a queue and fish in turns (Berkes 1987). In Newfoundland and in Japan, fishermen's councils decide who should occupy favoured fishing spots by holding annual lotteries (Matthew 1993; Ruddle 1989). In one area of Alaska, where the shifting form of the estuaries defies the establishment of long-term proprietary set-net sites, native fishermen compete for places by a 'challenge' or race to get their nets in the water, officiated by a fisheries enforcement officer who starts the race with a gunshot (Gmelch and Orth 1990). Although in this particular case the Fish and Wildlife Protection Officers were eventually ordered by their superiors to stay out of the potentially 'messy business' of refereeing these challenges, there is evidence that enforcement officers are sometimes happier to mediate disputes according to customary rights than to apply state law. From a series of interviews with officers of the Canadian Department of Fisheries and Oceans (DFO) in Newfoundland, John Phyne concluded that fishery officers act as mediators in areas where formal DFO rules are not used. In addition, some fishery officers have participated in the codification of local rules: although the settlement of gear disputes became part of fishery officers' duties in 1960, they try to settle conflicts on the fishing grounds and not in the courts. They argue that all inshore fishers have a right to make a living (Phyne 1990).

Unfortunately, this benign attitude is not universal. Zerner[2] describes a case in Majene Regency, Sulawesi, Indonesia, where the first crew to place their *roppong* (a raft designed to attract fish) in a certain spot severed the lines of a subsequent intruding *roppong* and dispatched it to sea. Under the existing customary rules they were entitled to do this. But the owner and crew of the original raft were found guilty of wilful destruction of property and fined for damages. The Majene court invalidated the traditional practices as obstructing national development and claimed they would provide an opportunity for individuals to play judge and so threaten national stability. Phyne, too, sounded a note of warning when he suggested that younger Newfoundland fishery officers, trained with the Royal Canadian Mounted Police in forms of what is known as deterrence-based policing, were less amenable to responding to the community, and keener upon the proactive enforcement of state directives.

Phyne's concerns, voiced in 1990, were pertinent, but on hindsight he can be seen to have been worrying about spilt coffee on a sinking ship. In 1993, the Newfoundland fishery collapsed completely (as many inshore fisherman had predicted that it would) and there is still a moratorium upon fishing in the region. Some 35,000 fishworkers have lost their jobs. The collapse was the result of gross mismanagement by the DFO, probably the most sophisticated fisheries management bureaucracy in the world, which permitted persistent overfishing by industrial trawlers owned by European and Canadian fishing firms. If the Newfoundland fishery ever gets back on its feet, there is a grave danger that the traditional community mechanisms for regulating the inshore fishing fleet, which operated sustainably for over two hundred years, will be forgotten or ignored.

Aggressive Trawling in Southeast Asia

The issues and conflicts surrounding the collapse of the Newfoundland fishery have been well reported (see especially Matthew 1993; and for a critique of Canadian fisheries scientists, Finlayson 1994) and it is not the purpose of this chapter to cover them in detail. It is observable that the force that precipitated the Newfoundland tragedy, namely an increasingly multinational and highly mechanized industrial fishing fleet, is extending its reach to many other parts of the globe, and creating havoc for inshore fishermen in many communities. In some areas where the local inshore fishery and the marauding trawler fleets rub shoulders, this has caused violent conflict on a scale that is unusual within fisheries. In other regions, particularly Africa, the level of differentiation between local fisheries and industrial fisheries has been so great that most violence has been incidental, and negotiation has been carried on at a diplomatic level.

Over the last quarter of a century recorded violence in the fishing industry has been centred around Southeast Asia and is associated with a rapid expansion of the trawler fleet that has radiated from Thailand in particular. In recent years Thai fishers have had confrontations with Malaysians, Burmese, Vietnamese and with their own compatriots. The fact that Thailand, a relatively small country with a relatively small seaboard, in 1994 replaced the USA as the world's leading exporter of seafoods, should not be regarded as entirely coincidental.

Trawling was first introduced into Thailand in the 1950s by private companies, but the industry began to expand in the 1960s with assistance from the Federal Republic of Germany and Japan, growing from 99 boats in 1960 to 5,284 in 1973 and 12,905 in 1990. At first trawling was extremely profitable; in 1961 the catch per unit of effort (CPUE) averaged 298 kg per hour but by 1980 the CPUE for Thai trawlers had declined to just 39 kg per hour. Moreover, the value of the fish caught declined substantially. In the early 1960s a high proportion of the catch consisted of large table fish, shrimp and lobsters, while 'trash fish' – juveniles and small species only suitable for fish meal – constituted just 10 per cent of the catch; by 1991, 39 per cent of the catch was trash fish (Baird 1993).

These figures demonstrate the classic symptoms of overfishing. In their attempts to locate fish, many of these trawlers have operated illegally within the 3 kilometre coastal zone which is the domain of the small-scale traditional fishers that make up some 70 per cent of the total number of fishers in the Gulf of Thailand. The trawlers break the gear of the traditional fishers and destroy the sea-bed. It is usually very difficult for the small-scale fishers to gain compensation, and confrontations frequently occur. The problem is so severe, according to Baird, that gunfire is sometimes exchanged at sea between desperate villagers and their commercial adversaries. In 1992 there were also protests by local fishermen against another destructive technology, clam dredging, which the villagers claimed was destroying the seabed habitat.[3]

The Thai trawler industry has also responded to the problems caused by its own overfishing by spreading its reach further abroad. Thai trawlers frequently trespass into the waters of countries such as Vietnam, Malaysia and Burma. Of 42 foreign boats detained by the Malaysian authorities in the first few months of 1994, 22 were Thai, while the remainder were Vietnamese and Indonesian.[4] Thai vessels have been subject to armed attacks by Vietnamese boats and by the Burmese authorities, although the Thai fleet has negotiated joint ventures with SLORC, the Burmese dictatorship. However, expansion of overfishing into other areas is not going to provide any permanent solution. Dr K. Kuperan of Pertanian University, Malaysia, warns: 'Look at Thailand, the seventh largest fishing nation in the world – it's in serious trouble. The Gulf of Thailand is completely overfished. There are too many boats and not enough fish, That's why Thai fishermen are caught all over the place for illegal practices. Some are in Malaysian jails.'[5]

The Thai model has been followed, with some variation, in several other countries in the region. In Malaysia resistance by the inshore fisheries to the trawling industry seems to have been considerably fiercer than in Thailand. Some of these fishermen had been smugglers or even pirates, and their boats and gear, while not as sophisticated as the modern trawlers, were nevertheless more advanced than those found in traditional fisheries. In 1962, having heard about the effects of trawling in neighbouring Thailand, some of these inshore fisherman seized the very first trawler to appear in Malaysia, burned it and threatened the life of its owner. 'Thus', writes E.N. Anderson Jr, 'began the great fishing war of the Penang and Perak coast … During our stay in Kampong Mee, a trawler was captured and burned. In this episode one fisherman was killed and another badly slashed. In another episode some 50 boats met in what amounted to a naval battle on the open sea.'

The Malaysian government eventually intervened and quelled the worst of the unrest by introducing a number of restrictions upon trawling. However, in Anderson's words, 'it would have taken a whole navy of utterly incorruptible and zealous police to oversee the Penang–Perak shore.' Violent confrontations continued to take place, and between 1970 and 1973 over sixty boats were sunk and twenty-three fishermen killed (Bailey 1986). Incursions into inshore Malaysian waters still occur, and there are persistent complaints from coastal and village fishers that their waters are being invaded and degraded by trawlers, some crews of which are armed with automatic rifles. In 1977, representatives of the inshore fisherfolk from nine local communities petitioned the Malaysian government to impose more restrictions upon the trawling fleet. One of their number stated:

> The present decrease in sources of protein is also due to trawler fishing. Ladies and Gentlemen, the trawlers approved by the Government 10 to 15 years ago are strongly opposed by the small inshore fishermen whose income is small and who use traditional nets. We should be concerned with the Government's policy of too much dependence on modern science and technology, to the extent of doing injustice to the inshore fishermen. Our initial opposition to trawler fishing has now been proved correct. We are now suffering the consequences of overfishing … It should be understood that the livelihood of our families is at stake. When the stomach is empty, anything can happen. This is not a threat. (Consumer Association of Penang 1980)

In the early 1980s, the Malaysian Government brought in additional measures to prohibit trawlers from inshore waters, but also embarked upon a programme of halving the number of inshore fishers and expanding the deep water fleet. Since then, various statistics have shown that local fishermen around Penang have seen their average daily catch decline to a third of previous levels (Consumer Association of Penang 1992); that the price of fish for the consumer has risen in real terms by 57 per cent (Balasegaram 1994); and that while the catch by the trawling fleet has been maintained in volume, about half of this catch is trash fish (Department of Fisheries 1994). By 1995, the Penang Inshore Fisherman's Welfare Association was calling for a complete ban on trawlers.[6]

The only country in the region that has introduced, and successfully enforced, a ban on trawlers is Indonesia – not a country habitually associated with measures to protect the environment and traditional use rights. Trawlers were introduced to Indonesia in 1966; by 1971 there were 800 operating in the Malacca Straits, but as a result of diminishing returns, the expansion of the fleet slowed down and a peak of 1,300 trawlers was reached in 1977 (Bailey 1986). Indonesia's fishing sector at the time was overwhelmingly small-scale: as late as 1982, 215,000 boats, over 70 per cent of the nation's fishing fleet, were powered only by sail or paddle. There also appears to be better evidence for the survival of local customary rights than in countries such as Thailand and Malaysia (Bailey 1991; also Zerner 1991). In Indonesia, as elsewhere, some of these small-scale fishermen resorted to violence in defence of their fishing grounds, by attacking trawlers with (amongst other things) Molotov cocktails, a particularly effective weapon when used at night against wooden boats at sea (Bailey 1986).

In response to this agitation the government in 1975 introduced restrictions on trawlers and in 1980 introduced a total ban on trawlers in the waters off Java and Sumatra, which was in 1983 extended to all Indonesian waters with the exception of the Arafura Sea. Because the ban was total it was considerably easier to enforce than the earlier restrictions.

The initial effects of the ban were lower harvests of demersal fish and a decline in the amount of shrimp available for export. However the demersal catch revived within two years, and actual earnings from shrimp exports increased by 15 per cent, partly because the small-scale fishers were landing shrimp of better quality. But perhaps the most significant effect was upon the welfare of fisherfolk. Between 1980 and 1982 the number of fishermen operating along the north coast of Java increased by 10 per cent and their average household income increased by 30 per cent (Bailey 1986). The trawler ban has not prevented Indonesia from building up a fleet of deep-sea trawlers, a number of which have been apprehended for fishing illegally in Malaysian waters. In this respect Indonesia may be said to be following in the footsteps of Japan, a country which protects its own local fisheries but ignores the rights of those in other countries.

In considering the conflicts between fishermen in Southeast Asia, one factor in particular needs to be borne in mind. Although these confrontations have often occurred between vessels of different nations, the impetus for the conflicts has not been national differences but sectoral differences. It makes little difference to a Malaysian fishing community whether a large boat trespassing on its waters is Malaysian, Thai, Vietnamese or Indonesian. What is important is the damage that such a vessel will inflict upon the community's fishing gear, fish stocks and marine habitat. Similarly, although ethnic factors have played a role in some of these disputes, this role has been an incidental one. In fact the main ethnic tension in the region, between immigrant Chinese on the one hand and indigenous Malays or Indonesians on the other, has operated in opposite directions in each of these two latter countries. In Malaysia, according to Anderson, many of the participants in the inshore fishery were 'poor and Chinese' (Anderson 1987) while in Indonesia, according to Bailey, many of the trawler owners and their crews were relatively wealthy ethnic Chinese (Bailey 1986). Thus while ethnic factors may have influenced the way in which the Malaysian and Indonesian governments responded to the crisis (that is, against Chinese interests in both cases), they have had little connection with the cause of the conflict, which is basically between the 'big fish' and the 'little fish'.

The unrest in Southeast Asia is by no means the only manifestation of such conflicts. Tensions between shrimpers in Mexico have culminated in riots, such as that on Black Thursday, 24 May 1990, in the city of Guaymas, when a conflict between two competing federations of fishing cooperatives led to the looting of offices, the burning of trucks and cars and the jailing of fisheries leaders. These conflicts have been in great part attributed to the damage caused by an off-shore trawling industry operating within a government policy that is hell-bent on increasing exports (McGuire 1991; McGoodwin 1987). Mention should also be made of the havoc wrought by the booming aquaculture industry, again largely for the export shrimp market, in Southeast Asia and Latin America. Displacement of peasants to make way for these fish farms has been carried out with considerable violence, notably in Bangladesh, where at least a hundred people have been killed by the hired goons of the shrimp pond owners. The law ignores these incidents and the police often support the owners (Tahmina 1995). This is not entirely a fishing issue since the people who are displaced are usually poor farmers, rather than fishers. However, the produce is destined for the same export market; many of the fish farms replace mangrove swamps, which are important breeding grounds for marine fish; and the farmed shrimp are fed upon fish meal, which may be manufactured from fish such as sardines that could be consumed by humans or from the trash fish provided by the trawling industry (Wilkes 1995).

In fact the violence and unrest in Southeast Asia, in Mexico and in Bangladesh are all bound up in the same dynamic: the production of export fish (with considerable emphasis on shrimp) for a market that supplies luxury products to wealthy countries who have long since exhausted their own fish supplies. This dynamic, as we have seen, is at its most dirty and violent when all the actors in the production process are from the less developed countries, since the 'civilized' nations which benefit can wash their hands of any direct involvement. But the dynamic is also pursued on another level: that of the international joint venture, which, although it is sanitized by international agreement, nonetheless evinces its own form of violence.

Joint Ventures

The collapse of the Newfoundland fishery was a disaster for the Canadian province's 35,000 fishworkers. But for the managers of Fisheries Products International (FPI), one of the two main firms responsible for the overfishing, it was little more than an occupational hazard. With the help of the Canadian overseas aid agency, CIDA, FPI sold off its redundant supertrawlers to countries in Latin America and Africa and bought into a number of companies supplying fish from other parts of the world. Whereas in the late 1980s FPI bought less than 2 per cent of its fish from outside Canada, by 1994 it was relying for 87 per cent of its supplies of cod, pollock and flatfish on imports from regions such as Russia, Scandinavia and Alaska. One of the new acquisitions gave FPI a foothold in the shrimp business, so that shrimp, most of it bought in East Asia and sold in North America, made up almost a third of FPI's business in 1994.[7]

FPI is one example of the new breed of multinational fishing firms which 'pulse fish' the world's waters in the same way that they play the world's markets: moving in while the going's good, pulling out when it gets bad (*The Ecologist* 1995). However the penetration of foreign waters by the fleets of industrial nations which have exhausted their own fishing grounds is achieved not only by playing the markets but also through international agreements imposed upon Third World countries with the sanction of the United Nations Convention on the Law of the Sea (UNCLOS). This mandates that surplus stocks in a nation's waters must be made available to foreign fleets if the country itself does not exploit them.

Thus the European Union (EU), while it officially aims to decommission 40 per cent of the capacity of its fleet to allay the effects of overfishing in European waters, is in fact providing 'exit grants' to fishing companies to relocate their boats somewhere else in the world that has not yet been fished to the point of economic and ecological breakdown. The EU has signed contracts to fish in the waters of countries such as Senegal, Morocco, Angola and Argentina, over the heads of the local fishermen in these countries. In 1994 the EU helped clear many diplomatic hurdles and provided grants to enable Spanish companies to secure a five-year agreement providing access to Argentine fisheries for up to seventy big trawlers involving joint projects worth US$230 million.[8] Mario Olaciregui, president of a leading Argentinian fishing concern, Harengus SA, had spoken out against the deal: 'EC grants would simply transfer the problem of idle tonnage from Spain to Argentina ... The only beneficiaries would be Spanish banks, whose unwise loans to finance shipbuilding would be repaid with EC taxpayer's money.'[9] Olaciregui's warning seemed to be confirmed when in 1995 the Spanish government moved to bail out Pescanova, a huge Spanish fishing company with 140 vessels in joint ventures in twenty countries, including Argentina, which had gone into debt to the tune of US$285 million.[10]

Senegal is one of several African countries that have contracted joint ventures with the EU. Agreements made in 1990, 1992 and 1994 have allowed European trawlers to catch specific tonnages of whitefish and shrimp and ferry most of the catch back to Europe. The agreements have not only met with opposition from the very active National Collective of Senegalese Fishworkers (CNPS) but have been greeted critically by the EU's own Verbeek Report to the Fisheries Sub-Committee, which claimed that the overexploitation of the stock and the 'economic difficulty facing Senegalese ship-owners' (low profitability and low average prices given the observable decrease in the average size of the species landed) 'pointed to an urgent need to cut back such activities.'[11]

What the Verbeek Report implies, and what the CNPS maintains, is that very similar pressures are being placed upon the Senegalese local fishermen by the European trawlers to those experienced by Southeast Asian coastal fishermen at the hands of the trawler fleets of Thailand, Vietnam, Indonesia and Malaysia. The reports of raking of the seabed, destruction of fishing gear, wasted fish and declining catches are similar. The main difference is that the freezer trawlers of the EU fleet are considerably bigger than the trawlers of the Southeast Asian fleets; and the pirogues operated by the local Senegalese are, if anything, rather smaller than those of their Southeast Asian counterparts.

The violence inherent in the Senegalese situation has therefore emerged in a manner that differs significantly from the Southeast Asian experience. There has been some active resistance to the arrival of the supertrawlers. In one instance an EU captain was taken hostage by artisanal fishermen after he was found fishing in an area reserved for artisanal fishing.[12] But on the whole the local fleet has been powerless to respond against the EU leviathans. Instead most of the violence has been 'incidental' and hence disguised. From 1990 to 1991 forty-eight fishermen died in collisions with industrial vessels. Some of these accidents took place in areas where trawlers were not permitted, whilst others took place outside this limit: the growing scarcity of fish obliges pirogues to venture ever further from the shore.[13]

To what extent these problems are reflected in other countries engaged in joint ventures with the EU is not clear, partly because many of these countries' fisheries do not have a fisherfolk organization that is as active and as well-organized as the CNPS. In India, where Government is engaged in negotiating joint ventures with multinational fishing companies on a bilateral level, there are several well organized fishing unions representing different sectors of the fishery. In November 1994 these different groups joined together in an *ad hoc* alliance called the National Fisheries Action Committee Against Joint Ventures and brought the entire fishing industry of the country to a standstill in a two-day strike against the proposed joint ventures – a show of force that caused the government to apply brakes to the entire project.[14]

However, one of the most extraordinary acts of resistance to the incursions of foreign trawlers was carried out not by local fishermen, but by the fledgling SWAPO government in Namibia. The incident, recounted in a document published by the Coalition for Fair Fisheries Agreements, is worth repeating in some detail because it illustrates how tenuous the rule of international law can be in many marine circumstances, and also how courageous a new and idealistic government can be before it gets caught up in the web of international negotiation.

Between 1970 and 1990 the rich fishing grounds off the coast of Namibia were systematically plundered by a fleet, largely consisting of Spanish and Russian vessels, which harvested over eight million tonnes of hake, worth some US$5 billion and considerable quantities of horse mackerel. In 1990, when Namibia was on the last leg of its road to independence, President-elect Sam Nujoma's request for all foreign fishing fleets to depart from Namibia's EEZ (national fishing grounds extending 200 miles from the shore) was complied with. Shortly after independence, however, surveillance flights revealed that a number of vessels had already returned to Namibia's EEZ. One vessel, the Spanish-registered *Frio Pesca Dos*, arrived back in Spain with 400 tonnes of Namibian fish.

As a result of the *Frio Pesca Dos*'s success about thirty Spanish vessels converged on Namibian waters and started fishing at the rate of about 20 tonnes per day.

The Namibian government was fully aware of this abuse, but at the time possessed only one ageing patrol vessel, the Oryx, which was no match for the sleek modern Spanish trawlers, which could easily pull in their nets and speed to the safety of Angolan waters. After considering arming local fishing vessels to apprehend the Spanish boats, the Namibian government decided upon an airborne operation. Unfortunately it did not have an airforce, but, with the aid of a loan from the local fishing industry in Walvis Bay, it managed to acquire the services of a helicopter. On the evening of 23 November the minister responsible for fisheries, Gert Hanekom, declared publicly that the government was regrettably powerless to stop the illegal incursions of Spanish trawlers – and secretly ordered the operation to go ahead. The operation was led by Johanne Van Rijhn, the senior inspector in the Ministry of Sea Fisheries, in command of a number of soldiers, none of whom had ever stepped on a fishing vessel in their lives and whose training for the operation had been limited to jumping backwards out of a helicopter whilst it was stationary on the ground.

At 7.00 a.m. on 24 November, the government's surveillance plane located two vessels fishing west of Mowa Bay. The helicopter went into action. To the complete amazement of the crew, Fisheries Inspector Johanne Van Rijhn was lowered onto the foredeck of the slowly trawling *Friolero*. He proceeded immediately to the bridge where he handed over a letter in both English and Spanish, informing the Captain of the arrest of his vessel. Having turned off the ships radio so that other vessels could not be tipped off, Van Rijhn was then lifted by helicopter to another Spanish vessel, the *Isla De Tambo*, where he again carried out his duties. Van Rijhn was then taken by the helicopter to Mowa Bay, whilst the two Spanish vessels under arrest were escorted to the port of Luderitz by the Namibian soldiers. However, on one of these vessels an arrested officer on the bridge suddenly broke into a haunting Spanish melody. Unbeknown to the supervising Namibian soldiers, the officer had discreetly switched on a Citizen Band radio and was singing poetically of how a helicopter had swept out of the eastern skies to arrest Spanish ships for fishing illegally in Namibia's EEZ, and how they were now under arrest and being taken to port. To the north of Mowa Bay a sister ship of the arrested Spanish vessel picked up the strange message and, half in jest, relayed it by radio telephone to the boats' owners in Spain.

Back at Mowa Bay, the task force was keen to press home its advantage before the Spanish fleet dispersed. However, a problem arose. The helicopter wouldn't start and so a truck had to be sent south to Terrace Bay to obtain a spare battery. Four critical hours were lost, and then more time was wasted as the helicopter had to fly back to Walvis Bay to refuel. The helicopter eventually arrived at Conception Bay to apprehend more of the Spanish trawlers 30 minutes after the trawlers had been warned, by radio from Spain, that arrest was imminent. Inspector Van Rijhn was successfully lowered onto the deck of the *Frio Pesca Uno*, the *Frio Pesca Dos* and the *Puente Belezar*. But when the helicopter tried to drop him on the *José Antonio Mores*, there was more determined resistance. As the helicopter approached, the captain ordered all officers and crew below deck, engaged the autopilot and turned the steering full to starboard. As a result the ship began spinning on its axis and although the helicopter approached the vessel three times it proved impossible to lower Inspector Van Rijhn onto the ship. The task force abandoned its attempt to arrest the *José Antonio Mores,* and returned to base content. Five supertrawlers in one day was a pretty good haul. The day after the seizures the surveillance plane was sent out and it reported that all the illegal vessels appeared to have fled Namibian waters. The Namibian authorities were jubilant. From a position of impotence, decisive action had been taken and results achieved far beyond expectations.

The atmosphere of operatic farce that tinges this account should not blind us to the significance of the event. In the court case that eventually followed, all of the fishing vessels were confiscated and fines were imposed upon the ships' captains totalling 1.65 million rand. The skipper of the *José Antonio Mores*, by executing that timely pirouette, saved his company considerable amounts of money. More importantly, the Namibian action showed fisherfolk around the world that an impoverished Third World government can make a stand against powerful transnational enterprises, and that the UNCLOS decision to confer jurisdiction over 200-mile zones around countries does carry weight.

The unusually detailed account of this episode should also serve to remind us of another point. All the other events cited in this chapter have been little more than statistics: 'over sixty boats were sunk and twenty-three fishermen killed between 1970 and 1973 in Malaysia', and so on. Any one of these sinkings and killings might have yielded a story more poignant or more extraordinary than the exploits of Inspector Van Rijhn – but these stories will never be told.

Commentators on the fisheries should not forget what fishermen know through experience: that every fisherman on the sea, whether skipper of a Spanish freezer-trawler or crewman on an African pirogue, is a simple mortal trying to gain a living by pitting his wits both with and against the elements, with and against the fishing bureaucracy, and with and against his fellow fishermen. By and large this competitive and cooperative occupation is carried out with considerable good humour. When it is not, then something has gone awry in the structure of the fishery, and that something needs to be addressed.

Reclaiming Marine Commons

The early part of this chapter alluded to Alaskan pot fishermen who dumped old cars on the sea-bed to obstruct the nets of trawlers. This spontaneous tactic may well be widespread: in 1995, the *Guardian* reported that inshore fishermen had created a no-go zone for trawlers in an area off Grimsby, in the UK, which, according to one fisherman 'contains all sorts of old junk, including cars. No one will take a trawler near that area for fear of losing their nets.'[15]

Several thousand miles to the east, in the waters of the Thai fishing village of Paak Baang Thephaa, a similar zone, called an *uyam*, has been created in a spot where the sea bed is naturally rocky. 'We enlarge it by adding more rocks, cement blocks and wood to the spot', says the village leader Jeseng Yisubo. 'The *uyam* prevents big trawlers from coming in close to the shore. If they do their nets will be destroyed by the pile of our *uyam*' (Ekachai 1995).

The *uyam*, or artificial reef as it is known in English, is being increasingly employed in countries such as Thailand, India and the Philippines, as a way of retaliating against trawler fleets. But it also serves another purpose. Piles of tyres, rocks or concrete blocks, like shipwrecks, also attract fish, providing them with a haven and breeding ground. The *uyam*, says another villager from Paak Baang Thephaa, 'is a true conservation method. We people need houses to shelter us. So do the fish. Small fish can live here without being disturbed. Squids also need shelter to lay eggs. Fish I haven't seen for a long time have come back. The *uyam* really works' (Ekachai 1995).

The artificial reef in Paak Baang Thephaa was initiated with the help of the Songhkia Small Fisherman's Group, a recently formed organization which has 200 members in eight villages. The organization has also helped to implement measures designed to protect fish stocks, such as limitations on mesh size.

Such organizations are often an attempt to re-create traditional management systems, which in many areas have disappeared or been eroded under pressure from modernization and immigration. In Senegal, the CNPS supports similar village-based groups. In Kayar, a large fishing village on the north coast, a committee of elders controls levels of fish catch to maintain prices.

> They have concluded that it is better to sell a box of *pageot* at 4,000 francs than three boxes at 1,000 francs. Fish stocks are better protected and the fishermen earn a better living ... Each pirogue fishing for high-priced species brings back only two boxes of *pageot* and not one more. Offenders beware! They risk having their pirogues grounded and being banned from fishing for several days.[16]

The CNPS has also mediated in a dispute between local fishermen and migrants from St Louis, Senegal, who lost the use of their traditional fishing grounds off Mauritania. The St Louis fishermen are now allowed to work out of Kayar, but must set aside the produce of one day's fishing as their contribution to the additional costs which their presence incurs. Kayar has not built an artificial reef; instead it has acquired a new radar installation to track trawlers intruding into its waters.

However, in Asia especially, it is the artificial reef which has become the most potent symbol of the growing solidarity of small-scale fishermen against the threat from more industrialized fisheries. Indeed, another contribution of the artificial reef may be its symbolic value to the community. The collective activity of defining a boundary reinforces the sense that a community can control its own resources; and it is more than mere coincidence that what creates a barrier to industrial boats simultaneously provides a favourable environment for fish. One cartoon in the international fishworkers' magazine *Samudra* (December 1994) depicts inshore fishermen fishing from an artificial reef built out of sunken trawlers – a marine equivalent of turning swords into ploughshares.

Notes

1. R.E. Johannes, cited in Zerner 1991.
2. C. Zerner, cited in Ruddle 1993.
3. *Bangkok Post*, 6 February and 26 April 1992.
4. Ang Su Ching, 'Dept; 400 Foreigners Fined for Illegal Fishing', *The Star*, 4 May 1994.
5. M. Balasegaram, 'Plenty of Fish in the Sea? Not Really', *Sunday Star*, 13 March 1994.
6. 'Fishermen Submit Memo to State Government', *The Star*, 6 February 1995.
7. B. Simon, 'A Tale of Debt and Survival on the High Seas', *Financial Times*, 14 January 1994.
8. *Seafood International*, January 1993, p. 4.
9. J. Barham, *Financial Times*, 7 October 1992, p. 28.
10. *Samudra* (journal of the International Collective in Support of Fishworkers), April 1995, p. 54.
11. *Fishing for a Future: Artisanal Fishing in Senegal and EU Fishing Agreements*, Coalition for Fair Fisheries Agreements, Brussels, 1993.
12. Ibid.
13. D. Corlay, 'No Cosy Relationship', *Samudra*, February 1994.

14. J. Kurien, 'Joint Action Against Joint Ventures', *The Ecologist*, vol. 25 no. 2/3, 1995.

15. 'Ministry Backs Reefs Made from Tyres to Protect Fish Stocks', *Guardian*, 16 January 1995.

16. *Fishing for a Future.*

Bibliography

Acheson, J., 1987, 'The Lobster Fiefs Revisited', in B. McCay and J. Acheson (eds), *The Question of the Commons: The Culture and Ecology of Communal Resources*, University of Arizona, Tucson.

Anderson, E.N., Jr, 1987, 'A Malaysian Tragedy of the Commons', in B. McCay and J. Acheson (eds), *The Question of the Commons: The Culture and Ecology of Communal Resources*, University of Arizona, Tucson.

Bailey, C., 1986, 'Government Protection of Traditional Resource Use Rights – The Case of Indonesian Fisheries', in D. Korten (ed.), *Community Management: Asian Experience and Perspectives*, Kumarian Press, West Hartford CT.

Bailey, C., 1991, 'Marine Fisheries Management and Development: Policies and Programs', in C. Bailey, A. Dwiponggo and F. Marahudin, *Review of Indonesian Marine Fisheries*, ICLARM Studies and Reviews, Directorate General of Fisheries and the Intenational Center for Living Aquatic Resources Management, Manila and Jakarta.

Baird, I., 1993, *Marine Capture Fisheries Development in Thailand: an Environmental and Socioeconomic Analysis*, Earth Island Institute, Thailand.

Balasegaram, M., 1994, 'Plenty of Fish in the Sea? Not Really', *Sunday Star*, 13 March.

Berkes, F., 1987, 'Common-Property Resource Management and Cree Indian Fisheries in Subarctic Canada', in B. McCay and J. Acheson (eds), *The Question of the Commons: The Culture and Ecology of Communal Resources*, University of Arizona, Tucson.

Berkes, F. (ed.), 1989, *Common Property Resources: Ecology and Community-Based Sustainable Development*, Belhaven Press, London.

Bryceson, I., 1994, 'A Skewed Kind of Development', *Samudra*, February.

Consumer Association of Penang, 1980, *The Malaysian Fisheries: A Diminishing Resource* (reprinted 1987).

Consumer Association of Penang, 1992, *Call for Stricter Controls on Trawling Activities*, press release, 5 December.

Department of Fisheries, 1994, *Annual Fisheries Statistics 1993*, Department of Fisheries, Ministry of Agriculture Malaysia, November, p. 63.

The Ecologist, 1995, 'Overfishing: Causes and Consequences', special issue, vol. 25, no. 2/3.

Ekachai, S., 1995, *Seeds of Hope: Local Initiatives in Thailand*, Thai Development Committee, Bangkok.

Finlayson, A., 1994, *Fishing for Truth: A Sociological Analysis of Northern Cod Stock Assessments*, Institute of Social and Economic Research, Memorial University of Newfoundland.

Gmelch, G. and G. Orth, 1990, 'A Tale of Two Rivers', *Marine Anthropological Studies*, vol. 3, no. 2.

Haakonsen, J., 1992, 'Artisanal Fisheries and Fishermen's Migrations in Liberia', *Marine Anthropological Studies*, vol. 5, no. 2.

Hardin, G., 1968, 'The Tragedy of the Commons', *Science*, vol. 162, no. 3859.

Matthew, D.R., 1993, *Controlling Common Property: Regulating Canada's East Coast Fishery*, University of Toronto Press, Toronto.

McCay, B. and J. Acheson (eds), 1987, *The Question of the Commons: The Culture and Ecology of Communal Resources*, University of Arizona, Tucson.

McGoodwin, J., 1987, 'Mexico's Conflictual Inshore Pacific Fisheries: Problem Analysis and Policy Recommendations', *Human Organization*, vol. 46, no. 3.

McGuire, T., 1991, 'Science and Destruction of a Shrimp Fleet', *Marine Anthropological Studies*, vol. 4, no. 1.

Olomola, A., 1993, 'The Traditional Approach Towards Sustainable Management of Common Property Fishery Resources in Nigeria', *Marine Anthropological Studies*, vol. 6, no. 1/2.

Pálsson, G., 1991, *Coastal Economies Cultural Accounts: Human Ecology and Icelandic Discourse*, Manchester University Press, Manchester.

Phyne, J., 1990, 'Dispute Settlement in the Newfoundland Inshore Fishery', *Marine Anthropological Studies*, vol. 3, no. 2.

Rajasingam, M., 1994, 'Fishing to the Tune of Gunfire', *Samudra*, February.

Ruddle, K., 1989, 'Solving the Common Property Dilemma: Village Fisheries Rights in Japanese Coastal Waters', in F. Berkes (ed.), *Common Property Resources: Ecology and Community-Based Sustainable Development*, Belhaven Press, London.

Ruddle, K., 1993, 'External Forces and Change in Traditional Community-Based Management Systems in the Asia Pacific Region', *Marine Anthropological Studies*, vol. 6, nos 1/2.

Ruddle, K., E. Hviding and R. Johannes, 1992, 'Marine Resources Management in the Context of Customary Tenure, *Marine Resource Economics*, 7, pp. 249–73.

Tahmina, Q., 1995, *Profit by Destruction*, International Workshop on Ecology, Politics and Violence of Shrimp Cultivation for Export, organized by Nijera Kori, UBINIG, ALRD and SEHD, 9–11 October, unpublished.

Wilkes, A., 1995, 'Prawns, Profits and Protein', *The Ecologist*, vol. 25, nos 2/3.

Zerner, C., 1991, 'Sea Change: Toward Community Management of Coastal Resources in Southeast Asia and the Pacific', draft manuscript.

8

Forests: Myths and Realities of Violent Conflicts

Larry Lohmann

Forests, many intellectuals assume, are threatened above all by two things: people and progress. 'If you took our planet and just put one human being on it', Lord Peter Melchett, Greenpeace's president, said in a recent interview,

> that human being would be consuming resources which otherwise would be available for nature – for wildlife, for wild animals, plants, whatever. Two human beings consume twice as much, and a million consume a million times as much.... Everything we do impacts on nature and to my mind what we need to concentrate on is limiting that impact. (Melchett 1997)

Environmentalists and others are accustomed to viewing the history of forests as one of continuous decline from some earlier, better-adjusted age, whether this is identified as pre-human, pre-agricultural, pre-industrial, pre-colonial or pre-development. They conclude that as forests become scarcer, the stage is set for more and more violent conflicts over the goods they provide. Some also claim that as ecosystems and traditional management systems deteriorate, 'primordial ethnic hatreds' are likely to resurface with devastating effect, particularly in the Third World. Thus journalist Robert Kaplan, in a 1994 article faxed by the US government to its embassies throughout the world, accounted for conflict in the forests of eastern and southern Sierra Leone by pointing to the anarchic results of what he perceived to be the natural proclivity of Africans to populate their countries to the point of environmental collapse (Kaplan 1994).

The weaknesses of such views of forest change and forest conflict are well known. Contesting the belief that there is an inherent tension between forests and human habitation, for example, historian Stephen Pyne has called attention to the way oak, pine, teak, sal, eucalyptus and other forests have evolved together with anthropogenic fire, pointing out that to ban human-made fire from a forest is typically not to 'restore a former, prelapsarian state, but to fashion an ecosystem that has never before existed' (Pyne 1982, 1995). Arriving at similar conclusions, anthropologists such as Melissa Leach, James Fairhead and Darrell Posey analyse instances in Africa and Latin America in which farming and local community management have caused forest islands, which might otherwise have disappeared or never arisen, to expand (Fairhead and Leach 1995, 1996; Posey 1985, 1990). Anthropologist Paul Richards, meanwhile, has disposed of Malthusian explanations for recent armed conflict in Sierra Leone and Liberia by showing that it is a response to political failures involving state recession and not to environmental changes, to which local people are well able to adapt through social and technical inventiveness (Richards 1996). More generally, a large and powerful grouping of historians and social scientists, among them scholars such as E.P. Thompson, Douglas Hay and Theda Skocpol, have rejected the view that violence, including forest violence, is a matter of the mechanical reactions of individuals to regularities visible from the office or laboratory – to population increases, economic stimuli or supposed primordial animosities (Thompson 1963, Hay 1975, Skocpol 1979). Rather, they have stressed, violence is generally either a subordinate part of larger structures of power tied up with languages, values, narratives and cultures, or the result of a breakdown of, or inability to extend, that power. Understanding violent conflict, on this view, means taking seriously the differences among specific societies and histories.

The 'people – progress – primordial hatreds' model of forest degradation and forest conflict, however, is simply too convenient for many intellectuals of a certain class or administrative bent to abandon easily. Its advantages are many. By appealing to supposed universal, impersonal human tendencies and a single line of 'progress' which all societies must follow, it enables bureaucrats to draw conclusions about any region from the comfortable distance of the meeting hall, classroom or laboratory. By invoking supposed inevitable, immutable, unreasoning aspects of human nature, it avoids sensitive political and economic issues, attributing conflict to natural forces and the tensions between a few eternally fixed 'ethnic identities' – neither of which can be changed, but only 'contained' by enlightened administration. Given the appeal of this model, it often seems beside the point to observe that it is usually worthless in accounting for any specific instance of violent conflict involving forests. That is not its function, which is not to explain so much as to mark boundaries between certain groups of middle-class intellectuals and the lower orders whose steps they wish to direct. However much evidence is offered against the model – and it would be impossible to discredit it comprehensively in the short space of one chapter – it is likely to crop up again and again in future discussions about the environment.

All the same, for observers without a prior stake in any single explanation of violent conflict involving forests, some specific examples may help suggest the shortcomings of the 'people – progress – primordial hatreds' account. The approach of this chapter will be simply to tell two such stories of forest violence and then to question the extent to which the model illuminates them. The implicit further question for readers' experience and common sense is whether the model is capable of explaining other cases of forest violence any better.

The first story is set in England. Here the course of forest violence over a period of 800 years refuses obstinately to be mapped onto population graphs or to follow directly any line of technical 'progress'. Here, too, forest conflict has shaped, as much as been shaped by, the politics of identity. In seeking to understand it, it is difficult to avoid coming to grips not only with, for example, how different regions responded to the industrial revolution, but also with such arcana as local cuisine and the role of commerce in forest animals in class differentiation.

A second story relates to a much briefer stretch of time, that of the Vietnam war. Here it is perhaps even more striking how little light is shed on forest violence by, for example, abstract theories of population–environment relations. More fruitful accounts must turn instead to such matters as international politics, the US culture of technocracy, and revolutionary strategy.

Forests in England: Unending Conflict

During the eighteenth century, the first part of the nineteenth and, to some extent, even some of the twentieth century, dwellers in forest-endowed parts of England lived off local woods to a degree difficult for urbanites to imagine today. Farmers, tenants and cottagers might release their livestock into forests to forage or graze them on wood-pastures, special landscapes where trees had been trimmed to allow crops of poles to sprout out of reach of grazing animals yet also encourage the growth of grass underneath. For the poor, this was often the only pasture available, and often made the difference between subsistence and destitution. Meanwhile, villagers might meet fuel needs by picking up dead wood from the ground or breaking off smaller branches of trees by hand or with a metal hook or a crooked pole. The expression 'by hook or by crook', as William Cobbett noted, still applies 'to those cases where people *will have a thing* by one means or another' (Cobbett 1930: I, 53). Gorse was meanwhile collected to fire brick or pottery kilns, lime kilns or bread ovens. Hazel poles were harvested and woven into frames used for gates and fishing weirs, and wood lopped or shredded off trees to be made into fences and carts. Timber might be cut to be used for ploughs or doors, furniture and frames of houses; wood taken away for hop poles, barns, baskets, wagons, spades, clothes pegs, brushes, ladders, and rakes; and wood ash used for potash and dyes. In the spring, bark was stripped and cleaned to be used for tanning or sometimes rope-making, or osier peeled for basket-making. In autumn, pigs might be let loose to fatten on acorns or beech mast; in the eleventh century woods were sometimes measured according to how many swine they could support. Autumn, too, was the season for cutting peat or turves for fuel, and the best time to collect mushrooms, hunt or snare rabbits, and gather bracken or fern for horse bedding or pig litter. Stone and gravel could be dug for house construction and clay for bricks and dams, as well as sand, marl, chalk, loam and iron ore. Fish could be caught in woodland streams, and rushes cut for thatching and lighting. In season, woods were also sources of honey, herbal medicines, watercress, blackberries, edible birds, birds' eggs, hazelnuts, fruit, briars, moss, and other useful goods. Forests drew specialized industries as well. Blacksmiths, glassmakers, bakeries, meat-smokers, smelters and mobile forges required easy access to wood or charcoal fuel; common English surnames such as Wright, Sawyer, Smith, Carpenter, Cutler, Fowler, Tanner, Wheeler, Cooper (barrel-maker) and Turner (maker of turned implements like dishes and cups) were concentrated early on in woodland zones (Rackham 1986; Kitteringham 1975; Birrell 1980; Stamp and Hoskins 1963; Eversley 1910).

Forest areas, with their abundant pastures, relatively scattered settlements, low density of gentry, and difficulty of cultivation, helped poorer rural dwellers to keep their distance from big landlords and agricultural improvers. In addition, although forest areas were also economically unstable and often dependent on grain imports, their comparative remoteness, inability to exclude outsiders, plentiful use-rights and opportunities for land and industrial employments attracted dispossessed or impoverished migrants and outlaws on the run; not for nothing was the forest the home of idealized rebel figures such as Robin Hood. This in turn often fostered further development of non-agricultural industries such as nail-making. The rural campaigner William Cobbett observed in his tours of the countryside in the early nineteenth century that the 'labouring people ... invariably do best in the woodland and forest and wild countries. Where the mighty grasper has all under his eye, they can get but little.' As elsewhere in Europe, the forest was the 'poor's overcoat', protecting not only against want but also against attempts to increase outside surveillance and control in cleared agricultural regions (Pettit 1968; Cobbett 1930: I, 233; Manning 1988: 255; Thirsk 1967: IV, 97–8; Appleby 1976; Westoby 1989).

Ordinary rural dwellers' need for forest access had to mesh not only with the claims of their fellows from the community and outside but also with those of manorial lords, monarchs and industry. In the forest, where commoners exercised rights to dead wood or turf or fodder, the local lord was likely, from at least as early as the eleventh century, to hold the soil, the minerals under it, and the trunks of the trees that grew on it, while the Crown might well have arrogated to itself the right to keep deer and, in order to protect them, appoint forest rangers, hold forest courts, and pocket fines for infractions of special forest laws (Rackham 1976: 174; Birrell 1987: 41).

Conflict was inherent in this situation. Over many centuries, at least two interrelated and overlapping but distinguishable types of economy hedged in or threatened, yet also helped indirectly to define, coincident forest use-rights. First, manorial lords and the Crown, as well as their agents, faced perpetual temptations, shaped in part by the ups and downs of the agricultural and wood economies, population decreases and increases, and pressures for more intensive agriculture, as well as the state of their own fortunes and alliances, to encroach on or tighten regulation of access to the forest for material or financial gain. Royal hunting forests and deer parks, for example, were made to yield a flow of fines from the middle ages, and in the thirteenth century rising prices and craving for luxuries motivated seigneurs to try to squeeze more income from forest commons through wood sales, clearance and fees for use. In the fourteenth century plague deaths led to labour shortages and wage rises, pushing lords into selling lands, which were then enclosed for sheep pastures, which expanded again in the sixteenth century following the growth of the European cloth industry. In the seventeenth century the Crown tried to raise money by leasing or selling royal forests to agricultural improvers, compensating commoners for lost coincident rights over large areas of 'waste' with small private plots of land, and attempts were made to enclose part of the Forest of Dean on the border with Wales for timber. Manorial lords and gentry meanwhile took over still more land in woodland areas to build and rent out cottages to the landless for profit. Commercial rabbit warrens became profit-making ventures at the expense of local pastures. Growing sanction and means for industrial capitalist enterprise further encouraged enclosure attempts. In the mid-eighteenth century in Cumbria, for example, some landowners' investments in mines, harbours, and other enterprises, together with a growing market for pit props, bobbins, shipbuilding, and charcoal for iron smelting and gunpowder, impelled them to new efforts to cash in on their forests, resulting in an assault on tenants' rights to take wood for repair or subsistence (Birrell 1987: 35, 41, 45; Manning 1988: 55; Sharp 1980; Hay 1975; Searle 1985: 127).

Throughout this process, the law slowly came to treat forest commons more and more as the marketable absolute property of landholders, with poorer commoners receiving little compensation for their loss. In 1235 the Statute of Merton had already given lords the right to take over forest commons on their estates, as long as enough was left for their tenants. Gateward's Case of 1607, in which judges ruled that rights to a local common belonged not to just any inhabitant, but only to those with an 'interest' in a house, also came to be used to divide poorer villagers from local forests. As the Industrial Revolution advanced, forest use-rights were threatened further as 'customs of manors were scrutinized in new ways by stewards and by lawyers, whose employers saw property in new and more marketable ways' (Thompson 1975b). The exercise of many commons rights was stigmatized, sharpening already-raging battles over rights to firewood. Parliamentary statutes in 1663 and 1671 made it an offence to gather wood from royal forests, and in 1766, when wood had grown even more commercially valuable, it became a statutory crime to cut or break branches off oak, beech, ash, or other timber trees. Intellectuals' attacks on commons rights, from Locke to Malthus and W.F. Lloyd, meanwhile became increasingly confident and peremptory.

Another set of conditions which often hemmed in and defined forest use-rights grew out of aristocrat-dominated economies of prestige, gifts, patronage and martial violence in which forests were either a prize, or an arena of contention, or both. For royals and their imitators, forests were from the middle ages onward a 'supreme status symbol and a source of gifts money could not buy' (Rackham 1986: 131–5). These gifts included above all deer. In English, the original meaning of 'forest' – which originally referred to an expanse of largely unwooded ground – was more political than biological: the word meant 'place of deer for royal use', not 'place of trees'; it was only by prevention of clearing and customary fire practices that such areas became more heavily wooded. Parks, meanwhile, were private, fenced-off deer preserves for a largely urban-based aristocracy. Landscape parks and gardens, the fashion for which also spread rapidly from royalty downwards, came to serve as additional marks of prestige; the word 'park', more than 'forest', has kept this connotation of exclusivity and urban-centredness through subsequent eras of city, national and wildlife parks, golf courses, biosphere reserves, and the growth of a global middle class. Other important transferable tokens of status connected with forests included hunting privileges, giant oaks and sinecures in the forest bureaucracy. In the fourteenth century, for example, the cash-strapped Edward III was able to get rid of a debt of what would be nearly $750,000 in today's money just by giving his creditor permission to hunt in Hatfield Forest. His successor Richard II rewarded faithful functionary Geoffrey Chaucer with the under-forestership of a minor royal forest in Somerset. Even as the cash nexus ramified and solidified, the 'deer and game nexus' connected with elite preserves remained important to hereditary elites partly because it offered them an arena of status competition in which they could hold an edge over *nouveaux riches* and other upstarts. Royals, peers and gentlemen worked hard to keep hunting privileges to themselves. Hunting, even on one's own land, was restricted in 1389 to those who possessed land worth 40 shillings a year, in 1670 to those with manors or incomes of at least 100 pounds a year from landed property. 'It is not fit that clowns should have these sports', James I reminded Parliament in the early seventeenth century (quoted in Manning 1993: 65). Eating the fruits of the hunt was also a mark of status: in the eighteenth century, gifts of game – which could not be legally bought or sold – remained 'one of the more delicate means by which the gentry expressed influence and solicited favour' (Thompson 1975b: 158; see also Hay 1975: 246–7; Chafin 1818; Manning 1993: 60). 'Nobody would care', Lord Londonderry reaffirmed in 1827, 'for a present which everybody could give' (quoted in Hay 1975). One of the incentives driving ambitious lower-middle-class males to join the colonial service was that in India and other overseas possessions they would be allowed to enjoy the status of participation in blood sports, which was denied to them at home (Rangarajan 1996: 154).

Also tied to the symbolic economy of hunting were recycled traditions of martial derring-do important to those at the top of the social pyramid. In the medieval and early modern period, aristocracy and gentry often provoked or settled internal rivalries through ostentatious, militaristic, ritualistic poaching on each others' parks, decked out in full war weaponry in zestful anticipation of skirmishes with keepers and at the head of mini-armies which included tenants and other commoners. Hunting was also sometimes conceptualized as an outlet for the aggressions of off-duty soldiers of noble rank or as a preparation for war, and martial rituals helped emphasize the boundaries between higher and lower orders of society (Manning 1993: 136). In this context, many grievances over use of hunting preserves, whether they concerned hunting privileges themselves, fees for forest use, deer eating local crops or competing with sheep for grass, or encroached land or restrictions on pasture, could be seen as challenges to elite standing. Reading them this way helped them become so.

Unsurprisingly, forests always seemed to ruling elites to present special challenges to discipline. One reason was political. From the fourteenth century, elites feared that unauthorized hunting parties could mask insurrections or be a cover for banditry, perhaps remembering how often in history they had been used as covers for military raids. And in fact rural rebellions in 1381 and 1549, as well as the Civil War of the 1640s, all saw pointed attacks on royal and aristocratic deer parks (Manning 1993: 49, 61; Charlesworth 1983). In addition, gentry sometimes led or provoked enclosure riots against political rivals. In the 1720s, legislators were concerned not only with 'attacks upon royal and private property' and a 'sense of a confederated movement which was enlarging its social demands', but also fears of political rebellion and 'repeated public humiliation of the authorities' by lesser gentry, yeomen and commoners reacting to the perceived abuse of manorial privileges by an *arriviste* class of landowners (Thompson 1975a: 190). Over the centuries, as the main source of threats to particular states moved downwards from disgruntled nobles to envious lesser gentry to smallholders and land-poor artisans, affrays in the woods involving more than a few people were consistently viewed by the courts as having an at least potential political meaning, and every period of popular rebellion was followed by new game laws. Hunting at night or in disguise were first made felonies in 1485; the Black Act of 1723 authorized the death penalty for more than fifty offences connected with hunting or defiance of hunting laws; and the game laws of 1828 made it not only possible but likely for any three men found in a wood together to be banished to Australia for fourteen years if even one of them had been carrying a gun or bludgeon.

The importance of game animals to elite identity was another incentive for game laws: deer, birds and rabbits had to be kept off limits to the lower orders. Yet such laws only generated fresh problems of discipline. Hard as it was to establish territories to hunt them in, direct enforcement of absolute ownership over the animals themselves was pretty close to impossible. The creatures could not easily be confined to a single territory nor stamped with their place of origin, and were never felt by ordinary people to be permanent property at all, a judgement with which many lawyers agreed. Nor was there any point in cashing them in to avoid the costs of enforcement, since it was precisely their non-exchange value which was vital to the elite status economy. What with such difficulties, the only way to enforce property claims on such animals was through the blunt instrument of laws which criminalized any circumstance in which they might be poached. Thus blanket bans were slapped on walking at night, for example, or on acquiring certain kinds of dogs. Sledgehammer-like penalties and crude technologies of terror like spring guns and man traps were additional, and not very successful, attempts to make up for the inherent difficulties of privatizing wildlife. The problem became particularly intractable in the early nineteenth century, when at a time of crisis in the rural economy pheasant-mad landowners packed their woods with forbidden 'tame and docile birds, whose gay feathers sparkled among the trees before the eyes of the half-starved labourers breaking stones on the road at half a crown a week' (Hammond and Hammond 1970: 163). What ensued was a virtual class war pitting plebeian poachers of birds and rabbits against landowners who had to suppress feuding among themselves in order to forge a united front to contain the lower orders. Although wood-stealing was probably the most common rural crime, game offences took up most of the time of many country magistrates in the eighteenth and early nineteenth centuries and interested Parliament deeply. Between 1827 and 1830 at least one in seven convictions in the country were Game Code violations. In time, the consequences of the criminalization of the most enterprising young men in the countryside began to frighten even some elements of the elite. In 1815 one self-identified gentleman, proprietor of game and magistrate wrote, following a killing on his manor, that

> the regular army, as it may be called, of Game keepers and their assistants are assailed in their nightly bivouac by the irregular tirailleurs of the bands of poachers, and the savage import and consequence of a war of posts are perpetuated in every village. All moral ideas of right and wrong are confounded; all love of the spirit of place and history are banished from the breasts of the contending parties; and even the shedding of a neighbour's blood is considered matter of triumph among their several advocates … That this condition of things should ultimately prepare the minds of the lower classes for every crime to which the circumstances of their station may tempt them is not surprising. (Anonymous 1815).

Among the 'crimes' in which lower-class poachers subsequently became involved were the risings of 1816 and 1830 (Hobsbawm and Rudé 1968: 63). In a parallel movement, some eighteen years previously Sir Frederick Eden had worried in a report on *The State of the Poor* about the consequences of the criminalization of the wood-collecting children of rural labourers. These 'young marauders', he wrote, who spared 'neither hedges nor trees', were 'calculated in the art of thieving, till, from being accustomed to small thefts, they hesitate not to commit greater deprivations on the public' (quoted in Bushaway 1982: 214). Here again, the difficulty of privatizing a good to which it was in principle difficult to restrict access (the space to be patrolled was huge, and much of the dead wood which the poor had traditionally had the right to collect was attached to live trees, leaving open large areas for contestation) had led to impossibly unwieldy regulation efforts.

Lower-grade threats – vagrancy, masterlessness, laziness, poverty, rowdiness, immorality, overbreeding and, not least, disrespect for authority – were also persistently associated with forest commons. One genteel seventeenth-century observer fulminated that forests were

> so ugly a monster as of necessity will breed ... more and more idleness, beggary and atheism, and conseqently disobedience to God and the King ... wherein infinite poor yet most idle inhabitants have thrust themselves, living covertly without law or religion, '*rudes et refractori*' by nature, among whom are nourished and bred infinite idle fry, that coming ripe grow vagabonds, and infect the Commonwealth with most dangerous leprosies. (quoted in Pettit 1965: 163).

Such heavy-duty abuse is not usually generated out of a comfortable ideological hegemony. There was something in the woods that touched a moral nerve in the elite of every era, and that wouldn't go away. When late-eighteenth-century apologists for agricultural improvement branded the commons a nest of indiscipline, when Malthus formalized his views of the breeding habits of the lower orders, when the Victorian middle class complained about the uncouth insults with which they were greeted when they walked across suburban heaths, they were building creatively on old traditions. Such traditions presumably owe their longevity to a number of enduring factors, economic and other: competition for land; need for safe, direct commercial routes; a wish not to face directly the social results of dispossession; the inappropriateness for a capitalist economy of forest dwellers' ways of organizing space and time; a yearning for a safe medium for unscrutinized middle-class movement; and no doubt many others.

Yet despite conflicts involving land, status and discipline, the relation between use of forest commons and elite-dominated economies was never one of simple opposition. Commoners of different statuses were accustomed to operating within, reshaping, and adapting the resources of, a variety of cultural systems. By the thirteenth century, for instance, tenants usually had to work within the legal fiction that they owed all their rights to the forest to the gracious grants of lords some time in the past. Yet the fact that the manorial courts which helped to police the exercise of such rights were composed mainly of commoners themselves and were 'seldom unduly favourable to the lord's interest' (Rackham 1986: 121) left a lot of room for manoeuvre; and grants by the nobility were appealed to by commoners on innumerable occasions. Commoners in one part of

Epping Forest near London, for example, defended their customary right of lopping trees from St Martin's Day (11 November) until St George's Day (23 April) by claiming that it originated in a grant from Queen Elizabeth I, though records indicate it was in fact much older (Fisher 1887: 248). At the same time, the martial culture of the hunt was often mined for useful materials by those further down the status hierarchy, who both imitated and mocked it. Not only did envious status-conscious lesser gentry, in the centuries preceding the Civil War, constantly lead aggressive poaching parties into the parks of the great, often injuring or killing keepers. Carefully prepared illicit hunts involving both gentry and ordinary commoners were also one way of carrying out community judgement on an encloser or emparker felt to be exploitative. The Church meanwhile evolved a role which not only mediated in disputes among commoners themselves but also provided them with some purchase in their conflicts with higher-ups. In Rogation week, the week following the fifth Sunday after Easter, clergy led annual mass 'perambulations' around parishes to reaffirm forest common boundaries, and these often provided not only much-needed legal evidence but also moral legitimation for popular claims. More generally, the whole arcane vocabulary of English commons rights – 'housebote' and 'cartbote' (the right to collect timber for house and cart construction, but only a certain quota), 'hedgebote' (the right to lops and tops for making hedges, but only a certain amount collected by certain methods), 'firebote' (the right to collect firewood in limited quantities), 'turbary' (the right to cut turfs in certain areas), 'pannage' (the right to set pigs loose in the wood in autumn, usually for a fee paid to the lord), not to mention rights of way and rights of access, which are still important common rights today – can be seen as a collective creation worked up out of the tension among different parts of the social hierarchy, none of which was able completely to dominate the others (Thompson 1990).

It was when such cultural webs could not be modified fast enough to contain emerging tensions that violence rose to unusual levels. Landlords might evict cottagers, fence out their animals, order officers to take brutal action against forest users, see to it that commoners were transported for forest use, or launch pre-emptive strikes against whole stands of trees to which commoners claimed use-rights to remove the cause of contestation. Forest officers and keepers, moreover, might abuse their authority when centralized controls lapsed. Commoners, especially those lacking the wherewithal to pursue matters through courts and petitions and unlikely to be compensated sufficiently for loss of pastures or firewood, might respond with tactics progressing from experimental invasions of fenced-off areas to anonymous threats to fence-breaking, forest raids, destruction of trees, animals, gardens and fields, arson, assaults on lords' or landowners' servants and mass riots. Raucous poaching raids, draining of fishponds, or pilfering of wood from enclosure hedges might combine material appropriation with symbolic protest, and assertion of right with criminal riot (Hopkins 1985).

All this went on for an astonishingly long period, and, encompassing thousands of recorded incidents sometimes linked in regional rebellions, looms large in the record of popular rural violence in England. In 1311, eighteen men broke down a fence in a wooded area of Staffordshire, claiming that the owner had enclosed land they were entitled to pasture their animals on (Birrell 1987: 22). Throughout the sixteeenth and seventeenth centuries, enclosure riots were widespread across the English landscape. In 1569, when the Forest of Westward in Cumberland in north-west England was rented out to local gentry and tenants to sublet, several hundred smallholders and labourers from nearby manors whose pastures were threatened pulled down the enclosures (Appleby 1976). Communities in and around at least seven royal forests erupted in the 1620s and 1630s over plans to convert them to farmland to gain income for the Crown. Miners and other commoners in the Forest of Dean rioted periodically over a 150-year period beginning in 1631 whenever enclosures were made or common rights restricted, and in 1831, when enclosures used to protect young trees were not thrown open to grazing after a suitable period, two thousand people with pickaxes and spades destroyed most of the fences (Charlesworth 1983: 42; Hart 1966: 214). On Cannock Chase in Staffordshire in central England, commoners protested the leasing of common pasture for rabbit warrens beginning in 1690; in late 1753, after further enclosures, 200 people including labourers, colliers, weavers, servants, tradesmen and artisans invaded the local nobleman's land and slaughtered between ten and fifteen thousand rabbits worth perhaps £3,000. The rioters had been encouraged by news that commoners in Charnwood Forest thirty miles away had defied troopers and police to dig up warrens on their own commons (Hay 1975; Thompson 1990). After the wall of the recently enclosed Richmond Park near London was breached several times in the 1750s by commoners concerned about the loss of rights of way and access to gravel, wood and water, a judge finally affirmed the validity of their claims (Thompson 1990). In 1784, poor commoners in Alice Holt Forest in Wiltshire, 'assembling in a riotous manner', seized the lops and tops of trees which a local lord had cut down, resulting in legal action against forty-five of them (White 1899: 24). In 1866, after part of Berkhamsted Common north of London was enclosed by a new manorial lord who wanted to add it to his park, a wealthy commoner hired 120 labourers to pull down two miles of iron fencing in the middle of the night as a demonstration and assertion of right; four years later his action was judged lawful in the courts, and the common remained open (Eversley 1910: 42–54). Today's well-reported struggles to protect commons and trees against state road-building projects at Twyford Down, Newbury, London and elsewhere should be seen – as they often are by their protagonists – as part of this longer history of defence of communally used land against the encroachments of elites.

Popular violence over forests in England, as in many other places, has generally brought repression or convictions. Yet, together with other, less visible, finer-grained, and more frequently employed forms of contestation, it also slowed the conversion of forests into commercial and state territories, often for decades and sometimes for centuries. Violence, together with other forms of contestation, was capable of weakening the rule of kings, and shaped the way commons were distributed when they were privatized. The mere threat of a mass of commoners ready to rise if their forest rights were undermined was a long-standing and potent influence on the decisions of the great. In April 1617 Fulke Greville, Chancellor of the Exchequer, noted that as a result of plans for a royal purchase of forest commons in Essex,

> the contry growing gealouse of some further intention of inclosing their comons began to mutyne ... what a showre of Shrewes [the surveying official] encountred with I leave to the stories of his own letters. Wherein ye may see how easilie this tight Sea of busie people is raysed up with every wynde; so as a tender proceeding with them can be no preiudice. (quoted in Fisher 1887: 37)

In the next century, Queen Caroline asked her prime minister, Sir Robert Walpole, how much it would cost to fence St James's Park in London. He replied, 'Only a *crown*, Madam.' The existence of St James's and other London parks, which the stubbornness of commoners helped preserve up until the time they were taken over by public managers, is evidence visible even to casual visitors to the country today of the power and longevity of the often violent confrontations over forest rights which at one time raged across the country, and which are continued in new forms in today's protests against road and other construction projects (Thompson 1990: 111, 125–6; Eversley 1910).

The USA in Vietnam: At War with the Land

'Power and violence are opposites', Hannah Arendt wrote:

> where the one rules absolutely, the other is absent. Violence appears where power is in jeopardy, but left to its own course it ends in power's disappearance ... to speak of nonviolent power is actually redundant. Violence can destroy power; it is utterly incapable of creating it. (Arendt 1970)

The defeat of the United States in Vietnam, well under way at the time Arendt wrote these words, is the most spectacular demonstration in recent times of the weaknesses of violence when inadequately supported by power. Between 1965 and 1973 the United States military dropped between 8 and 15 million tonnes of munitions from aircraft on Southeast Asia, the equivalent of between four and eight times the tonnage it dropped in the Second World War, or the explosive force of between 600 and 1,200 nuclear weapons of the size dropped on Hiroshima (Gibson 1986: 319, 495). The amount of munitions used per US soldier was twenty-six times that of the Second World War (Kolko 1994). Almost two tonnes of explosive per Vietnamese civilian were expended in the region surrounding Saigon, 775 kilogrammes per person in Laos (Westing 1976: 9). Between 1.4 and 2 million lives were lost within the borders of Vietnam alone, over 96 per cent of them Vietnamese. Yet in 1975 the United States was forced to withdraw in disarray.

As in many other wars, attacks on people quickly spread to include direct attacks on forests. In Vietnam, forests fell victim to US campaigns to reduce cover for enemy forces, to destroy installations, communications and roadside areas, to depopulate the countryside and create refugees, and to destroy crops. The scale and some of the technology employed, however, were unusual. In South Vietnam alone, herbicide applications, bulldozing, and intensive conventional and incendiary bombing stripped perhaps 5,700 square kilometres entirely of their forest cover and heavily damaged an additional 56,000 square kilometres of forest land. Together, this comes to some 59 per cent of the south's pre-war forest cover (Westing 1976: 9). 'Only we can prevent forests', went the slogan painted on the sides of C-123 transport planes used to spray defoliants. The US air force, one Vietnamese politician remarked, seemed 'at war with the very land of Vietnam' (quoted in Weisberg 1970: 53). The damage was all the more telling given that in many parts of rural Vietnam, as in many parts of England before the latter part of the twentieth century, farming families depended for part of their livelihood on local forests (Condominas 1977; Ireson and Ireson 1996).

This forest violence was clearly not due to 'overpopulation' or 'the inexorable march of progress'. Its character and scale, on the other hand, did owe a great deal to the technocratic institutions and thinking which came to prominence in the USA in the 1950s and 1960s. Robert McNamara, previously head of Ford Motor Company and subsequently President of the World Bank, took over the US Defense Department in the early 1960s at the head of a self-confident team of university and think-tank intellectuals whose institutional upbringing disposed them to claim that all political and military problems could be neatly divided into means and ends, with rational action being exclusively a matter of applying appropriate quantities of available means to given goals. Progress toward those goals, on this view, could be evaluated and achieved numerically, from a distance. The assurance and glibness with which McNamara's technocrats and their allies pressed this vision intimidated senior officials, politicians and military officers alike (Kolko 1994: 144–5). Institutions concerned with war-making occupied themselves increasingly with creating a numerical reality with which office-bound theoreticians were comfortable.

This situation created an inherent bias against examining either long-term goals – which remained abstract, fixed, and undiscussable – or the nature, rather than the quantity, of the means used to achieve them. Patrician bureaucrats eager to uphold US international dominance defended the view that at some stage increasing quantities of violence – the commodity they happened to have in their hands in abundance, thanks partly to the post-Second World War decision to offer massive subsidies to weapons-producing corporations as a lead sector of the economy – would be transformed into power in the form of Vietnamese submission, enabling the USA to 'speak in Viet Nam on many topics and in many ways' (*Pentagon Papers* 1972: III, 311), and ensuring recognition of US determination and legitimacy by a world public. Unable to quantify legitimacy or influence directly, the US war apparatus obsessively tallied up accumulated bodies, artillery shells expended, sorties flown, and hectares of forest defoliated. Even the Central Intelligence Agency, which was often more sceptical about US prospects than other agencies, maintained in 1966 that 'there presumably is a point at which one more turn of the screw would crack the enemy resistance to negotiations' (quoted in Gibson 1986: 97).

While violence is often measurable, however, power is not. To the professed puzzlement of US technocrats and politicians alike, Vietnamese revolutionaries 'irrationally' failed to respond in numerical proportion to the violence used to 'communicate' with them and failed to realize when the costs of resistance outweighed the benefits (Gibson 1986: 98). Yet instead of attempting to come to grips with this apparent anomaly, US leaders piled more and yet more baroque and counterproductive technical fixes onto the 'problem', engendering an unfalsifiable logic of escalation. Partly through the mechanism of ecological destruction, peasants were forced out of their homes on the premiss that depopulating the countryside would simplify the war physically for the US side and, in the words of establishment pundit Samuel P. Huntington, help replace the 'Maoist-inspired rural revolution' with an 'American-sponsored urban revolution' (Huntington 1968: 645). By 1973, 10 million refugees had been pushed at one time or another into strategic hamlets, cities or camps, causing many peasants to take up arms on the revolutionary side. Whereas in 1955 some 85 per cent of South Vietnam's people had lived in rural areas, in 1970 only 40 per cent did so, and the population of Saigon had swelled from 300,000 to 3 million (Kolko 1994: 239, 464; Weisberg 1970). US combat soldiers were meanwhile treated largely as bait in high-tech traps. 'You don't fight this fellow rifle to rifle', one US Army general said. 'You locate him and back away. Blow the hell out of him and then police up' (quoted in Kolko 1994: 179). When massive bombing failed to turn the tide of the war, it was claimed that yet more bombing had to be carried out, partly in order to save the credibility of the quantitative model itself (Kolko 1994: 149). Even attempts to 'win hearts and minds' were mainly technical in orientation, as witnessed by the surrealistic flood of consumer goods – refrigerators, movie cameras – which helped swamp South Vietnam in corruption.

The US military's possession of large-scale, coarse-grained, energy-intensive technologies of violence motivated strategists to attempt to create an abstract, simplified battlefield suitable for their use. In addition to alienating rural dwellers and destroying their forests, land and watercourses, this strategy failed even in military terms. The failure, however, was generally more visible to US soldiers on the ground than to theorists higher up. One GI criticized the practice of clearing forest on both sides of roads to prevent ambushes, a technique that the elites of medieval and early modern England had found effective against bandits but which met an unexpected twist in Vietnam:

> Let me tell you about that defoliation programme. It didn't work.... Some idiot somewhere sold somebody the idea that if the gooks couldn't hide, then they couldn't ambush you, and they bought the idea, I mean really bought it. The trouble with the whole thing is that the Viet Cong and North Vietnamese Army use guns in their ambushes instead of bows and arrows. Nobody mentioned that. They don't have to be sitting on top of you to pull off an ambush. An AK-47 is effective up to 1,500 metres and accurate up to 600. So we'll hit an area, like along a busy road, billions of gallons of the stuff, and pretty soon there's nothing except for some dead bushes for 50 or even 300 metres on both sides.... So the gooks will start shooting at you from 300 metres away instead of five, only now you're the one that ain't got no place to hide. Ever try running 100 metres or 200? It takes time, and they're firing at you the whole way. (quoted in Gibson 1986: 123–4)

In reality, the landscape could never be stripped down in a way which would enable US technology to be able to transmute violence into power. Jet aircraft, however effective they might be over a large area on a bare plain, were vulnerable when they had to slow down to enter narrow, short valleys. Similarly, while Cu Chi near Saigon was a good place to station US tanks and trucks because it was perched high above the water table and would remain dry even during the rainy season, the dry ground could also support a vast system of secret tunnels. A revolutionary officer described US soldiers' bewilderment when they first encountered an attack from Vietnamese hidden in the earth:

> They … did not hide or take defensive positions. They did not know where the bullets had come from. We kept on shooting… . Although their fellows kept falling down, they kept on advancing. They should have retreated. They called for artillery. When the first shells landed we simply went into the communications tunnels and went on to another place.… [The tunnels] are something very Vietnamese and one must understand what the relationship is between the Vietnamese peasant and the earth, his earth. Without that, then everything here is without real meaning. (quoted in Gibson 1986: 123)

Chemical defoliation was one of the first experiments aimed at simplifying the difficulties of counter-insurgency warfare which was tested in Vietnam. Singled out as the most promising compounds among hundreds of possibilities, 2,4–D and 2,4,5–T – the components of Agent Orange – had been synthesized during the Second World War for possible use against Germany and Japan and tried out in India and Australia. After field tests in Kenya and the former Tanganyika, the British military used the two compounds together with another herbicide in the mid-1950s in what was then Malaya, with consultation from ICI, partly to deprive guerrillas of cover, partly against crops. In Vietnam, herbicides were first employed in 1961, this time with consultation from the ex-director of British defoliation operations in Malaya, who worked with the British Advisory Commission to South Vietnam between 1961 and 1965 (Luber 1990). Although the US military at first feared 'charges of barbarism for waging a form of chemical warfare', the spraying programme in fact attracted little attention in the USA until late 1965 (Buckingham 1982).

The Vietnam war was conducted by numbers, and there are plenty of numbers to describe the prodigious extent of herbicidal use. The area sprayed each year with defoliants increased from 24 square kilometres in 1962 to 6,800 in 1967. Over a nine-year period approximately 14–20 per cent of South Vietnam's terrestrial forests and 36–41 per cent of its mangrove forests were sprayed (Westing 1984; Kolko 1994). In terms of land area, over 17,000 square kilometres were treated one or more times, with the bulk of the attacks being directed against forests rather than food crops. Between 1965 and 1969, between 380 and 800 square kilometres of Laos were also secretly sprayed, violating US law, as well as a considerable area of Cambodia, where Kompong Cham province was also severely affected by chemicals drifting across the Vietnamese border (Westing 1984; Pfeiffer 1982: 24; Neilands, Orians, Pfeiffer et al. 1972:

120, 177–205). In all, nearly 55,000 tonnes of active herbicidal ingredients were dispensed (Westing 1984).

The effects on plant life, not so easily expressible in numbers, are less clear, and began to be studied only belatedly. A single spraying of herbicide was enough to defoliate virtually all non-bamboo trees, killing at least 10 per cent outright and gravely injuring a much larger proportion. Because soils in tropical forests cannot hold many of the nutrients released by dead leaves, this resulted in immediate loss of nutrients to the whole ecosystem, and soil erosion also increased. Approximately one-third of the forests treated were sprayed more than once, and the tree mortality rate was far higher here: 25 per cent for an area sprayed twice, 50 per cent for one sprayed three times, and up to 100 per cent for an area hit four times (Westing 1976: 31). In coastal mangrove forests, meanwhile, virtually nothing remained alive after even a single spraying. Because mangroves serve as breeding or nursery grounds for marine and some riverine fish, the effects were also felt by the fishing fleet. Long-term effects are uncertain, but it is estimated that it will take between eighty and a hundred years for a dense inland forest sprayed even once or twice to recover to a state comparable to that of the original stand. In areas sprayed more than twice, soil erosion, nutrient loss and repeated fires have changed the landscape permanently. In the 1,240 square kilometres of South Vietnam's mangroves devastated by herbicides, only about 11 per cent had been rehabilitated by 1983, mainly through replanting rather than natural regeneration (Westing 1984).

Direct effects on human biology are even more uncertain. Although in 1961 McNamara assured the Joint Chiefs of Staff that herbicides used in Vietnam would not be harmful to humans or livestock, in 1963 the USA began to study an especially deadly and persistent dioxin contaminant of Agent Orange – the herbicide which constituted more than 60 per cent of the defoliants used in the war. This dioxin, known as TCDD, was suspected of causing cancer, birth defects, and other grave problems. By 1967 it was clear that these fears were grounded; today dioxins are suspected also of adversely affecting reproduction, development and the immune system (Pfeiffer 1982; *Environmental Science and Technology* 1995). Anecdotal reports from the ground in Vietnam and Cambodia from the late 1960s, however, remained uninvestigated by US officials. Highlanders in Kontum and Pleiku provinces, for example, reported an unusually high number of deaths, especially among children, in areas that had been sprayed, and also complained of abdominal pains, diarrhoea, vomiting, respiratory symptoms, rashes and dizziness. Domestic and wild animals, including fish, were also killed (Hickey 1982: 255, 308–19; Neilands, Orians, Pfeiffer et al. 1972). It took a good deal of political activism, moreover, before any effects on US policy were discernible even from certified laboratory research. As late as 1968, John S. Foster, Director of Defense Research in the Defense Department, claimed that 'herbicides would not have a long term negative impact on South Vietnam's people or its interests', and it was not until 1970 that use of Agent Orange was finally stopped by President Nixon. Only in 1972 did Foster advise the Secretary of Defense that that all Agent Orange remaining in Vietnam be recalled to the US, since 'known impurities in Agent Orange preclude its use by the South Vietnamese'. On 8 April 1975, an official order banning the military use of herbicides was promulgated (Pfeiffer 1982; Neilands, Orians, Pfeiffer et al. 1972). To what extent this law has been and will be followed is a matter for investigation, but it is clear that the issue of Agent Orange's long-term destructive effects on human health will remain a contentious issue for some time, thanks in part to the protests of affected US veterans. Dioxin dispensed during the war, having an environmental half-life of at least three years, is meanwhile still present in Vietnamese soils. Most affected is the former Military Region III outside Saigon, where 16.3 litres of herbicide per person were sprayed over the landscape (Westing 1976: 9).

Another technology of deforestation employed by US forces in Vietnam was the Rome plough – a heavy caterpillar tractor equipped with a large blade designed to split, sever, fell and push aside trees of all sizes. By 1968 some 100–300 metres of forests had been cleared on either side of many major road systems in the south, and the tractors were being increasingly employed to remove whole forests suspected to be capable of harbouring guerrillas, for example in Bien Hoa, Binh Duong and Tay Ninh. Some 3,250 square kilometres of forests were scraped clean of trees by Rome ploughs in South Vietnam – 2 per cent of its entire land area. Soil erosion and wildlife loss were immense. Bombing, in addition, created approximately 250 million craters across the landscape, displacing 3 billion cubic metres of soil and obliterating at least 1,000 square kilometres of forest. It is estimated that over 45 million trees were killed directly or indirectly by shrapnel, with a proportional toll of animal life (Westing 1976: 20, 46, 70).

Conclusion

After this brief look at cases from England and Vietnam, it ought not be necessary to stress at length the limitations of generalizing about forest violence using standard-issue concepts such as 'population increase', 'resource scarcity' and 'primordial identities'. Who is violent, when and why, and what that violence brings about, depends on specific social and historical contexts.

Rising population, for example, hardly seems to be to blame for the violence which tore apart many of Vietnam's forests during the war, and the concept seems largely beside the point in accounting for the ups and downs of strife over forests in medieval and modern England as well. In the fourteenth century, for example, increased enclosure and competition over land may have been spurred by declining population, as higher wages pushed landowners to seek new sources of income. Similarly, the upsurge in popular forest violence in 1720s' Berkshire had more to do with new state policies than with growing human numbers. As E.P. Thompson remarks,

> It would have been easy to have explained [it] by some gesture towards an (unprovable) demographic crisis, precipitating increasing demands upon the forest's resources. But there is no convincing evidence as to any such crisis, demographic, ecological or agrarian. Farmers and forest officers had rubbed along together, in a state of running conflict, for many decades and they were to continue to do so for many more. What appears as crisis was a conflict in the broadest sense political. (Thompson 1975a: 99)

Yet it is almost as difficult to offer universally valid political generalizations about, say, the relationship between forest violence and the state. In the Vietnam of three decades ago, for instance, US state technology devastated forests and dispossessed or killed many of those who lived in or near them, yet in seventeenth-century England, Crown control of forests was often, from the point of view of commoners who revolted in order to retain forest use-rights, comparatively benign. Nor is it necessarily particularly illuminating to assume that forest conflicts are attributable to cultural differences between social groups. In England, certain group identities seem to have been as much created out of forest conflict as they inflamed it. Landlords who chose to preserve game for competitive massacre and to press for increasingly vicious laws against poaching and wood-stealing in the early nineteenth century not only widened class gaps but also helped forge and articulate the identity of 'forest criminals' and of themselves. 'Criminal' may not in this case be an ethnic identity, but the point is not necessarily irrelevant to so-called 'ethnic conflicts' being waged elsewhere today.

A more defensible generalization is perhaps Arendt's: 'those who hold power and feel it slipping from their hands, be they the government or be they the governed, have always found it difficult to resist the temptation to substitute violence for it' (Arendt 1970: 87). Violence is never sufficient and often unnecessary for power, and while it usually appears together with power, if 'left to its own course it ends in power's disappearance'. It does not follow, however – as many forest users in England and Vietnam would attest – that it is always unnecessary.

Note

Many thanks for comments to David Underdown and an anonymous copyeditor for Zed Books, and for financial support to Heinrich-Böll-Stiftung and the Program in Agrarian Studies at Yale University.

Bibliography

Anonymous, 1815, *A Letter on the Game Laws, by a Gentleman and Game Proprietor*, privately printed, London.
Appleby, Andrew B., 1976, 'Common Land and Peasant Unrest in Sixteenth Century England: A Comparative Note', *Peasant Studies Newsletter*, pp. 20–23.
Arendt, Hannah, 1970, *On Violence*, Harcourt, Brace and World, New York.
Birrell, Jean, 1980, 'The Forests of Medieval England', *Journal of Forest History*, April, pp. 78–85.
Birrell, Jean, 1987, 'Common Rights in the Medieval Forest: Disputes and Conflicts in the Thirteenth Century', *Past and Present* 117.
Buckingham, William, 1982, *Operation Ranch Hand: The Air Force and Herbicides in Southeast Asia 1961–1971*, Air Force, Washington DC.
Bushaway, Bob, 1982, *By Rite: Custom, Ceremony and Community in England 1700–1880*, Junction Books, London.
Chafin, William, 1818, *A Second Edition of the Anecdotes and History of Cranbourn Chase*, J. Nichols, Son and Bentley, London.
Charlesworth, Andrew (ed.), 1983, *An Atlas of Rural Protest in Britain 1548–1900*, Croom Helm, London.
Cobbett, William, 1930 [1830], *Rural Rides*, edited by G.D.H. and Margaret Cole, Vol. I, Peter Davies, London.
Condominas, George, 1977, *We Have Eaten the Forest*, Hill & Wang, New York.
Environmental Science and Technology, 1995, vol. 29, no. 1.
Eversley, Lord, 1910, *Commons, Forests and Footpaths*, Cassell, London.
Fairhead, James and Melissa Leach, 1995, 'False Forest History, Complicit Social Analysis: Rethinking Some West African Environmental Narratives', *World Development*, vol. 23, no. 6, pp. 1023–35.
Fairhead, James and Melissa Leach, 1996, 'Enriching the Landscape: Social History and the Management of Transition Ecology in the Forest–Savanna Mosaic (Republic of Guinée)', *Africa*, vol. 66, no. 1, pp. 14–36.
Fisher, William Richard, 1887, *Forest of Essex: Its History, Laws, Administration and Ancient Customs and the Wild Deer which Lived in It*, Butterworth, London.
Gibson, James William, 1986, *The Perfect War: Technowar in Vietnam*, Atlantic Monthly Press, Boston MA.
Hammond, J.L. and Barbara Hammond, 1970 [1911], *The Village Labourer 1760–1832*, Harper, New York.
Hart, Cyril E., 1966, *Royal Forest: A History of Dean's Woods as Producers of Timber*, Clarendon Press, Oxford.

Hay, Douglas, 1975, 'Poaching and the Game Laws on Cannock Chase', in D. Hay, P. Linebaugh, J.G. Rule et al. (eds), *Albion's Fatal Tree: Crime and Society in 18th Century England*, Pantheon, New York, pp. 189–253.

Hickey, Gerald Cannon, 1982, *Free in the Forest*, Yale University Press, New Haven CT.

Hobsbawm, Eric and George Rudé, 1968, *Captain Swing: A Social History of the Great English Agricultural Uprising of 1830*, Norton, New York.

Hopkins, Harry, 1985, *The Long Affray: The Poaching Wars in Britain 1760–1914*, Secker & Warburg, London.

Huntington, Samuel P., 1968, 'The Bases of Accommodation', *Foreign Affairs* 46, July.

Ireson, Carol J. and W. Randall Ireson, 1996, 'Cultivating the Forest: Gender and the Decline of Wild Resources among the Tay of Northern Vietnam', East–West Center Working Paper, Honolulu.

Kaplan, Robert D., 1994, 'The Coming Anarchy: How Scarcity, Crime, Overpopulation and Disease are Rapidly Destroying the Social Fabric of Our Planet', *Atlantic Monthly*, February, pp. 44–76.

Kitteringham, Jennie, 1975, 'Country Work Girls', in Raphael Samuel (ed.), *Village Life and Labour*, Routledge & Kegan Paul, London.

Kolko, Gabriel, 1994, *Anatomy of a War: Vietnam, the United States and the Modern Historical Experience*, New Press, New York.

Luber, Burkhard, 1990, *When Trees Become the Enemy: Military Use of Defoliants*, Georg Olms Verlag, Hildesheim.

Manning, Roger B., 1988, *Village Revolts: Social Protest and Popular Disturbances in England, 1509–1640*, Clarendon Press, Oxford.

Manning, Roger B., 1993, *Hunters and Poachers: A Social and Cultural History of Unlawful Hunting in England, 1485–1640*, Clarendon Press, Oxford.

Melchett, Lord Peter, 1997, interviewed in *Against Nature*, Channel 4 television broadcast, 7 December.

Neilands, J.B., Gordon H. Orians, E.W. Pfeiffer et al., 1972, *Harvest of Death: Chemical Warfare in Vietnam and Cambodia*, Free Press, New York.

The Pentagon Papers: The Senator Gravel Edition, 1972, Beacon Press, Boston MA.

Pettit, P.A.J., 1968, *The Royal Forests of Northamptonshire, 1558–1714*, Northants Record Society.

Pfeiffer, E.W., 1982, 'Operation Ranch Hand: The US Herbicide Program', *Bulletin of the Atomic Scientists*, May.

Posey, Darrell, 1985, 'Indigenous Management of Tropical Forest Ecosystems: The Case of the Kayapo Indians of the Brazilian Amazon', *Agroforestry Systems* 3, pp. 139–58.

Posey, Darrell, 1990, 'Cultivating the Forests of the Amazon: Science of the Mebengokre', *Orion Nature Quarterly*, vol. 9, no. 3, pp. 16–23.

Pyne, Stephen, 1982, *Fire in America: A Cultural History of Wildland and Rural Fire*, Princeton University Press, Princeton NJ.

Pyne, Stephen, 1995, *World Fire: The Culture of Fire on Earth*, Henry Holt, New York.

Rackham, Oliver, 1976, *Ancient Woodland*, J.M. Dent, London.

Rackham, Oliver, 1986, *The History of the Countryside*, J.M. Dent, London.

Rangarajan, Mahesh, 1996, *Fencing the Forest: Conservation and Ecological Change in India's Central Provinces 1860–1914*, Oxford University Press, Delhi.

Richards, Paul, 1996, *Fighting for the Rain Forest: War, Youth and Resources in Sierra*

Leone, James Currey, Oxford.

Searle, C.E., 1985, 'Custom, Class Conflict and Agrarian Capitalism: The Cumbrian Customary Economy in the Eighteenth Century', *Past and Present* 110.

Sharp, Buchanan, 1980, *In Contempt of All Authority: Rural Artisans and Riot in the West of England, 1586–1660*, University of California Press, Berkeley.

Skocpol, Theda, 1979, *States and Social Revolutions: A Comparative Analysis of France, Russia and China*, Cambridge University Press, Cambridge.

Stamp, L. Dudley and W.G. Hoskins, 1963, *The Common Lands of England and Wales*, Collins, London.

Thirsk, Joan, 1967, 'The Farming Regions of England', in H.P.R. Finberg (ed.), *The Agrarian History of England and Wales*, Vol. IV, Cambridge University Press, Cambridge.

Thompson, E.P., 1963, *The Making of the English Working Class*, Gollancz, London.

Thompson, E.P., 1975a, *Whigs and Hunters: The Origin of the Black Act*, Pantheon, New York.

Thompson, E.P., 1975b, 'The Grid of Inheritance: A Comment', in Jack Goody, Joan Thirsk and E.P. Thompson (eds), *Marriage and Inheritance*, Cambridge University Press, Cambridge, pp. 328–60.

Thompson, E.P., 1990, 'Custom, Law and Common Right', in *Customs in Common*, J.M. Dent, London.

Weisberg, Barry (ed.), 1970, *Ecocide in Indochina: The Ecology of War*, Harper & Row, San Francisco.

Westing, Arthur H., 1976, *Ecological Consequences of the Second Indochina War*, Almqvist and Wiksell International, Stockholm.

Westing, Arthur H. (ed.), 1984, *Herbicides in War: The Long-term Ecological and Human Consequences*, Taylor & Francis, London.

Westoby, Jack, 1989, *Introduction to World Forestry*, Blackwell, Oxford.

White, Gilbert, 1899 [1788], *The Natural History of Selbourne*, Appleton, New York.

9

Climate Change and Violent Conflicts

A. Atiq Rahman

The world is fast approaching a new millennium. This decade can be best defined as the post-Cold War and post-UNCED world experiencing increasing globalization. The end of the Cold War has seen the breakdown of the Soviet empire; at the same time a series of conflicts between emerging nation-states and ethnic groups manifested themselves in the Balkans and in the newly emerging states previously subsumed in the Soviet bloc. The grotesque concept and in many cases execution of 'ethnic cleansing' resurfaced in the daily vocabulary, as well as on the television screens, of an increasingly interconnected world. Simultaneously dreadful scenes of human atrocity, violence and genocide also took place in Rwanda and Burundi. Sporadic and often isolated violence on a significant scale has been evident in many countries.

At the same time the 1990s saw the emergence of a series of development and environment conventions. The most important amongst these was the UN Conference on Environment and Development (UNCED) held in Rio de Janeiro in 1992, popularly known as the Earth Summit. Its spirit was encapsulated in the concept of 'sustainable development'. The concept has been defined in various ways. But it essentially contains the elements of integrating environment and development, inter-generational equity, including intra-generational equity, maintaining the capacity of future generations to develop, and integrating the external costs of production and consumption over processes, space and time.

The Earth Summit saw the convergence of almost all the global political and civil society leadership in an amazing conglomeration of issues, activist groups and national and international fora. The outputs of UNCED were a set of well-argued and agreed inter-governmental documents, with the limited participation of global civil society. These documents are of two types: (i) non-binding voluntary agreements such as the Rio Declaration and Agenda 21; (ii) legally binding commitments such as the United Nations Framework Convention on Climate Change (UNFCCC) and the United Nations Framework Convention on Biodiversity (UNFCB). A third UN Framework Convention on combating desertification was also agreed upon.

The voluntary agreements lacked teeth and there was little obligation regarding implementation, though they created a groundswell of awareness and interlinkages. Agenda 21 was followed by the creation of the UN Commission for Sustainable Development (CSD). All three UNCED conventions have now come into force. The Desertification Convention lacks serious financial commitment for implementation, and hence has made limited progress. The Biodiversity Convention, for its part, has made significant progress, with an increasing strengthening of the science and acceptance of concepts and obligations beyond those demanded by traditional conservation activists and has a framework for negotiation in place.

Greatest progress has been made in the Climate Convention, with three conferences held by the end of 1997. There has been a flurry of activity on different concepts and mechanisms, and the establishment of a financial mechanism called the Global Environment Facility (GEF), which also covers biodiversity issues. In 1997 the Kyoto Protocol, with legally binding obligations, was also initiated.

This chapter will be mostly confined to the UNFCCC and the issues, concerns, opportunities and potential challenges and risks for conflicts and violence therein. The first section considers such global environmental phenomena in the context of overall globalization.

Globalization: Opportunities, Challenges and Potential Conflicts

In the post-Cold War, post-UNCED world, where sustainable development has become a widely accepted principle and objective, there is a rapid and increasing trend towards globalization. This globalization is occurring at various levels and involves different aspects of the socio-economic and ecological systems. The implications of globalization are beyond the scope of this chapter. The following is a brief illustration of the types of globalization and their key interlinkages. Efforts have been made to expand on the aspects of global climate change.

Economic and financial globalization

The dominant mode of economic interaction and transaction has become the capitalist system, with greater emphasis on privatization, and the emergence of a 'free' market and market forces. This has increased the flow of trade, seen the emergence of the World Trade Organization (WTO), and created a dominant role for financial organizations such as the World Bank (WB) and the International Monetary Fund (IMF). The UN system and its agencies have been focusing more on development and conflict-resolution concerns.

At the same time, financial transactions are being made faster and easier, including increasing direct foreign investment, international loans and bank transfers, and the dominant role and influence of multinational businesses. For example, each of the world's richest one hundred companies has a capital larger than the world's poorest one hundred countries. This simplistic example demonstrates that economic and financial globalization is likely to play an increasing role where nation-states are becoming weaker as the functional units of decision-making.

The recent decline of the economies of the Asian tigers, such as Korea, Thailand and Indonesia, demonstrates their potential vulnerability and the increasing risks of political unrest, threats and violence. The violence can be of a direct type where national power has to confront the weakening economic capabilities of its citizens through the reduction of economic stability and the loss of purchasing power of individuals, particularly the poor. The Indonesian crisis is a case in point.

Commodity globalization

The increase in international trade, and the demand for a homogenized market through better communication, advertisement and rapid financial exchanges, create a greater demand for exchange of commodities. Every country, in a bid to capture the growing market, tries to increase exports. In the effort each tries to find specific relative advantages. While industrialized countries try to take advantage of their wealth and technology, many developing countries attempt rapid exploitation of their natural resources, even at the risk of threatening their own sustainability. Some of the poorer countries try to sell their labour cheaply to enter this global commodity market. This can give rise to exploitative practices that perpetuate a quiet violence on low-income labour and other vulnerable groups such as the poor, women and children.

Globalization of inequality

In the recent stage of globalization there has been a significant increase in global wealth, unprecedented in the history of mankind. At the same time, over one-third of the world population has to survive in poverty with less than $1 per capita per day. Despite increasing global wealth, there is a frightening increase in poverty, with malnutrition present across the developing world, particularly in Africa and South Asia.

Recognizing that the central issue of poverty had been sidetracked in Rio, a group of activists aimed to bring the issue of poverty back to the centre stage of global discussion. This is encapsulated in the Declaration on Environment and Poverty and associated analyses as described below, as enunciated by the Global Forum on Environment and Poverty (GFEP). The last two demands in the Declaration on Environment and Poverty have major implications for global economics and equity. These are that 'the rich must pay the full ecological cost of their consumption', and that 'all people, including the poor, must have equal rights to global commons including the atmosphere and the oceans'.

Information globalization

With the rapid development in communications technology, where the satellite and computer revolutions are progressing at an unprecedented rate, the information world is becoming highly globalized. This rapid transfer of information has very serious implications for all other forms of globalization. Money, jobs, information on events, including political debate, natural disasters, weather predictions, can be instantly communicated worldwide. The Internet is emerging as a dominant mode of information exchange, leaving behind conventional postal communication and even fax exchanges, which cannot compete for speed.

Attempts to control Internet exchanges can give rise to conflicts across countries and between individuals and interest groups. New laws will be needed to handle and organize the developing field. It appears that the advance of technology and thirst for using instant communication are outpacing institutions, legal systems and the capacity of nation-states to adjust. Further, these technologies are likely to increase inequity unless poorer societies can leapfrog with the new and emerging hardware and software. Caution will have to be exercised in order to avoid the conflicts that may emerge out of these aspects of globalization.

Environmental globalization

Global phenomena such as climate change, loss of biodiversity, ozone-layer depletion and transboundary migration pollutants are a few examples

Box 9.1 Declaration on Environment and Poverty

'There can be no sustainable development without eradication of poverty'

Demand for a poverty convention

The global concern for environment emerges from the fact that the environment affects all people and future generations. The vast majority of the world's population is living in absolute poverty without any security of food, shelter, health, education and other basic survival needs.

Unsustainable consumption of resources in the North and rampant poverty in the South are the greatest threats to the achievement of sustainable global development. The poor are the most vulnerable and main victims of environmental degradation and ecological disasters.

The declaration:

We believe that

- There can be no sustainable development without eradication of poverty.
- The rights of all people to have access to food and other basic requirements for a healthy and meaningful life are inalienable.
- The poor, both men and women, must be able to make decisions about their own local environments and natural resources.
- Although poverty must be addressed at a global scale, there can be no solution without the direct participation of people at the local and national levels.

We demand that

- A Global Convention on Poverty be convened immediately. The two UNCED conventions, on Biodiversity and Climate Change, do not address the central environmental problem of the majority of the global population, which is poverty.
- The peace dividend in a post cold war era must be assessed and re-directed towards global poverty eradication.
- Efforts must be undertaken to remove the most outstanding obstacles to poverty eradication and environmental conservation.
- The rich must pay the full ecological costs of their consumption.
- All people, including the poor, must have equal rights to global commons including the atmosphere and the oceans.

The following analysis forms an integral part of the Declaration on Environment and Poverty initiated in the first GFEP workshop during UNCED in Rio on 4 June 1992 and discussed and developed by hundreds of participants at UNCED. It was finalized in the second GFEP workshop held on 11 June 1992 at UNCED. It was signed by hundreds of delegates and participants in Rio at UNCED and many more subsequently:

Basic issues in environment and poverty

Poverty eradication

The existence, intensification and perpetuation of poverty represents a serious problem that must be attacked frontally, rather than accepting these as an inescapable fact of life. Poverty eradication is an end in itself.

Development models

Prevailing development patterns in the North as well as the South have led to the perpetuation of poverty as well as the exacerbation of environmental degradation. Their effect has been intensified by indiscriminate adjustment policies imposed under the present unjust economic order. A model of truly sustainable development must take into account equitable sharing and governance of global commons. It should be based on the quality of life and not on economic growth alone. The poor must play a key role in defining these models as well as planning and implementing them.

Institutions

The absence or weakness of participatory, decentralized and democratic institutions of collective decision making in the South as well as the North constitutes yet another fundamental obstacle to the pursuit of development that is socially as well as environmentally sustainable. Existing centralized institutions are biased towards vested interests at the national as well as global levels. New institutional mechanisms are needed to coordinate local, national and global actions and to articulate grassroots activities as well as macro level policies.

Consumption and population

Ever increasing consumption is an obstacle to sustainable development. In order to be sustainable, consumption must be stabilized both from above (over-consumption) and below (under-consumption). In making the necessary adjustments, the consumption of the poor to meet their basic human needs must be distinguished from the luxury consumption of the rich. Population stabilization can only be reached by improving the living conditions of the poor and not through coercion.

Gender

The marginalization of women in the present economic and social development process, and their involuntary displacement from their traditional and natural roles is yet another obstacle to sustainability. Empowerment of women is a fundamental step in eradicating poverty and halting environmental degradation. Women should not be the 'victims' of population control programmes. The unique potentials of both genders must be tapped and nurtured for a more wholesome society.

Demilitarization

Militarization and wars are major threats to the environment. The financial and human resources wasted on militarization are more than enough to eradicate world poverty now. These financial and human resources should be diverted towards the goals of peace and development.

Technology

Access to environment-friendly technology by the world's poor must be assured and subsidized.

North–South relations

Poverty in the South and in the North demands a common solution. Eradication of poverty in the South must be an integral part of North–South relations. The obscene flow of financial resources from the South to the North must be reversed in favour of the poor.

Values and attitudes

The values and attitudes of consumerism and acquisitiveness need to be replaced with values which emphasize sharing, caring, solidarity and enhancement of quality of life for all.

of globalization in the field of environment and ecology. Pollution of oceans, overexploitation of marine fisheries, and increasing greenhouse gas emission are a few examples of encroachment upon global commons such as atmosphere and oceans and their capacities to adapt to rapid changes. Deforestation is a similar threat which can have far-reaching global implications. Environmental globalization has been a constant process; the key issue is the rate and scale at which it is now happening. There is now a far greater understanding of the interlinkages and awareness of some of the consequences; these include a threat to sustainability and the risk of violence and conflict.

Globalization of governance

The basic and fundamental unit of governance today is the nation-state. However, there is an increasing influence exerted by the private-sector business community and civil society, particularly non-government organizations (NGOs). This is happening at local, national and global levels.

Following UNCED, a series of global conferences has taken place where governments have addressed several of the key developmental concerns. These include the Social Summit at Copenhagen, the International Conference on Population and Development in Cairo, the International Conference on Women and Development at Beijing, the International Declaration on the Rights of Children, the Habitat meeting at Ankara, amongst others. These meetings and declarations are the beginning of a set of emerging agreed principles: the seeds for future global governance. Several multilateral environmental agreements (MEAs) are also laying the ground for global environmental governance.

UN and Bretton Woods institutions are increasingly playing an important role, particularly in developing countries, to harmonize national practices with the global system. Many critics argue that international financial institutions such as the World Bank, the International Monetary Fund, the World Trade Organization and the regional banks tend to serve the interests of the industrialized world rather that the developing countries. Many critics argue further that these institutions tend to increase poverty and environmental degradation. Nevertheless, whatever the equity implications, a regime of global governance is slowly emerging. The implications of these developments for inciding violence will not be discussed here.

The missing link in globalization and the forbidden frontiers

Efforts to increase globalization in finance and capital, commodities and trade are continuing apace; environmental processes and degradation, too, are on the increase. Early concepts of global governance are also being pursued. Yet one critical component of production, the globalization of labour, is being discouraged vehemently: all possible efforts are being made to confine labour forces in their respective countries. If true free market forces are to prevail, this must include the free transfer and open globalization of labour. The implication of this would be, say, that if a woman from Chad, Sudan or Laos can work in a hamburger joint in New York, London or Bonn cheaper and better then she must have the right to do so. If the globalization of labour is encouraged, or not actively discouraged, then this would probably have the greatest implication for poverty and inequity, and also for the costs of production. To make the world more fair, to reduce inequality, and arguably to achieve global sustainability, the globalization of labour has to be permitted and encouraged. This missing link in globalization is the forbidden frontier that demands proper analysis and consideration. Many ecological phenomena such as rising sea levels and desertification are likely to create environmental refugees; these and the victims of other trends in globalization could be best served by the globalization of labour and population. The implications of these developments for the overall level of violence and conflict deserve urgent attention from scholars and from policy and opinion formers.

Global Climate Change: Issues and Concerns Leading to Kyoto

Global climate change is the focus of this chapter. The following is a commentary and an analysis of the UNFCCC approach to the issue of global climate change. It is necessary to focus on the essential elements of the climate negotiations to appreciate how the impact of climate change may encourage or affect conflicts and violence. The phenomena and science of climate change are adequately dealt with in the relevant and rapidly increasing literature. Therefore comments will be restricted to the nature of the climate change negotiations.

The climate change discourse is a science-driven policy of truly global dimension. The 'greenhouse effect' has in fact always been there; it is the rapid anthropogenic intervention that has created the growing threat. The emission of so-called greenhouse gases by individuals, communities, industrial enterprises, and so on are intimately connected to lifestyle, energy systems, agriculture, transport, forestry and housing practices. It is thus an integral part of the production–consumption pattern of populations.

The negotiations on Climate Change Convention and the emerging science

There were critical and consequential stages in the development of the climate negotiations. These are as follows:

1. Evolution of the early Scientific Consensus leading up to the Second World Climate Conference.
2. Initiation of the Climate Negotiation (INC).
3. Agreement on the Climate Convention (INC 1–INC 6).
4. Signing of the UNFCCC in Rio in June 1992 at UNCED.
5. UNFCCC coming into force and First Conference of Parties (COP-1) at Berlin and establishment of the Adhoc Group on the Berlin Mandate (AGBM).
6. Second Conference of Parties and agreement to initiate a legally binding protocol.
7. Development of Kyoto Protocol at COP-3, Kyoto, in December 1997.

The analysis that follows is located in time just before COP-3 and includes the key issues and concerns leading up to the Kyoto Protocol. The negotiations process for UNFCCC was set up in 1990 and lasted for eleven sessions. After six sessions the Climate Convention was an agreed document and signed by all important countries and ratified soon thereafter by an adequate number.

The main thrust of the negotiations was undertaken by two main blocks. The first block, the industrialized countries, took the major responsibility for causing the change in global climate; the second block, the developing countries, comprised the Group of 77 and China. This followed established UN practice. Nevertheless, the issues and the impact of climate change cut across these traditional UN negotiating blocks. Hence the vulnerable groups, particularly small island states, formed a new block within the G77, the Alliance of Small Island States (AOSIS), which presented the elements of a protocol in the first conference of the parties. On the other side stood the least developed countries, most of which are very vulnerable with little voice due to lack of leadership, no coherent strategy and lacking the capacity to negotiate, or to appreciate and take advantage of the science.

Due to the character of the negotiations, with their science–policy interface, few of the world's prominent civil society organizations attended the negotiations. Furthermore, given that any attempt to contain the global climate change would involve shifting energy uses and practices, particularly hydrocarbons such as oil, coal and natural gas, few of the most powerful companies and businesses, particularly the oil and coal exporters and users, took part. Thus the climate negotiations became one of the most vociferous arenas for debate between science and what was often non-science and non-sense. Much time and effort were needed to differentiate between the scientific information and misinformation.

The Intergovernmental Panel on Climate Change (IPCC) was entrusted with the responsibility of scientific assessment. The two five-yearly assessments by the IPCC advanced the scientific consensus with the usual caution exercised by a group of scientists, whose tendency is to be conservative. Nevertheless, the quality of these assessments added tremendous credibility to the negotiations.

After eleven arduous negotiation sessions, the Convention came into force at the First Conference of Parties at the Berlin Climate Summit which produced the Adhoc Group on Berlin Mandate (AGBM). This negotiating mechanism conducted the process which led to the Third Conference of Parties (COP-3), held in Kyoto in December 1997. It is helpful to follow the account given in *Clime Asia*, the newsletter of the Climate Action Network South Asia, which provides a critical analysis of the issues and events. What follows is a summary of this account as published in the July–September 1997 and October–December 1997 issues of *Clime Asia.*

Issues and concerns in climate change: the march towards Kyoto

In order to ensure a consistent approach to what was a very wide-ranging debate with divergent perspectives and a plethora of issues, it seems best to adopt a viewpoint that represents a southern and civil society perspective.

The North must act; the South is acting

The Third Conference of Parties (COP-3) of the United Nations Framework Convention on Climate Change (UNFCCC) in Kyoto in December 1997, presents a great challenge; it is also a great opportunity to take the necessary, practical and tangible steps to reduce the threat of global climate change. COP-3 has been described by leading members of the global negotiations as the most important environmental meeting since UNCED in Rio in 1992. While the call from global scientists and the expert community is for a 20 per cent cut in greenhouse gas (GHG) emissions by 2010 from 1990 levels, the reality is that in the five years since Rio there has been an increase in excess of 12 per cent.

AGBM 8: time to overcome obstacles

The eighth session of the Adhoc Group on Berlin Mandate (AGBM 8), commencing in October 1997 in Bonn, was the last negotiating session before the Ministerial Summit in Kyoto. The negotiations and practicable compromise have so far been blocked by a group of industrialized countries led by the USA, the emissions of which constitute 20 per cent of the world's greenhouse gases or heat-trapping gases, with only 4 per cent of world population. Japan, the host country of COP-3, has been accused of poor leadership and criticized for its inability to put forward its own significant GHG reduction target. Japan, however, along with many others wants to ensure the participation of all countries in a legally binding Kyoto Protocol. Several OPEC countries led by Saudi Arabia and Kuwait within the Group of 77 and China have been accused of being obstructionist during the process of developing a common position for developing countries, most of which are especially vulnerable to the impacts of climate change, such as rising sea level, extreme weather events, threat to food security and mass migration.

Opt for maximum reduction target

Before the negotiators of this difficult session were a series of options. The Alliance of Small Island States (AOSIS) proposed a 20 per cent reduction from 1990 levels of GHG emission by Annex 1 countries by the year 2010. This was supported by many developing countries, by the global community of civil society actively participating in the climate negotiation, and by most of the scientific community. The European Union proposal called for a 15 per cent reduction in GHG emissions by 2010 and a 1.5 per cent reduction by 2005. The Brazilian proposal was very similar to the EU proposal in terms of targets and timetable.

Experts call for action

The global consensus of scientists through the Inter-governmental Panel on Climate Change (IPCC) in their Second Assessment Report (SAR) called for deeper cuts to stabilize and reduce the GHG concentration caused by human actions.

They also pointed out the factor of the time lag in the response of large systems such as the atmosphere and oceans and called for early reduction. More recently over 2,400 scientists and 2,000 economists in the USA and other countries endorsed the findings of IPCC and urged the global leadership to take prompt action. President Clinton in Washington DC on 6 October 1997 asserted: 'I am convinced that the science of climate change is real. Although we do not know everything, what we do know is enough to warrant responsible action.' But he refrained from making any announcements on targets and timetables that would make Kyoto a serious beginning in combating the threats of climate change.

Profit, costs and 'dis-informercials'

The debate has seemed to be forever shifting and at times manipulated, be it by the scientific concerns and ecological imperatives or due to the uncertainty of the economics of action. The enormous ecological, economic, security, social and human costs of inaction had often been kept out of the calculations.

The oil and coal industries felt threatened that their profits would be reduced if northern countries were to reduce fossil fuel consumption. Ellen Goodman of the *Boston Globe* wrote in the *International Herald Tribune*:

> The same industry that told us that climate change was bunk is now shelling out $13 million in ads to convince the public that, even if it isn't bunk, it will cost us too much to deal with it.

Goodman compared the campaign by the coal and oil lobby to that of the tobacco industry and concluded:

> For a long time, doubts were fueled, if you will excuse the expression, to undermine public belief. But the public had learned something from its encounters with the tobacco folks. It is a bit of post-industrial skepticism about industry-financed science and corporate dis-informercials. So most of us have now signed on to the belief honed in the title of Ross Gelbspan's important book *The Heat is On*. (9 October 1997)

Developing countries are acting

One of the critical issues that stalled progress in the climate change negotiations prior to Kyoto was the perception that developing countries together will become the major contributor of GHG emission in the future, some time during the period between 2020 and 2050. 'So they must undertake some commitment', cried some of the obstructionists in the Kyoto negotiations, while most others demanded that those who committed themselves under UNFCCC and are mainly responsible (i.e. Annex 1 or industrialized countries) must commit themselves to significant GHG reduction first. 'Most developing countries are already taking significant voluntary steps to integrate climate change and GHG reduction', said the leader of a key developing country delegation recently. 'Such a call [for developing countries to undertake commitment] at this point is a deviation tactic. It is also a violation of both the UNFCCC and the COP-1 outcome, i.e. AGBM. This is not helpful at all.' The fear of job losses is not an issue, as many new jobs will be created from opportunities arising from a decarbonized economy. For example, the workforce had been doubled in Solarex, a solar-energy-related company in Maryland, USA.

Two recent initiatives testified to the fact that most developing countries were in fact undertaking actions which show their serious commitment towards reducing GHGs and thus to the objectives of the convention.

The first initiative was by World Resources Institute, Walter Reid and José Goldenberg report: 'Are developing countries already doing as much as industrialized countries to slow climate change?' (*Climate Notes*, July 1997). The report stated that 'Developing countries are already effective participants in global efforts to reduce greenhouse gas emissions. Indeed, since the signing of the 1992 Framework Convention on Climate Change (FCCC) developing countries may have achieved greater carbon dioxide emission savings than industrialized countries.' They emphasized that 'Even without commitments to limit emissions, developing countries are already taking significant steps to rein in greenhouse gas emissions.' Exemplifying the case of China, the WRI study states that

> The most significant carbon savings over the past decade had occurred in China, which accounts for 12 per cent of total world energy-related CO_2 emissions, second only to the United States. Although annual carbon emissions grew by 228 MtC between 1980 and 1990, emissions would have been 155 MtC higher in 1990 without the energy efficiency gains achieved over this period. The World Bank estimated in 1996 that further efficiency gains in China have the potential of yielding savings of 1,000 to 1,700 million tonnes of coal equivalents per year by 2020, an amount greater than China's total energy consumption in 1990.

The study also illustrated that, 'Within the past six years, India, Mexico, South Africa, Saudi Arabia, and Brazil – all of which rank among the top 25 countries for industrial CO_2 emissions – also cut fossil fuel subsidies significantly. An additional 19.5 MtC in savings should result from fuel price reforms on petroleum products in China over this same time period.' The study concluded: 'Much of the growth in emissions in developing countries results from the provision of basic human needs for their growing populations, while that in industrialized countries contributes to growth in a standard of living that is already far above that of the average person worldwide.'

New North–South dialogue on good practices

In another major initiative, a consortium of environment/development organizations involved in global climate change research started a series of regional workshops in Africa, Latin America and Asia involving representatives from governments, the private sector, NGOs, and the research community from the North and South with a view to creating a 'New North–South Dialogue on Climate Change: good practices, technology innovation and new partnership: challenges and opportunities to implement climate change.' These organizations included the Bangladesh

Centre for Advanced Studies (BCAS, Dhaka, Bangladesh) and the Pacific Institute for Studies in Development, Environment, Security (Oakland, California), the Woods Hole Research Centre (WRC, Massachusetts), Environment and Development Africa (ENDA, Dakar, Senegal) and COPPE, the Graduate School of Engineering at the Federal University of Rio de Janeiro, Brazil.

They held a series of workshops in Africa (Dakar, 30 August–1 September 1997), Latin America (Rio de Janeiro, 3–5 October 1997) and an Asian Regional Workshop (Dhaka, 8–10 November 1997). In addition, they reported their early conclusions to the AGBM during its 8th Session in Bonn on 22 October, and looked forward to holding the final workshop in Kyoto during COP-3 on 3 December 1997.

Their effort was supported by ten other collaborating institutes from North and South, and by financial support from four northern countries and the European Union. The initiative based its report on some twelve country studies, which demonstrated a large number of existing good practices both supportive of their own development process and yet making a significant contribution to GHG reduction. The studies and the regional workshops demonstrated the opportunities and potential for technology cooperation in the area of combating climate change. It was clearly evident that most developing countries had initiated institutional measures to develop the capacity to address the issues at governmental, academic, NGO and community levels. There was significant interest from the private sector and they are waiting for appropriate profit signals in these efforts. Peoples and communities were themselves taking a large number of steps, whether in energy efficiency, use of improved cooking stoves, better and low-carbon housing, afforestation, reforestation, fuel switching, transport or cogeneration. This was happening in most developing countries, making a significant contribution to local environmental benefits and global carbon reduction.

Achieving the dual objectives of UNFCCC

It has to be emphasized that the UNFCCC has two clear objectives: (a) achieving sustainable development; and (b) reducing GHGs. Most developing countries are attempting to achieve sustainable development and in the process reduce GHG emission. The socio-economic realities may not permit them to prioritize GHG reduction as a prime motive force for development, but they are consciously contributing to the reduction of GHGs. A country like Bangladesh, which is one of the countries most vulnerable to global climate impact, including rising-sea-level-related inundation and enhanced drought has mobilized its government and non-government agencies in a nationwide tree plantation and reforestation campaign. Early calculations showed that due to this massive social forestry campaign, Bangladesh in 1995 and 1996 had become a net 'absorber' of CO_2 and not an emitter. India has initiated a massive programme on wind energy. India's 1992–97 Five-Year Plan also includes a National Energy Efficiency Programme, which has the potential to save 5,000 MW in the electricity sector and 16 million tonnes of oil in the petroleum sector over the plan period. Brazil's use of ethanol from sugarcane for the transport sector and its PROCEL programme were described at the recent Rio workshop. This programme will avoid the installation of 1,600 MW of new electricity generation at one quarter of the cost of generating the additional power.

From futility to action: don't 'cop out'

It is futile to take the planet hostage and not act in the best interest of all populations and future generations, in the false assertion that developing countries are not acting responsibly. In fact, they have been taking responsible actions in both the letter and the spirit of UNFCCC. There is a strong case for developing countries to work even harder in this direction, and for that the UNFCCC clearly allows for provision of 'new and additional funding'. Industrializing and developing countries must all act to save the planet from the threat of climate destabilization by GHG emission, but Annex 1 countries must first make their commitment to a significant reduction. 'Opting out' from commitment at COP-3 is not an option.

Northern Commitments: The Central Issue

The key concerns were highlighted in the post-Kyoto Protocol issue of *Clime Asia*, on which the following account draws.

The battle lines were drawn over the commitments to targets and timetables for reduction of greenhouse gases, in order that the planet can be saved from the threat of global climate change. The eighth session of the Adhoc Group on the Berlin Mandate (AGBM 8) held in Bonn in October 1997 witnessed the formal presentation by individual or groups of countries on reduction targets under the Quantified Emission Limitation Reduction Objectives (QELRO) of the United Nations Framework Convention on Climate Change (UNFCCC). This was the centrepiece of decision-making and negotiations on which the Third Conference of Parties (COP-3) will make or break. As was expected, the commitment to reduce greenhouse gases, the heat-trapping gases in the atmosphere responsible for global warming and climatic changes, varied widely between countries or groups of countries.

The Second Assessment Report of the Intergovernmental Panel on Climate Changes (IPCC) concluded that major reductions of GHG will be required to stabilize the atmosphere and protect it from the anthropogenic intervention that threatens ecosystems and food security and consequently the potential for sustainable development for all citizens of the planet. The Group of 77 and China, representing the developing world, demanded a 15 per cent reduction of greenhouse gases by the year 2010 from the 1990 level; with 7.5 per cent reduction by 2005 and subsequent further reduction beyond 2020.

Poor and fragile commitments

The United States, the largest emitter of GHGs, declared that they would commit themselves to achieve only stabilization at the 1990 level between 2008 and 2012 and to no reduction prior to Kyoto. Japan, the host country of COP-3, made the meagre commitment to a 5 per cent reduction, which when recalculated is in fact closer to a 2 per cent reduction.

Prior to Kyoto, the European Union (EU), representing fifteen countries, had committed itself to a 15 per cent reduction from the 1990 level by the year 2010. Of the Annex 1 countries which had agreed to undertake a commitment under UNFCCC. Only the EU put forward at AGBM 8 in Bonn in October 1997 a set of policies and measures and an analytical framework to demonstrate how they could achieve such a reduction. It is true that a set of supportive circumstances enabled the EU to undertake this collective commitment as a 'European Bubble'; nevertheless, the intricacies of intra-EU allocation had not been easy and the undertaking represents a significant achievement in international environmental politics and negotiation. But they made it clear that if other Annex 1 countries do not reach this level of commitment, they are not obliged to implement it on their own. This implied that the USA, Canada, Japan, Australia and New Zealand, along with other Annex 1 countries, must make the same commitment. Every country has its own internal pressures, vested interest groups and political reality. However, the growing scientific consensus represented by IPCC is that the climatic and ecological stability of the planet is dependent on every Annex 1 country acting now to effect a reduction that at least matches, and preferably exceeds, the EU commitment. Anything less than this will be equivalent to taking the planet hostage, to which no responsible government or state should be party. Failure to reach agreement would amount to risking a major conflict.

The current problem: deadlock to be unlocked

Negotiations on implementation of the UNFCCC reached deadlock in the months leading up to the Third Conference of the Parties (COP-3, Kyoto,

December 1997). The Rio spirit of cooperation, partnership and a shared commitment to protecting the global environment had dissipated, replaced to some extent by an atmosphere of confrontation, rife with countervailing accusations about who is responsible for global climate change.

In the five years following Rio, industrial countries failed to fulfil the promises of emissions reductions and financial support for technology transfer that they made at the Earth Summit. Many of these countries allege that developing countries are doing little or nothing to reduce the shared risks of global climate change. In this context, some industrial countries ignore the challenges of their own commitments and argue that, since emissions are growing most rapidly in developing countries, these Parties should now make commitments for future emissions reductions.

Developing countries counter that neither the UNFCCC nor the Berlin Mandate (agreed at COP-1, Berlin, March–April 1995) require reductions in their emissions. Indeed, they note that the Convention specifically recognizes that developing country emissions must increase as these Parties pursue essential programmes of national economic development. They argue that industrial countries have grown rich through profligacy with no regard for the global commons, and now wish to lock the world's poor into generations of future penury and economic servitude.

All the actors demanding action

The climate negotiations are essentially an intergovernmental process. Almost all the important member states of the UN are now Parties to the UNFCCC and offer the largest representation in any global environmental negotiation. Thus the climate negotiations are one of the most important steps towards formulating a strategy to save the planet from a threat that affects us all.

The non-governmental communities represented by scientists, environment and development NGOs, the private sector and the media are also playing their part. Despite a campaign of misinformation by a few, the corporate sector is seeing the emergence of a new set of industries such as renewable energy; the insurance industry and even some key oil companies are appreciative of the scientific developments. All agree on the need to act to achieve a world with low carbon emission and cleaner technologies. Above all, communities in many countries are taking significant steps to introduce good practices, and thereby contribute to the reduction of GHGs.

Voice of the vulnerable

Before COP-3 the Bangladesh Minister for Environment and Forestry addressed the Asian Regional Meeting of the 'North–South Dialog on

Climage Change' in Dhaka on 9 November 1997. She epitomized the voice of the vulnerable, stating:

> You are aware that climate change is one of the greatest challenges that humanity faces today. It also threatens the lives and livelihood of millions. This is also the most important environmental problem that we face here in Bangladesh. The global impacts of climate change on the environment and ecosystem will not spare any country, whether big or small. However, the greatest threat is to the small island states and highly populated countries. Bangladesh is one of the countries most likely to be severely affected by global climate change. According to the Second Assessment Report of the Inter-governmental Panel on Climate Change (IPCC, 1996) about 17.5 per cent of Bangladesh land-mass will be inundated due to the sea level rising by one metre. Besides this flooding, the incidence of flash floods, cyclones, tidal bores, excessive rainfall, drought and salinity is likely to increase. Studies in Bangladesh on global climate change show that intense cyclone and storm surges will increase over southern areas. Above all, these will have a devastating impact on our socio-economic system and the lives of the people.

A truly global problem

Urging a global solution, the Bangladeshi minister emphasized that the problem of global climate change is not that of any single country, as global climate change has no geographical boundary. Whatever may be the cause, the threat of change affects us all across the whole world. It is becoming clearer that the primary source of the problem is the industrialized countries; nevertheless, the main sufferers will be the poor countries. Every year, 80 per cent of the global emission of carbon dioxide is from the industrialized countries, in which only 20 per cent of the world's population lives. That is why industrialized countries must act first to solve this problem. Without a change in consumption patterns and luxury lifestyles, it will not be possible to overcome the threat of climate change. The threat will keep on growing as emissions increase. They must demonstrate their sincerity by implementing their commitments as enshrined in the Convention. At the same time, they must extend their hand of cooperation to the developing world to initiate different programmes for combating climate change.

The North must act now: call before Kyoto

The leader of the Bangladeshi delegation to COP-3 in Kyoto, the Bangladeshi environment minister, emphasized that

> the reality is that industrialized countries have not been able to reach the greenhouse gas reduction target required to combat climate change. Rather, in many countries emissions have increased. Industrialized countries have not increased their financial commitment towards developing countries for environmentally

> sound development either. On the other hand, they could not set appropriate targets and timetables to combat the threats of climate change. While the industrialized countries are primarily responsible for the problem, an agreement is yet to be reached between developed and developing countries to increase financial cooperation and transfer of appropriate and necessary technology for combating these threats. This is most urgent in the present-day context.

Addressing the international participants, the Minister said

> Despite the fact that Bangladesh makes an insignificant contribution to greenhouse gas emission, as a full participant in the global community we have given serious consideration to this problem. We have already evaluated our greenhouse gas inventory, which shows that we have one of the lowest per-capita emission values in the world. The study has shown that our vulnerability is one of the highest. To address this vulnerability and to undertake adaptation we need the support of the world community. Before that we need to determine a global target and timetable for greenhouse gas reduction. We also need to achieve a greater level of technology cooperation, and procure additional funding from the industrialized to the developing countries. Otherwise, the more we delay, the greater will become the vulnerability of the coastal areas of Bangladesh and the island states. Many of the areas of these countries may disappear into the ocean due to inundation. Many elements of civilization and communities would vanish. This is not acceptable to anyone.

Global Responsibility versus Narrow Economic Costing: Economic Action

The dual objectives of the Climate Convention are to achieve (a) sustainable development and (b) greenhouse gas reduction. These objectives must be mutually reinforcing whenever possible. That is the primary responsibility of the parties to the convention, under the framework of the principle of 'differentiated responsibility'. Recently efforts have been made to focus the debate on the costs of action and to persuade certain sectors and economic interests of some countries, particularly some of the major polluters among the Annex 1 parties. Often the costing has been too narrowly defined, and in the domain of economic modelling many subjective assumptions have been made. The same interest groups that use the uncertainty in the science of climate change as an excuse for inaction have been benefiting from the results of economic modelling. Economic modelling is fraught with greater uncertainties: in the pricing of commodities, the vagaries of international trade, and the possible trends in future technological development and diffusion. Different studies have shown that GHG reduction of more than 20 per cent was possible in industrialized countries, which would stimulate economic growth and employment, and bring many other social and environmental benefits. Many who wanted to use these results to delay action failed to take into consideration the enormous potential cost of inaction. Economic efficiency and a least-cost approach are essential for sound global and national environmental planning. A failure to carry out costings will not only delay action, but in the long run produce greater cost and defeat the twin objectives of the Convention. Thus the citing of cost in order to delay action for reasons of narrow self-interest would also be tantamount to taking the planet hostage. Such a tactic would see the further increase of greenhouse gases in the atmosphere and intensify the threat of global climate change. The time to act is now.

Joint implementation must not become carbon transfer

Soon after signing the Climate Convention, the Annex 1 countries decided that they were not serious about 'new and additional funding' to developing countries for achieving the objectives of climate mitigation, adaptation, technology transfer and progressing towards sustainable development.

Joint implementation, a mechanism of financial transfer primarily through the private sector to pay for the additional costs of climate-related activities, was put forward as a mechanism of financial transfer against carbon credits. This was not welcomed by developing countries and consequently did not progress very far. A variation 'without credit' was agreed at COP-1 in Berlin as the 'grand compromise', wherein Activities Implemented Jointly (AIJ) will be undertaken during a five-year pilot phase.

The private-sector joint-implementation dollars never materialized

These activities did not meet the expectations of their proponents either. The private sector, moved predominantly by the profit motive, did not come up with the 'billions of dollars' expected of it. The AIJ/JI modality became one of the most controversial and emotive concepts in climate change. A number of problems – including conceptual, accounting, baseline related, methodological, ownership, sovereignty issues, availability of finance, institutional capacity building in host and investor countries, the legal position of private-sector investment vis-à-vis parties that are nation-states – thwarted the advance of the AIJ/JI mechanism.

Despite all the problems, AIJ/JI made some progress with a few projects. But the basic need of COP-3 was to reduce GHG, not just transfer the source of gases from rich to poor countries. Further, AIJ/JI should not become an excuse for inaction at home. Only a very small amount of GHG could be considered under such a modality while the principal reduction must be made at home by Annex 1 countries. Carbon transfer was not a solution to climate change.

The North–South Dialogue and its four regional workshops concluded that technology, considered in the right perspective and when supportive of low emission and sustainable development, offered a major means to address the challenge of climate change. The North must develop both low-energy and low-carbon pathways and reduce carbon intensity. A study presented in the workshops shows that Latin America could achieve an increase in GDP that would match that of the USA, with only one-third of the carbon emission.

From technology cooperation to technology empowerment

The countries of the South that need to develop further must use low carbon and lower energy pathways. Low emission and emerging technologies can offer these opportunities. But it is technological cooperation that could lead to technological empowerment in the South that offers the best opportunity for achieving GHG reductions and sustainable development alike.

The challenge to all concerned and particularly to the COP-3 negotiators is: how do you maintain and improve the quality of life for citizens globally, where at least everyone's basic needs are met adequately, without increasing the carbon content in the atmosphere? For now, the objective must be for the present generation to assist in reducing the concentration of CO_2 in the atmosphere, to help achieve the eradication of poverty and improve the quality of life for today's citizens and tomorrow's generation.

Transition to sustainability

The above challenge can be met within the financial and technological resources of the planet today. The lesson from the new North–South dialogue is that this is possible. Technology backed by adequate financial transfer offers such an opportunity.

It is futile to take the planet hostage based on narrow self-interest. The imperative is to act now and avert a global climate disaster for future generations and the ecosystems in which they will live. The resources and technology at our disposal, if mobilized wisely, can begin to assist in the transition to sustainability. We need a social mobilization process based on a paradigm of a civilization based on low energy, low carbon and high quality technologies. The new North–South dialogue has indicated that this is within the realm of possibility. The negotiators at COP-3 should seize the opportunity for change, and begin the transition to sustainability; that is what the citizens of the world expect from them.

The outcome of Kyoto: the Protocol

The above discussion preceded the Kyoto Summit. The Kyoto Protocol came out with a legally binding document specifying for the first time a quantitative commitment for industrialized (Annex 1) countries to reduce greenhouse gas emission. The insistence on a degree of voluntary commitment from developing countries was dropped from the wording of the final Kyoto Protocol. Instead the Climate Development Mechanism and some trading on carbon emissions were proposed. The details of these are yet to be resolved. The Kyoto Protocol initiated the process of Annex 1 commitment, though this is insufficient to meet the requirement of scientific findings. Its implementation will determine whether the planet will begin the process of carbon reduction. Unless serious reduction is demonstrated, developing countries are unlikely even to consider any commitment on their part. This would open the way to confrontation and conflict.

The potential for conflict

Early conflict arose from the concept of 'responsibility': the emission of greenhouse gases and commitment to their reduction. Responsibility for anthropogenic greenhouse gas emission in the post-industrial period up to the present has been accepted by the industrialized countries by virtue of their agreement to be Annex 1 countries under the Climate Convention (UNFCCC), but this did not imply any liability. Indeed, the concept of 'liability' was kept out of the Convention. The Convention also accepted the dual objective of enabling sustainable development and reduction of greenhouse gases. Nevertheless, the Annex 1 parties have done everything to delay action to reduce GHGs. It was only under the Kyoto Protocol that the first agreement to an overall reduction in the emission of GHGs, with some Annex 1 countries' emissions excepted, was agreed. This has yet to begin the long journey to implementation. The second area of contention has been over the 'uncertainty' in the science and the cost of action. In this process the cost of inaction has hardly been addressed.

The knowledge domain and capacity

The Intergovernmental Panel on Climate Change (IPCC) has produced two highly laudable and credible assessments of the science of climate change in its First and Second Assessment Reports and is engaged in work towards the Third Assessment Report. Given the nature of the task of assimilating scientific knowledge, the IPCC was only able to access peer-reviewed published literature. Many scientists and activists believe that action on climate change will have to be undertaken by societies in both industrialized and developing countries. A great deal of knowledge resides with traditional and rapidly changing communities and peoples, who can hardly afford the luxury of publishing in peer-reviewed literature. Furthermore, the social science issues at stake have been addressed in only a very limited way. Thus there has been a call for the incorporation of traditional knowledge, community practices and initiatives to strengthen the IPCC. However, the nature and terms of reference of the IPCC do not permit that. Hence its findings may be biased towards the Northern published literature and sources of information; this may be detrimental to the interests of the South, which is likely to be disproportionately affected by climate change.

The other conceptual and practical issue is the capacity of southern governments, NGOs, and even the private sector to participate effectively in the process. A lack of information, human resources, finance and institutional mechanisms has prevented developing countries from becoming equal partners in these negotiations. Furthermore, the reality of addressing other more pressing and urgent issues of poverty, public health and nutrition, demographic pressure, the need for education and infrastructure, as well as coping with natural hazards and conflicts, has preoccupied policy-makers; for them climate change is likely to seem a much more distant threat than day-to-day crises. Despite the fact that the sustainability of many of today's efforts may be severely compromised by the impact of climate change on their ecosystem and economic productivity, many governments lack the capacity to address climate change concerns.

Threatened sovereignty

The concern of nation-states on the issue of sovereignty over their territory is another emerging issue. Many low-lying island states such as Maldives and Kiribati could be obliterated by the impact of a one- or two-metre rise in the sea level. A rise in the sea level is one of the more certain and imminent consequences of climate change. It could give rise to conflicts in a number of ways. Political consequences attach to the loss of sovereignty by small island states facing inundation and obliteration. Similarly, vulnerable coastal areas will be inundated, thus challenging sovereignty over that part of national territory and involving the displacement of people.

The United Nations Charter, the preamble of which begins 'We the people', has become a discussion body where the people and nations have been replaced by 'we the governments'. The main purpose of the UN has become the protection of the sovereignty of its member states, represented by their respective governments. Yet global climate change challenges the very existence of land-based nation-states, and consequently of their governments. 'If my country and all my islands are inundated, who is going to protect my sovereignty', asked a head of government of a threatened small island state. This is an area of potential major conflict and violence in the future.

Environmental refugees

Inundation as a result of rising sea level could displace millions of people, who would have to migrate, hence becoming environmental refugees. For example, studies have shown that over 15 million people in today's population would be displaced from the coastal area of Bangladesh alone in the event of a one-metre rise in sea level. These potential environmental refugees probably present the greatest challenge in terms of conflict and violence. Countries with excess land may be able to accommodate this displaced population in other areas, despite a degree of conflict. However, countries such as Bangladesh or city states that have a high-density population will be faced with out-of-country migration that will carry severe political and human costs and attendant conflict. Social and ecological adaptation may serve to reduce the extent of the potential tension and conflict; nevertheless, residual problems will have to be faced by the society and the governments.

There is a second aspect to this. The Netherlands' coasts, to take an obvious example, are also vulnerable to a rise in sea level. For their part, the government and social structures of the Netherlands have the financial, institutional, managerial and social capacity to build and manage infrastructural barriers against sea-level rise. In comparison, the ecology of the Bangladesh coast and many coastal islands will not permit such infrastructure, and above all the country will not have the financial and other resources to tackle the issue. This raises the fundamental question of increasing inequity, which in its turn threatens sustainability – a key objective of the Climate Convention.

The threat to food security

Another decisive and threatening impact of global climate change will be the shift in agro-ecological zones, and the consequent reduction in food productivity and the threat to food security. The emerging literature is increasingly addressing this question. There is likely to be a reduction in food yield area, due to inundation by the sea, and a change in appropriate optimal growing conditions for the various crops – cereals, rice, wheat, maize, soya, and so forth. Crop yield is likely to be affected by temperature change, increase in carbon dioxide (CO_2 fertilization) and shifting precipitation. The prediction is that the impact will be mostly negative, with the potential for positive yield in crops in some places. The changing cropping patterns would have to be adjusted by adaptability on the part of farmers and their support institutions. The key question is: can these social organizations adapt to the rapidity of change in temperature, precipitation and CO_2 concentration?

Lester Brown of World Watch Institute, in his recent book *Tough Choices: Facing the Challenge of Food Scarcity*, has indicated that food scarcity is emerging as the defining issue of the new era that is now unfolding, much as ideological conflict was the defining issue of the historical era that has recently ended. More fundamentally, food scarcity may be the first major economic manifestation of an environmentally unsustainable global economy.

> An early hint of the shift to an economy of scarcity came in late April 1996, when wheat prices on the Chicago Board of Trade soared above $7 a bushel, the highest level in history and more than double the price a year earlier. Corn prices also doubled, moving above $5 a bushel, a new record. And the price of rice, the other major grain, was climbing. Densely populated countries, such as China, India, and Indonesia, will have to decide whether to use land for automobile-centered transportation systems or to satisfy food needs. In a world where the need for seafood and grain for the 90 million people being added each year is being satisfied in part by reducing consumption among those already here, the world has little choice but to try and quickly slow population growth. Historically, farmers and fishermen bore the primary responsibility for balancing supply and demand. Now with the fish catch no longer expanding and with the growth in grain production slowing, the principal responsibility rests with the family planners.

Thus the threat to food security as a consequence of global climate change is a likely area of serious conflict, from the net reduction of crops to the distribution of them in different geographical areas. It is not the increase of population pressure but the per capita consumption that remains the central issue in climate change. Nevertheless, the threat to food security is a real one.

An increased number of extreme weather events

Global climate change is expected to alter precipitation regimes, with a consequent impact on extreme events such as floods, cyclones and tidal surges. A cyclone in April 1991 devastated the coastal area of Bangladesh, causing the deaths of over 130,000 people, as well as the destruction of infrastructure and the ecosystem. A similar cyclone in 1991 devastated the coastal area in Florida, USA; deaths were few, but the infrastructure and consequently the insurance industry were devastated.

One implication of the increasing greenhouse effect is an intensification of extreme weather events.

The impact of these extreme weather events on society depends on the intensity of the event and the capacity of the social and ecological system to cope and adjust. Thus, as scientific understanding increases, it may be possible to discern to what extent the impact is due to factors influenced by climate change. Besides the human misery, economic and ecological dislocation and devastation caused, countries and societies may demand compensation. This will raise the question of identifying responsibility, and open up the possibility that victims of global climate change will seek recompense from the perpetrators. These considerations are another potential source of disputes, which in turn could lead to conflict and possibly violence.

Who emits – and how much?

One area of conflict that is already visible is the question of the responsibility for emitting greenhouse gases in the past, today and in the future. Several northern countries claim that key and large developing countries such as China, India and Brazil will be the major emitters in the near future. Hence they assert that the developing countries must take mitigation measures and make some commitment immediately to reduce greenhouse gas emission. The latter group of countries respond that, although their total emission may become larger to meet the needs of their increased development, their per capita emission will remain very low compared to UNFCCC Annex 1 countries. What is more, the Annex 1 countries that have made the commitment in UNFCCC to reduce their emissions have not yet done so; indeed GHG emissions have increased since the Rio Climate Convention. In addition, Annex 1 countries promised to provide 'new and additional' funding, which has not yet materialized. These vexed questions may give rise to more intensive debate, and to consequent conflict.

Impacts, Conflict and Violence

In conclusion, the UNFCCC has been a way forward in identifying the concerns and establishing a framework for future negotiations to combat the threat of climate change. The Kyoto Protocol, for its part, is a broad-based statement of intent to implement certain measures of a limited kind. A lot of human effort has gone into the process so far. It appears that of all the instruments coming out of the Rio process, the Climate Convention has made the greatest progress. Yet the global challenge of confronting the detrimental impacts of global climate change on societies and countries, ecosystems and infrastructures, food security and economic productivity, choice of technology, technology transfer and empowerment, requires that the efforts be consolidated, strengthened and reinforced at a rate faster than the nation-states have demonstrated so far. It is a race between the rate of global climate change and the speed with which the social, economic, ecological and institutional systems can react to offset the negative impacts. If efforts to combat climate change are insufficient, the consequence would be a series of major conflicts that may initially follow the traditional North–South pattern, but that may soon give way to uncharted territory – new forms of alignment, confrontation, conflict and violence.

From quiet to vocal violence

A form of quiet violence in the form of massive poverty, malnutrition and environmental degradation is already being faced by a third of the global population. Global climate change and its impact are likely to place additional pressure on already severely stressed societies and ecosystems. Thus global climate change may transform this quiet violence into a situation which an increasingly globalized and interconnected society may not be willing to tolerate. This may unleash a type of violence that will challenge the capacities of weak nation-states. It is thus necessary, in the interest of all, North and South, to address this global threat as responsible global citizens who appreciate the urgency that the emerging science of climate change is indicating.

Bibliography

Agarwal, A. and S. Narain, 1992, *Global Warming in an Unequal World: A Case of Environmental Colonialism*, Centre for Science and Environment, New Delhi.

Banuri, T., K. Goran-Maler, M. Grubb, H.K. Jacobson and F. Yamin, 1996, 'Equity and Social Considerations', in J. Bruce, L. Hoesung and E. Haites (eds), *Climate Change 1995: Economic and Social Dimensions of Climate Change; Contribution of Working Group III to the Second Assessment Report of the IPCC*, Cambridge University Press, Cambridge, pp. 79–124.

BCAS/RA/Approtech, 1994, *Vulnerability of Bangladesh to Climate Change and Sea Level Rise: Concepts and Tools for Calculating Risk in Integrated Coastal Zone Management*, Resource Analysis and Approtech Consultants Limited, Bangladesh Centre for Advanced Studies, 1994.

Brown, L., 1996, *Tough Choices: Facing the Challenge of Food Security*, World Watch Institute, Washington DC.

Brundtland, G.H. et al., 1987, *Our Common Future*, Report of the World Commission on Environment and Development, Oxford University Press, Oxford.

Clime Asia, 1997a, 'Global Experts Call for Actions', *Clime Asia*, AGBM-8 Issue, July–September, Bangladesh Centre for Advanced Studies, Dhaka.

Clime Asia, 1997b, 'Don't Take the Planet Hostage: Make COP-3 An Opportunity for Change', *Clime Asia*, COP-3 Special Issue, October–December, Bangladesh Centre for Advanced Studies, Dhaka.

Comean, L., 1995, 'Don't Trade Technology Transfer for JI', *ECO* (Berlin), vol. 89, no. 2, March.

Delft Hydraulics, 1992, *Sea Level Rise: A Global Vulnerability Assessment*, Ministry of Transport, Public Works and Water Management, The Hague.

Downing, T.E. (ed.), 1996, *Climate Change and World Food Security*, NATO AI Series, vol. 1, no. 37, Springer Verlag, Berlin and Heidelberg.

Government of India, 1992, *Eighth Five Year Plan, 1992–97*, Vols I and II, Planning Commission, New Delhi.

Haider, R., A. Rahman and S. Huq (eds), 1991, *Cyclone '91: An Environmental and Perceptional Study*, Bangladesh Centre for Advanced Studies, Dhaka.

Haider, R. (ed.), 1992, *Cyclone '91 Revisited*, Bangladesh Centre for Advanced Studies, Dhaka.

Houghton, J.T., G.J. Jenkins and J.J. Ephroums (eds), 1990, *Climate Change: The IPCC Scientific Assessment*, Cambridge University Press, Cambridge.

Houghton, J.T., L.G. Meira Filho, B.A. Callander, N. Harris, A. Kattenberg and K. Maskell (eds), 1996, *Climate Change 1995: The Science of Climate Changes*, Cambridge University Press, Cambridge.

Huq, S., A.U. Ahmed and R. Koudstaal, 1996, 'Vulnerability of Bangladesh to Climate Change and Sea Level Rise', in T.E. Downing (ed.), *Climate Change and World Food Security*, NATO ASI series, vol. 1, no. 37, Springer Verlag, Berlin and Heidelberg, pp. 347–79.

Hyder, T.O., 1992, 'Climate Negotiations: The North/South Perspective', in I.M. Mintzer (ed.), *Confronting Climate Change: Risks, Implications and Responses*, Cambridge University Press, Cambridge, pp. 323–36.

Lunde, L., 1990, *The North/South Dimension in Global Greenhouse Politics – Conflicts, Dilemmas, Solutions*, Report 1990/9, Fridtjof Nansen Institute, Kysaker.

Maya, S. and J. Gupta (eds), 1996, *Joint Implementation: Carbon Colonies or Business Opportunities? Weighing the Odds in an Information Vacuum*, Southern Centre for Energy and Environment, Harare.

Mintzer, I.M. (ed.), 1992, *Confronting Climate Change: Risks, Implications and Responses*, Cambridge University Press, Cambridge.

Ong'wen, O., 1994, 'Poverty and Climate Change: Putting the Record Straight', *Impact*, nos 13/14, 2–8 September.

Pachauri, R.K. and M. Damodaran, 1992, '"Wait and See" versus "No Regrets": Comparing the Costs of Economic Strategies', in I.M. Mintzer (ed.), *Confronting Climate Change: Risks, Implications and Responses*, Cambridge University Press, Cambridge, pp. 237–51.

Parikh, J., 1992, 'IPCC Strategies Unfair to the South', *Nature*, vol. 360, 10 December, pp. 507–8.

Parikh, J., K. Parikh et al., 1991, *Consumption Patterns: The Driving Force of Environmental Stress*, Research Paper No. 3, Indira Gandhi Institute of Development Research, Bombay.

Parry, M.L., 1990, *Climate Change and World Agriculture*, Earthscan, London.

Parry, M.L. and M.S. Swaminathan, 1992, 'Effects of Climate Change on Food Production', in I.M. Mintzer (ed.), *Confronting Climate Change: Risks, Implications and Responses*, Cambridge University Press, Cambridge.

Preston, L.T., 1992, *Reducing Poverty and Protecting Development: A Call to Action*, United Nations Conference on Environment and Development, Geneva.

Rahman, A. (ed.), 1998, *Environment and Poverty: The Key Linkage in Sustainable Development*, University Press Limited, Dhaka.

Rahman, A., I. Mintzer, A. Leonard and K. Ramakrishna, 1997, *A New Initiative for North–South Dialogue on Climate Change: Good Practices, Technology Innovation and New Partnership for Sustainable Development*, Bangladesh Centre for Advanced Studies, Dhaka.

Rahman, A., N. Robins and A. Roncerel, 1998, *Exploding the Population Myth: Consumption vs. Population*, University Press Limited, Dhaka.

Rahman, A. and A. Roncerel, 1994, 'A View from the Ground Up', in I.M. Mintzer and J.A. Leonard (eds), *Negotiating Climate Change: The Inside Story of the Rio Convention*, Cambridge University Press, Cambridge, pp. 239–77.

Reid, W. and J. Goldenberg, 1997, 'Are Developing Countries Already Doing as Much as Industrialized Countries to Slow Climate Change?', *Climate Notes*, July, World Resources Institute.

Shiva, V., 1992, *Why GEF is an Inadequate Institution for UNCED*, Earth Summit Briefings No. 19, Third World Network, Penang.

United Nations, 1977, *Kyoto Protocol To the United Nations Framework Convention On Climate Change*, FCCC/CP/1997/L.7/Add.1, United Nations, 10 December.

United Nations, 1992a, *Non-Legally Binding Authoritative Statement of Principles for a Global Consensus on the Management, Conservation and Sustainable Development of All Types of Forest*, UNCED, June.

United Nations, 1992b, *Rio Declaration and Agenda 21*, Report on the UN Conference on Environment and Development, Rio de Janeiro, 3–14 June, UN doc. A/CONF.151/26/Rev.1 (Vols. I–III).

United Nations, 1992c, *United Nations Conference on Environment and Development*, Document Number A/Conference WI/L.b, June.

United Nations, 1992d, *United Nations Convention on Biological Diversity*, United Nations, Rio de Janeiro, 5 June.

United Nations, 1992e, *United Nations Framework Convention on Climate Change*, United Nations, New York, 9 May.

Warrick, R.A. and A.A. Rahman, 1992, 'Future Sea Level Rise: Environmental and Socio-political Considerations', in I.M. Mintzer (ed.), *Confronting Climate Change: Risks, Implications and Responses*, Cambridge University Press, Cambridge, pp. 97–112.

Watson, R.T., M.C. Zinyowera, R.H. Moss and D.J. Dokken, 1996, *Climate Change 1995: Impacts, Adaptations and Mitigation of Climate Change: Scientific–Technical Analyses*, Cambridge University Press, Cambridge.

10

Mining, Environmental Degradation and War: The Bougainville Case

Völker Böge

Bougainville is an island in the South Pacific, with an area of 8,800 square kilometres and approximately 180,000 inhabitants. Geographically it is the biggest island of the Solomon Islands archipelago. Politically, however, it belongs to the state of Papua New Guinea (PNG), because in colonial times it was always governed together with mainland New Guinea, first under German, then under Australian rule (since 1914). When PNG became independent in 1975, Bougainville became its so-called North Solomons Province (NSP), together with some minor islands.

Bougainville is covered with inaccessible mountain ranges and tropical rainforest; so its inhabitants live a remote life based upon subsistence agriculture and hunting and gathering. The traditional society was widely egalitarian, clan-relations structuring the social life in small villages with descent being an important principle governing access to land. Widespread matrilineal descent provided an important role for women in the social life of the clans, and gender relations tended toward complementarity rather than hierarchy. Contact with the colonial world was only sporadic in the beginning, with people living on the east coast having some contact with tradesmen, administrative officers, missionaries and planters. Since the beginning of the twentieth century, in the coastal regions there existed some major copra and (later) cocoa plantations, producing for export purposes (Wesley-Smith and Ogan 1992).

It was only in the Second World War that the modern world massively disturbed the life of the people on Bougainville, the island becoming a battleground for Japanese and allied forces. People were forced to abandon their villages and gardens, and many inhabitants were killed. During the war no part of PNG suffered more than Bougainville (Wesley-Smith and Ogan 1992); after the war the Australian administration was not very committed to the reconstruction and development of the island, as Bougainville was the district most distant from the administrative centre in Port Moresby.

However, things on the island began to change dramatically in the 1960s. In 1964, Conzinc Riotinto of Australia (CRA), one of the world's largest mining companies, began exploration on Bougainville in search of copper. This was successful, and in 1967 Bougainville Copper Limited (BCL) was established with CRA being the majority shareholder (53.6 per cent, the PNG central government holding 19 per cent). Development of the Bougainville Panguna mine in the Crown Prince Range southwest of the town of Kieta began in 1969, and in 1972 production started (Howard 1991). BCL was granted leases for mining, tailings disposal, building roads, town and port facilities, the leases affecting a significant proportion of the provincial population. Panguna mine was a very large mine by world standards in terms of both production and size, ranking among the ten biggest copper mines in the world at that time. For BCL, and that means for CRA also, Panguna was an extraordinary success story; profits deriving from it were enormous, making it CRA's most profitable single venture in the 1970s and BCL the most successful company in Australian corporate history up to that time (Moody 1991).

But, on the other hand, mining caused enormous environmental degradation. In the mining process a crater of 7 km^2 by 500 metres deep was dug, and referred to as 'the second biggest hole in the world'. Tailings disposal covering vast areas contributed severely to the loss of land, and mining operations replaced agricultural land on a large scale. As early as 1974 a study regarding the disposal of mining waste on Bougainville stated: 'The most serious source of environmental pollution concerns the disposal of about 150,000 tonnes of rock waste and tailings a day from the mine area' (Brown 1974). Between 1973 and 1983, 768 million tonnes of ore and waste were processed, rich in copper and iron pyrites. Of the 373 million tonnes of processed ore, just under seven million were exported as concentrate, and the remainder deposited in the valley of the Jaba river, the tailings lease area (some 10,000 hectares). Loss of land meant also loss of sources of, for example, drinking water and timber. Disposal of tailings blocked tributary systems, causing erosion, flooding and loss of fish. Fish stocks became substantially depleted due to river pollution by sediment from the mining process as the sediment loads in rivers became very high. The aforementioned study of 1974 stated: 'In addition to the vastly increased sediment load of the Kawerong–Jaba river system, the disposal of tailings has resulted in chemical pollution, particularly by heavy metals such as zinc, copper, cadmium, mercury and molybdenum' (Brown 1974), the washes also being high in sulphur and arsenic.

As a consequence, 'the sediment-choked Kawerong–Jaba rivers [had] no more fish living in them. Also, the fish are dying in the fresh tributaries of the Jaba, principally the Pagana and upper Jaba rivers, because they cannot migrate to the sea to spawn' (Brown 1974). The entire 480 km^2 tributary system became essentially devoid of fish. River water could no longer be used by villagers. The depletion and pollution of the bush reduced traditional hunting and gathering activities. Wild pig and possum populations declined drastically, and the flying fox population disappeared totally in 1987. In villages close to the mine, air pollution became a problem. Dust contaminated drinking water. Chemical pollution caused by the mine also had a negative impact on fishing on the west coast of Bougainville. Dumping of chemicals into the sea severely disrupted fish stocks, which were a very important source of protein for people living on the coast. In addition malaria increased because of the swampy conditions that developed in some areas as a result of tailings disposal (Connell in Polomka 1990; Connell and Howitt 1991). To summarize:

> Copper mining on Bougainville has resulted in serious pollution of the tropical environment. Rivers have become choked with sediments, large areas of rainforest have been destroyed, fish have been killed, and the rivers and seas are being contaminated with heavy metals. The spread of tailings has threatened several villages, deprived the people of both agricultural land and areas of rainforest traditionally important for hunting and building materials, and the people have lost access to fish in the rivers. (Brown 1974)

At the end of the 1980s, there existed the imminent danger that additional areas of the island would be destroyed in the future. For BCL was pressing to lift a moratorium on further exploration, the intention being to exploit new copper deposits; the central government in Port Moresby had no principal objections (Wesley-Smith 1990).

Reasons for the Environmental Devastation

Open-pit mining is always environmentally damaging, and this is especially true in a highly sensitive environment such as tropical rainforest, which covers much of Bougainville. This was particularly the case in this instance, as no environmental impact studies were conducted before mining started, and BCL initially provided hardly any environmental safety measures, since there were no such corresponding laws in the territory at the time mining began.

While three pieces of legislation did incorporate some environmental regulations, they were completely inadequate (an agreement of 1967 obliged BCL to revegetate tailings piles and overburden; an agreement of 1971 was intended to compel BCL to minimize copper pollution and expedite land restoration [but it lapsed in 1980]; and the 1974 agreement empowered the government to collect environmental data from the company, but did not say what type of data). There might as well have been no legal attempts at all to limit environmental damage (Moody 1991).

Conditions for BCL to follow such a course in ignoring the environmentally detrimental effects of its mining operations were good because the Australian administration and, after independence, the PNG government showed no interest in imposing environmental standards on BCL. In addition the people directly affected on Bougainville did not have the knowledge and power to do so themselves. The continually growing volume of tailings and the increasing size of the hole at the mine site were both far beyond anything local residents had possibly imagined at the start. For them it was only over the years that 'the absolute loss of land and the physical and chemical impacts of mining on the environment became the most important issues as the sheer size of the hole and the volume of the tailings became more and more apparent' (Connell and Howitt 1991). Concern began to grow among Bougainvilleans that at the end of the mine's life Bougainville would be a lifeless island, with an enormous hole at it's centre, and its surrounding areas of land and the adjacent sea depleted of wildlife and fish and therefore useless to human beings (Connell, in Polomka 1990).

What was destruction for the people on Bougainville was meant to bring 'development' to the new state of PNG as a whole, for the country's central government based its strategy for development heavily on the mining sector. PNG is a poor developing country, rich in natural resources, especially the minerals copper and gold. PNG's development philosophy (as with similar developing countries) focuses heavily on the export of those minerals as a means of gaining resources for the development of the country. This world-market-oriented development approach is firmly supported by the International Monetary Fund and the World Bank, and since independence in 1975 the key role played by large mining projects has been explicitly stated in the government's planning and budget documents and in policy statements: that these projects should raise capital which can be used to achieve desirable development aims (Seib 1994).

The economic importance of the Panguna mine to the central government in the past cannot be overestimated in this context. Since 1972, BCL has contributed about 16 per cent of PNG's internally generated income and 44 per cent of its exports (Connell, in Polomka 1990).

'Between 1972 and 1985 BCL had a gross surplus of K980 million, out of which K466 million was paid in taxes (excluding the income tax paid by its employees and import duties), and the PNG government additionally received dividends through its 20 per cent equity holding' (Jackson, in Connell and Howitt 1991). Thus 62 per cent of BCL gross revenue went to the central government. Foreign shareholders received approximately 33 per cent; only 4 per cent went to the NSP provincial government; and 1 per cent to local landowners (1972–89) (Quodling 1992). This means that the distribution of revenues was highly unbalanced. Landowners developed a strong view that an insufficient proportion of the profits went to them, and that the total amount of compensation (K17 million from 1969 to 1988) was very small in relation to the wealth produced by the mine and the revenue gained by BCL and the central government (Connell, in Connell and Howitt 1991). This was emphasized by the relative deprivation experienced by villagers close to the mine site. Finally, there was a growing recognition of the enormity of the hole and the tailings; where once there had been assumptions that only some land would be used, and that after the mine and lease ended the land would revert to its traditional owners, it now became clear that the land had been destroyed and could never be of any economic or social use again (Connell, in Connell and Howitt 1991).

The significant reduction of land available for agricultural production and the declining yield were perceived as serious threats to the very survival of the people's traditional way of life, which is closely connected to the land. The importance of land for Melanesian social structures cannot be overestimated. Land provides livelihood and the most reliable security for the clan. Land is communally owned by the clan, either on a matrilineal (as in the case of major parts of Bougainville) or patrilineal basis. No concept of individual ownership exists, nor of land as a commodity. Land belongs to the whole group, and the villagers' rights are those of users only (Polomka 1990). The overwhelming importance of land was well expressed by some Bougainvilleans in 1974:

> Land is our life. Land is our physical life-food and sustenance. Land is our social life; it is marriage; it is status; it is security; it is politics; in fact, it is our only world. When you [the Administration] take our land, you cut away the very heart of our existence. We have little or no experience of social survival detached from the land. For us to be completely landless is a nightmare which no dollar in the pocket or dollar in the bank will allay; we are a threatened people' (Dove et al., quoted from Connell, in Connell and Howitt 1991).

On Bougainville, local people were alienated from their land due to mining. There were several village relocations from the mine site and from tailings-affected areas. For resettled villagers the land situation became critical since the amount of land available shrank to a small proportion of the land area before resettlement. Moreover, some of the resettled villagers had to live in very poor conditions: rotten housing, overcrowding and so on (Connell, in Polomka 1990).

Further important aspects of the disruption of the land-related social order of traditional life on Bougainville were the population growth and urbanization that came along with the mine. The population of Bougainville rose from 80,000 in 1970 to 130,000 in 1980 and approximately 180,000 in 1988. The annual population growth rate in mine-affected areas was higher than 3 per cent. Urbanization followed mining development, too. The mine generated two completely new towns, Arawa and Panguna, with populations of 15,000 and 3,500 respectively. The majority of the overall urban population were young male foreign mine workers. The proportion of indigenous Bougainvilleans in the towns remained low, not more than one-third of the total. That means that the towns were characterized by male migration from outside, so that they were far from being balanced communities in sex or age structure (Connell, in Polomka 1990). This was due to the fact that BCL mostly employed labourers from mainland PNG, so that there was a massive influx of foreign manpower (the top direct employment at the mine site numbering 4,300 workers, out of which only 30 per cent were Bougainvilleans [1980]); during the construction phase in the early 1970s there came some 10,000 construction workers from abroad onto the island; and the overall management of the mine remained expatriate (Australian) over the whole time (Wesley-Smith and Ogan 1992; Howard 1991). This in turn obviously led to an upsurge of law and order problems: rape, assault, rascalism, prostitution, alcohol abuse and traffic accidents, formerly almost unknown to Bougainville, began to spread throughout the island. Indigenous Bougainvilleans blamed the rise in crime on the establishment of the mine and the subsequent increase in the number of single young men from abroad (Connell, in Polomka 1990).

The problem became even more serious because there was also an inherent ethnic dimension to it. One of PNG's main problems as a state is the diversity of its people. PNG has more than seven hundred language groups and significant ethnic divisions. The indigenous population of Bougainville in particular is ethnically different from that of the remaining PNG. Bougainvilleans are black-skinned people, similar to those of the western islands of the neighbouring Solomon Islands, with whom they share some cultural characteristics and with whose people there exist direct family ties. Many Bougainvilleans felt strangers to the rest of the people of PNG, referring to Papuans from mainland PNG as 'redskins', whereas people from mainland PNG, on the other hand, often show great dislike of the 'blackskin' Bougainvilleans (Havini, in Polomka 1990; Lawson 1992). (On the other hand, one has also to take into consideration that the people of Bougainville are not ethnically homogenous either; there exist nineteen different linguistic groups on the island). These ethnic differences contributed to friction between the indigenous island population and migrants from mainland PNG attracted by the Panguna mine. All the more so as the migrant workers benefited from the mine, whereas indigenous landowners had to suffer from environmental damage caused by mining operations.

To summarize the social effects of mining and its environmental implications, it can be said that the whole traditional way of life of indigenous rural Bougainvilleans based upon traditional values and subsistence economy (and to a certain extent also based upon smallholder cash-crop production already [cocoa, copra], which had been carried out very successfully before mining commenced) came under severe pressure. It is true that some social changes were perceived as being positive: expansion of the education system and health services; construction of roads, providing villagers with better access to markets and a range of services; better communication and increased mobility. In fact, in general, incorporation into a wider economy and society was widely welcomed, and Bougainvilleans are unlikely to seek to withdraw towards self-sufficiency and subsistence economy. But, on the other hand, the above-mentioned negative social and environmental effects of mining activities were widely perceived as being predominant. The gains were not perceived as outweighing the losses; on the contrary, gains and losses were assessed as being distributed extraordinarily unevenly. Bougainvilleans were convinced that they were being neglected and exploited for the benefit of others, especially BCL, foreign workers and the PNG central government.

The main reason for this conviction was that the land issue was not dealt with adequately. Although compensation had been paid for land leased and damaged, much debate arose over the extent of the damage and the level of compensation payments (Connell, in Connell and Howitt 1991). One has to take into account that the question of compensation is a highly sensitive and very complex issue: in traditional societies things are not as simple as in the modern capitalist society of the West, with its principle of private property, which is also the principle governing access to land. This notion that land is a commodity that can be bought and sold, that one can give away land for money, is not an element of the traditional world-view (Wesley-Smith 1990). Even the term 'landowners' is therefore problematic in this respect: it is a simplifying modern term, introduced from outside in order to describe traditional tenure systems which are much more complex. In reality there exists a complex web of primary and subsidiary rights to land which simple payments of money can hardly take into account (Wesley-Smith and Ogan 1992; Hyndman and Stratigos 1993). Furthermore, it seems highly dubious whether there can be such a thing as 'just' and 'adequate' monetary compensations for the environmental, social, cultural and psychological damage inevitably resulting from modern large-scale mining on the lands of traditional societies. Conflicts regarding compensation issues seem unavoidable anyhow, and this includes conflicts within the traditional society too. For suddenly questions arise such as: who is going to receive compensation payments, and who gets how much? (Filer 1990; Wesley-Smith 1990).

The status and role of women in particular seems to worsen, because the leadership of the mining company and the administration are men who 'naturally' negotiate with the men of the indigenous population; and in so far as the company has to offer jobs to earn money, these jobs will be given to men. Further cleavages develop within the traditional society: between generations; between those who receive compensations and those who do not; between men with a job at the mine and those without. Or, to put it in other words, the homogenous traditional society begins to disintegrate into social classes (Wesley-Smith and Ogan 1992).

The mining company is interested in keeping the amount of compensation money as low as possible, of course. And as far as Panguna is concerned, BCL was very successful in this respect for a long time. But over time, discontent among landowners rose considerably, and the compensation issue escalated in the late 1980s, essentially due to the emergence of intergenerational problems within the landowning community: the compensation money was received by traditional landowners and family heads (850 so-called land title holders), but those children who became adults during the time of mining operations found access to that money difficult, and, furthermore, increasing population meant that particular sums had to be shared between more and more people, so that for most households the annual payment of compensation money was spent extremely quickly and was unlikely to be of long-term benefit for the succeeding generations. Thus, a kind of generational conflict emerged among landowners, with the successor generation being afraid of getting even less out of Panguna and being left with hardly any economic opportunities (Filer 1990; Connell, in Connell and Howitt 1991).

The leaders of this next generation were willing to take a more radical stance regarding demands towards BCL and the central government. The generation split between landowners led to the establishment of a new organization advocating landowners' demands in 1987, namely the 'new' Panguna Landowners' Association (PLA) as compared to the 'old' PLA, which had been established in 1979 and which was dominated by older landowners who had become more moderate over the years and were accused of being bought out by BCL (of having become a 'comprador bourgeoisie', so to speak) by the younger folk (Okole, in May and Spriggs 1990). The new PLA proved to be the decisive actor, 'with which nobody had really reckoned-in the process of re-negotiating the Bougainville Copper Agreement in 1988' – which actually turned out to be a process of non-negotiation. This agreement had been signed in 1967 and revised in 1974. The revised agreement required the parties (BCL, the central and the provincial government) to meet every seven years to consider whether the agreement was 'operating fairly to each of them', and to discuss any apparent problems (Wesley-Smith 1992). The first review had commenced in 1981, but had soon fallen into disarray. The 1988 review never even got under way because of the intervention of the hitherto widely ignored local landowners, now reorganized into the new PLA.

In 1981 as well as in 1988, BCL and the central government had no major disagreements (the government side in particular did not raise the problem of environmental damage) and were quite content with things as they were (having only minor differences regarding taxation), and were planning further mineral explorations of Bougainville in order to locate and exploit new reserves of ore in the future. They were seeking ways of reducing energy costs in order to counter the effects of rising operating costs on profitability. The obvious way to do this was by substituting cheap hydroelectricity for the power produced by the company's oil-fired generators, and indeed a site for a hydroelectricity facility was selected on the Laluai river in southeast Bougainville. Of course, both the building of a dam for hydroelectricity purposes and further explorations would have led to even more environmental degradation and social disruption on the island. But clear signs that at least some of the local landowners were objecting to the Laluai hydropower project began to emerge (Wesley-Smith 1992).

Opposition came not only from the landowners but also from the NSP provincial government. Within its ranks two tendencies can be identified. On the one hand there was the desire to capture a greater share of mining revenues for the province. This was, so to speak, the 'modernist' tendency: to take part in and profit from the economic and social transformations which the mine brought about. Hence the demand for direct control of a portion of tax revenues and an increase in the mineral royalties rate, and so on. These demands were rejected outright by the central goverment, because accepting them would have deprived it of important resources. On the other hand, a 'traditionalist' tendency could be identified: a general suspicion and opposition regarding large-scale development projects, advocating the protection of traditional institutions and small-scale village-based projects instead (Wesley-Smith 1992).

The affected landowners also espoused the two aforementioned streams of thought. On the one hand they demanded a higher share of any mining revenues; the provision of roads, electricity, schools and health services; and the exclusion of 'redskins'. On the other they complained about the environmental and social problems connected with mining. Hence, in the second half of the 1980s, there emerged a rather complex coalition of forces driven by varying motives in opposition to BCL and the central government. That this coalition finally pushed BCL and the central government out of Bougainville was due to the consistent action of the younger generation of local landowners organized in the new PLA.

Deeply dissatisfied with the non-results of years of talk (in which they were not allowed to participate directly), the new PLA proceeded towards radical demands and radical action in 1988. First and foremost, they made two major financial demands: a demand for a general compensation payment of K10 billion to offset the amount of environmental destruction caused by mining operations so far, and a demand that the landowners acquire the 20 per cent share of the mining project currently owned by the central government (which was justified by the belief that the central government had never paid for this shareholding in the first place). These general demands were accompanied by a number of more limited demands, which were seen to require more immediate action: an increase in employment, training and business opportunities for the landowners; an improvement in the monitoring of environmental damage and in actual control of chemical pollution, soil erosion, and so on; an overall improvement of the living standards, especially housing standards, of the landowners, particularly those who had been resettled by BCL; a new survey of customary land titles in order to rectify a number of mistakes which were thought to have been made in the original surveys; and an amendment of the agreement regarding compensation payments, because it was in conflict with the matrilineal inheritance customs of the local clans (Okole, in May and Spriggs 1990).

During the spring and summer of 1988 the new PLA succeeded in putting the old PLA on the defensive with these demands, and in gathering mass support from local Bougainvilleans. BCL and the central government rejected the new PLA's demands, and, as a reaction, militant landowners started operations against mine installations in November 1988, aiming at the closure of the mine. This was the origin of the Bougainville Revolutionary Army (BRA), which from then on waged a fierce war against the forces of the PNG central government in the years to come.

The BRA leadership, which arose from the new PLA's leadership, started the war as a conflict motivated primarily by environmental concerns. An early declaration of the BRA reads:

> Our land is being polluted, our water is being polluted, the air we breath[e] is being polluted with dangerous chemicals that are slowly killing us and destroying our land for future generations. Better that we die fighting than to be slowly poisoned. (Polomka 1990)

For years the central government was painfully unsuccessful in dealing with the Bougainvillean revolt. It tried to achieve a military 'solution' to the conflict, sending out its troops to destroy the BRA. These military forces receive comprehensive assistance from Australia: Australia and PNG have defence cooperation agreements which provide for the equipment and training of PNGDF by Australia, and Australian military aid was substantially increased in recent years in order to enable the defence forces to fight the rebels successfully. In particular, Australia equipped the PNGDF with Iroquoi helicopters, which are designed for anti-guerrilla warfare; they were also used as gunships to fire upon civilians (Amnesty International 1993). The Australian government, being highly interested in the integrity and stability of PNG, is afraid that Bougainville secessionism might spread to other parts of PNG and thus endanger the very existence of the state of PNG (Lawson 1992; Smith, in Polomka 1990). Yet, despite massive Australian military assistance, the first phase of the war ended with a major defeat for the central government.

The complex situation on the island made attempts to achieve a peaceful resolution very difficult, though there were some endeavours to dampen or even resolve the conflict. Initial attempts at resolution in 1989 were unsuccessful because they were countered by military actions by one side or the other. So it became clear that a ceasefire was the first step necessary in order to find a solution. And, indeed, after the failure of 'Operation Footloose' the central government was willing to accept a ceasefire. So too did the BRA, demanding that cessation of hostilities be internationally supervised, preferably by the United Nations (UN). As UN involvement was rejected by the central government, an international supervision team was established instead, composed of personnel from the Commonwealth Secretariat in London, and diplomatic staff from embassies in Port Moresby and Canberra. Invited by the PNG government, this supervisory team actually went to Bougainville in order to control the process of ending hostilities. The ceasefire went into effect on 2 March 1990 and the international supervision of the handing in of arms from the BRA's side as well as the withdrawal of PNGDF from the island actually occurred during the following two weeks. But the second phase of the process, the negotiations, did not go ahead, a key point of dispute being the status of police forces on the neighbouring island of Buka (Wallensteen 1991; Kemelfield, in May and Spriggs 1990).

Following the imposition of the blockade in April and the unilateral declaration of independence in May, at the end of July both sides accepted an offer from New Zealand to negotiate on board the ship *The Endeavour*, belonging to the New Zealand navy. Negotiations resulted in the so-called 'Endeavour Accord' of 9 August (Polomka 1990). But this agreement had no lasting effect, mainly because defence forces landed on Buka in September and thus scotched the attempts to achieve a political solution (Amnesty International 1993; Howard 1991).

In January 1991, representatives of both sides met again in Honiara, capital of the neighbouring Solomon Islands. On 24 January, after two days of talks, they agreed upon the so-called Honiara Declaration on Peace, Reconciliation and Rehabilitation on Bougainville. Although the Honiara Declaration was welcomed as a breakthrough to peace by outside observers, this agreement left open the essential issues in dispute, 'namely the future of the Panguna mine and the future political status of NSP,' and did not provide for the conditions of actual peace negotiations. Thus the war resumed when the PNGDF landed on the northern shore of Bougainville in March 1991.

In the following years there were several series of talks between PNG and BRA representatives in Honiara, but without results. All these attempts failed because either one side or the other always alleged that the adversary did not fulfil agreed obligations, or else resumed military operations. One might suspect that neither side was always able to control 'hawkish' elements within their ranks, so that these elements were able to thwart the respective attempts. To put it more generally, one might even say that these failures are expressions of the weakness of the respective 'states': the 'state' of PNG and the 'state' of Bougainville.

The next real chance for peace came in the summer of 1994. At the end of August there was a change of government in PNG, and the new prime minister, Sir Julius Chan, immediately declared that he was willing to hold peace talks; the other side accepted. Thus high-level talks between PNG government representatives and BRA leader Sam Kauona were held at Honiara, starting on 27 August. These culminated in the signing of the Honiara Commitments to Peace on Bougainville by Sir Julius Chan and Sam Kauona on 3 September. The commitments declared peace on Bougainville with immediate effect, freezing the opposing forces in their current positions. It was agreed to create an international South Pacific peacekeeping force to oversee the ceasefire and to guarantee the security of participants in peace negotiations on Bougainville. A peace conference should take place on the island not later than 10 October. In fact, a ceasefire was officially enacted on 8 September, and a South Pacific peacekeeping force composed of military personnel from Fiji, Tonga and Vanuatu was established, with substantial support provided by Australia. The 400 soldiers of the peacekeeping force arrived on Bougainville at the beginning of October, and the peace conference was scheduled to commence on 10 October.

However, the BRA/BIG leadership did not attend the conference in Arawa. They complained that the government side had violated agreements obtained in Honiara (for instance, the PNGDF did not retreat from the Arawa area) and that their personal safety could not be guaranteed during the peace talks. They also accused Australia of being involved in the peacekeeping force in a much more comprehensive way than originally planned and agreed upon. The BRA's boycott of the peace conference in Arawa resulted in its failure, and it 'ended in confusion and frustration on 14 October' (Spriggs 1994). The South Pacific peacekeeping force left the island soon afterwards.

Nevertheless, the Arawa conference gave new momentum to a peace process on Bougainville: only a few days after the end of the conference an agreement was reached between a breakaway BRA faction led by North Nasioi traditional leaders and the PNG government, and on 25 November 'The Charter of Mirigini for a New Bougainville' was signed by the central government and representatives of PNGDF-controlled areas of Bougainville. This charter aimed, *inter alia*, at the establishment of a transitional legal body for Bougainville, a so-called 'Bougainville Transitional Government', and at a 'programme of reconciliation, reconstruction and restoration of services in Bougainville'.

After some delay, the Bougainville Transitional Government (BTG) was established in April 1995. Theodore Miriung became its prime minister (he had been with the BRA until October 1994, but had left the secessionists with other North Nasioi leaders when it became clear that the BRA/BIG leadership was not willing to participate in the Arawa conference). The BRA/BIG was also invited to name a number of representatives for the BTG, but they turned down the offer, claiming that the BTG was nothing but a puppet on the string of PNG's central government.

The developments that followed, however, showed that the BRA's assessment of the situation was somewhat simplistic. Under Miriung's leadership the BTG in fact turned out to be an important third player trying to strike a path between the PNG government on the one side and the BRA/BIG on the other. Miriung put forward independent proposals for solving the Bougainville crisis and thus won the support of many Bougainvilleans. Concerning the future status of Bougainville, the BTG and the central government differed widely, with Miriung advocating as high a degree of autonomy as possible for Bougainville 'short of independence'. Furthermore, Miriung was well aware that the BRA/BIG would have to be included in any peace process, because a lasting and sustainable peace could never be achieved otherwise. The central government, on the other hand, was against autonomy for Bougainville and against negotiating with the BRA/BIG. Thus negotiations between the BTG and the PNG central government, which started with a first round of talks in May 1995, proved to be very difficult. At the same time, the BTG declared its willingness to talk to the BRA/BIG as well. At first, the central government tried to prevent any direct contact between the BTG and the BRA/BIG. However, in mid-1995 its attitude changed. This was probably due to Australian influence, since at that time Australia finally became convinced that only a political solution to the crisis would be sustainable.

Thus in September 1995 representatives of the BTG, the BIG and Bougainvillean members of PNG's national parliament met for five days in Cairns, Australia. The meeting was hosted by the Australian government with the consent of PNG's central government. It resulted in a joint press communique expressing satisfaction at its outcome and declaring a mutual willingness to hold further talks. And indeed, in December 1995, both sides met again in Cairns, along with representatives of the UN and the Commonwealth Secretariat. They agreed upon a joint communique, including an agenda for future peace talks, and a round of talks to be held in March/April 1996.

These talks, however, never took place. Instead, the peace process endured major setbacks in the course of 1996. The first occured when the BIG delegation to the December Cairns talks was attacked by PNGDF soldiers on its return from Cairns to Bougainville; the delegates were very fortunate to survive. The PNG central government called the incident a 'misunderstanding', but any trust the BIG/BRA had placed in the central government was shattered. In the following weeks and months the situation on the ground deteriorated seriously, with clashes between BRA and government forces intensifying. In June 1996 the central government launched a major offensive, 'Operation High Speed II', aimed at the total destruction of the BRA and the capture or annihilation of its leaders, whom the PNG government once again termed 'criminals'. That offensive turned out to be a disaster. The PNGDF were defeated by the BRA, and in August 1996 'Operation High Speed II' came to an inglorious end. Another major setback to the peace process was the assassination of the BTG's prime minister, Theodore Miriung, in October 1996. An independent inquiry into the assassination established that members of the defence forces and the anti-BRA 'resistance fighters' were responsible.

The attack on the BIG delegation, the failure of 'Operation High Speed II', Miriung's assassination and other developments caused the stance of the PNGDF on Bougainville to deteriorate drastically during 1996, all the more so as members of the defence forces continued to commit gross human rights violations (documented in a report published by Amnesty International in February 1997). In early 1997, the situation on the island was in grave danger of deteriorating even further, as the central government hired more than a hundred mercenaries from Sandlines International, a British company, and Executive Outcomes, a South African company, to fight and defeat the BRA. But a massive wave of protest both within PNG and overseas prevented the mercenaries from acting. In fact, the mercenary issue triggered a major domestic crisis in PNG, just a few months before the general election of June 1997.

The situation on the ground in Bougainville remains strained. The blockade of BRA-controlled areas is still in force, and tens of thousands of people suffer from it. In areas controlled by the PNGDF, about 60,000 people still live in so-called care centres. Education, health and other basic services are still inadequate. Lack of funds and personnel prevents further improvements. The lack of opportunities for young people in terms of education, jobs and so forth is most critical. If they are not given the chance to live a fulfilled life under conditions of peace, there will always be a danger that they will run back to the bush and resume fighting.

However, there are signs of hope, especially at the local level. The churches, women's organizations and other non-governmental organizations, as well as traditional village leaders, are very active in organizing local peace processes. It is vital that these positive approaches at the local level be supplemented by similar processes at the provincial level (talks between the BTG and BRA/BIG) and the national level (talks between the BTG, BRA/BIG and the central government of PNG). It is also vital to consider involving international players via the UN and/or other international bodies. Only such a process of negotiation will lead to genuine peace on and for Bougainville, and it is perfectly clear that without the participation of the BRA/BIG leadership in such a process there will never be stable and lasting peace.

Negotiations will not be easy, since the positions of the parties involved are very diverse:

- The BIG/BRA still insists upon the right of the people of Bougainville to self-determination, and this has to leave open the option of full political independence. They demand the complete withdrawal of the PNGDF from Bougainville as a prerequisite for negotiations.

- The BTG is not in favour of full independence but wants a high degree of autonomy for Bougainville in the framework of the state of PNG.
- The central government of PNG is not willing to concede either autonomy or independence to Bougainville. On the contrary, it is striving for increased political centralization.

These problems need to be resolved politically. The past years have shown clearly that it is a dangerous illusion to believe in a military solution.

Without a political solution it will be impossible to tackle the underlying causes of this protracted conflict – namely, the environmental and social disruptions connected with large-scale mining operations. Thus, after years of fighting, which have drawn the opposing factions further and further away from the essential concerns that originally started the conflict – namely, the grievances of the local landowners and the interests of the provincial government – attention should shift back to these concerns. This means that negotiations regarding a peaceful solution will, at later stages, also have to focus on the future of the Panguna mine, environmental restoration and social reconstruction.

There are at least two preconditions for such negotiations on these issues. The first is the internationally monitored demilitarization of the island. Many people on Bougainville want the PNGDF withdrawn from the island. On the other hand, many people do not trust the BRA either, because of the bad experiences they had with them in the early 1990s. Thus most people would be in favour of a third independent force coming in to guarantee security. This means that the PNGDF must be withdrawn from Bougainville, the BRA and the resistance fighters must be disarmed, and an international peacekeeping force must supervise this process of withdrawal and disarmament, as well as guaranteeing the security of the people and providing for negotiations to be undertaken in an atmosphere of safety and trust for all participating sides. Second, there must be a process of democratization, enabling the people of Bougainville to say what they want. At present, all sides claim to represent the will of the people, but at the same time they all shy away from letting the people decide – for example, by means of a referendum on Bougainville's future.

Although the war is continuing at present, the urgent desire for peace is alive on all sides. And it is obviously clear that Bougainville needs peace now for the sake of those who suffer most in this war (as in all modern wars): the women, the children and the old folk.

Bibliography

Amnesty International, 1993, 'Under the Barrel of a Gun', Bougainville, Papua New Guinea, 1991 to 1993.

Brown, M.J.F., 1974, 'A Development Consequence Disposal of Mining Waste on Bougainville, Papua New Guinea', *Geoforum*, vol. 5, no. 18, pp. 19–27.

Connell, John and Richard Howitt (eds), 1991, *Mining and Indigenous Peoples in Australasia*, Sydney University Press, Sydney.

Filer, Colin, 1990, 'The Bougainville Rebellion, the Mining Industry and the Process of Social Disintegration in Papua New Guinea', *Canberra Anthropology*, vol. 13, no. 1, pp. 1–39.

Fitzpatrick, Brenda, 1993, 'Stories of Bougainville. Report of Women's Team Visit', July, World Council of Churches' Programme Unit IV, Geneva.

Forster, Mike, 1992, 'The Bougainville Revolutionary Army', *The Contemporary Pacific*, vol. 4, no. 2. pp. 368–72.

Howard, Michael C., 1991, *Mining, Politics, and Development in the South Pacific*, Westview Press, Boulder CO.

Hyndman, David, and Christine Stratigos, 1993, 'Mining, Resistance and Nationalism in the Republic of Bougainville', *Social Alternatives*, vol. 12, no. 1, pp. 55–62.

Lawson, Stephanie, 1992, 'Ethnonationalist Dimensions of Internal Conflict: The Case of Bougainville Secessionism', Australian National University Peace Research Centre Working Paper No. 121, Canberra.

May, R.J. and M. Spriggs (eds), 1990, *The Bougainville Crisis*, Crawford House Press, Bathurst.

Moody, Roger, 1991, 'Plunder!', presented by a global network of people opposed to the activities of the RTZ Corporation, Partisan/CAFCA, London.

Polomka, Peter (ed.), 1990, *Bougainville: Perspectives on a Crisis*, ANU, Strategic and Defence Studies Centre, Canberra.

Premdas, Ralph R., 1990, 'Decentralisation, Development and Secession: The Case of Papua New Guinea', in Ralph R. Premdas et al. (eds), *Secessionist Movements in Comparative Perspective*, Pinter, London.

Quodling, Paul W., 1992, 'Bougainville: Some Financial and Ownership Issues', *The Contemporary Pacific*, vol. 4, no. 2, pp. 345–54.

Regan, A.J., 1996, 'The Bougainville Conflict: Origins and Development, Main 'Actors', and Strategies for its Resolution', unpublished paper, Port Moresby.

Seib, Roland, 1994, *Papua-Neuguinea zwischen isolierter Stammesgesellschaft und weltwirtschaftlicher Integration*, Unstitut Für Asienkunde, Hamburg.

Spriggs, Matthew, 1994, 'The Failure of the Bougainville Peace Talks', *Pacific Research*, vol. 7, no. 4, pp. 19–23.

Wallensteen, Peter, 1991, 'Third Parties in Conflict Resolution', in Karen Lindgren (ed.), *States in Armed Conflict*, Department of Peace and Conflict Research, Uppsala University.

Wesley-Smith, Terence, 1990, 'The Politics of Access: Mining Companies, the State, and Landowners in Papua New Guinea', *Political Science*, vol. 42, no. 2, pp. 1–19.

Wesley-Smith, Terence, 1992, 'The Non-review of the Bougainville Copper Agreement', in Donald Denoon and Matthew Spriggs (eds), *The Bougainville Crisis*, updated edition, Crawford House Press, Bathurst, pp. 92–111.

Wesley-Smith, Terence and Eugene Ogan, 1992, 'Copper, Class, and Crisis: Changing Relations of Production in Bougainville', *The Contemporary Pacific*, vol. 4, no. 2, pp. 245–67.

11

Food Crises: Their Roots in a Country's Political and Developmental Crises

Abdel-Galil Elmekki

The purpose of this chapter is to explain the roots of, and the relationship between, food crisis and environmental degradation and social conflict in the Sudan. Its premiss is that both food insecurity and environmental degradation are products of the same socio-political and economic factors. National development policies have been designed to serve the interests of large-scale commercial farmers. These policies have exposed small peasant producers and pastoralists to enormous economic and political pressures. In their response to these pressures, rural communities have resorted to adjustment mechanisms that have been damaging not only to their long-term food security but to the environment as well. This is reinforced by the profit-oriented practices of the state-supported commercial and agrarian bourgeoisie, which has emphasized its short-term interests at the expense of the long-term reproduction of the natural environment. The exhaustion of natural resources and its social impact was precipitated by profit maximization on the part of the state and the commercial/agrarian bourgeoisie, on the one hand, and by the response of rural population to 'external' pressures, on the other.

A major irony in Sudan's development and politics is that the peasant producers who are now starving are those who managed in the past to feed their households and deliver cheap food to urban areas and for export. Peasant farming areas in the western regions of Darfur and Kordofan and the eastern regions of Kassala and the Red Sea are the hardest hit by the food crisis and the socio-political breakdown associated with it. What it is necessary to address is the question: why is it that producers of food are the first and most seriously affected by famine?

Famine is primarily a product of a collapse of the national food security system, which in turn is a result of a serious decline in both production and exchange entitlements of peasant communities. The process of deteriorating food security in Sudan reached its climax in the early 1980s when the dream of transforming Sudan into the 'breadbasket of the Middle East' came to a shattering end. By 1984 hundreds of thousands of Sudanese had starved to death and millions were forced by the spectre of hunger to move towards the major cities. After a year of massive relief deliveries from all over the world and one good harvest in 1986 the critical phase was over. Although it has receded from news headlines – something governments in Khartoum had always sought to achieve – the food crisis in Sudan continues. Starvation persists as a widespread phenomenon in the country. In 1990 over 50 per cent of the population in north Sudan were facing either chronic or transitory food security problems (World Bank 1990). The fate of the country's population in the south represents a shocking human tragedy as the population remains hostage to the civil war and the famine associated with it.

The situation in the late 1990s remains critical, especially in the western states of Darfur and Kordofan. According to the Food and Agriculture Organization/World Food Programme the output of rain-fed crops in the 'traditional' peasant subsector in 1991/92 'was inadequate to meet even the subsistence needs in the states of Kordofan, Darfur, parts of Eastern state and in a number of other areas' (FAO/WFP 1991). The same report states that an estimated 7 million people, representing almost 30 per cent of the country's total population, remained seriously affected by famine and in need of food aid for all or most of the year 1992/93. The total cereal deficit for 1991/92 was estimated by the mission at almost 1 million tonnes (FAO/WFP 1991).

The most fundamental factor in explaining this situation is that the access of peasant communities to food is declining at both production and exchange levels. At the level of production, peasant communities in eastern and western Sudan are no longer capable of producing enough sorghum and millet. This is a result of land degradation and externally induced changes in production processes and labour allocation. At the exchange level, peasant communities cannot afford to buy cereals produced in the large-scale mechanized farms or the irrigated schemes in central Sudan because of the high market price, on the one hand, and the declining cash incomes of peasant households, on the other. One example here is that while the country as a whole produced a surplus in sorghum in 1992/93, the FAO estimated that almost 2 million people were threatened by serious starvation.

Most of this sorghum was produced in the irrigated sector and the mechanized farms of Gedaref. It was a result of a combination of price incentives to big farmers and a shift from cotton to cereals in the irrigated schemes. While aggregate figures indicate a considerable surplus at the national level, the regions of Darfur, Kordofan and of course the south faced grain deficit as a result of crop failures, national market imperfections and lack of cash at the disposal of peasant households. Instead of tackling this national problem head-on, the military government 'donated' sorghum to the Islamic fundamentalists in northern Somalia and exported wheat and sorghum to Iran in return for military equipment. The peasant food system became fragile and vulnerable to any temporary hazard. This has been the case in the Sudan since the mid-1980s. The state's responses to the crisis are again determined and handicapped by the state's social foundation and orientation; therefore these responses have avoided touching the real roots of the crisis.

With acute crisis looming, radical recovery requires a rethinking of development policies and political power relations rather than a reliance on short-term relief and limited market reform. This is because the food crisis is essentially a political and developmental crisis which involves not only peasant communities but other social forces as well. Finally, the current crisis situation has now generated a new political reality in rural Sudan where peasant communities are developing new forms of political institutions through which they express demands and their dissatisfaction with the established order of economic development and politics.

To test the above hypotheses this chapter examines the following areas: the transformation of peasant production and peasant communities within the framework of Sudan's agrarian development process through both colonial and post-colonial policies; the way issues of food security have been perceived in national development policies; the mechanisms and effects of pressures exerted on peasant communities by the state and non-peasant social forces; how peasant communities resist and adjust to these pressures, and state responses to the current food crisis.

The Context of Food Insecurity and Ecological Crisis

The food crisis in Sudan is not an overnight phenomenon. It has been building up for some time, and the immediate causes of the sudden decline in food production, for example drought and desertification, are the products of historical processes encompassing complex social, political and economic factors. The food crisis and the widespread environmental degradation are two faces of the same coin and they are products of the same socio-economic and political forces. In addition, the dynamics of the relationships between the state, crop merchants and moneylenders on the one hand, and peasant farmers on the other, provide the sharpest focus for the analysis of the current food crisis in Sudan, specifically because peasant communities have been allocated a marginal position in national development policies under both colonial and post-colonial rule.

The Sudanese agricultural sector is composed of three subsectors, each with its own historical development, organization, objectives, social relations of production and forms of relations to the state and political power. The mainly cotton-producing subsector was established in the mid-1920s by the colonial state in collaboration with the then powerful British Cotton Growers Association and the British Textile Association of Lancashire. The objective was simply to secure a source of regular supply of high staple cotton in order to reduce the dependency of the British textile industry on the United States. The large-scale rain-fed mechanized subsector was established by the colonial authorities in the mid-1940s and developed into its present shape by the early 1950s. Its objective was to produce sorghum on a large scale to feed the growing labour force of the cotton schemes. Finally, the small peasant subsector has undergone tremendous transformations under a policy that was carefully designed by the colonial state and carried over by the post-colonial one. As early as the 1930s, this subsector was fully incorporated into the market economy, as will be shown later. The rural labour market is the main link between these heterogeneous agricultural subsectors. As far as labour is concerned, the irrigated and the large-scale mechanized subsectors are totally dependent on the peasant subsector. Migratory workers based in adjoining peasant communities supply almost 70 per cent of the work in the irrigated schemes (Wohlmuth and Oesterdiekhoff 1983) and 100 per cent of the labour input in the mechanized schemes.

Each of the three subsectors is specialized in one or two crops. The irrigated schemes produce mainly cotton; the mechanized subsector produces sorghum and some sesame and sunflower, with 89 per cent of the total area allocated to sorghum; and the peasant subsector combines food production (sorghum and millet) with export crops (mainly groundnuts and sesame). In terms of relative weight the peasant subsector accounts for an average of 52 per cent of the total area cultivated in the country, the irrigated production 13.7 per cent, and mechanized farming 34.3 per cent. However, this does not reflect the relative political weight, as will be explained below.

The above distribution of area cultivated by different subsectors also does not reflect the relative real and potential contribution of each subsector to national food security, especially in the case of mechanized farming, the produce of which is basically geared towards the export market and urban consumers, who make up less than 20 per cent of the total population. The rural population have no access to sorghum produced in mechanized farming schemes because it is offered at prices not affordable by peasants. Between 1984 and 1992 domestic prices of sorghum produced in the mechanized schemes increased fifteenfold, and between 1989 and 1992 alone these prices quadrupled. The usual explanation given by the state and mechanized scheme farmers for this increase is the rise in the cost of imported spare parts and fuel. However, a more fundamental explanation is the nature of the sorghum market itself and the government policy which fixes a minimum price for the sorghum produced in mechanized schemes. This minimum price, which the actual price normally exceeds, is supposed to cover the cost of production and to secure a comfortable profit margin for mechanized scheme farmers who are themselves sorghum traders. The normal practice, fixed by the Ministry of Commerce, is based on recommendations made by the Union of Mechanized Scheme Farmers, which is one of the most powerful political lobbies in the country.

Peasant farming

The peasant subsector is the largest in Sudan's agriculture. In the past it produced most of the food and contributed considerably to the export economy. However, this subsector is now undergoing a process of rapid disintegration, which became much more visible after the beginning of the current food crisis in the country. This process is a cumulative effect of the development strategies followed by both colonial and post-colonial states. One of the components of these strategies was the full incorporation of peasant producers into the export economy in order for their surpluses to be channelled through the 'national' accumulation circuit. The subsistence and self-sufficiency cycle of peasant production was subsequently broken and peasant producers were exposed to pressures through the market. Consequently they lost their historically developed survival and reproduction strategies.

The household makes up the basic unit of labour, production and consumption in the peasant subsector. Land is the major object of labour, and holdings are not equal but there are no landless. Although all the rainlands of Sudan are 'legally' owned by the state, in practice they are mainly privately owned, and only in a few cases communally owned; it is up to local leaders (tribal chiefs) to distribute rights of land use to peasant households. Until recently access to and acquisition of land was only determined by the household's labour resources and the capacity of a household to clear new land (Bernal 1988). Therefore there was a clear correlation between a household's landholding and the size of the household. However, this advantage is now diminishing as a result of expansion by mechanized farming into land reserves.

With the introduction of cash-crop production during the first quarter of this century and the emergence of seasonal wage labour with the establishment of cotton schemes and mechanized farming, a process of differentiation was undergone by peasant production, and the single subsistence circuit was replaced by a new structure combining subsistence with commodity and wage-labour circuits. There has been a continuous conflict between them. The most fundamental reason for the food crisis was the marginalization of the subsistence circuit and a growing dependence on the market. However, the same food crisis is now leading to a 'revival' of the food production circuit although the tension is ongoing, especially between the subsistence circuit and wage labour. A major source of this tension is that market dependence has become too deeply rooted; it is objectively impossible for peasants to exit the market economy. They are dependent on the market not only for the sale of labour and crops and purchase for consumption but also for the purchase of agricultural tools and sometimes seeds. The author's field research in western Sudan found that 88 per cent of peasant farmers purchase their tools from the market.

Large-scale mechanized farming

This is the subsector which attracts most attention so far as food security and environmental degradation are concerned. It was originally intended to contribute to development through the satisfaction of the following objectives: positive contribution to food security, contribution to balance of payments by producing exportable surpluses of sorghum and sesame, and broadening the rural labour market. Until the mid-1970s the supply of relatively cheap sorghum for the domestic market was the leading objective of mechanized farming. The aims of this policy were to allow the allocation of a maximum portion of resources in the irrigated schemes to cotton; to supply cheap sorghum to urban centres in order to depress, or at least stabilize, wages in the small industrial sector; to deliver 'affordable' sorghum to peasant producers in order to divert a greater portion of their land resources and labour power to cash crop production as well as to seasonal labour in the other subsectors. When the so-called breadbasket strategy was launched, contribution to food security ceased to be an objective of mechanized farming; contribution to balance of payments became the top objective.

There are five categories of actors involved in the organization of production in the mechanized farming subsector: the state, the leaseholders and/or capital owners, farm managers, and agricultural labour. The state is the legal owner of land, and allocates schemes of 1,500 feddans each to leaseholders at a nominal rent. In addition, the state supplies leaseholders with concessional credit facilities for equipment and working capital through the Mechanized Farming Corporation (MFC) and the Agricultural Bank of the Sudan (ABS). The state also grants leaseholders an incentive exchange rate for purchases of equipment and inputs. Finally, in most cases the state takes over the losses of MFC and ABS caused by low repayment ratios. The sate bias towards mechanized farming is clearly reflected in the budget figures of the Ministry of Agriculture. In 1979–80, for example, 85 per cent of total expenditure was allocated to mechanized farming, while the Range Management Administration received only 1 per cent, the Wildlife Administration 3 per cent, and the Forestry Department 11 per cent (Department of Agricultural Economics and Statistics, Ministry of Agriculture).

Neither leaseholders nor financiers are directly involved in on-farm management. In all cases mechanized farms are run by salaried managers who supervise labour and conduct the various farm operations. This is why leaseholders and financiers are sometimes labelled 'suitcase farmers': they both lack any experience in farming and the majority of them are traders and civil servants. It is a common argument that this 'absentee landlordism' is in itself a major reason behind the seriously damaging impact of mechanized farming on the environment. Both policies have shown no interest in conserving soil fertility and ecological balance, because for them mechanized farming is a business venture which should be conducted along the lines of a 'merchant logic'.

The state policy towards various agricultural subsectors has been extremely unbalanced. The state attitude towards every subsector is, in the final analysis, determined by the patterns of political power distribution. Mechanized farming has, since the 1950s, been the base for the most powerful fraction of the Sudanese bourgeoisie. Moreover, it has been the subsector in which the top bureaucrats and the bourgeoisie takes its solid material form. It is the subsector in which the top bureaucrats are transformed from being mere 'instruments' of the ruling class(es) to being an organic component of it. This thesis is crucial to the explanation of the state's policies towards mechanized farming, which range from uncontrolled horizontal expansion to encroachment into peasant territories.

To conclude, the state-subsidized mechanized farming subsector has made an insignificant contribution to national food security and has contributed to the current environmental crisis in the following ways:

exports and foreign exchange earnings rather than food security have been the priority of this subsector; inappropriate technology and inappropriate commercial/agricultural practices have led to exhaustion of the soil, with a negative impact on yields and ecology; the unplanned and uncontrolled expansion of the sector has led to the total and irreversible destruction of grass cover and tree-stock; commercial farming – encouraged by state policies – has expanded into ecologically fragile zones and therefore contributed to desertification; small peasant producers and pastoralists have been pushed by commercial farming into areas of poor soil and low rainfall, leading to the collapse of the peasants' food system.

The state-controlled irrigated sector

The three schemes of the Gezira, Halfa-Elgirba and El Rahad make up 90 per cent of the irrigated subsector, with cotton as the leading crop. The Gezira model was more or less mechanically reproduced in the other schemes. Production relations are based on a crop-sharing arrangement between the state and tenant farmers with the latter contributing family labour, and some capital in the case of wealthier tenant households. For the majority of the tenant farmers the share in the cash proceeds of the cotton is essentially the equivalent of a wage, which in most cases is below the real value of their labour time expended on producing cotton. To compensate for this, farmers are allowed to grow sorghum and vegetables as a food security measure in parts of their tenancies without having to share the crop with the state.

The state and food security: policies and responses

State policies during both colonial and post-colonial rule have been characterized by:

- too much emphasis on large-scale government-controlled irrigated schemes, to which most of government development spending has gone;
- encouragement of large-scale private production of sorghum in the savannah rainlands with massive concessions from the state and foreign donors;
- total neglect of the peasant sector, which accounts for the absolute majority of the country's population;
- a total absence of any clear 'food policy'.

One striking feature of Sudan's political economy is the absence of a 'food policy'. Issues of food security are only occasionally referred to in development strategies. During the colonial period food issues were handled from purely a security perspective and only when a food shortage touched the immediate issue of stability. The colonial agricultural policy was primarily based on the supremacy of export production and therefore all the development efforts were directed to the cotton-producing irrigated sector. Since independence the post-colonial state has totally neglected food security. Food production was only emphasized when it appeared to be an attractive area for investment; when it becomes less profitable it is abandoned.

The predominant development policy has always been geared towards maintaining the colonial pattern of primary export production. When sorghum production was boosted during the 1960s and 1970s, the reason was simply because it was comfortably accommodated in the export orientation of the national economy. The state is still dealing with food security from a short-term perspective which does not go beyond disaster management and immediate relief. It was only in 1987 that a Food Security Unit was established, but it is already failing because of feuds among different government departments.

Pressures on Peasant Communities: The Roots of Crisis

The food crisis and environmental collapse in Sudan are a product of the historical evolution of Sudanese agrarian structures and especially the process of transformation undergone by peasant communities. State policies and state responses (or lack of responses) to the crisis are crucial variables in explaining the food situation in the country. Marginalization of the peasant communities in national development and politics, the expansion of mechanized farming, the creation of a market-dependent peasant economy, and the operation of crop and credit markets exposed peasant communities to severe pressures. In their response to these pressures these communities sometimes resorted to mechanisms which exhausted and overexploited their natural and labour resources as well as their environmental set-up. The ultimate result is a collapse of the food security system and the exposure of peasant communities to further pressures and deepening of their subsistence crisis.

The neglect of the 'traditional' peasant farming sector by both the colonial and post-colonial states provides the historical context for the current dilemma of peasant communities. The colonial state's major concern was to attract peasant producers to the production of export crops and to participation in cotton production through supplying seasonal labour. In colonial times, according to Wohlmuth and Oesterdiekhoff,

> a policy of neglect towards the traditional sector prevailed, modified only by providing 'pull' factors to increase migration in order to cater for the demand

> of temporary labour necessary for growing export production (especially cotton in private and government-owned irrigation schemes). (Wohlmuth and Oesterdiekhoff 1983)

This perspective did not change after independence. The 'traditional' sector continued to be seen as a labour reserve and as a source of cash crops siphoned into the export economy through merchant capital. It 'received little or no assistance from the state and very little technical aid to improve farming methods' (Fruzzetti and Oster 1990). However, it is through the operation of merchant capital that Sudanese peasant production was kept under control, as will be shown later.

The interests of peasant communities are never expressed in national development policies, unlike those of capitalist farmers in the mechanized sector and the tenant farmers in the irrigated schemes. Mechanized rain-fed agriculture was stimulated indirectly by low land rent, subsidized credit and by buying up sorghum at a guaranteed minimum price. On the other hand, 'the "traditional" peasant sector has totally been neglected, by and large, with the exception of some "pilot projects"' (Institute of Social Studies 1989). The bias against peasant farmers in development policy is expressed in the traditional/modern dichotomy which has dominated development thinking in Sudan since the establishment of the Gezira irrigated scheme in the 1920s. The assumption has always been that since the return on investment is far greater in the 'modern' sector (that is, in irrigated schemes and large scale rain-fed mechanized schemes) than in its 'traditional' (that is, peasant) counterpart, investment should be concentrated mainly in the 'modern' sector with almost total neglect of the peasant sector (Kursany 1983).

Uneven access to state power and influence on state policy are determined by the relative power of different social groups. While farmers in the mechanized sector make up the core of the Sudanese bourgeoisie and are always in alliance with the state bureaucracy, the tenant farmers in the irrigated schemes have benefited from being well organized as a result of their involvement in an industry-like production organization. While the Mechanized Farming Union and the Gezira Tenant Farmers' Union have been powerful factors in Sudanese politics since the early 1950s, the peasant farmers of western and eastern Sudan never had this influence.

The peasant farmers are geographically dispersed. They see neither a common interest nor a clearly defined common enemy. Also until recent changes stimulated by the crisis situation, peasant communities had never articulated their relationship to the state. They used to see the state as an insignificant factor in their lives as it did not enter into direct confrontation with them. Rather, the state was represented by people from within the community after they had been incorporated in the state apparatus through forms ranging from the Native Administration to local people's courts. The state functions of tax collection, organization of markets, settlement of land disputes, and maintenance of law and order were taken care of by local people who disguised their contradictions with their communities through primary loyalties of ethnicity and religion. State power was there but the state itself was invisible.

The marginalization of peasant farmers in national development policies and politics was a result of lack of organization; lack of clarity in the way peasant communities perceived the state, the crop merchant and the moneylender; and lack of interest in influencing state policy. This marginalization provided the context for pressures imposed on peasant communities by the state and other social forces. However, as will be shown below, peasant communities are undergoing tremendous political change as a result of the famine situation, which makes social contradictions much more visible, and it is no longer possible for ethnicity and religion to disguise it.

Coping with Stress: From Adjustment to Resistance

Food shortages have been a periodic phenomenon in Sudan throughout this century, partly as a result of droughts and partly due to specific grain production and marketing policies. Throughout this period peasant households and communities have accumulated tremendous coping mechanisms for food shortages. However, coping with temporary and seasonal shortages is quite different from coping with an acute food crisis such as the current one. Peasant communities, especially in western Sudan, utilized their accumulated coping experience, which worked relatively well during the first years of the current crisis. Now, however, there is a growing awareness among these communities that the 'old' coping mechanisms are no longer sufficient in the present situation and that such strategies have contributed to deepening their socio-environmental stress. Indeed the common assumption in 'coping studies', that coping capacities of peasant communities are almost infinite, could not be further from the truth. The exhaustion of the old coping strategies raises the question of what are the possible alternative strategies and could they be different from the old ones. The author's field research in western Sudan shows that while the old mechanisms are still in use alternative strategies are now being developed, as will be shown below.

Conventional household coping strategies

The central assumption in this chapter is that peasant producers were exposed to extreme pressures from the state, and from merchant and finance capital, and in their response and adjustment to these pressures they resorted to certain mechanisms which exacerbated their food situation and damaged their environment. The most important adjustment mechanisms in this regard are: changing labour and cultivation practices, overcultivation, cultivation of marginal lands, the search for supplementary cash income sources by excessive cutting of trees and charcoal burning, and the overconsumption of wild grass and wild seeds, which contributes to desertification. The first fall-back strategy during periods of stress was the 'asset path of coping'; in other words, selling animals was the first response by peasants to the food crisis. During the famine years, animal population in most north Darfur villages diminished to almost zero. This did not help much because the terms of exchange of animals and grain were extremely unequal. While under normal circumstances the price of a goat would buy a sack of millet, in 1991 buying one sack required the sale of twenty goats. Thus the option of selling animals to buy grain was exhausted during the first years of famine. In 1986, for example, the cattle population in some villages dropped to 1.3 per cent (De Waal 1989). During the 1980s animal prices were so low that Khartoum-based export companies increased their profits by a minimum of 1,000 per cent.

Reorganization of labour within a household had always been one of the most 'efficient' coping mechanisms, especially with the commercialization of the peasant economy and the emergence of an agricultural labour market in the cotton-producing schemes and the mechanized sorghum-producing areas. Peasant households are composed of three labour circuits: a subsistence circuit where a portion of the household's labour time is used in producing food crops; a commodity circuit where some labour is used for producing cash crops; and a wage labour circuit where a portion of the household's labour time is 'liberated' and offered for sale. Competition among these three circuits is tough. The subsistence circuit dominated peasant production until the 1960s, when it was overtaken by the commodity and wage labour circuits. This was a result of the commercialization of peasant production during colonialism and the expansion of the national agricultural labour market.

The dissolution of the subsistence circuit of production has been one of the fundamental reasons for the food crisis, especially because the commodity and wage labour circuits have failed to achieve food security the way the subsistence circuit had always done. Cash returns from the sale of peasants' crops (especially oilseeds) and labour were too low to meet peasants' food purchase requirements. The structure of the crop, commodity and labour market has a clear bias against peasants.

The acute food crisis of the 1980s and 1990s further intensified the conflict among the three circuits. There is clear evidence now that the cash crop circuit is vanishing and that competition is now basically between the food and the wage labour circuits. On the one hand, peasants are now allocating an increasing portion of their land and labour to food production. On the other hand, they have to engage in wage labour because their food crop yields are low as a result of ecological degradation and deterioration in soil fertility, and also because their subsistence has become market-dependent to the extent that they cannot easily exit the market economy. This is one of the paradoxes of peasant communities under conditions of severe stress: there is no way to exit the market, yet there is no way to depend fully on it. The tension continues between these two tendencies.

Field data reveals that cash crops such as sesame, groundnuts, watermelon seeds and hibiscus have almost disappeared, and millet and sorghum are becoming the only crops. This process has had serious negative effects on the country's exports and on the accumulation base of merchant capital, which has historically dominated the capital accumulation circuit in the country. A major reason for abandoning export crops is the deterioration in terms of trade since the early 1980s. Research in north Darfur shows that the same amount of groundnuts could buy 10 per cent of the volume of sorghum and millet in 1991 as compared to 1983. While originally diversification meant a combination of food and cash crops, now it means diversification of food crops. An average of six varieties of sorghum and millet are now sown in each plot and the tendency is towards growing fast-maturing and drought-resistant varieties.

Peasant households are increasingly willing to offer a larger portion of their labour time to off-farm income-generating activities. However, the labour market is too limited, while there is an oversupply of labour. The classical pattern of migration to cotton and mechanized sorghum-producing areas has increased dramatically. Migration begins earlier than usual; the rates of migration have risen rapidly; the age and sex composition of participants has shifted, including an increase in whole-family migration, which is indicative of the stress phase of migration (Teklu 1991). As a result the migration option seems to have become exhausted. Food and employment opportunities are diminishing in regional towns and in central Sudan. In addition, the state, for its own short-sighted political interests, has become too brutal against the famine-displaced people in the urban centres, and especially around Khartoum, where over 2 million famine- and war-displaced people reside in shantytowns and engage in marginal jobs in the city. Peasants interviewed in Darfur in 1991 expressed their intention to migrate in search of food but did not expect anything better anywhere else.

It is also noted that more and more people are engaged in 'petty trade' – selling items such as water, charcoal and fuel wood, grass and wild food. However, not every household can engage in petty trade, because in most trading activities, owning a donkey or a camel and a small amount of capital is a basic requirement. The majority of households, especially in north Darfur, have either lost their animals or sold them for cash or grain.

Extensive wood cutting and charcoal burning have been among the adjustment mechanisms that are most devastating so far as depletion of natural resources and environmental degradation are concerned, because the annual fuelwood off-take rate in Sudan has already exceeded natural regeneration, and therefore energy and nutrient cycles are seriously affected (Whitney 1986). It has been estimated by geographers that in the period between 1960 and 1980, the amount of deforestation attributable to household fuel consumption rose from nearly 7,500 to 28,000 square kilometres per year (Whitney 1986). The consumption of wood per family in the northern Darfur region is estimated to be some 330 trees of middle height per year for both fuel and hut-building purposes (El Mangouri 1990). However, this seems to be only part of the problem. Although rural household energy use is considered by many to be a major source of desertification, extensive tree overcutting and charcoal burning became a serious problem only when it was commercialized and rural communities resorted to it as an adjustment mechanism. This situation was made much more serious by the emergence of a profitable large-scale charcoal business as a result of the growing urban demand for charcoal, especially since the early 1970s.

What makes charcoal-burning the most feasible cash-earning activity is the fact that wage labour opportunities in villages are limited and therefore wages are extremely low especially when compared with grain prices. A day's labour, which could buy 10 kilograms of millet in north Darfur in the early 1980s, could only buy 1.5 kilograms in October 1991. Labour opportunities in villages are only available during the peak periods of weeding and harvest. Households that hire labour are mainly those with access to considerable cash incomes, either from a trade or remittances sent by some of the household members working in Libya (especially in the case of Darfur), Saudi Arabia and the Gulf. Wage labour opportunities are better in southern Kassala and southern Kordofan provinces, which are the main locations for large-scale mechanized farming.

In the case of Darfur, most of the wage labour in the villages and nearby locations is left for women and children, while adult males travel longer distances in search of work. Almost 60 per cent of agricultural wage labour in western Darfur is done by women (Tully 1988). However, in the Gedaref, Damazin and Habila areas, where mechanized farming schemes are located in the middle of peasant areas, women's and children's share in the labour market is rapidly increasing. Employment in these schemes under famine conditions is especially attractive to women and children because wages are partly paid in food (sorghum flour, dried okra, dried fish and salt). This changing position of women and children is a stress-related phenomenon; traditionally female and child labour was confined to the household and farm. The emergence of this new category in the labour force has contributed to a further decline in rates of wages. On average, the wage paid to women and children, whether in cash or in kind, is half that paid to adult males.

The competition between food production and wage labour is clearly reflected in the organization of households' labour. Although most of the land resources are now committed to cereals, peasants cannot afford to commit all their labour to this activity because they still need cash. It is interesting to note that now there is an oversupply of off-farm peasant labour, while demand is sharply declining as a result of the decline in mechanized farming and cotton-production sectors. There are two reasons for this oversupply of peasant labour. First, the shift from cash to food crops has reduced the amount of on-farm labour requirements because sesame and groundnuts (which have been abandoned) were labour-intensive compared to cereals: a hectare under groundnuts in Darfur requires a labour input of an average of 69.5 adult work days while a hectare under millet requires 33.5 work days (Tully 1988). Second, farming practices are adjusted in such a way as to liberate a larger portion of labour power for sale in the market. One important adjustment is reduction in the number of weedings from the normal three to one. The decline in yield as a result of this practice is at least temporarily compensated for by horizontal expansion. In addition, peasants in eastern Sudan have resorted to greater tractor hiring in order to reduce the time spent in seeding and weeding and save it for wage labour in the nearby large-scale mechanized farms. In most cases tractor hiring is done on credit at high interest rates; in other cases peasants pay the cost in labour to the tractor owner, who is normally the operator of a mechanized farming scheme.

In addition to the shift from cash crops to food crops, peasants resort to a number of other adjustment mechanisms, which include changing crop and seed variety mixes, changes in inputs, variation in planting practices, and the cultivation of more than one plot in different locations because of high local variability of rain. Of the households surveyed in Darfur, 64 per cent reported planting three plots; 29 per cent planted two plots; and only 7 per cent planted one plot, because they could not physically move too far from their villages. These results are confirmed by other surveys in Kordofan, where 70 per cent of peasant households cultivate more than one plot (Ahmed 1983). This tendency is now radically changing the nature of land as an asset. From essentially being a free good, the control of which has been limited only by the amount of labour available to cultivate, land has come to be a limited good, and apparently a land market will soon emerge.

The horizontal extension of cropping areas under peasant production has been confirmed as one of the main reasons for environmental degradation. Poor peasant households are forced by economic and political factors to expand into the marginal lands of low, unreliable rainfall (Horowitz and Salem-Murdock 1987). Clearing of the savannah in these areas for cropping exposes the land to increased risk of desertification, and there is clear evidence of declining productivity in northern Darfur province, as the area under millet production increased threefold from 1960 to 1975 (El Mangouri 1990). According to Ibrahim:

> The transgression over the agronomic dry boundaries is the main cause of desertification [in western Sudan]. For the preparation of the fields for millet cultivation means the felling of all the trees and the extraction of all the fields. The soil is then loosened and made exposed to strong deflation. The repetition of this process leads finally to an irreversible destruction of the natural vegetation cover and enhances the erosion of fertile topsoil. Soil degradation leads to the diminution of productivity. The land cultivator is thus obliged to shorten the rotation of cultivation and fallow, and ultimately plants the land continuously. The soil becomes gradually exhausted, because all plant nourishment is used up. (Ibrahim 1978)

Overcultivation as another adjustment mechanism has had equally devastating consequences as that of horizontal expansion of cropping areas. In the perimeters of most settlements land is cultivated annually without allowing for a fallow period for soil regeneration. After five or six years, the production decreases so much that the farmer is forced to give up cultivating the plot (Ibrahim 1978). Instead of being the result of enormous population increase, as Ibrahim argues, this tendency is basically one of the mechanisms used by peasant producers to compensate for the negative impact of overcommercialization of peasant agriculture and the pressures exerted by the state and merchant capital on peasant communities.

From Karama to a new political setting

The intensification of the food crisis during the past decade has led to a number of significant socio-economic changes, with important political repercussions on the political development of the country.

First, it has become clear that the old coping strategies are no longer working. Developed for coping with short-term periods of stress, the old mechanisms are unable to adapt to the present one, which has been too long and too severe. The mechanisms of reorganization of household labour; dispossession of assets; changing consumption patterns; modifying production processes; and eating wild fruits, leaves and roots – all worked perfectly during the first years of the current drought and famine, but now they are no longer feasible.

Second, there is a growing awareness that the current food crisis and collapse of agricultural production have a wider political and social dimension. While at the beginning of the famine in the early 1980s peasants would explain the whole phenomenon as nothing but an act of God. However, during the author's field research at the end of 1991 most of the respondents attributed the crisis to *al-hakooma wa al-tijjar* – the government and merchants. This change in peasants' perception of their reality is clearly reflected, as will be shown below, in the way they are now perceiving their position in the national framework of economic and political development and in the way they are rethinking their relations with other social forces in the country. This does not mean the emergence of a fully fledged 'peasant consciousness' but the beginning of a process in which peasants no longer look at themselves as self-contained communities without any 'external' factors determining the course of their communities' development. This embryonic consciousness is already posing a challenge to the legitimacy of the established authority despite the fact that the concrete political expressions of this consciousness are still in the making. However, at least now the official explanation of famine in terms of natural factors and acts of God makes no sense to those communities affected by famine.

Regional political organizations like the Beja Congress in the east, the Nuba Mountains Union in southern Kordofan, and the Darfur Renaissance Front have contributed considerably to bringing a peasants' awareness to the connection between the food crisis and the nature of the political and development course of the country. The concept of marginalization, which is the backbone of these organizations' programmes, is now becoming popular in all the regions affected by the food crisis and the social hardships associated with it. Although this awareness of marginalization has its origins in the 1960s it is now gaining a much wider platform as a result of the food crisis. During the 1986 democratic elections the issues of famine and marginalization were the focus of political mobilization programmes to the extent that even the traditional political parties like the Umma and the Democratic Unionist parties were forced to adopt at least the jargon.

The most articulate expression of this new awareness at the national level was the formation in 1987 of the Rural Forces Solidarity (RFS) as an umbrella organization accommodating the interests of the marginalized rural forces. The formation of RFS pushed the old urban-based left-wing organizations, especially the Sudanese Communist Party, to rethink their political strategies and their social foundation. On the other hand the formation of the RFS posed a real threat to the old political parties, especially the Umma and the Democratic Unionist Party (DUP). What consolidated the fear of these parties was the fact that the RFS was adopting a popular democratic ideology similar to that of the Sudan People's Liberation Movement (SPLM) in the south. Moreover, the RFS was targeting the same social groups with whose support the Umma and the DUP had dominated Sudanese politics.

The third change brought about by the intensification of the food crisis was the awareness among peasant communities of the inefficiency of the old household coping strategies in dealing with the present crisis. Now the tendency is towards consolidating some of the old community-based strategies as well as initiating new ones. There is a clear preference now for community-based survival mechanisms over household-based ones. The people in many of the villages visited by the author suggested that even NGO relief should be delivered on a village basis rather than the conventional household one, and that it should be left to the village community to organize its consumption, preferably through *karama* meals. This idea is not seen as attractive by NGOs, who have not yet understood the potential capacities of community support systems.

What is noticeable here is that peasant communities are developing these new community-based strategies on the assumption that the state is absolutely hopeless, and that they should not expect any support from it. This is basically a product of the growing awareness of the responsibility of the state in creating the crisis situation, as well as the experience of the past ten years, during which the state not only acted with indifference but also made it difficult for the foreign NGOs who were willing to help by delivering food relief or by helping peasants to rehabilitate their productive capacities. The peasant communities are thus holding the state responsible for the roots of the crisis as well as for the lack of response to it. During the author's field research it was noticed that the consistent denial of famine by the state was the major source of frustration of peasant communities in Darfur, who were at the time facing one of the worst phases of their decade-long food crisis.

The fourth change is the transformation of the concept of coping from mere adjustment to the existing political set-up to that of politically organized resistance. In this framework, some of the old community-based coping strategies like Islamic *zakat*, *nafir* (reciprocal work parties) and *karama* (communal feasts) are being developed in new political settings with their objectives going beyond dealing with temporary hardships to rethinking peasants' political relations with other social forces. Of most interest here is the way the *karama* meeting is gradually being transformed into a platform not only for expressing the political interests of peasant communities but also for articulating these interests and initiating mechanisms for implementing them as concrete projects. In this process new leadership emerges, new forms of popular participation are developed, and new organizational frameworks are innovated. It seems that the severe hardships associated with the food crisis are not only consolidating communal bonds but also leading to changes challenging the old ideas that peasant communities are not innovative, but stagnant and politically passive.

The *karama* feast is one of the oldest means of community support during periods of hardship. In Darfur, people mentioned that it became particularly important during the famine of 1913–15 when the region faced a critical food shortage and there was no possibility of external support as Darfur was still beyond the control of the central colonial state. It became even more important during the 1980s, when very little support reached the region as a result of the central government's denial of the existence of a famine. All villages organize a communal meal whenever the need arises. Each household contributes whatever is available, and those who have nothing to contribute join the meal without any stigma as it was organized for them in the first place. Usually the meal is preceded by prayers for God to lift hardships and bring rain. However, attending the prayers is not a requirement for joining the meal.

In most cases the imam of the village mosque has the responsibility of organizing the event and, of course, leading the prayers. The ideological context is the concept of Islamic reciprocity, which is why the imam is the centre of leadership. In its original format, the *karama* was little more than a communal meal. Issues of limited scope, like family disputes, were discussed and resolved. It is only recently that political issues and major community concerns have come to dominate the agenda.

With the intensification of hunger the sources of food for the *karama* have changed. Hunger is no longer confined to the weakest households in a village and, therefore, the food locally available is no longer sufficient to supply a *karama* meal. The little food available to some households, mainly through transfers from outside the community, is supplemented from other sources, which include wild food; NGO relief, if any; and, in the case of Darfur, 'robbing' the trucks on the way from Libya. One of the community leaders interviewed by the author in north Darfur identified the sources of food as: *mukheit* (wild berries), *al-munazzama* (Save the Children and Oxfam, UK) and the Kalashnikov (machine gun).

He openly admitted that a group of youths from the village were organizing an 'armed bandit' for robbing truckloads of food on the way from Libya to the region's towns, mainly El-Fasher. The food acquired through this means is offered for communal consumption in *karamas*. When asked about the compatibility of this action with Islamic ethics the short reply was that, during years of famine, Muslims are allowed to acquire food through whatever means, and the hungry have the right to seize food owned by the rich. To support his argument he referred to a well-known incident during the reign of Omar Ibn Al-Khattab, the second Khalifa to prophet Mohammed. This perception of armed theft of food, which has been a widespread phenomenon in Darfur during the past ten years, is in clear contrast to the state's perception of the problem. While peasant communities look at it as a justified coping mechanism, the state never refers to the social basis of the phenomenon and always looks at it from a narrow security perspective.

Thus, while the format of the *karama* has been maintained, its essence has undergone tremendous changes in terms of objectives, leadership and political orientation. In al-Sayyah, a village in north Darfur, the *karama* meetings were centred around a development project in late 1991 utilizing a *wadi* (valley stream) running across the village during the rainy season. Because rain-fed farming was no longer feasible, the idea was to construct a dam by communal work in order to capture the water for spreading irrigation. The village community contacted the regional government, but received no positive response, and therefore decided to do it their own way. One of the ideas adopted by the meetings was the establishment of a communal project for the production of millet and vegetables. The people who had claims to the land around the *wadi* agreed to transfer their rights to the community. The millet crop and the cash proceeds from selling vegetables were brought under the control of a communal granary and a village fund (*sandoog*), and a committee was elected for each of these 'institutions'. Also, in one of the *karama* meetings a person was assigned to contact the ILO's Food for Work programme and the German GTZ agency for support.

Similar initiatives were reported in different parts of the region. In the cases where there was no *wadi*, like the one in al-Sayyah, people dug shallow wells and organized cooperative production of millet and vegetables. In al-Sayyah itself the village women established a cooperative project around two shallow wells, the crop was stored as a community reserve, the vegetables were sold in the nearby town of Millit, and the cash proceeds were kept for communal security.

Other issues discussed in the *karama* meetings included, for example, assignments for liaison with other villages, NGOs and the regional government; organization of wild food collection; redistribution of seeds available in the village at planting time; and handling of relief deliveries. One problem discussed in a particular *karama* meeting was how to contain attempts made by some individuals to enclose fields of *koraib* and *mukheit* (wild seeds and berries). The meeting passed a resolution that all wild food should be a communal property and any individual attempting to 'privatize' it would be penalized by exclusion from the village community. A similar move was made in Dar Zaghawa in Darfur in 1980 (De Waal 1989). The only difference was that in the case of this dispute it was settled by a panel of local sheikhs, while in 1991 the resolution was passed by a public *karama* meeting.

The yard of the village mosque is still where *karama* meetings are organized, and praying for rain remains a component of the event. However, the imam of the mosque is no longer the absolute leader. With the change in the social and political character of the event a new type of leadership is emerging. Previously, the religious factor provided the context for the meeting and the meal. Now the objectives are no longer confined to the religious domain, and therefore a new breed of secular leadership is replacing the religious one. It is also noticeable that the new leadership does not derive its legitimacy from an old source of tribal authority or native administration. Neither the village sheikh nor the *omda* or *shertie*, or any of those attached to the state structure, are in control of the new economic and political settings. Most of the people in command of the new settings derive their power from their dedication and commitment to the common concerns of the community and their awareness of the complex context of famine and agricultural crisis. The leaders who are most popular in the new settings are those who are openly critical of the central and regional state as well as the old power structures of tribal native administration. This is the source of the conflicts between the new settings, on the one hand, and the state and old local political structures on the other.

The new settings and its leadership are in conflict with the central government, regional government, state local administration, religious authority, and the organizations affiliated to the National Islamic Front. The most acute conflict is with the National Islamic Front (NIF) because the latter now controls central and regional government and is held responsible for the aggravation of the food crisis in rural Sudan by the denial of famine and prohibition of relief deliveries. The NIF is also associated with the big grain merchants who have controlled the market since the beginning of the crisis in 1983, when they made use of their access to funding from the Islamic banks. Furthermore, the version of Islam adopted by the NIF seems to be too radical to be accepted by the rural population in Sudan, who prefer the milder and more moderate version of the Sufi orders, especially the Tijjaniyya in Darfur and the Khatmiyya in eastern Sudan. Finally, the NIF is associated in the popular mind with the practices of the NIF-affiliated relief agencies, especially the Islamic African Relief Agency, which has used relief to buy support for NIF since 1983. NIF supporters are thus struggling to establish an alliance with some tribal chiefs and *omdas* against the growing new rural leadership, which is often accused of being anti-Islamic.

The most overt expression of the above conflicts is the tense relationship between the leadership of the new settings and the NIF-affiliated popular committees. The central government has appointed these committees in almost every village in the country and has passed a law assigning them a wide range of functions, including intelligence and security and granting them absolute immunity protection. However, these committees are very unpopular because they are too closely associated with the government and the NIF. In some villages in Darfur the regional leadership of the NIF has thus failed to find enough people to form a committee. Being closely associated with the state authority and security organs, the popular committees pose the most serious threat to the new local settings. Most of the arrests of leaders of new political settings have been made on the basis of reports by members of NIF-affiliated popular committees. However, inside the *karama* meetings the members of popular committees are extremely unpopular not only because they are adopting a different version of Islam but because they never talk about the real and immediate interests of local communities.

In addition to the severe hostility of the state to the new political settings, these settings are suffering a number of limitations. First, the dominant idea in these settings is that the central state is irrelevant and it would be better to do without it. This idea could intensify the state pressure on these settings and could reduce any positive potential impact of these settings on public policy. Second, there is a general disappointment with national political organizations, even those that are dedicated to the interests of famine-affected rural communities. Again this could lead to a weakening of both local settings and national organizations and could make it much easier for the state to crush both of them. Third, new political settings are still confined to village community levels with very little coordination between different settings. However, community leaders are gradually becoming aware of this issue. In one of the *karama* meetings in al-Sayyah village a community leader suggested contacting twelve other villages to which the proposed dam project was relevant because they share the valley stream.

Concluding remarks

First, unlike the general tendency in the available literature to focus on the crisis of mechanized farming production, the best way to account for the current food crisis in Sudan is through an analysis of the historical transformation undergone by peasant communities in terms of the pressures imposed on them by national development strategies, and the ways peasant communities have responded to these pressures. This chapter shows that the food crisis is nothing but the crisis of a development pattern in which peasant producers, the majority of the population, are marginalized and subjected to severe pressures.

Second, the food crisis and the collapse of the environmental equilibrium are two faces of the same coin; both are products of the same socio-economic and political processes.

Third, the state, under both colonial and post-colonial regimes, has been central to the food crisis both in terms of the agricultural development policies pursued and in its responses to the crisis. What worries the state most now is that peasant communities are becoming increasingly aware of the role of the state. This awareness would lead to a serious threat to the legitimacy of the state.

Fourth, with the intensification of the crisis the old household coping strategies have been exhausted and they are no longer relevant in alleviating the stress. The state, development agencies and NGOs should rethink their strategies on the basis of these new developments. What the Sudan's case shows is that there is a wide gap between the way peasant communities perceive the food crisis and their coping capacities and the way NGOs understand these capacities and develop their strategies accordingly.

Fifth, peasant communities are now resorting to community-based strategies with a clear political perspective and a clear awareness of the political roots of the crisis. The emergence of new political settings in rural Sudan pose challenges not only to the established regime of political power distribution but also to rural development theories and to political organizations claiming to represent the interests of peasant communities.

Finally, new agendas for research in rural political economy are now being opened and should be taken seriously. These include the capacities of rural communities to adjust to stress and the potential for the transformation of these adjustment mechanisms to political resistance and strategies of political change. In this regard, the old notions of peasants' inherent conservatism should be rethought.

Bibliography

Abdel Ati, H.A., 1988, 'The Process of Famine', *Development and Change*, vol. 19, no. 2, pp. 267–33.

Abdelkarim, A., 1992, *Primitive Capital Accumulation in the Sudan*, Frank Cass, London.

Ahmed, Awad El Seed, 1983, 'Traditional Agriculture in the Northern District of Southern Kordofan Province', in M.H. Awad (ed.), *Socio-economic Change in the Sudan*, Khartoum University Press, Khartoum.

Ali, T.M.A., 1982, 'The Cultivation of Hunger: The Political Economy of Agricultural Development in Sudan', Ph.D. Thesis, University of Toronto.

Barker, J. (ed.), 1984, *The Politics of Agriculture in Tropical Africa*, Sage Publications, London.

Barker, J., 1989, *Rural Communities Under Stress: Peasant Farmers and the State in Africa*, Cambridge University Press, Cambridge.

Bascom, J.B., 1990, 'Food, Wages and Profits: Mechanised Farming Schemes and the Sudanese State', *Economic Geography*, 66, pp. 140–55.

Barnett, T. and A. Abdelkarim (eds), 1989, *Sudan: State, Capital and Transformation*, Croom Helm, London.

Barnett, T. and A. Abdelkarim, 1991, *Sudan: The Gezira Scheme and Agricultural Transition*, Frank Cass, London.

Bennet, J. and S. George, 1987, *The Hunger Machine: The Politics of Food*, Polity Press, Cambridge.

Bernal, V., 1988, 'Coercion and Incentives in African Agricultural Development: Insights from the Sudanese Experience', *The African Studies Review*, vol. 31, no. 2, pp. 89–108.

Bernal, V., 1990, 'Agricultural Development and Food Production on a Sudanese Irrigation Scheme', in M. Salem-Murdock, M. Horowitz and M. Sella (eds), *Anthropology and Development in Africa and the Middle East*, Westview Press, Boulder CO.

Berry, S., 1984, 'The Food Crisis and Agrarian Change in Africa', *The African Studies Review*, vol. 27, no. 2, pp. 59–112.

Borton, J. and E. Clay, 1988, 'The African Food Crisis of 1982–86: A Provisional Review', in Douglas Rimmer (ed.), *Rural Transformation in Tropical Africa*, Belhaven Press, London.

Bothomani, I.B., 1984–85, *The Food Crisis in East and Central Africa*, IMF Staff Papers 21, pp. 148–55.

Brandt, H., 1987, 'The Food Crisis in Africa: A Discussion of the Proposals of Remedying It', *Economics* (Tubigen), 36, pp. 89–99.

Brandt, H. et al., 1987, *The Potential Contribution of Irrigated Agriculture to Food Security in Sudan: The Case of the Gezira Irrigation Scheme*, The German Development Institute, Berlin.

Bush, R., 1985, 'Drought and Famines', *Review of African Political Economy*, 33, pp. 59–63.

Bush, R., 1988, 'Hunger in Sudan: The Case of Darfur', *African Affairs*, vol. 87, no. 346, pp. 5–23.

Campell, D.J., 1987, 'Strategies for Coping With Severe Food Deficits in Northeast Africa', *Northeast African Studies*, vol. 9, no. 2, pp. 43–54.

Campbell, D.J., 1990, 'Strategies For Coping With Severe Food Deficits in Rural Africa: A Review Of The Literature', *Food And Foodways*, vol. 4, no. 2, pp. 143–62.

Central Economic Board, 1909, *Annual Report*, Sudan Government, Khartoum.

Chada, B. and R. Jeja., 1990, 'The Macroeconomics of Famine', *Finance and Development*, vol. 27, no. 1, pp. 46–8.

Clute, R.E., 1987, 'The African Food Crisis: The Need For Reform', *Journal of Developing Societies*, vol. 3, no. 2, pp. 156–73.

Cohen, R. (ed.), 1988, *The Commercialisation of African Agriculture*, Rienner, London.

Commins, S.K. (ed.), 1988, *Africa's Development Challenges and the World Bank: Hard Questions, Costly Choices*, Lynne Rienner, Boulder CO.

Commins, S., M. Lofchie and R. Payne (eds), 1986, *Africa's Agrarian Crisis*, Lynne Rienner, Boulder CO.

Craig, G.M. (ed.), 1991, *The Agriculture of the Sudan*, Oxford University Press, Oxford.

De Souza, F. and J. Shohan, 1985, 'The Spread of Famine in Africa', *Third World Quarterly*, vol. 7, no. 3, pp. 515–31.

Davies, S. et al., 1991, *Food Security and the Environment: Conflict or Complementarity?*, IDS Discussion Paper No. 285, Institute of Development Studies, University of Sussex.

De Waal, A., 1989, *Famine That Kills*, Clarendon Press, Oxford.

Duffield, M., 1990a, *Sudan at the Cross-roads: From Emergency Preparedness to Social Security*, IDS Discussion Paper No. 275, Institute of Development Studies, University of Sussex.

Duffield, M., 1990b, 'Absolute Distress', *Middle East Report*, vol. 20, no. 5, pp. 4–11.

Duffield, M., 1991, 'Where Famine Is Functional', *Middle East Report*, vol. 21, no. 5, pp. 26–30.

Dunmoye, R.A., 1989, 'The Political Economy of Agricultural Production in Africa: State, Capital and the Peasantry', *Peasant Studies*, vol. 16, no. 2, pp. 87–105.

Eicher, C.K., 1988, *Food Security Battles in Sub-Saharan Africa*, Department of Agricultural Economics, Michigan State University.

El Mangouri, Hassan, 1990, 'Dryland Management in the Kordofan and Darfur Provinces of Sudan', in John Dixon, David James, and Paul Sherman (eds), *Dryland Management: Economic Case Studies*, Earthscan, London.

Elmekki, A.M., 1985, 'Peasants and Capital: The Political Economy of Oilseeds Marketing in Sudan', Ph.D. dissertation, University of Toronto.

Elmekki, A. and Jonathan Barker, 1993, 'Marketing, Politics and Agrarian Crisis in Sudan', *IDS Bulletin*, vol. 24, no. 3, pp. 68–73.

Elmekki, A.M. and K.A. El-Amin, 1991, *Peasants' Coping Strategies With Drought and Famine in North Darfur*, research report presented to the UNICEF, Khartoum.

Elmekki, A.M. and S.E. Ibrahim, 1990, *Off-Farm Income Generating Activities in Rural Sudan*, research report presented to the ILO/JASPA, Addis Ababa.

El Moghraby, A. et al., 1987, 'Desertification in Western Sudan and Strategies for Rehabilitation', *Environmental Conservation*, Sudan Energy Research Council, Khartoum, vol. 14, no. 30, pp. 227–31.

FAO/WFP, 1991, *Special Report on Crop and Food Assessment in Sudan*, FAO, Khartoum.

Fruzzetti, L. and A. Ostor, 1990, *Culture and Change Along the Blue Nile*, Westview Press, Boulder CO.

Glantz, M.H. (ed.), 1987, *Drought and Hunger in Africa*, Cambridge University Press, Cambridge.

Hansen, A. and D. Macmillan (eds), 1986, *Food in Sub-Saharan Africa*, Lynne Rienner, Boulder CO.

Harrison, G.A. (ed.), 1988, *Famine*, Oxford University Press, Oxford.

Holy, Ladislav, 1980, 'Drought and Change in a Tribal Economy: The Berti of Northern Darfur', *Disasters*, 4, pp. 65–71.

Holy, Ladislav, 1987, 'Cultivation as a Strategy of Survival in Ecological Crisis: The Berti of Darfur', in D. Johnson and D. Anderson (eds), *The Ecology of Survival: Case Studies from the History of North East Africa*, Crook Green, London.

Horowitz, M. and M. Salem-Murdock, 1987, 'The Political Economy of Desertification in White Nile Province, Sudan', in P.D. Little and M.M. Horowitz (eds), *Lands at Risk in the Third World*, Westview Press, Boulder CO and London.

Ibrahim, F.N., 1978, *The Problem of Desertification in the Republic of the Sudan with Special Reference to Northern Darfur Province*, Development Studies and Research Centre Monograph Series No. 8.

Ibrahim, F.N., 1983, 'The Role of Nomadism in the Desertification in Western Sudan', *Applied Geography and Development*, 22, pp. 46–57.

Ibrahim, Fuad, 1986, 'Ecology and Land Use Changes in the Semiarid Zone of the Sudan', in P.D. Little and M.M. Horowitz (eds), *Lands at Risk in the Third World*, Westview Press, Boulder CO and London.

International Labour Organization, 1986, *After the Famine: A Programme to Strengthen the Survival Strategies of Affected Populations*, ILO, Geneva.

International Labour Organization/JASPA, 1986, *Employment and Economic Reform: Towards A Strategy for Sudan*, ILO, Geneva.

Institute of Social Studies Advisory Service, 1989, *Food Security in the Sudan*, ISS, The Hague.

Jamal, V., 1988, 'Getting the Crisis Right: Missing Perspectives on Africa', *International Labour Review*, vol. 127, no. 6, pp. 655–78.

Jaycox, E.V.K., 1988, 'Ending Hunger In Africa', *Africa Report*, vol. 33, no. 5, pp. 15–18.

Kaspar, Ph. and W. Moll, 1986, 'The Case of Sudan', in Klaus Klennet (ed.), *Rural Development and Careful Utilisation of Resources: The Cases of Pakistan, Peru and Sudan*, Nomos Verlagsgesellschaft, Baden Baden.

Khogali, M.M., 1983, 'The Grazing Resources of the Sudan', in Ooi Jin Bee (ed.), *Natural Resources in Tropical Countries*, Singapore University Press, Singapore.

Kursany, I., 1983, 'Peasants of the Nuba Mountain Region', *Review of African Political Economy*, 26, pp. 35–44.

Larson, B.A., 1991, 'Natural Resource Prices, Export Policies, and Deforestation: The Case of Sudan', *World Development*, vol. 19, no. 10, pp. 1289–97.

Leach, G. 1990, 'Agroforestry and the Way Out for Africa', in *Greenhouse Effect and Its Impact on Africa*, Institute for African Alternatives, London.

Lemma, A. and P. Malaska (eds), 1989, *Africa Beyond Famine*, Tycooly Publishing, London and New York.

Lemma, H., 1985, 'The Politics of Famine in Ethiopia', *Review of African Political Economy*, 33, pp. 44–58.

Little, P.D. and M.M. Horowitz, 1987, 'Social Science Perspectives on Land, Ecology, and Development', in P.D. Little and M.M. Horowitz (eds), *Lands at Risk in the Third World*, Westview Press, Boulder CO and London.

Lofchie, M., 1975, 'Political and Economic Origins of African Hunger', *Journal of Modern African Studies*, vol. 13, no. 4, pp. 551–67.

Mafeje, A., 1987, 'African Agriculture: The Next 25 Years – Old Problems, Old Solutions and Scientific Foibles', *Africa Development*, vol. 12, no. 2, pp. 5–34.

Markakis, J., 1987, 'Famine and Politics in the Horn of Africa', *Capital and Class*, 31, pp. 17–23.

Maxwell, S., 1989, *Food Insecurity in North Sudan*, IDS Discussion Paper No. 262, Institute of Development Studies, University of Sussex.

Maxwell, S. (ed.), 1991, *To Cure All Hunger*, Intermediate Technology Publications, London.

Mengisteab, K., 1985, 'Food Shortages in Africa: A Critique of Existing Agricultural Strategies', *Africa Today*, vol. 32, no. 4, pp. 39–53.

Mengisteab, K., 1988, 'Africa's Food Crisis: A Challenge to Existing Development Theories', *Journal of Developing Societies*, vol. 4, no. 2, pp. 166–79.

Ministry of Finance, 1988, *Proceedings of National Food Security Workshop*, Khartoum, Sudan.

Mohamed Salih, M.A., 1989, 'Ecological Stress, Political Coercion and the Limits of State Intervention: Sudan', in A.H. Ornas and M.A. Mohamed Salih (eds), *Ecology and Politics: Environmental Stress and Security in Africa*, Scandinavian Institute of African Studies, Uppsala.

Mohamed Salih, M.A., 1990a, 'Perspectives On Pastoralists and the African States', *Nomadic Peoples*, 25–27, pp. 3–6.

Mohamed Salih, M.A., 1990b, 'Pastoralism and the State in African Arid Lands', *Nomadic Peoples*, 25–27, pp. 7–18.

Mohamed Salih, M.A., 1990c, 'Government Policy and Options in Pastoral Development in the Sudan', *Nomadic Peoples*, 25–27, pp. 65–78.

Moll, W., 1986, 'Basic Aspects of Development and Ecology in the Sudan', in Klaus Klennet (ed.), *Rural Development and Careful Utilisation of Resources: The Cases of Pakistan, Peru and Sudan*, Nomos Verlagsgesellschaft, Baden Baden.

Novicki, M.A., 1985, 'Ethiopian Drought and Famine Crisis', *Africa Report*, 30, pp. 47–9.

O'Brien, J., 1978, 'How Traditional is "Traditional Agriculture"?', *Sudan Journal of Economic and Social Studies*, vol. 2, no. 2, pp. 1–10.

O'Brien, J., 1980, 'Agricultural Labour Force and Development in Sudan', Ph.D. thesis, University of Connecticut.

O'Brien, J., 1981, 'Sudan: An Arab Breadbasket?', *MERIP Report*, 99, pp. 20–26.

O'Brien, J., 1983a, 'Formation of the Agricultural Labour Force', *Review of African Political Economy*, 26, pp. 15–34.

O'Brien, J., 1983b, 'The Political Economy of Capitalist Agriculture in the Central Rainlands of Sudan', *Labour, Capital and Society*, vol. 16, no. 1.

O'Brien, J., 1985, 'Sowing the Seeds of Famine', *Review of African Political Economy*, 33, August, pp. 23–32.

O'Brien, J., 1987, 'The Calculus of Profit and Labour in Sudanese Peasant Agriculture', *Journal of Peasant Studies*, vol. 4, no. 3.

Okigbo, B.N., 1988, 'Food: Finding Solutions to the Crisis', *Africa Report*, vol. 33, no. 5, pp. 13–18.

O'Neill, N. and J. O'Brien (eds), 1988, *Economy and Class in Sudan*, Avebury, Aldershot.

Onimode, B., 1988, *The Political Economy of The African Crisis*, Zed Books, London.

Osterfield, D., 1985, 'Famine in Africa', *The Journal of Social, Political and Economic Studies*, vol. 10, no. 3, pp. 259–74.

Pankhurst, D., 1988, 'Hunger in Western Sudan', *Capital and Class*, 33, pp. 19–28.

Picard, L., 1984, 'Self-sufficiency, Delinkage, and Food Production: Limits on Agricultural Development in Africa', *Policy Studies Review*, 4, pp. 311–19.

Raikes, P., 1988, *Modernising Hunger*, James Currey, London.

Rau, B., 1991, *From Feast To Famine: Official Cures and Grassroots Remedies to Africa's Food Crisis*, Zed Books, London.

Saeed, Abdelbasit, 1982, *The State and Socio-Economic Transformation in the Sudan: The Case of Social Conflicts in Southern Kordofan*, University Microfilms, Ann Arbor MI.
Sen, A., 1976, 'Famines and Failure of Exchange Entitlements', *Economic and Political Weekly*, 11, pp. 1273–80.
Sen, A., 1977, 'Starvation and Exchange Entitlements: A General Approach and its Application to the Great Bengal Famine', *Cambridge Journal of Economics*, 1, pp. 33–59.
Sen, A., 1980, 'Famines', *World Development*, vol. 8, no. 9, pp. 613–21.
Sen, A.K., 1981, *Poverty and Famines: An Essay on Entitlement and Deprivation*, Clarendon Press, Oxford.
Sen, A.K., 1982, 'The Food Problem: Theory and Practice', *Third World Quarterly*, vol. 4, no. 3.
Sen, A. and J. Dreze (eds), 1990, *The Political Economy of Hunger*, 3 vols, Clarendon Press, Oxford.
Shenton, R. and M. Watts, 1979, 'Capitalism and Hunger in Northern Nigeria', *Review of African Political Economy*, 15/16, pp. 53–62.
Shepherd, A., 1983, 'Capitalist Agriculture in the Sudan Dura Prairies', *Development and Change*, 14.
Shepherd, A., 1988, 'Case Studies of Famine: Sudan', in D. Curtis, M. Hubbard and A. Shepherd (eds), *Preventing Famine*, Routledge, London and New York.
Shields, T., 1991, 'A Tragedy in the Making', *Africa Report*, March/April, pp. 54–7.
Skalnes, T., 1989, 'Group Interests and the State: An Explanation of Zimbabwe's Agricultural Policies', *The Journal of Modern African Studies*, vol. 27, no. 1, pp. 85–107.
Stone, J., 1955, *Sudan Economic Development*, Sudan Economic Institute, Khartoum.
Swift, J., 1989, 'Why are Rural People Vulnerable to Famine?', *IDS Bulletin*, vol. 20, no. 2, pp. 8–15.
Tapasoba, E.K., 1991, *Food Security Issues in West Africa*, FAO Economic and Social Development Paper No. 93.
Teklu, T., 1991, 'Responses to Declining Food Entitlement: The Experience from Western Sudan', unpublished paper.
Teklu, T., J. von Braun and E. Zaki, 1991, *Drought and Famine Relationships in Sudan: Policy Implications*, IFPRI, Washington DC.
Tully, D., 1988, *Culture and Context in Sudan: The Process of Market Incorporation in Dar Masalit*, State University of New York Press, Albany.
Wallace, T., 1985, 'Refugees and Hunger in Eastern Sudan', *Review of African Political Economy*, 33.
Wallach, B., 1989, 'Improving Traditional Grassland Agriculture in Sudan', *The Geographical Review*, vol. 79, no. 2, pp. 143–60.
Watkins, R., 1985, 'Sudan's Hidden Tragedy', *Africa Report*, vol. 30, no. 6, pp. 19–21.
Watts, M., 1983, *Silent Violence: Famine and Peasantry in Northern Nigeria*, University of California Press, Berkeley.
Whitney, J.B.R., 1986, 'Impact of Fuelwood Use on Environmental Degradation in the Sudan', in P.D. Little and M.M. Horowitz (eds), *Lands at Risk in the Third World*, Westview Press, Boulder CO and London.
Winer, N., 1989, 'Agriculture and Food Security in Ethiopia', *Disasters*, vol. 13, no. 1, pp. 1–8.
Wohlmuth, K. (ed.), 1983, *The Development of the Sudan: The Limits of the Breadbasket Strategy*, Munich.
Wohlmuth, K. (ed.), 1989, *Structural Adjustment in the World Economy and East–West–*

South Economic Co-operation, Institute For World Economics and International Management, Bremen.

Wohlmuth, K. and P. Oesterdiekhoff, 1983, 'The "Breadbasket" is Empty: The Options of Sudanese Development Policy', *Canadian Journal of African Studies*, vol. 17, no. 1, pp. 35–67.

Woldemeskel, G., 1990, 'Famine and the Two Faces of Entitlement: A Comment on Sen', *World Development*, vol. 18, no. 3, pp. 491–5.

World Bank, 1990, *Sudan: Toward an Action Plan for Food Security*, World Bank, Washington DC.

Zahlan, H. (ed.), 1986, *The Agricultural Sector of the Sudan*, Cornell University Press, London and Ithaca NY.

Part III

Conflict Resolution

12

Sowing the Seeds of Cooperation in Environmentally Induced Conflicts

Katrina S. Rogers

Why Study Cooperation?

This chapter is not about conflict mediation, conflict resolution or conflict management. It is about the dynamics of cooperation and how it is possible to foster these dynamics in environmentally induced conflicts. A starting point in understanding cooperation is Kenneth Boulding's observation (1962) that peace is a socially learned behaviour; by analogy this idea can be applied to cooperation.

It is an unfortunate truth that many disciplines, including but not limited to political science, sociology, peace studies, psychology and conflict resolution, focus their theoretical work on conflict (war) much more than on cooperation (peace). Cooperation, like peace, is more often seen as a 'non-event', and researchers tend to look for events to study. The oft-quoted phrase, 'for every page written on peace, there are forty written on war', can also by analogy be applied to the topic of co-operation. Worse still, from a conceptual standpoint cooperation and conflict are usually seen as two sides of the same coin. This is ill-considered. The absence of war may not be peace, and the absence of peace is not necessarily war. The absence of conflict does not *de facto* mean that cooperation is evident; nor is the absence of cooperation necessarily a prelude to conflict.

In assessing the literature for this chapter, I was struck by the limited role that cooperation played in discussions of conflict prevention and resolution. Notable exceptions include the work of Rummel (1972) and

Ward (1982), both of whom discuss the dynamics of conflicts, as distinct from cooperation, in terms of interstate interactions. Others who have discussed the circumstances under which conflict can occur within a cooperative framework and where cooperation can occur in the midst of conflict include Axelrod (1984) and Mansbach and Vasquez (1981).

At the outset of this discussion I would like to state my belief that environmental cooperation does not have properties distinct from other types of cooperation. Cooperation operates with certain dynamics which are evident whether the issue to be resolved is an environmental one, such as the case of a dispute over water resources, or a non-environmental one, such as in a dispute over political boundaries. It is, however, important to appreciate the particular subtleties that characterize cooperation over environmental problems. Scenarios which include cooperation over environmental issues are likely to have the following characteristics:

- multiple decision-making fora;
- involvement of multiple actors;
- multiple issues;
- technical complexity;
- scientific uncertainty;
- power and resource disparities;
- public/political arenas for problem-solving.

In addition, decisions over an environmental dispute often involve fundamental alterations to the physical environment, and one side often controls the scientific data (O'Leary in Blackburn et al. 1995).

The Cultural Context of Cooperation

Cooperation emerges out of productive conflict (Deutsch, in Schellenberg 1996). Productive conflict refers to the idea that conflict is a form of socialization and inherent in society (Simmel 1955). In this view, groups within societies require disharmony as well as harmony, dissociation along with association. Conflict functions both as a process and as a structure for group formation, within a group and among groups in any given society. Building on Simmel's work, Lewis Coser observed the following aspects of conflict in society:

- Conflict helps to establish and maintain the identity and boundary lines of societies and groups.
- Conflict with another group contributes to internal group cohesion and unity.
- Conflict may be a way that a society balances competing ideas and maintains its dynamic.

- Conflict is not always dysfunctional in a relationship; it is often necessary to maintain and clarify the tension of a relationship.

One way to view cooperation is to see it as a process which, when viewed in a conflict situation, turns a potentially destructive or violent conflict into a productive one. Productive conflict is characterized by actors' willingness to think about their problems in creative ways, to consider mutual problem-solving mechanisms, to give those they disagree with the benefit of the doubt, and to negotiate cooperative commitments. Cooperation, therefore, exists within an interacting system of relationships, relying both on communicative and on contextual mechanisms. The presence of open communication, a past relationship of goodwill (or at least not hostility), an issue that is relatively small or straightforward, an avoidance of rigid ideological stances on the part of the actors, and a conscious effort to focus on the more objective aspects of the conflict are all indicators of cooperation. The more these elements are present, the more likely is it that cooperation will occur.

The dynamics of cooperation are also located within a cultural context. The underlying context (the common ground) of a dispute needs to be understood in order to explain cooperation and foster its elements. There are many ways to discuss cultural context, and there is increasing recognition that culture plays an important role in conflict, conflict management and conflict resolution (Lund, Morris and Duryea 1994). Utilizing the literature on high- and low-context cultures, for example, helps to clarify the context within which productive conflict/cooperation takes place. Low-context cultures generally refer to groups characterized by individualism, overt communication and heterogeneity. The USA, Canada, and central and northern Europe are described as areas where low-context cultural practices are most in evidence. High-context cultures feature collective identity-focus, covert communication and homogeneity. This approach prevails in Asian countries including Japan, China and Korea, as well as Latin American countries (Jandt and Pedersen 1996).

A misreading of context can lead to prescriptions which have neither specific applicability nor general universality. For example, some studies call for the importance of conciliation and mediation by third parties (Rangarajan 1985). This recommendation may only work for low context cultures such as the United States; in high-context cultures such as Korea insiders are preferred to outsiders in most cases for help in resolving conflict (Duryea 1992). A survey across a large number of different cultures reveals that there are many and different preferred ways to resolve conflicts: arbitration, avoidance, adjudication, divination, feuding, litigation, management, mediation, negotiations, and toleration. In analysing a hundred case examples, Jandt and Pedersen (1996) concluded that differentiation between high context and low context cultures was an important factor in successful mediation. High-context cultures paid attention to historical relationships and long-term outcomes. Low-context cultures focused on conflict resolution or mediation toward immediate solutions, minimizing relationships between parties, and dealing with resolution/mediation at an abstract rather than contextual level (Jandt and Pedersen 1996). From this basis, Jandt and Pedersen developed a series of seventeen hypotheses about conflict management and mediation, of which four are listed as examples:

(i) In low-context cultures, individual participants must first accept and acknowledge that there is a conflict before resolution/mediation can begin.
(ii) In high-context cultures, traditional groups must first accept and acknowledge that there is a conflict before resolution/mediation can begin.
(iii) In low-context cultures, conflict and the resolution/mediation process must often be kept private.
(iv) In high-context cultures, conflict is not private and must be made public before the resolution/mediation process can begin.

The Dynamics of Cooperation in Microcosm

What is happening when cooperation is taking place? The most straightforward path to answering this question is to focus on the simplest form of human interaction: that of two individuals. In the simplest interactions, the dynamics of cooperation are brought to light, making the process easier to understand. This informs our knowledge; whether the dynamics can then be extrapolated to multiple-actor environmentally induced conflicts is taken up in the last part of this chapter. An assumption made here is that the participants do not always behave in a completely rational manner, and it is important to keep in mind that negotiators are not neutral (see Rangarajan 1985 for an elaboration on this point). Additionally, focusing analysis at the individual level emphasizes the importance of individuals in devising theoretical models about cooperation. There are many historical examples that demonstrate the importance of particular individuals at critical moments in politics. For example, Jean Monnet's vision of European unity was crucial to developing post-Second World War cooperation in Europe; Konrad Adenauer's determination to establish a positive relationship with France provided critical cement for the European Coal and Steel Community; and Nelson Mandela's role as a conveyor of non-violence in South Africa has been essential to the fledgling democracy there. Groups, however, can just as easily be substituted for the term 'individual' here, particularly as this scenario is also relevant for high-context cultures.

Consider neighbours living side by side, neither in conflict nor in cooperation; each farming and taking sufficient nutritional sustenance from the land; each taking what they need from the stream that meanders through both properties. Their properties are not well defined. This may be a place where private property is not well defined, a place where there are few people and just enough resources to go around. But as all things change, so too does this situation. One of the neighbours discovers that by growing a different crop, he/she can earn money in the marketplace: enough remuneration to provide for their nutritional needs, and for other things besides. This crop, however, is water intensive. At first, nothing seems to change, even though this neighbour is using more water from the stream. Over time, however, the water level of the stream drops, and the other neighbour becomes concerned. Not only is he/she concerned about the scarcity of water, but he/she also decides he/she wants to grow this crop. Unfortunately, there is not enough water in the stream for both neighbours to grow the same crop.

In this simple scenario, several choices are available to the neighbours. It is at this point that choices are made which bring into play the dynamics of conflict or the dynamics of cooperation. As Mansbach and Vasquez have argued elsewhere (Mansbach and Vasquez 1981; Vasquez 1995), there are three dimensions of conflict and cooperation which reinforce each other over time. These dimensions are:

(i) agreement versus disagreement (a similarity or difference in opinion);
(ii) positive versus negative acts (behaviour that is seen as desirable or undesirable);
(iii) friendship versus hostility (attitudes reflecting psychological affect).

In the case of the neighbours, any or all of these dimensions may be brought into play at any given time. They may agree about the water but disagree about the solution. One may block access to the stream, seen by the other as a clearly hostile act, and so on. The critical point to be made is that actors do not simply behave in a cooperative or conflictive fashion, but rather they relate to each other in conflictive or cooperative ways (Vasquez 1995: 140). It is the emerging relationship which shows the dynamics of cooperation.

If these are to be understood in this hypothetical scenario, several assumptions must be made: both neighbours perceive that there is a problem brewing (or one sees it and brings it to the other's attention);

both neighbours are willing to discuss the issue, and there is an element of trust. Viewing these assumptions, it should be clear that the underpinnings of any type of cooperation will include the ability of the parties to perceive a problem, the willingness to engage in communication, and the willingness to trust the other party. Perception, communication and trust are fundamental human behaviours which can be learned and created.

If it is assumed that the neighbours are communicating and trusting, then the dynamics of cooperation will become evident. Communication will require a willingness to see the issues relevant to each neighbour, and the ability to see that they may 'agree to disagree'. Communication will take time as well; the most positive dialogues will take place in a setting where the space has been created for the neighbours to learn about each other and their differing priorities. The quality of communication is also important. This should not be a forum for the second neighbour to nurse the grievance or dredge up past injuries. In an atmosphere of trust, communication should encourage better understanding of the nature of the problem.

At the heart of the scenario is the fact that the second neighbour feels increasingly insecure about the quantity of water in the stream. For the second neighbour the water in the stream may even be a metaphor that the first neighbour is advancing along a material scale, using a resource that, until now, was common to them both. This perceived inequity and real insecurity is at the heart of most conflicts, particularly where the environment plays a role. Communication between the neighbours needs to address the issues of insecurity and inequity even more than the physical issue of the water between them.

Any attempt at limiting conflicts must address these feelings of insecurity. Insecurity often is the result of a sense of powerlessness, nurtured grievance or perception of threat. Uncertainty breeds insecurity, which causes people to view the future with fear. Since dependence produces insecurity, its alleviation can only come from promoting feelings of interdependence. Displays of power emphasize the powerlessness and subordinate position of others. Showing that dependence is matched by counter-dependence neutralizes that feeling (Rangarajan 1985). Building trust is essential for effective cooperation.

In learning from the lessons that emerge from the negotiations literature (Rangarajan 1985), two sequences have been identified that could end in violence. Individuals, groups or nations feel vulnerable either because they perceive their excessive dependence on others or because a perceived threat makes them feel insecure. Prolonged vulnerability degenerates into fear, leading to desperation. Feelings of dissatisfaction are aroused in an individual, group or nation when unfairness or inequity is perceived. In addition, sometimes failure to get what is seen to be attainable also produces dissatisfaction. A grievance nurtured leads to frustration. Aggressive behaviour is one of the outlets for frustration which turns into desperation. Grievances and feelings of insecurity often go together.

An insecure or a dissatisfied person (group or nation) may voice his/her grievance as a demand for redress. The demand is addressed to those in the environment in a position to ameliorate the situation or remove the perceived threat. But these individuals (groups or nations) may then feel that they have to make a sacrifice, and feelings of dissatisfaction are seeded in them. When such a conflict of interest is perceived, all concerned can either negotiate about it or do nothing. The presence of insecurity gives rise to a desire for order. When a conflict is perceived, the desire for order motivates people to negotiate about it.

Simultaneously, people are reluctant to forgo what they already possess; giving up entails a reduction in power. This fundamental conflict between the desire to reduce insecurity and the desire to maintain power and possessions is ever present. Though it may be rational to negotiate, say, about the conservation of human and material resources that could be irrevocably destroyed, people also fear that the outcome may be disadvantageous to them. The feedback from other negotiators can reinforce these apprehensions. The contradiction between wanting an agreement and fearing its outcome is also ever-present.

One of the conclusions based on this understanding of human interaction is the clear importance of reducing uncertainty. A reduction in uncertainty, or an increase in predictability, crucially depends on trust, which is built up as a perception of past actions. This is especially true of conflicts between states, because there is no judicial enforceability of agreements. The unity of coalitions with multiple actors also depends on trust.

Conflict limitation is possible only if we reduce the number of issues and the number of people (negotiators and mediators) to the minimum. Every conflict has to be tackled first by attempting to shrink the bargaining space and by reducing the number of negotiators. International practice is often the opposite. In demanding a new international economic order, the developing countries have put into the bargaining space everything they can think of – commodity trade, trade in manufactured goods, transfer of technology, aid, shipping, patents, and so on. Since no one can negotiate on all of these as a single package, negotiations do not take place and rhetoric takes over (Rangarajan 1985).

The neighbours, having chosen not to physically fight over the water, still face several options. These options include: the first neighbour stops growing the new crop, returning the stream to its original state; the first neighbour gives some of the crop to the second one in recognition of the water use; the neighbours divide the water so that both grow limited quantities of the new crop; and the second neighbour participates with the first in growing the crop and they share the proceeds. In all of these cases, the neighbours assume that any solution is better than leaving the situation the way it is.

Cooperation does not automatically lead to the best solution, but if cooperation is evident (and not just used as a stalling tactic), then at the simplest level it helps to avoid violent conflict, which is always a positive outcome. But this interpretation again sees cooperation as the flip side to conflict, a view which has limited utility. More importantly, cooperation over the water in the stream creates positive reinforcement for behaviour which can then be evidenced for other more problematic and disturbing environmental problems.

The Dynamics of Cooperation in a Broader Context

Our neighbours show, in the most basic terms, how it is that two individuals cooperate over a human-induced problem with a natural resource. In considering a more complex subject, this chapter now turns to the issue of development and the environment – an issue area that is an important item on the international agenda and one full of potential conflict.

There are many objectives of development, but perhaps the most fundamental were expressed by Ball:

> [to] reduce poverty and ensure an adequate standard of living for all members of society. This involves meeting basic material needs such as those for food, housing, education, and health and medical care, as well as certain non-material requirements, such as the ability to participate in economic and political decisions affecting the course of one's life. (Ball 1988)

Caught up in the task of development is the issue of the environment: how to develop without disrupting natural ecological processes; how to do no harm; how to leave resources for future generations while dealing with the very real needs of present generations. These questions are particularly challenging in societies where people are closely connected to the natural environment, both in securing their food and in deriving their livelihood from it. In these countries development and protection of the environment are often seen as polar opposites. The aggressive use of the environment is seen as necessary to development. At the same time, there is a recognition that the overall goals of environmental protection and development are essentially the same; that is (to paraphrase the Brundtland Report), the improvement of the human quality of life and welfare for present and future generations. Phrases like the 'integrated approach to environment and development', 'sustainable and environmentally sound development', and 'alternative patterns of development and lifestyles' reflect the need for integration of environmental dimensions into development planning and strategies (Bartelmus 1986). To some extent, this shows that environment and development contain the elements of the dynamics of both conflict and cooperation.

In order to consider environmental protection and development as partners in a common goal, developing countries first need to perceive this linkage. Second, they need to have or develop the communicative skills to pursue environmental strategies. Third, they must have the tools available to implement strategies. An interesting example of the simultaneously conflicting and compatible goals of environmental protection and development is provided by examining the issue of conservation in pursuing the protection of biodiversity. The following two examples are condensed from Morse and Stocking (1995; in particular Chapter 6, Stocking et al.).

Conservation policy in past decades has concentrated on protecting species as well as their habitats from further intrusion. This intrusion was usually in the form of people, which meant that much of the energy in conservation was directed at keeping local people away from the resource. In terms of biodiversity, local resource users were seen as the primary culprits in the loss of biodiversity. This attitude pitted local users against conservationists in an adversarial stance and in a conflictive setting. One example of this is in the Ngorongoro Conservation Area (NCA) in Tanzania, which was established in 1959 and set up as a multiple-use area. Conflict has plagued the NCA, with hard-line conservationists portraying the multiple-use aspects of the area as an ecological disaster. Other problems that have become evident in the last few decades are increasing competition for grazing between wildlife and domestic animals, demands by the communities for better infrastructure, and complaints that there has been a lack of material and financial benefits directly to local communities from the management system.

A second case study comes from the Usambara mountains, also in Tanzania, where, in an attempt to preserve the biological diversity and tropical forest in this isolated area, the East Usambaras Agricultural Development and Environmental Conservation Project was set up in 1987. The objective of the project was to link conservation and development by establishing as priorities the organization of communal tree nurseries, village forest reserves, and village pit-sawing groups. These village-based activities were seen as ways in which public forest land could be protected and managed sustainably while also giving direct benefits to groups. Unfortunately, the organization of these group efforts proved frustrating to project management. The nurseries provided few seedlings of plantable quality and local institutions were unwilling to organize controlled and limited legal exploitation of public land.

Lessons Learned from Case Studies

Both of these examples show that the people most affected by the conservation, the locals, are also the ones that paid most in terms of loss of that resource in order to satisfy basic development needs. A growing consensus among a number of actors involved in similar conservation projects now recognizes that local people have legitimate needs (going back to our scenario where perception becomes apparent as a presupposition of cooperation), and that a different strategy is needed. This different strategy involves linking conservation goals and action with development, by

> arguing that one is contingent upon another, by showing the 'true' value of conservation and what it can contribute to development, and by developing a more flexible approach to protected areas. The means of linkage are usually through externally funded projects, institutions and government initiatives. (Stocking et al. 1995)

These two examples from Tanzania demonstrate how cooperation functions in an environmental context. First of all, there is a recognition that local participation is important in conservation and development. The neighbours need to participate, and there has to be a perception on the part of outside actors that this participation is valid and necessary. These lessons from past experience show that without local participation the people who are expected to implement the project will not sustain it once the outside planners are gone from the scene. An important secondary point, however, is that with more participation the incompatibility between conservation and development becomes more pronounced and the project cycle, the amount of time required to complete the project, needs to be extended. This implies an axiom for cooperation: good communication takes time.

Another lesson to be drawn from these case studies is that integrated conservation and development projects are extremely complex and difficult to manage. Coordinating these projects involves a delicate balance between conservation goals and development priorities. By analogy, this complexity holds true for environmentally induced conflict, particularly where a multiplicity of stake-holders and competing priorities are involved. Since the human mind does not deal effectively with more than two or three interrelated issues simultaneously, it may be useful to take a page from the lessons learned in negotiation theory that breaking up the issues into discrete parts (while still seeing them as part of a related whole) will promote better communication and useful dialogue. Increasing complexity leads to failure, and a decision is more difficult to reach the larger the number of people negotiating together (see Rangarajan 1985).

The examples of conservation and development point out that at the most fundamental levels a change in attitude in required on the part of all actors in order to link conservation and development. The authors issue a call for training, education and research through monitoring of activities (Stocking et al. 1995). I would like to echo this call, with the observation that cooperation is a learned behaviour which begins with training and education.

Lastly, these case studies highlight the point that possible solutions to conflict include multiple-use areas and local control of resources. Both of these solutions require cooperation on the part of actors to share responsibility for the use of resources.

Learning Cooperation: Implications for Environmentally Induced Conflicts

Keeping in mind our hypothetical scenario of the two neighbours, a rough outline of the set of stages relevant to cooperation can be constructed:

(i) *Latent stage*: the conditions of a conflict emerge, such as the decreasing quantity of a resource, which leads to a social conflict.
(ii) *Emergent stage*: the social conflict becomes evident as our two neighbours begin to perceive that there is a problem to be settled.
(iii) *Escalation stage*: this is the point where the dynamics of cooperation are evident. The neighbours communicate with each other about the problem; willingness to negotiate, communicate, and trust each other become important indicators of cooperation.
(iv) *Settling stage*: this is where the neighbours settle on a solution or series of solutions to the stream and attempt to settle some aspects of the conflict.
(v) *Outcome stage*: the situation appears to have been settled.
(vi) *Post-conflict stage*: the solutions to the problem either work or do not work. If they work, then this builds trust for future cooperation. If they do not, then the likelihood of renewed negotiation becomes high.

In this outline of the stages, the distinction between cooperation and conflict is evident only from stage (iii) onward. In a conflict, evidence of cooperation would be absent from the escalation stage, and might include violence as an element of escalation. In addition, a de-escalation stage would also be necessary as moves are made to reduce the level or extent of the dispute.

Embedded in these stages is the recognition that cooperation is based on a series of learned behaviours. These behaviours emphasize: listening to others, valuing their contributions, cooperation with others, affirmation of self and others as a necessary basis for resolving conflict, speaking for oneself rather than accusing others, trying to understand others' points of view, using a creative problem-solving approach to work on conflicts, looking at all the options before deciding, and looking for a win/win solution.

Cooperation is often difficult to achieve because it is a behaviour as well as a process which requires a series of actions that, in general terms, most individuals have not learned. Nor have they been trained to engage in these actions in these positive preventive ways. Cooperation requires perception, high-quality communication, trust and time. Skills which facilitate cooperation include the ability to perceive another's problem or issue. This empathetic understanding can be developed in individuals as well as collectively in communities. Communication is also a learned skill, one in which positive interaction is demonstrated. High-quality communication is when parties in disagreement are able to focus on the issue at stake rather than engage in past grievances or tangential complaints. Trust builds as sustained interaction results in positive, or at least non-negative, outcomes. Interaction occurs when actors interface either in a physical space or over issues. Over time, positive interaction builds trust. This issue of time is an important one. Temporality locates people within a context, a context which then become a basis for cooperation.

In recent years, much attention has been paid to using arts education as a way to develop practical and applicable techniques in problem-solving and cooperation. One area where skills relevant for cooperation are being taught is in the arts. Arts approaches can provide special opportunities to develop and practise many of these skills in the following ways. For instance, they involve participants actively in interfacing with the subject matter, which allows participants to explore a wide range of emotional and intellectual responses. Also, the engagement in an external activity can provide and teach distancing, a skill which is particularly useful in difficult and emotive issues such as is often the case with the environment. Using the arts as a forum for self-discovery, people can try out different options and ways of being without endangering their position, whether using drama, movement, music or painting. Involvement in the arts also engages the whole person speaking from his/her intuitive and visceral grasp of the media, which helps to develop empathetic understanding. Cooperative projects can also teach participants skills in working together to resolve conflict, and can assist in developing communication skills, such as listening, clarity of thought and expression, and mutual problem-solving (Liebmann 1996).

Cooperation can be created and nurtured, even in highly conflictive situations such as a disagreement involving humans and the environment. As I have suggested here, the literature, research and practical application in the area of conflict resolution, psychology and sociology offer political scientists many ways to engage in understanding cooperation. This chapter has taken the opportunity to clarify the proposition that cooperation can be fostered within conflict through a variety of means, including, but not limited to, measures such as reducing underlying bases for conflict; reducing inequalities and/or differences in values; building trust and confidence among constituencies through repeated interaction and positive communication, and teaching cooperative skills such as communication, listening and developing understanding.

Bibliography

Axelrod, R.K., 1984, *The Evolution of Cooperation*, Basic Books, New York.

Ball, Nicole, 1998, *Security and Economy in the Third World*, Princeton University Press, Princeton NJ.

Bartelmus, Peter, 1986, *Environment and Development*, Allen & Unwin, Boston MA.

Bercovitch, Jacob (ed.), 1996, *Resolving International Conflicts: The Theory and Practice of Mediation*, Lynne Rienner, Boulder CO.

Blackburn, J. Walton, Willa Marie Bruce et al., 1995, *Mediating Environmental Conflicts*, Quorum Press, Westport CT.

Boulding, Kenneth E., 1962, *Conflict and Defense*, Harper & Row, New York.

Coser, Lewis A., 1956, *The Functions of Social Conflict*, The Free Press, Glencoe IL.

Duryea, M.L.B., 1992, *Conflict and Culture: A Literature Review and Bibliography*, University of Victoria Institute of Dispute Resolution, Victoria BC.

Hopman, P. Terrence, 1996, *The Negotiation Process and the Resolution of International Conflicts*, University of South Carolina Press, Columbia SC.

Jandt, Fred E. and Paul B. Pedersen et al., 1996, *Constructive Conflict Management: Asia-Pacific Cases*, Sage Publications, London.

Katz, Mark N., 1995, 'Mechanisms of Conflict Resolution', in I. William Zartman, Victor A. Kremenyuk et al., *Cooperative Security: Reducing Third World Wars*, Syracuse University Press, Syracuse NY, pp. 315–30.

Kremenyuk, Victor A. and I. William Zartman, 1995, 'Prospects for Cooperative Security and Conflict Reduction', in I. William Zartman, Victor A. Kremenyuk et al., *Cooperative Security: Reducing Third World Wars*, Syracuse University Press, Syracuse NY, pp. 331–41.

Kriesberg, Louis, 1995, 'Applications and Misapplications of Conflict Resolution

Ideas to International Conflicts', in John A. Vasquez, James Turner Johnson, Sanford Jaffe, Linda Stamato et al., *Beyond Confrontation: Learning Conflict Resolution in the Post-Cold War Era*, University of Michigan Press, Ann Arbor, pp. 87–102.

Liebmann, Marian (ed.), 1996, *Arts Approaches to Conflict*, Jessica Kingsley Publications, London.

Lund, B., C. Morris, M. LeBaron Duryea et al., 1994, *Conflict and Culture: Report of the Multiculturalism and Dispute Resolution Project*, University of Victoria Institute of Dispute Resolution, Victoria BC.

Mansbach, R.W. and Vasquez, J.A., 1981, *In Search of Theory: A New Paradigm for Global Politics*, Columbia University Press, New York.

Morse, Stephen, Michael Stocking et al., 1995, *People and Environment*, University of British Columbia Press, Vancouver.

Rangarajan, L.N., 1985, *The Limitation of Conflict: A Theory of Bargaining and Negotiation*, St Martin's Press, New York.

Rummel, R.J., 1972, 'US Foreign Relations: Conflict, Cooperation, and Attribute Distances', in B. Russett et al., *Peace, War, and Numbers*, Sage Publications, Beverly Hills CA, pp. 71–113.

Schellenberg, James A., 1996, *Conflict Resolution: Theory, Research, and Practice*, SUNY Press, Albany NY.

Simmel, Georg, 1955, *Conflict*, trans. Kurt H. Wolff, The Free Press, Glencoe IL.

Smock, David R., Chester A. Crocker et al., 1995, *African Conflict Resolution: The US Role in Peacemaking*, US Institute of Peace, Washington DC.

Stocking, Michael, Scott Perkin and Katrina Brown, 1995, 'Coexisting with Nature in the Developing World', in Stephen Morse, Michael Stocking et al., *People and Environment*, University of British Columbia Press, Vancouver, pp. 155–85.

Vasquez, John A., James Turner Johnson, Sanford Jaffe, and Linda Stamato et al., 1995, *Beyond Confrontation: Learning Conflict Resolution in the Post-Cold War Era*, University of Michigan Press, Ann Arbor.

Vasquez, John A., 1995, 'Why Global Conflict Resolution is Possible: Meeting the Challenges of the New World Order', in John A. Vasquez et al., *Beyond Confrontation: Learning Conflict Resolution in the Post-Cold War Era*, University of Michigan Press, Ann Arbor, pp. 131–53.

Ward, M.D., 1982, 'Cooperation and Conflict in Foreign Policy Behaviour: Reaction and Memory', *International Studies Quarterly*, 26, March, pp. 87–126.

Zartman, I. William, Victor A. Kremenyuk et al., 1995, *Cooperative Security: Reducing Third World Wars*, Syracuse University Press, Syracuse NY.

13

Conflict versus Cooperation in a Regional Setting: Lessons from Eritrea

Arthur H. Westing

Eritrea finally gained its independence from Ethiopia in 1993 following thirty long years of deadly and disruptive conflict (Cobb 1996; Fre 1991; Gebremedhin 1997; Giorgis 1993; Pool 1993). In that same year it joined the United Nations (UN) in ebullient spirits despite a greatly damaged infrastructure and an abjectly impoverished condition. Eritrea is now striving to establish a viable multi-ethnic, secular state, *inter alia* by rebuilding its natural-resource base and economic and political systems to achieve self-sufficiency in basic needs, participatory governance, and a harmonious alliance within the family of nations.

With the appallingly destructive war of independence still fresh in everyone's memory, Eritrea recognizes that its current efforts to achieve sustainability would be greatly hampered, if not prevented, by engaging in further armed conflicts. Even in the absence of any major future military actions, Eritrea additionally recognizes that its sustainable development would be subverted by maintaining a substantial military sector, owing of course to the resulting demands on the scarce material, financial and intellectual resources it so desperately needs within its civil sector.

The present chapter examines the hurdles that Eritrea must overcome in order to attain the national security it desires, doing so in the context of its eco-geographical and political positions within the Horn of Africa, the Red Sea drainage basin, the Nile drainage basin, and beyond. Starting afresh – and with the nation-wide camaraderie and momentum that has been generated by three arduous decades of struggle – Eritrea has, in fact, the rare opportunity to achieve its goals.

Eritrea as a Sovereign State

As one of the youngest and poorest sovereign states in both its region and the world, the Eritrean government and people now face the Herculean task of developing a viable system that will obviate recourse to civil war by ensuring basic human rights and necessities for all. Such a dual obligation implies the need for Eritrea to maintain or establish a number of crucial social prerequisites, among them especially a corruption-free form of participatory governance at both national and local levels and a structure of justice built upon a robust legal system and equal treatment for all irrespective of gender, religion or race. These principles reflect the stated desires of Eritrea, and a constitution is now being drafted accordingly, one that is meant formally to confirm and nurture those rights and necessities within a framework of non-violence (Eritrea 1996). However, they will not be easy to achieve or maintain in the light of Eritrea's own current deficiencies or scarcities and in the midst of the generally poor records and conditions of Eritrea's neighbours and near neighbours.

Within the framework of national security just outlined, the Eritrean government recognizes that it has the further responsibility to enable each citizen to achieve a standard of living and level of personal safety that secures his or her health and well-being from birth to death. Those obligations in turn imply a panoply of additional social and environmental conditions that must be met, as outlined below.

Chief among the additional social conditions to be met are education (fewer than 20 per cent of Eritrean adults are literate), old-age insurance, medical care, housing, and employment opportunities for all, as well as a regionally appropriate defensive military force and adequate transportation and communication infrastructures. Moreover, the current severe nationwide shortages in arable land, urban infrastructure, housing (both rural and urban), and employment opportunities make the repatriation of perhaps as many as 150,000 Eritrean refugees still remaining in the Sudan a particularly intractable problem. These shortages also make it most difficult for any of the 50,000 or more Eritreans now living in Europe or North America to return and assist in reconstructing the economy.

Chief among the additional environmental conditions to be met are: access by all to clean water (now available to less than 10 per cent of all Eritreans), air that is fit to breathe, availability of adequate fuel supplies, arable land to produce a sufficiency of staple foods and an appropriate fraction of the nation's territory devoted to providing necessary ecosystem services. The last noted obligation should simultaneously serve to provide satisfactory habitat for the protection of biodiversity and of nature in general. Within its limited means, Eritrea is, in fact, already striving to achieve environmental security in its various crucial dimensions (Eritrea 1995).

At present the Eritrean people – about 80 per cent rural and 20 per cent urban – depend for their well-being on a substantial continuing influx of foreign aid. For example, the country now produces less than 50 per cent of its staple food requirements, and must therefore consider the achievement of food security as one of its very highest priorities (Gebremedhin 1996). Similarly important is the achieving of fuelwood security. To accomplish these dual aims will require restoration and continued maintenance of the now widely prevalent degraded lands through improved agriculture, silviculture and coastal fisheries on the one hand, and effective population control measures on the other. Moreover, the nurturing of democratic rule appears to be a prerequisite for permitting the still much needed foreign aid to be utilized to good effect (Boone 1996).

The rural land reformation measures adopted by Eritrea in 1995 – despite some potential difficulties – are a major step towards achieving food security (Joireman 1996). They establish the necessary continuity of sedentary agricultural tenure, provide for land essential to wood production, create opportunities for foreign investors, and, most importantly, institute equal land rights for men and women. On the other hand, they fail to provide safeguards for the small fraction of nomadic pastoralists among the rural population (concentrated in the relatively large arid coastal lowlands) and they require governmental vigilance to enforce environmental safeguards in the areas to be given over to foreign investment.

As a member of the UN, Eritrea has agreed to eschew aggressive military actions, as have all of its eleven neighbours and near neighbours, and most other countries as well. Nonetheless, many of Eritrea's neighbours have politically unstable and consistently bellicose records, so that Eritrea must on the one hand strive to win its region over to non-violent norms in both external and internal affairs, and on the other to maintain an adequate defensive force to safeguard the integrity of its own recently enunciated non-violent standards. Aside from the inevitable loss of life, damage to infrastructure, and disruption of the environment associated with armed conflict, the resources expended in the region by the military sector are, as already noted, urgently needed to help achieve better standards of living. Moreover, in order to safeguard its nascent democracy, Eritrea is well advised to keep its military sector distinct from, and subservient to, its civil sector (Luckham 1996).

As important as it is for Eritrea to strive for self-sufficiency in its basic needs and legitimate desires, it is impossible for any country – especially a small and poor one – to achieve self-sufficiency and further affluence in a vacuum. Eritrea forms an intricate part of various social and natural systems from which it simply cannot divorce itself. That is, of course, the case because numerous problems beyond military threats, as well as a host of opportunities, do not respect national boundaries, and must therefore be addressed in concert by two or more states. In addition to the need for cooperating bilaterally with each of its three contiguous neighbours, Eritrea must also function within three eco-geographical regions, as well as within the community of nations in general. Those four domains are discussed separately below.

Eritrea and the Horn of Africa

Eritrea is one of five states in the Horn of Africa, shares borders with three of them, and represents 3 per cent of the regional area and 4 per cent of its population. The overall Horn is a semi-arid, environmentally degraded, poverty-stricken, and strife-torn part of the world, representing about 15 per cent of the area of Africa (i.e. almost half the size of Europe). The Horn has few exploitable mineral or natural resources suitable for export. All five states within the Horn are plagued with exploding population growth, which makes any attempt for them to achieve self-sufficiency in the production of staple foods or of fuelwood extraordinarily difficult if not impossible. Of the four states with which Eritrea shares the Horn, it now has the very good fortune of enjoying a warm and productive relationship with Ethiopia. On the other hand, as is outlined below, there has been some tension with Djibouti and seriously strained relations with the Sudan; Somalia has added additional regional stresses.

Djibouti has been experiencing some internal unrest (Wallensteen and Sollenberg 1996), but this appears to be kept from escalating by the permanent presence of French troops. Moreover, recent militarized border problems between Eritrea and Djibouti, Eritrea's smallest and presumably least militarily threatening neighbour, now seem to be yielding to non-violent resolution (HoAB 1996b).

The Sudan, the largest and one of the poorest states in Africa, is particularly troublesome for Eritrea and its other neighbours. The Sudan, which has experienced five violent changes of government since its establishment in 1956 (in 1958, 1964, 1969, 1985 and 1989), remains under autocratic military rule. Greater or lesser levels of warfare within the Sudan – in large part between the government in the north and one or more insurgent groups in the south – have been the norm for much of the time since its independence, especially during 1953–72, and again ever since 1983, leading, *inter alia*, to huge numbers of fatalities (Sivard

1996; Wallensteen and Sollenberg 1996). The internal conflict in the Sudan is widely ascribed to some combination of religious, ethnic and political animosities, in part a legacy of colonial rule exacerbated by pervasive corruption (Westing 1994). On the other hand, the population of the country has virtually tripled since independence, leading to an over-exploited and deteriorating natural resource base and ever more wide-spread social malaise. There is thus some merit to the suggestion that at least the current phase of this internal conflict is in significant part over the control of the country's increasingly abused and scarce natural resources (Suliman 1993).

Eritrea severed diplomatic relations with the Sudan in December 1994 (as did Uganda in April 1995). It appears that the militant Islamic government of the Sudan is fomenting trouble within Eritrea, lending encouragement and material support there to a fundamentalist Muslim anti-government group (Lefebvre 1995). In response, Eritrea is said to be providing non-military support to the secularist forces within the Sudan that are attempting to overthrow the current Sudanese regime.

Somalia, although not sharing a border with Eritrea, is another focus of anarchy and upheaval within the Horn (Sivard 1996; Wallensteen and Sollenberg 1996). Somalia waged war against Ethiopia during 1964 and again during 1977–79, invading Ethiopia in an attempt to acquire the Ogaden region (to which it refers as 'Western Somalia'), but was driven back. Ethiopia was at war with Somalia in 1982, again in 1987, and once again in 1996. As to its intrastate affairs since independence, Somalia underwent a violent change of government in 1969. More recently, there has been more or less continuous fighting within the country for control of the government since about 1988 (brought to world attention for a time during the inauspicious UN operation in Somalia [UNOSOM], especially so from 1993/94). Additionally, the northern portion of Somalia has considered itself independent since 1991 under the name of Somaliland, with Hargeisa its capital.

Because of the various foci of conflict within the Horn, one useful vehicle for fostering both environmental and political components of the national security aims of Eritrea within this region could be the recently revitalized Intergovernmental Authority on Development (IGAD), with headquarters in neighbouring Djibouti. Eritrea joined the Authority in 1993 and has now begun to take a very active role in that potentially key Horn organization (HoAB 1996c). The Association for Strengthening Agricultural Research in East and Central Africa (Entebbe), bringing together since 1994 the directors of agricultural research of twelve states, including all five from the Horn, could complement and reinforce the role of the IGAD (Anderson 1996).

Non-governmental organizations, such as the InterAfrica Group Networking Service in Addis Ababa and the Pastoral and Environmental Network in the Horn of Africa (PENHA) (also in Addis Ababa), play valuable roles in fostering regional security both by complementing the intergovernmental agencies and by serving in something of a watchdog capacity. Among the cross-border issues of environmental concern in the Horn that would lend themselves especially well to bilateral or multilateral regional cooperation are:

- the exploitation of trans-frontier fresh water systems (e.g. the headwater streams of the Atbara that flow from Eritrea into the Sudan);
- the utilization by nomadic pastoralists of trans-frontier rangelands;
- the supervision of environmental refugee movements across national boundaries;
- the control of the ever recurring regional locust infestations;
- the management of migratory game species and other wildlife that do not respect national borders;
- the sharing of regionally limited environmental research and educational facilities.

The safeguarding of ecosystems and biodiversity is not as yet well served in the Horn, with only about 4 per cent of the area under formal protection as natural areas, about one-third of what it ought to be. Djibouti and Somalia are especially deficient in this regard. Moreover, the 1968 African Convention on the Protection of Nature and Natural Resources could become a valuable vehicle for regional cooperation, but to date from among the five Horn of Africa countries only Djibouti and the Sudan belong.

Eritrea and the Red Sea Drainage Basin

Eritrea represents 2 per cent of the combined areas of the seven Red Sea states and 3 per cent of their combined populations. This is a community of nations exhibiting a wide range of wealth and power and with unfortunate political and religious incompatibilities. Most of them share a propensity to resort to violence for conflict resolution, including Egypt, Israel, Jordan, the Sudan and Yemen (Sivard 1996; Wallensteen and Sollenberg 1996). Egypt and the Sudan have a 2 million hectare contested border region (the Halaib Triangle), which resulted in a military clash in 1995 (Westing 1995c). They are also all burdened with unsustainable rates of increase in their population sizes, flagrantly so in the cases of Jordan and Yemen. Eritrea makes only a minor contribution to this community in terms of size, population or wealth, but is nonetheless an important partner because its coastline represents fully 20 per cent of the perimeter of the Sea. The Red Sea itself has an area of almost 44 million hectares and is a particularly warm and saline body of water, with coral reefs and islands prevalent, especially in its southern half. To the south, the Sea is connected to the Indian Ocean via the Gulf of Aden; and to the north, it has been connected since 1869 to the Mediterranean Sea via the Suez Canal. The Sea is burdened with heavy tanker traffic and considerable associated pollution. Artisanal fishing is widely prevalent.

The 1982 Red Sea Conservation Convention (with headquarters in Jeddah) could become a most useful compact for cooperation among the littoral states to protect that eco-geographical region if its pernicious exclusionary clause were purged from it. In the meantime, the United Nations Global Environment Facility (GEF) has supported a number of projects aimed, at least in part, at protecting the marine environment of the Red Sea (GEF 1996; Land 1994).

Eritrea must strive to take increased advantage of its splendid coastal location at the least by further developing its coastal fishery, its sea salt production, and its opportunities for tourism – doing all this, of course, with due regard to maintaining the integrity of its still relatively unspoiled littoral environment. Such pursuits will be able to contribute variously to food security, to bolstering the export sector, and to attracting foreign capital.

Roughly 3 per cent of the Red Sea drainage basin is now formally reserved on behalf of ecosystems and biodiversity, a value that should be increased perhaps fourfold. Only Israel has to date set aside a sufficient area for nature, and Somalia and Yemen are egregiously deficient in this regard. As to the sea itself, at present only about 0.2 per cent, a pitifully small fraction, is under formal protection. Elsewhere I have suggested that the conflict between Eritrea and Yemen over the Hanish archipelago (Plaut 1996) could be resolved amicably by setting aside the contested sovereignty issue in favour of a jointly administered, and sorely needed, protected natural area (Westing 1996).

Eritrea and the Nile Drainage Basin

Eritrea is one of ten states within the Nile drainage basin, its portion of that basin representing about 1 per cent and its contribution to the waters of the Nile roughly 3 per cent. Of those ten states, five are considered of special relevance to present concerns. Eritrea represents 2 per cent of the combined areas of those latter five states, and 2 per cent of their combined populations as well. This group of five is an asymmetric community in terms of wealth and power but, once again, what most of them have in common is the resolution of conflicts by resorting to deadly violence, including Egypt, Ethiopia, the Sudan, and Uganda (Sivard 1996; Wallensteen and Sollenberg 1996; Westing 1995a). And they all share an urgent need to control their population sizes if they are to entertain any serious hope of approaching sustainability.

The Nile, at almost 6,700 kilometres, is among the longest rivers in the world. Its drainage basin covers 10 per cent of the area of Africa. The Nile is important as a transportation artery and for hydropower, but its foremost value by far in semi-arid to arid and over-populated north-eastern Africa is for irrigating agriculture. The Nile has been the life-blood of Egypt for perhaps the past six millennia, which, although it contributes nothing to the stream flow, now withdraws about 70 per cent of the total current abstraction. In the years to come, as upstream countries develop more than their now generally rather modest needs for the Nile waters, this is certain to lead to a demand that exceeds the supply and thus to regional discord. Indeed, Egypt quite recently went so far as to warn the upstream states that it would go to war in response to upstream diversions of its traditional supplies (Starr 1986). Regarding these matters, it may be of interest to note here that in early 1997 Egypt embarked on a huge (and much criticized) engineering project to divert waters from its portion of the Nile in order to develop a portion of its western desert for agriculture.

The main trunk stream of the Nile is formed in the Sudan, at Khartoum, where the Blue and White Niles join. The Blue Nile receives its waters largely from the summer rains in north-western Ethiopia (especially from Ethiopia's Lake Tana), together with some drainage from south-western Eritrea; the Atbara (an intermittent stream) rises in Ethiopia and Eritrea, to enter the main trunk somewhat north of Khartoum. By contrast, the White Nile receives its waters, year round, largely from Lake Victoria via the extensive southern marshes of the Sudan – known as the Sudd, Arabic for floating vegetation – and thus predominately originates from Kenya, Tanzania and Uganda. The main trunk of the Nile in northern Sudan (before it enters the lake formed by the Aswan High Dam) has a mean annual flow (based on the 1945–84 period) of about 93 thousand million cubic metres; of which about 63 (68 per cent) is contributed by the Blue Nile, 18 (20 per cent) by the White Nile, and 11 (12 per cent) by the Atbara (Conway and Hulme 1993). A planned 360-kilometre channel (the Jonglei Canal) to circumvent the Sudd and thereby reduce evaporative loss would, it is estimated, increase the annual flow of the White Nile by perhaps 7,000 million cubic metres (Moghraby 1982). The civil warfare in the Sudan has kept this barely initiated project in limbo for more than fifteen years.

A Nile treaty, open to all drainage basin states, is sorely needed as a means of avoiding future armed conflicts relating to water allocations. Such an instrument would not only have to provide in a peaceful and non-coercive manner for equitable allocations of the Nile waters, but would also need to address questions of water pollution, of the sustainable utilization of fisheries, and of the protection of riverine biodiversity. Needless to say, the 1959 Utilization Agreement (an agreement only between Egypt and the Sudan) is thoroughly inadequate for facilitating amicable relations among the Nile basin states.

Ecosystems and biodiversity are not now adequately safeguarded in the Nile drainage basin, with only about 4 per cent of the combined land areas of the five states under consideration here currently under formal protection – one-third of what is needed. Egypt is especially inferior in this regard. As is the case with the Horn of Africa, the 1968 African Convention on the Protection of Nature and Natural Resources could become a valuable vehicle for regional cooperation, but to date only Egypt, the Sudan and Uganda belong from among the Nile basin countries under consideration here.

Eritrea and the Community of Nations

Although many of Eritrea's national security concerns derive either from within its borders or else from the three eco-geographical regions of which it is a component, some of course transcend those areas. It must thus share in the global necessity for improving world order in such more or less closely connected and overlapping realms of concern represented by humanitarian, environmental and human rights treaties. To that end, Eritrea has both the opportunity and responsibility to join with other nations in at least a relatively small number of key multilateral treaties meant to foster the most important humanitarian, environmental and human rights aims.[1] Such action by Eritrea will not only contribute to the amelioration of the global problems being addressed – a number of which are potential causes of conflict – but will additionally serve as an example to its regional partners to do likewise, some of which are unduly recalcitrant in this regard.

Conclusion

If Eritrea is to survive and prosper within its now generally hostile physical and political surroundings, it must continue to act constructively on several fronts – national, regional and global. At the national level, Eritrea must achieve both social and environmental security, each being a function of the other (Westing 1989; 1991; 1995b). The attainment of national food security and national fuelwood security are of course clear priorities. In order for these goals to succeed, they must go hand in hand with the safeguarding of ecosystems and biodiversity, the maintenance of a corruption-free government and a race-blind and gender-blind society, as well as the establishment of national and local democratic institutions and a robust legal system.

At the regional level, Eritrea must regrettably continue to maintain a defensive (non-provocative) military force, but simultaneously has to strive by example and otherwise for the regional acceptance of non-violent means of dispute resolution, both within and across national borders (Doornbos et al. 1992; Hutchison 1991). The fostering of regional co-operation on environment-related opportunities and problems can become one of the more useful means of building regional political confidence and security (Westing 1993; 1995a).

At the global level, Eritrea can become an important partner in – and, indeed, example to – the as yet semi-anarchic community of nations by actively cooperating with other states in protecting the environment and in fostering humanitarian and human rights goals (Ahmad et al. 1991).

Whether measured in terms of size, population, wealth or power, there is no denying that Eritrea represents only a very modest fraction of any of its several eco-geographical regions (Horn of Africa; Red Sea drainage basin; Nile drainage basin) and but a minuscule fraction of the world at large. But as is the case for every sovereign state, in order for Eritrea to achieve sustainability and other aspects of national security, it must be able through population controls and otherwise to bring into balance its basic needs with its available resources. However, given its wartime damage and physical limitations, Eritrea's long-term survival and prosperity will additionally depend on the establishment of amicable relations especially with its neighbours and near neighbours – and, concomitantly, on the promotion of regional peace and stability.

Notes

The author is pleased to acknowledge useful suggestions from Naigzy Gebremedhin (Asmara) and Carol E. Westing (Putney).

1. Multilateral treaties of regional or sub-regional extent that are of environmental relevance to Eritrea include especially:

(a) The 1986 Agreement Establishing the Inter-governmental Authority on Drought and Development in Eastern Africa (UNTS, not registered) – revitalized in 1995, and in 1996 renamed the Intergovernmental Authority on Development (IGAD) – comprises as states parties: Djibouti (1995),

Eritrea (1995), Ethiopia (1995), Kenya (1995), Somalia (1995), the Sudan (1995) and Uganda (1995).

(b) The 1968 African Convention on the Conservation of Nature and Natural Resources (UNTS #14689) is limited to Africa; the states parties from among Eritrea's eco-geographical partners include: Djibouti (1978), Egypt (1972), the Sudan (1973) and Uganda (1977).

(c) The 1982 Regional Convention for the Conservation of the Red Sea and Gulf of Aden Environment (UNTS, not registered) includes five of the seven littoral states: Egypt (1990), Jordan (1989), Somalia (1988), the Sudan (1985) and Yemen (1985). However, neither Eritrea nor Israel is eligible to join inasmuch as this UN sponsored Convention is, incredibly, not open to all of the littorals but restricted to members of the League of Arab States.

(d) The 1959 Agreement for the Full Utilization of the Nile Waters (UNTS #6519) is a pact between Egypt and the Sudan only. It proclaims the following allocation of waters: Egypt, 55.5 × 109 m^3; the Sudan, 18.5 × 109 m^3 (the former representing *c.* 60 per cent of the 1945–84 92.8 × 109 m^3 mean flow of the upper main trunk, and the latter *c.* 20 per cent of it). At least Ethiopia, Kenya, and Uganda have voiced formal rejections of this Agreement (regarding a recent statement by Ethiopia, see HoAB, 1996a).

Multilateral treaties of regional extent that are of human rights relevance to Eritrea include especially:

(a) The 1969 African Convention Governing Refugee Problems (UNTS #14691) is limited to Africa; the states parties from among Eritrea's eco-geographical partners include: Egypt (1980), Ethiopia (1973), the Sudan (1975), and Uganda (1987).

(b) The 1981 African Charter on Human and Peoples' Rights (UNTS #26363) is limited to Africa; the States parties from among Eritrea's eco-geographical partners include: Egypt (1986), Somalia (1986), the Sudan (1986) and Uganda (1986).

Bibliography

ACDA, 1996, *World Military Expenditures and Arms Transfers 1995*, US Arms Control and Disarmament Agency, Washington DC.

Ahmad, Y.J., M. Kassas, J.B. Opschoor, I.M. Thorsson and A.H. Westing, 1991, 'Disarmament, Environment, and Development and Their Relevance to the Least Developed Countries: An Approach to Sustainable Development with Equity', in A.H. Westing (ed.), *Disarmament, Environment, and Development and their Relevance to the Least Developed Countries*, Research Paper No. 10, United Nations Institute for Disarmament Research, Geneva.

Anderson, I., 1996, 'African Nations Sow Seeds of Hope', *New Scientist*, vol. 152, no. 2051, p. 11.

Boone, P., 1996, 'Politics and the Effectiveness of Foreign Aid', *European Economic Review*, 40, pp. 289–329.

CIA, 1995, *World Factbook 1995*, US Central Intelligence Agency, Washington DC.

Cobb, C.E., Jr, 1996, 'Eritrea Wins the Peace', *National Geographic*, vol. 189, no. 6, pp. 82–105.

Conway, D., and M. Hulme, 1993, 'Recent Fluctuations in Precipitation and Runoff over the Nile Sub-basins and Their Impact on Main Nile Discharge', *Climatic Change*, 25, pp. 127–51.

Doornbos, M., L. Cliffe, A.G.M. Ahmed and J. Markakis (eds), 1992, *Beyond Conflict in the Horn: Prospects for Peace, Recovery and Development in Ethiopia, Somalia and the Sudan*, Institute of Social Studies, The Hague.

Eritrea, 1995, *National Environmental Management Plan for Eritrea*, Government of Eritrea, Asmara.

Eritrea, 1996, *Draft Constitution of Eritrea*, Constitutional Commission of Eritrea, Asmara.

Fre, Z., 1991, 'Legacy of War', in O. Bennett (ed.), *Greenwar: Environment and Conflict*, Panos Institute, London, pp 131–42, 156.

Gebremedhin, N., 1997, 'Reconstruction and Development Following Armed Conflict: The Case of Eritrea', *Environment and Security*, vol. 1, no. 2.

Gebremedhin, T.G., 1996, *Beyond Survival: The Economic Challenges of Agriculture and Development in Post-independence Eritrea*, Red Sea Press, Lawrenceville NJ.

GEF, 1996, *Global Environment Facility Quarterly Operational Report*, November, UN Global Environment Facility, Washington DC.

Giorgis, A.W., 1993, 'Human and Ecological Consequences of the War in Eritrea', in T. Tvedt (ed.), *Conflicts in the Horn of Africa: Human and Ecological Consequences of Warfare*, Research Programme on Environmental Policy and Society, Department of Social and Economic Geography, Uppsala University, Uppsala.

HoAB, 1996a, 'Ethiopia to Develop Nile Basin Regardless of Egyptian–Sudanese Agreement', *Horn of Africa Bulletin*, vol. 8, no. 4, p. 11.

HoAB, 1996b, 'Eritrea: Border Dispute with Djibouti', *Horn of Africa Bulletin*, vol. 8, no. 3, pp. 5–6.

HoAB, 1996c, 'IGAD Council of Ministers Elaborates Priorities for Expanded Cooperation', *Horn of Africa Bulletin*, vol. 8, no. 3, p. 2.

Hutchison, R.A. (ed.), 1991, *Fighting for Survival: Insecurity, People and the Environment in the Horn of Africa*, World Conservation Union [IUCN], Gland, Switzerland.

IUCN, 1994, *1993 United Nations List of National Parks and Protected Areas*, World Conservation Union [IUCN], Gland, Switzerland.

Joireman, S.F., 1996, 'Minefield of Land Reform: Comments on the Eritrean Land Proclamation', *African Affairs*, 95, pp. 269–85.

Land, T., 1994, 'New Fuel in the Middle East', *Contemporary Review*, 264, pp. 123–8.

Lefebvre, J.A., 1995, 'Post-Cold War Clouds on the Horn of Africa: The Eritrea–Sudan Crisis', *Middle East Policy*, vol. 4, nos 1–2, pp. 34–49.

Luckham, R., 1996, 'Democracy and the Military: An Epitaph for Frankenstein's Monster?', *Democratisation*, vol. 3, no. 2, pp. 1–16.

el Moghraby, A.I., 1982, 'Jonglei Canal: Needed Development or Potential Eco-disaster?', *Environmental Conservation Now*, 9, pp. 141–8.

Plaut, M., 1996, 'Clash for Control in the Shipping Lanes', *World Today*, 52, pp. 46–7.

Pool, D., 1993, 'Eritrean Independence: The Legacy of the Derg and the Politics of Reconstruction', *African Affairs*, 92, pp. 389–402.

Sivard, R.L., 1996, 'World Military and Social Expenditures 1996', 16th edn, World Priorities, Washington DC.

Starr, J.R., 1986, 'Water Clock Ticking for People of the Nile', *International Herald Tribune*, 11 June, p. 14.

Suliman, M., 1993, 'Civil War in the Sudan: From Ethnic to Ecological Conflict',

The Ecologist, 23, pp. 104–9.

UN, 1978, *Register of International Rivers*, United Nations Department of Economic and Social Affairs, New York; Pergamon Press, Oxford.

UN, 1995, *World Population Prospects: The 1994 Revision*, 14th edn, Publication No. ST/ESA/SER.A/145, Population Division, United Nations Department for Economic and Social Information and Policy Analysis, New York.

UNDP, 1996, *Human Development Report 1996*, 7th edn, UN Development Programme and Oxford University Press, New York.

Wallensteen, P. and M. Sollenberg, 1996, 'The End of International War? Armed Conflict 1989–95', *Journal of Peace Research*, 33, pp. 353–70.

Westing, A.H., 1989, 'Environmental Component of Comprehensive Security', *Bulletin of Peace Proposals* [now *Security Dialogue*], 20, pp. 129–34.

Westing, A.H., 1991, 'Environmental Security and Its Relation to Ethiopia and Sudan', *Ambio*, 20, pp. 168–71.

Westing, A.H., 1993, 'Building Confidence with Transfrontier Reserves: The Global Potential', in A.H. Westing (ed.), *Transfrontier Reserves for Peace and Nature: A Contribution to Human Security*, United Nations Environment Program, Nairobi, pp. 1–15.

Westing, A.H., 1994, 'Environmental Change and the International System: An Overview', in J. Calließ (ed.), *Treiben Umweltprobleme in Gewaltkonflikte?: Ökologische Konflikte im internationalen System und Möglichkeiten ihrer friedlichen Bearbeitung*, Loccumer Protokoll No. 21/94, Evangelische Akademie Loccum, Rehburg-Loccum, pp. 207–28.

Westing, A.H., 1995a, 'Environmental Approaches to the Avoidance of Violent Regional Conflicts', in K.R. Spillmann and G. Baechler (eds), *Environmental Crisis: Regional Conflicts and Ways of Cooperation*, Occasional Paper No. 14, Environment and Conflicts Project, Swiss Federal Institute of Technology, Center for Security Studies and Conflict Research and Swiss Peace Foundation, Zurich, pp. 148–53.

Westing, A.H., 1995b, 'National Security for Eritrea as a Function of Environmental Security', *Environmental Awareness*, 18, pp. 83–7.

Westing, A.H., 1995c, 'Rare Chance for Egypt–Sudan Accord', *New York Times*, 6 July, p. A20.

Westing, A.H., 1996, 'The Eritrean–Yemeni Conflict Over the Hanish Archipelago: Toward a Resolution Favoring Peace and Nature', *Security Dialogue*, 27, pp. 201–6.

14

Conflict Resolution among the Borana and the Fur: Similar Features, Different Outcomes

Mohamed Suliman

The relatively tranquil settings of the Jebel Mara massif in northern Darfur in western Sudan and the Boran area in southern Ethiopia were profoundly disrupted during the 1980s by prolonged drought, which had persisted with minor interruptions since 1967.

In the past, when faced with deteriorating natural conditions, people would move to a nearby virgin area (mobility being a way of African life). There were enough empty corridors then. Now there are practically none. Climatic variations, large-scale mechanized agriculture for export purposes and urban consumption, as well as large increases in human and livestock populations, have all conspired to limit or deny access to new resources. Ultimately, these ecological buffer zones have gradually lost their distinction as areas of refuge and as borders of cooperation among neighbouring peoples.

With the persistence of the drought, pastoral groups, in the Fur as well as in the Boran areas, began to fall apart. Livestock died in large numbers and their owners began to dispose of the rest for next to nothing. Soon after 'the year of meat' ended, 'the year of famine' began and the city merchants turned away from the collapsing economies, leaving them to their own fate. Abandoned by both nature and the market, life became a real struggle. These rural societies became ripe for dislocation, turbulence and, ultimately, war. At the height of the drought, in the mid-1980s, violent conflicts erupted in the Boran and Fur areas. A closer look at the two conflicts reveals great similarities in their ecological, political and social aspects.

In both conflicts, pastoralists suffering from persistent drought (the Zaghawa and others in Darfur and the Abore and others in the Boran area) were seeking refuge in the lands of the Fur and the Borana respectively, which are richer in water and pasture. The conflict is, therefore, taking place along the ecological borders between rich and impoverished ecozones, the so-called 'desert versus the oasis syndrome'.

The current need of the pastoralist groups and their animals to stay for unspecified long periods in the lands of the Fur and the Borana has led to the breakdown of all previous mutual agreements that allowed pastoralists limited access, in times of scarcity, to pasture and water. For example, the Arab pastoralists were previously allowed to enter Jebel Mara from January to the first rains, usually in May.

In both cases, there were no inherent ethnic or religious differences between the two adversaries. The Fur and Arabs are Muslims, the Borana and their opposing fourteen volksgroups have similar traditional religions. Ethnic barriers were easy to surmount; for example, an Arab pastoralist who settled among the Fur soon became one, with all duties and rights of a typical Fur, and the opposite was also true. Ethnic dichotomies are more a product of the conflict than a cause of it.

As these areas are far away from the capital city and now with little appeal to traders, government intervention in both conflicts was relatively limited. In essence, we are dealing here with armed conflicts of local people against each other. Mutual also is the introduction of modern arms in the traditional conflict arena, especially in Darfur, where the proximity of the Chadian/Libyan war brought in large amounts of cheap modern weapons as well as the possibility of military training of combatants from both sides of the conflict divide. (The price of an AK47 with accessories was about US$40, far less than its international price. It was estimated that in 1990 there were more than 50,000 modern weapons available in Darfur, one for every man above 16 years of age.)

Since their inception, several attempts at resolving the conflicts through peace conferences initiated by central and regional governments have failed to bring peace to the regions.

The Fur and Boran conflicts are typical of the Sahel and Horn of Africa regions. Weakened by prolonged drought, pastoralists and their animals move into areas of better pasture and more water with the apparent intention of staying there for as long as it takes to recover. Previous agreements that allowed limited and temporary sharing of water and land resources become no longer binding. The inhabitants of the relatively richer lands refuse entry to the desperate pastoralists, and whenever there are no mitigating powerful third parties the friction ultimately leads to violent confrontation.

The Borana Conclude Peace, while the Fur Continue the Fight

In March 1993, in a great traditional religious ceremony, the Borana blessed a peace agreement with the Abore and the fourteen ethnic groups (the Konso, Tesmay, Hammer, Dasenech etc.), against whom they were fighting in and around the Umo valley, in the south of Ethiopia near the Kenyan border (Bauerochse 1993). A year later the Borana concluded a similar agreement with their Somali enemies, the Garri.

After years of violence around water holes and grazing lands, and after all appeals to the government failed to solicit any positive response, the elders of the Abore and the Hammer decided it was time to meet the elders of the Borana to settle the conflict in a fair and equitable way. The first meeting went well, and so, on 13 January 1993, ten young Borana visited the Abore to negotiate details of the peace accord. Meanwhile, and as a prelude to peace, all livestock were allowed free access to the buffer zone between the Borana and the rest.

Next, it was agreed that the peace between the Borana and the Abore would not be complete without the inclusion of all affected parties. All fourteen ethnic groups were therefore invited to the final and crucial general assembly in the homeland of the Abore. The meeting took place on 8 March 1993, in Gonderaba, a traditional religious centre of the Abore people.

The peace conference affirmed two fundamental principles to be strictly adhered to in making peace in the region:

> First principle
>
> The Abore and all other ethnic groups agree that the Borana have all traditional rights over their land. Traditional right over land is understood as right of use, not absolute ownership.
>
> Second principle
>
> The Borana accept that all rival groups and their animals have an inalienable right to survival.

To adhere to both principles, it was decided that the other groups and a limited number of their animals can access Boran lands after harvest time and stay there for a limited period, depending on the rain situation. Further measures were decided upon, namely:

- The agreement shall be overseen by a council of forty members representing all ethnic groups.
- A boarding school shall be built for the children of all groups so that they may know more about each other and befriend each other.
- An agricultural centre should be established to improve the health of the herds.
- Water management schemes in the area should be supported.

Improving the quality of life of the people and their herds was thus considered vital for lasting peace, because it entailed greater social security.

What this peace settlement shows is that in areas or in times of scarcity the prerequisite for peace is temporary, asymmetric and sustainable sharing of contested resources, and the respect for the fundamental right of stricken people and their animals to survive. 'The winner-[owner-]takes-all' mentality and an insistence on so-called historic rights, which totally exclude all others in need, is a sure recipe for confrontation. Three years later, peace is still holding in the Boran land.

Why Did the Fur Conflict Fail to Reach Peace?

The most obvious cause of failure to reach peace in the Fur conflict is the exclusion of local leadership from peace negotiations. All meetings and peace conferences were dominated by professionals from both sides of the conflict: teachers, lawyers, medical doctors and so on – that is, by 'the boys from town' (Suliman 1994). The boys from town were not able to understand the significance of two crucial principles associated with the conflict:

1. In spite of their apparent temporary economic insignificance, pastoralists and their animals do constitute an organic and important part of the economic and ecological systems of the region: the desert and the oasis are inherent parts of the same ecosystem. The problem should not be seen as 'us against them', but as live and let live. This solidarity is necessary for both sides and not an act of sheer generosity of one side towards the other.
2. Land right was understood as absolute ownership of land (i.e. as mere economic space). The boys from town consistently argued in terms and concepts of Western and town law, namely that ownership allows absolute hegemony over land. Most rural Africans understand customary land right as right of use, not as absolute, unrestricted ownership. For them land is living space, the soil, the grass, the trees, the hills, the river, the ancestral burying ground, and the place for rituals. Land is thus economic, social and spiritual space; or simply, land is life. Because of these two principles, it is possible for local leadership to understand the necessity for temporary, asymmetric sharing in times of need – namely, the right of other peoples and their animals to survive.

However, instead of dealing with the most pertinent issues of sustainable sharing of the contested natural resources, the boys from town spent valuable time quarrelling about the sharing of political power in regional and central government. They were more concerned with their own town interests than with those of their respective peoples.

Lessons to Learn from this Comparison

The first lesson to be learnt from this comparison of two very similar violent conflicts and their diametrically opposite conclusions is that in localized conflicts local leaders should be the major actors in conflict resolution. Left to themselves, most people tend to choose cooperation most of the time, and if provided with the right assistance, all people will choose cooperation all the time.

The second lesson is that the principle of temporary, asymmetric and sustainable sharing in times of crisis is a necessity for conflict resolution and for long-term survival, not only for the suffering side, but for both adversaries.

The third lesson demands that outsiders appreciate the particular understanding of land ownership of most traditional African societies, namely – that of right of use, rather than right to absolute ownership.

The insistence on so-called historic rights to ownership of land and other natural resources and the imposition of urban concepts of ownership on societies in turmoil cannot facilitate the processes necessary to resolve simmering or raging conflicts.

May the Borana and Abore wisdom prevail in all similar conflicts!

Bibliography

Bauerochse, Lothar, 1993, 'Bauchspeck für den Frieden', *Der Uberblick*, 3, p. 63.
Suliman, Mohamed, 1994, *War in Darfur*, IFAA Publications, London.

About the Contributors

Günther Baechler is a political scientist (Free University of Berlin) with a focus on peace and conflict research. He is director of the Swiss Peace Foundation and the Institute for Conflict Resolution. He is currently the head of an action-oriented research project in the Horn of Africa. The author and editor of many books and papers on ecology and conflict, his latest publication is *Violence Through Environmental Discrimination* (Kluwer, 1999).

Völker Böge is a historian and peace researcher working at the Unit for the Study of Wars, Armaments and Development, University of Hamburg. He was a member of the international research team of the Environment and Conflict Project (ENCOP), 1991–96.

Abdel-Galil Elmekki is a prominent Sudanese political scientist. He taught at the University of Khartoum and is now senior programme officer at the International Development Research Centre (IDRC), Ottawa, Canada.

Simon Fairlie was a co-editor of *The Ecologist.* He works with the land rights campaigning group, The Land Is Ours. He is co-author of *Whose Common Future?* (Earthscan, 1993) and author of *Low Impact Development* (Jon Carpenter, 1996). He has also worked as a commercial fisherman in North America.

Nicholas Hildyard is former editor of *The Ecologist* and one of the founders of the Corner House. He is a powerful and influential writer on social justice, sustainable development and peace.

Stephan Libiszewski is a political scientist and research associate at the Centre for Security Studies and Conflict Research, Swiss Federal Institute of Technology, Zurich. He has researched the political role of water in the Arab–Israeli conflict within the Environment and Conflict Project (ENCOP). He is a co-author of *Environmental Degradation: War or Cooperation?* (Agenda Verlag, 1993). He is currently project coordinator of International Relations and Security.

Larry Lohmann works with the Corner House, a UK-based organization concerned with democracy and resource issues. He is co-author, with Ricardo Carrere, of *Pulping the South: Industrial Tree Plantation and the World Paper Economy* (Zed Books, 1996), and co-editor, with Marcus Colchester, of *The Struggle for Land and the Fate of the Forests* (Zed Books, 1993).

Fatima B. Mahmoud is an academic and author, former associate professor of political science at the University of Khartoum. Former director of the MSc Programme on Planning and Development at the University of Bristol. She is the chairperson of the Pan-African Women's Liberation Organisation. She currently works as a senior research fellow and consultant on development issues at the Institute for African Alternatives in London.

A. Atiq Rahman is the director of the Bangladesh Centre for Advanced Studies. He is currently the chairman of the steering committee of the Asia–Pacific National Council for Sustainable Development (APNCSD). Rahman has written extensively on sustainable development and people's participation.

Katrina S. Rogers is a well-known peace researcher.

Wolfgang Sachs is a project director at Wuppertal Institute for Climate, Energy, and the Environment, Wuppertal, Germany.

Mohamed Suliman is the director of the Institute for African Alternatives, London. He writes on environment, politics and violent conflict in the Horn of Africa.

Arthur H. Westing is a leading name in conflict research. He has worked as a consultant to the United Nations Environment Programme, at the United Nations Institute for Disarmament Research, at the International Committee of the Red Cross, and for the government of Eritrea.

Index